offbeat king's Indian

by Krzysztof Panczyk
and Jacek Ilczuk

EVERYMAN CHESS

Gloucester Publishers plc   www.everymanchess.com

First published in 2004 by Gloucester Publishers plc (formerly Everyman Publishers plc), Northburgh House, 10 Northburgh Street, London EC1V 0AT

British Library Cataloguing-in-Publication Data
A catalogue record for this book is available from the British Library.

ISBN 1 85744 361 6

Distributed in North America by The Globe Pequot Press, P.O Box 480, 246 Goose Lane, Guilford, CT 06437-0480.

All other sales enquiries should be directed to Everyman Chess, Northburgh House, 10 Northburgh Street, London EC1V 0AT
tel: 020 7253 7887 fax: 020 7490 3708
email: info@everymanchess.com
website: www.everymanchess.com

Everyman is the registered trade mark of Random House Inc. and is used in this work under license from Random House Inc.

EVERYMAN CHESS SERIES (formerly Cadogan Chess)
Chief advisor: Garry Kasparov
Commissioning editor: Byron Jacobs

Typeset and edited by First Rank Publishing, Brighton.
Cover design by Horatio Monteverde.
Production by Navigator Guides.
Printed and bound in the US by Versa Press.

CONTENTS

BIBLIOGRAPHY

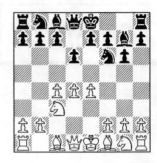

Books

Encyclopaedia of Chess Openings volume E, 3rd Edition (Sahovski Informator 1998)
Szachy od A do Z, W. Litmanowicz, J. Gizycki (Warsaw 1987)
Staroindiyskaya zashchita, E. Geller (Moscow 1980)
Staroindiyskaya dlinoyu v zhizn, E. Gufeld (Moscow 1980)

Periodicals, Magazines and Websites

Chess Informators
New in Chess Yearbooks
64 Shakhmatnoye Obozrenye
Przeglad Szachowy
MegaBase 2002
ChessBase Magazines
The Week in Chess
Ajedrez de Estilo

INTRODUCTION

The move 1...♘f6 after 1 d4 was mentioned by K. Jaenisch in his *A New Analysis* as far back as 1842/43. In 1848 a German chess magazine, *Deutsche Schachzeitung*, published a game starting with 1 d4 ♘f6, and in 1875 published a game beginning in this way which had been played by two Brahmins (Sauncheri-Moonshander). Hence the name of the defence, which was invented by Saviely Tartakower in the 1920s.

In 1880 in an international tournament in Wiesbaden the game A.Schwarz-L.Paulsen went 1 d4 ♘f6 2 c4 g6 3 ♘c3 ♗g7 4 g3 d6 5 ♗g2 0-0 6 ♘f3 ♘bd7 7 0-0 e5 (published by *Deutsche Schachzeitung* in 1881)

This is the first time that this position, now a common sight at all levels, was seen.

The King's Indian was used first by one of the best players of this era in Leipzig in 1879 when the German player and theoretician Louis Paulsen faced Adolf Schwarz in a match. Towards the end of the nineteenth century Mikhail Chigorin joined Paulsen in employing the defence and, as the years passed in the twentieth century, a number of the so-called hypermodern school continued the trend, with Tartakower, Nimzowitsch, Réti, Grünfeld and Euwe among the recruits.

An important turning point in the development and assessment of new ideas, as well as the creation of new systems, came with analysis and tournament practice of the outstanding Soviets grandmasters Boleslavsky, Konstantinopolsky, Bronstein, Geller, Yudovich and others, all achieving very good results as Black. Then Fischer made a further contribution, playing the defence dynamically (for example in his candidates matches against Taimanov and Larsen in 1971) and earning victories against a number of the world's top players.

Toward the end of the twentieth century the King's Indian enjoyed more popularity thanks to Garry Kasparov's use of the defence against Karpov, although Kasparov was later to unexpectedly put one of his main weapons on hold, perhaps influenced by his two defeats to Kramnik (Novgorod 1997 and the Moscow blitz in 1998, both in the Classical System with 9 b4!). Not surprisingly this led to the King's Indian losing some of its followers.

Opening trends in the modern game can be influenced as much by fashion as hard evidence, and the King's Indian continues to be a faithful friend to a host of today's successful players, among them Radjabov, Bologan and Ye Jiangchuan, while Svidler, J.Polgar, Shirov and Movsesian (and – occasionally – Topalov and Ivanchuk) are strong players for whom the King's Indian forms part of their repertoire, albeit not exclusively so.

There are two schools of playing chess, each with fundamentally different approaches to the struggle. The first, 'classical' philosophy assumes that Black should play rather carefully, opting for defensive systems that are geared more towards establishing a more or less level footing as the middlegame phase begins. This involves minimal strategic risk and revolves around staking some kind of claim for a presence in the centre. The other, modern attitude sees a deliberate 'neglecting' of the centre, allowing White to set up camp there provided that this sector can then be attacked. This kind of thinking clearly brings with it an element of risk and, not surprisingly, tends not to lead to 'level' positions – any equality would be described as dynamic rather than static. These two trends predominate periodically, one after the other, and, for the moment, classical chess is prevailing. We hope – it is high time – that the situation changes.

The King's Indian definitely belongs to the modern, more combative theory of playing the game, White usually having some extra space but his centre being susceptible to attack. Consequently many players – particularly those with a more aggressive outlook – use the King's Indian regularly. Typical counterplay after closing the centre, for example, often comes in the form of the no-nonsense ...f7-f5. Moreover the defence is also attractive in that it is apparently simple to play – game after game Black often employs the same series of moves such as ...♘f6, ...g7-g6, ...♗g7, ...d7-d6, ...0-0 and ...e7-e5, after which a number of plans, each with its own logic, is available. Life, of course, is not that easy. White has a choice of concrete set-ups that demand accurate treatment from Black. It seems that the main problem for Black is the Classical System, especially the variation with 9 b4 (Kramnik's choice against Kasparov), although this does not mean that the Classical secures White a guaranteed advantage. In fact other types of position have become areas of discussion.

In the real world not every player is ready to delve into such systems as the Classical or Sämisch, where it is quite normal for the real battle to begin only around the twentieth move (or later...). And herein lies the idea of this book. We are going to present a collection of seldom used systems for White which can surprise the opposition and which, importantly, can contain much venom. These are: 5 ♘ge2, 5 ♗d3, 5 h3 (Makogonov System) and 5 ♗e2 followed by 6 ♗g5 (Averbakh System). Obviously the Averbakh is the most extensive theme and will therefore be afforded appropriate attention.

As for the playing strength of the reader, the book is designed not only for club players who do not have enough time to properly prepare the 'main' lines, for more advanced players can also benefit from the set-ups on offer, especially in view of the transpositional possibilities. A good knowledge of these systems allows for a useful level of flexibility, depending on circumstances.

The nature of the chess book means that the vast amount of material from which to make selections has to be considerably condensed (we think that it is worth 2-3 books), so it is not possible to provide a magical 'winning' recipe for every given move or situation. Rather we have tried to demonstrate how to treat this or that scenario, as well as what to avoid. This is not a compendium of knowledge about all the systems but a guide to the ideas which may occur, a manual that explains strategic principles and eases the journey around tactical themes.

Note that we do not discuss transpositions to the Classical System (or other variations with ♘f3), the Sämisch System, lines with g2-g3 and the Modern Benoni unless specific situations are untypical or clearly advantageous for either side.

We encourage all players – especially those who like non-standard play – to incorporate these systems in their opening repertoire.

CHAPTER ONE

5 ♘ge2

1 d4 ♘f6 2 c4 g6 3 ♘c3 ♗g7 4 e4 d6 5 ♘ge2

This move has been played since as early as the beginning of the 20th century, when Ha-kansson-Sjoberg, Gothenburg 1919 and Sämisch-Schoenman, Berlin 1920 saw 5 ♘ge2. However, for a long time this development of the knight had little independent significance, being used only as an introduction to other systems, mainly the Sämisch or those systems involving a kingside fianchetto. Only in the 1950s did a new idea connected with the transfer of the knight to g3 appear (Steiner-Pedersen, 1950 Dubrovnik Olympiad). Subsequently the variation was analysed and popularised by Hungarian players at the beginning of the 1960s.

Nowadays it is not unusual for White to throw in an early h2-h4 in order to generate a kingside offensive. Of course the knight's journey from g1 to g3 takes time, and the new post might even appear a little unnatural. Moreover, White also has to deal with the sometimes annoying ...h7-h5-h4.

Apart from the Hungarian veterans Forintos and Kaposztas today's most notable followers of 5 ♘ge2 are Serper, Novikov and Jakab, while well-known GMs who occasionally include the variation in their armoury are Hort, I.Sokolov, Korchnoi and M.Gurevich.

Game 1
Serper-Dzindzichashvili
CITS New York 1996

---

1 c4 g6 2 d4 ♗g7 3 e4 d6 4 ♘c3 ♘f6 5 ♘ge2 c5

This thrust is more usual after ...0-0 because now Black must be prepared for a queenless middlegame in which his king will be deprived of castling rights.

6 dxc5

6 d5 b5 leads to non-standard positions of the Benko Gambit – 7 cxb5 and now:

a) 7...0-0 8 ♘g3 a6 9 ♗e2 (9 a4 axb5 10 ♗xb5 ♗a6 11 0-0 was an edge for White in Grabowski-Doda, Jachranka 1987) 9...axb5 10 ♘xb5 ♘e8 (10...♘a6 11 0-0 ♘d7 12 ♖b1 ♘c7 13 ♘c3 slightly favoured White in Ador-jan-Doda, Polanica Zdroj 1970 but was agreed drawn) 11 0-0 ♘c7 12 ♘c3 ♗a6 13 ♗g5 ♘d7 14 ♕d2 ♖e8 15 ♖ab1 ♕b8 16 ♖fc1 and White retained a pull in Kaidanov-Gufeld, Las Vegas 2001.

b) 7...a6 8 ♘g3 h5 9 h4 (9 ♗e2 h4 10 ♘f1 was seen in Poluljahov-Strelnikov, Krasnodar 2001, and now Christiansen's 10...h3 is unclear) 9...♘bd7 10 a4 0-0 11 ♗f4 (11 ♖a3 ♘g4 12 ♗e2 axb5 13 ♘xb5, or 11 ♕c2 or 11 ♗e2 and in all variations Black must prove that he has compensation for the pawn) 11...♕a5 12 ♖a3 ♘g4 13 ♗e2 ♕b4 14 ♖b3 ♕d4 15 ♗xg4 hxg4, Zueger-Christiansen, Lucerne 1989. Now 16 b6 would have been excellent for White.

6...dxc5 7 ♕xd8+ ♔xd8 8 e5

A good alternative is 8 ♗e3!?, with the following possibilities:

a) 8...♘bd7 9 f3 b6 10 0-0-0 ♘e8 11 g3 e6 12 ♗h3!? ♔e7 13 ♖hf1 ♗b7 14 f4 ♘d6 15 f5 ♘xc4 16 fxe6 ♘de5? (16...fxe6 17 ♗g5+ ♘f6 18 ♘f4 is very poor for Black) was the course of Beckwith-Nakamura, Southampton (USA) 2003, when 17 ♖xf7+! ♘xf7 18 ♖d7+ ♔f8 19 ♖xf7+ proved decisive.

b) 8...♘fd7 9 0-0-0 b6 10 h4 ♗a6 11 b3 h5 12 g3 ♘c6 13 ♗h3 e6 14 f4 ♗h6 15 ♖d3 ♔e7 16 ♖hd1 ♖ad8 17 a3 and White had an edge in Formanek-Fedorowicz, Philadelphia 1992. However, this edge is rather symbolic as the extra space and temporary control of the d-file are hardly significant. After 17...♘de5 18 ♖xd8 ♖xd8 19 ♖xd8 ♔xd8 Black could have been close to equality.

8...♘fd7

The pseudo-active 8...♘g4 9 f4 ♘a6 10 h3 ♘h6 11 ♗e3 ♗d7 12 0-0-0 ♔c8 13 ♘e4 b6 14 g4 ♗c6 15 ♘2c3 in Dochev-Spassov, Bankia 1991 led to a clear advantage for White due to the two misplaced knights and White's considerable extra space.

9 f4 f6

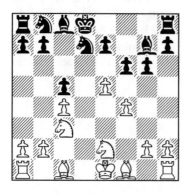

Let us assess the diagram position. Al-

though White is unable to maintain his centre his position nevertheless deserves preference. The most important factor here is that there is no convenient home for Black's king; the point is not that it might come under attack, rather it hampers development.

10 exf6 ♘xf6

No better is 10...exf6 11 ♗d2 ♘c6 12 0-0-0 f5 13 ♘d5 with the better prospects for White.

11 g3 ♗d7 12 ♗e3 ♗c6 13 0-0-0+ ♘bd7 14 ♖g1 ♔e8

Black plans to evacuate the king to f7. Another option is 14...♔c7, although this is no better than the text.

15 g4

Another way of developing an initiative is 15 ♗h3!? h5 (15...b6 16 ♘d5 ♘xd5 17 cxd5 ♗a4 18 b3 ♗b5 19 ♖ge1 favours White, while 15...♔f7 walks into 16 ♘d5) 16 ♖ge1 b6 17 ♘d5 and White has the upper hand.

15...♔f7?!

15...♖d8, deserves attention, defending the d7-knight and preparing to meet 16 g5 with 16...♘e4. After 16 h3 ♘e4 17 ♘xe4 ♗xe4 18 ♗g2 ♗xg2 19 ♖xg2 White has a small advantage.

16 g5 ♘e8

16...♘h5 17 ♗h3 ♖hd8 18 ♗g4 might be a lesser evil.

17 ♗h3

Black must lose the c5-pawn.

17...♘d6 18 ♗xd7 ♗xd7 19 ♗xc5 ♖ac8 20 ♗xd6 exd6 21 ♘e4

The sensible 21 b3 looks preferable in this position.

21...♖xc4+ 22 ♘2c3 ♖c7 23 ♘xd6+ ♔f8 24 ♖d3?!

Again White can improve with the more precise 24 ♔b1 ♗xc3 (24...♗e6 25 ♘d5) 25 bxc3 h6 (25...♖xc3 26 ♘xb7 ♖c7 27 ♘d6) 26 c4 etc.

24...h6 25 ♖g2?!

25 ♖f1 hxg5 26 fxg5+ ♔g8 27 ♖f2 keeps White ahead.

25...hxg5 26 fxg5 ♖h3

26...♗e5!? leads to a draw after 27 ♖e2 (27 ♖f2+ ♔g7) 27...♗f4+ 28 ♔b1 ♖xh2 29 ♖f3 ♖xe2 30 ♘xe2 ♔e7 31 ♘xf4 ♔xd6 32 ♖d3+ ♔e5 33 ♘xg6+ ♔f5 34 ♘f8 ♗c8 35 ♖d5+ ♔g4 etc.

27 ♖f2+ ♔g8 28 ♖xh3 ♗xh3 29 ♘e8 ♖c5 30 ♘xg7 ♔xg7

White has no way to make the extra pawn tell.

31 ♖f3 ♗e6 32 h4 ♗xa2 33 b4 ♖c8 34 ♔d2 ♗c4 35 ♖f4 ♖d8+ 36 ♔c2 ♗e6 37 ♘b5 a6 38 ♘d4 ♗f7 39 ♘f3 ♖e8 40 ♔c3 b6 41 ♔d4 ♖d8+ 42 ♔c3 ♖c8+ 43 ♔d3 ½-½

> *Game 2*
> ## Miles-Romanishin
> *Tilburg 1985*

1 d4 ♘f6 2 c4 g6 3 ♘c3 ♗g7 4 e4 d6 5 ♘ge2 c6 6 ♘g3

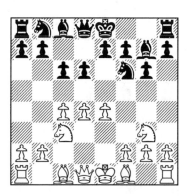

The most common treatment of this system in modern practice, although this does not necessarily mean that the text is the best move. In fact a transposition to ♗g2 systems or the Sämisch is worth consideration.

Also possible is 6 ♗g5, when Black has a plan involving ...a7-a6 and ...b7-b5, which is a remedy in various systems of the King's Indian. Note that Black often gets queenside mobilisation under way before castling in order to save a tempo, particularly if White has e4-e5. After 6...a6 play can continue 7 ♕d2 h6

8 ♗h4 (8 ♗e3 meets with 8...♘g4) 8...b5 9 f3 0-0 (9...bxc4!?) 10 g4 e5 11 ♗f2 as in Conquest-Hebden, Clichy 2001, when 11...b4! would have favoured Black. Notice here that 7...h6 was made possible by Black's avoiding automatic castling.

6...♘bd7 7 ♗e2 h5

This thrust is a key feature of Black's counterplay.

8 ♗g5 a6

8...h4!? 9 ♘f1 ♕a5 is interesting, when 'unclear' is a fair assessment.

9 ♕d2 b5 10 f3 0-0 11 ♖d1 e5 12 dxe5

After 12 d5 b4 Black intends to trade on d5 with equality (Miles).

12...dxe5 13 0-0 ♖e8 14 a3

14 c5 ♕a5! (Miles).

14...♕c7 15 ♖c1?

Better is 15 b4 ♘f8! 16 ♕d6 (16 ♗d3!?) 16...♕a7+ 17 ♖f2 (17 ♔h1 ♘e6 is an edge for Black) 17...♘e6 18 ♗xf6 ♗xf6 19 cxb5 cxb5 20 ♘d5 ♗g7 with the better prospects for Black, while 15 ♕e3 ♘f8 16 ♘h1 ♘e6 17 ♘f2 ♘d4 looks unpleasant for White.

15...♘c5

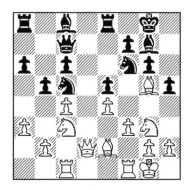

Not only did White lose a tempo after 15 ♖c1, but now there is the threat of the fork on b3.

16 ♕e1

16 cxb5 ♘b3 17 ♕e3 or the immediate 16 ♕e3 are preferable, but Black already has at least a small advantage.

16...♘b3 17 ♖d1 ♗e6

Now or on the next move Black might consider 17...♕b6+ 18 ♕f2 ♕xf2+ 19 ♖xf2 ♗e6 20 cxb5 axb5 with a definite pull.

18 cxb5 axb5

Pressure on the c4-pawn has induced an exchange on b5 which, from a strategic point of view, benefits Black. The point is that the d5-square is still protected by the c6-pawn, while the d4-square is in Black's hands.

19 ♗d3 ♖ad8

19...♘d7!? looks good for Black.

20 ♕f2 ♖d7 21 ♗b1 ♘d4 22 ♗a2 ♗xa2 23 ♘xa2 ♘h7 24 ♗e3 ♘f8 25 ♘c3?!

The more circumspect 25 ♘b4 is called for.

25...♘fe6

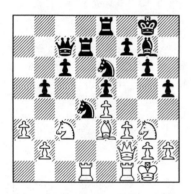

Black is gradually increasing his advantage, and White has nothing with which to counter his opponent's tightening grip.

26 ♘ge2 ♖ed8 27 ♔h1 ♕b7 28 ♖d2 ♘b3 29 ♖xd7 ♖xd7 30 f4

30 ♖d1 ♖xd1+ 31 ♘xd1 ♕d7 32 ♘dc3 ♘a5 is decisive (Miles).

30...exf4 31 ♘xf4 ♘xf4 32 ♗xf4 b4 33 axb4 ♕xb4 34 ♗g5 ♘c5 35 ♗f6 ♘xe4 36 ♕f4?

36 ♘xe4 ♕xe4 37 ♗xg7 ♔xg7.

36...♕d6 37 ♕xd6 ♘xd6 38 ♗xg7 ♔xg7 39 ♖d1 ♖e7 40 ♔g1 ♘f5 41 ♖c1 ♔f6 42 b4 ♖e5 43 ♔f2 ♔e6 44 g3 ♘d4 45 ♖d1 ♖f5+ 46 ♔g2 ♘c2 47 ♖b1 ♘a3 48 ♖c1 ♘c4 49 ♘e2 ♘e3+ 50 ♔g1 ♔d5 51 ♘f4+ ♔d6 52 ♘e2 ♖d5 53 ♘c3 ♖e5 54 ♔f2 ♘g4+ 55 ♔g2 f5 56 h3 ♘f6 57 ♔f3

♘e4 58 ♖d1+

58 ♘xe4+ ♖xe4 59 ♖b1 ♔c7 60 b5 c5 61 b6+ ♔b7 62 ♖b5 c4 63 ♖b4 c3 (Miles).

58...♔c7 59 ♘e2 ♖b5 60 ♖d4 ♘g5+ 61 ♔g2 ♘e6 62 ♖c4 ♖d5 63 h4 ♔b6 64 ♖c3 ♖d2 65 ♔f1 ♘c7 66 ♔e1 ♖d6 67 ♘f4 ♔b5 68 ♘d3 ♘a6 0-1

Game 3
Poluljahov-Milov
Aeroflot Open, Moscow 2003

---

1 c4 g6 2 d4 ♘f6 3 ♘c3 ♗g7 4 e4 d6 5 ♘ge2 ♘bd7 6 ♘g3 e5

Extremely complicated positions arise after 6...c5 7 d5 a6 (7...h5 8 h4 ♘e5 9 ♗e2 ♗g4 10 f3 ♗d7 11 ♗g5 a6 12 ♕d2 ♕a5 was unclear in M.Ivanov-Jiretorn, Reykjavik 2002) 8 a4 (8 ♗e2 h5 9 h4 ♘e5 10 0-0 ♘h7, intending ...♗f6 with counterplay, Flear-Makropoulou, Manila Olympiad 1992) 8...h5 9 ♗e2 h4 10 ♘f1 ♘h5 11 ♗g5 ♕a5 12 ♕c2 (12 ♗d2!?), Barczay-Ortega, East Berlin 1968, and now 12...♘hf6 leaves the situation well balanced.

7 d5 h5

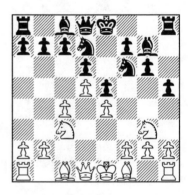

With the centre closed Black prepares the thematic offensive on the kingside. He can often exchange his passive dark-squared bishop by ...♗h6.

An alternative is 7...a5, when Nikolaidis-Haritakis, Korinthos 1998 continued 8 h4 h5 9 ♗g5 ♘c5 10 ♗e2 ♗h6!? 11 ♗xh6 ♖xh6 12 ♕d2 ♖h8 13 0-0-0 (13 f3 ♗d7 14 ♘f1 ♕e7 was equal in Nikolaidis-Grivas, Aegina 1996) 13...♕e7 14 ♔b1 ♗d7 15 f3 0-0-0?! (15...a4!? is unclear) 16 ♘f1 ♘g8 17 ♘b5 b6 18 ♘e3 ♔b7 19 ♗d3 ½-½, although White has an albeit modest lead here. 8 ♗e2 h5!? 9 ♗g5 ♗h6 10 ♗xh6 ♖xh6 11 ♘f1! h4! 12 ♘d2 was Serper-Bologan, Philadelphia 1999, when 12...♘c5!? merits attention.

8 ♗e2

8 h4 can be met with 8...♘h7 when White has to withdraw his knight in view of the threat to pick up the h-pawn with ...♗f6. After 9 ♘ge2 a5 10 g3 ♘c5 11 ♗e3 0-0 12 ♗g2 ♘f6 both sides had chances in Mukherjee-Guizar, E-mail 1999.

8...♕e7

A new idea. 8...h4 is more popular, e.g. 9 ♘f1 ♘c5 with the following position:

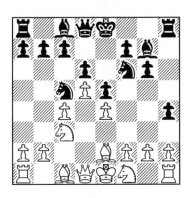

Here we have a typical struggle for this structure in which the result will depend on whether the h4-pawn is a strength or a weakness.

a) 10 f3 a5 11 ♗g5 (11 ♗e3 ♗h6 12 ♗xh6 ♖xh6 13 ♕d2 ♖h8 was unclear in Pottornyai-Vigh, Budapest 1998) 11...♕d7 12 ♘d2 ♘h5 13 ♗e3 ♘f4 14 0-0 ♕e7 (14...♗h6!? 15 ♔h1 ♕e7 favours Black) 15 ♔h1 ♕g5 16 ♖f2 ♘fd3, Nikolaidis-Mastrokoukos, Athens 1996, when 17 ♗xc5 ♘xc5 leaves Black with a pull.

b) 10 ♗g5 with a further branch

b1) 10...a5 11 h3 (11 ♕c2!? ♗f8 12 b3 b6 13 ♖g1 ♗e7 14 ♗e3 ♘h5 15 g3 ♗g5 was interesting in Serper-Akopian, Moscow 1991)

11...♗d7 (11...♗h6 12 ♗xh6 ♖xh6 13 ♘d2 ♘h5 makes more sense) 12 ♕c2 (12 ♗g4 looks a shade better for White) 12...♗f8 (there is no other way to unpin, keeping the h4-pawn) 13 ♘h2 ♗e7 14 ♗e3 and White enjoyed the superior prospects in Kovacevic-Hulak, Pula 2000.

b2) 10...♗h6 again comes into consideration. Prevenios-Bergamini, E-mail 2000 led to chances for both sides after 11 ♗xh6 ♖xh6 12 ♘d2 a5 (12...♘h5 13 b4 ♗d7 14 ♗xh5 ♖xh5 15 0-0, Novikov-Gelfand, Uzhgorod 1987, is given as slightly better for White by Novikov in ECO) 13 ♕c2 g5 14 h3 ♖g6 15 ♖c1 ♗d7.

9 ♗g5 ♗h6 10 ♗xh6 ♖xh6 11 h4 ♖h8 12 ♘f1

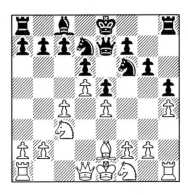

Black has realised his plan, albeit at the price of two tempi. White has some extra space and a slight initiative, although he must be careful not to be left with the potentially passive light-squared bishop (and therefore weak on the dark squares).

12...♘c5 13 ♘d2?!

More logical is 13 f3 a5 14 ♘e3 because e3 is the appropriate square for the f1-knight. Then 14...♘fd7 15 ♕d2 ♘b6 16 0-0-0 ♗d7 17 ♔b1 0-0-0 is interesting, while 14...♔f8 15 ♕c2 ♔g7 16 0-0-0 ♘fd7 17 g3 ♘b6 18 f4 promises White some kind of initiative.

13...a5 14 ♕c2 ♔f8 15 0-0-0

15 ♘b3 ♘fd7 16 0-0-0 ♘xb3+ 17 ♕xb3 ♘c5 18 ♕c2 a4 19 ♔b1 ♔g7 is another possibility.

15...♔g7 16 f3

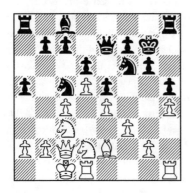

16...♗d7?!

Milov's recommended improvement looks preferable: 16...c6 17 ♘b3 ♘a6! 18 ♘xa5 (18 ♔b1 cxd5 19 cxd5 a4! with initiative) 18...cxd5 19 cxd5 ♘b4 20 ♕b3 ♘xa2+! 21 ♕xa2 ♕c7 with play for Black, although 17 ♖dg1!? ♗d7 18 g4 a4 19 ♔b1 ♖hc8 is complicated.

17 ♘f1 c6

One tempo too late! Now White's knights will be on the right squares just in time.

18 ♘e3 cxd5?!

Black should have maintained the tension in the centre.

19 ♘exd5 ♘xd5 20 ♘xd5 ♕d8 21 f4

White might consider 21 ♘c3 with a view to attacking the weak d6-pawn, e.g. 21...♖a6 22 ♔b1 ♗e6 23 ♕d2 ♕e7 24 ♘b5 ♖d8 25 ♕e3 and the prospect of pushing the g-pawn offers White the better chances.

21...♗a4 22 b3 ♗c6 23 ♖hf1?

This time Milov proposes 23 fxe5 dxe5 24 ♕c3 ♕d6 25 ♕e3 ♘e6 ('unclear'), or 23 f5 ♗xd5 24 ♖xd5 ♕b6 with counterplay.

23...♕xh4 24 ♕b2?

24 ♖h1 ♕g3 is strong (Milov).

24...♘xe4 25 ♔b1?!

25 fxe5 ♕g5+ etc.

25...♖ae8?

Milov gives 25...♗xd5 26 ♖xd5 ♘g3 27 ♖f3 ♘xe2 28 ♕xe2 exf4 29 ♕b2+ (29 ♖xd6 ♖he8) 29...♕f6.

26 f5?

Black would have to settle for a slight lead after 26 fxe5 ♗xd5 27 exd6+ f6 28 d7 ♖e5 29 ♖xd5 ♖xd5 30 cxd5 ♕g5 according to Milov.

26....♗xd5 27 ♖xd5 ♘g3 0-1

Game 4
Bertok-Tatai
Reggio Emilia 1967/8

1 c4 g6 2 d4 ♘f6 3 ♘c3 ♗g7 4 e4 d6 5 ♘ge2 e5 6 d5

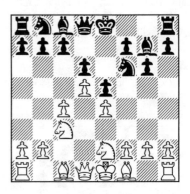

Closing the centre. In this game we are going to investigate themes for Black which are based on either delaying castling, or not castling at all. Of course there is nothing to prevent Black from entering more usual lines by simply castling at some point.

White has a number of alternatives to 6 d5:

a) Nothing special is achieved by 6 ♗g5 h6 7 ♗h4. Apart from 7...exd4 8 ♘xd4 0-0 9 ♗e2 ♘bd7 10 0-0 c6 11 ♔h1 ♕b6 which was fine for Black in Garcia-Corradine, Bogota 1990, there is also a different course in 7...g5 8 ♗g3 ♘h5, e.g. 9 dxe5 dxe5 10 ♕xd8+ ♔xd8 11 0-0-0+ ♘d7 12 ♘d5 c6 13 ♘e3 ♔c7 14 ♘f5. We are following Botvinnik-Smyslov, Leningrad/Moscow 1941. Now 14...♘xg3!? 15 ♘exg3 ♗f8 has been suggested. Instead the game continued 14...♗f8 15 ♖xd7+! ♔xd7 16 ♗xe5 f6 17 ♗c3 ♔e6 18 g4 ♘f4 (18...♗g7!?) 19 ♘xf4+ gxf4 20 ♗d3, with sufficient compensation according to *ECO*.

b) The trade 6 dxe5 dxe5 7 ♕xd8+ ♔xd8 is

harmless for Black, e.g. 8 ♗g5 c6 9 f3 (9 b4 ♗e6 10 ♘c1 h6 11 ♗d2 ♘bd7 was equal in Edery-Molinsky, Correspondence 1990) 9...♕c7 10 ♘g3 ♘bd7 11 ♗e3 h5 12 h4 ♘f8 13 ♗d3 ♘e6 with a very good ending for Black, Lomakina-Kadar, Zalakaros 1995.

6...c6

Alternatively:

a) 6...♘h5?! 7 h3 and White wants to play g2-g4. Since 7...f5 runs into 8 exf5 gxf5 9 ♘d4 ♘f6 10 ♘e6 Black has an unpleasant choice to make between losing two tempi or sacrificing a pawn. 7...0-0 8 g4 ♘f4 9 ♘xf4 exf4 10 ♗xf4 ♕e7 11 ♕e2 ♖e8 12 ♖c1 ♗xc3+ 13 ♖xc3 ♕xe4 14 ♕xe4 ♖xe4+ 15 ♗e3, as in I.Polgar-Portisch, Budapest 1965, is given as an edge for White in *ECO*. The same evaluation can be made of 7...♕e7 8 g4 ♘f4 9 ♘xf4 exf4 10 ♗xf4 ♗xc3+ 11 bxc3 ♕xe4+ 12 ♕e2 ♕xe2+ 13 ♗xe2, which was the course taken in Efimov-Pedersen, Saint Vincent 2000.

b) 6...♘bd7!? 7 ♗g5 (7 ♘g3 transposes to Game 3) 7...h6 8 ♗h4 0-0 9 f3 a6 10 g4 ♘b6 11 ♕b3 c6 12 ♗f2 ♘fd7 was unclear in Szabo-Gligoric, Buesum 1969.

c) 6...c5 7 h3 a6 (7...h5 8 a3, Bertok-Minic, Ljubljana 1960, and now Minev – in *ECO* – proposes 8...♘h7, intending ...♗f6, with an assessment of an edge for White) 8 a4 h5 9 g3! ♗h6 10 ♗xh6 ♖xh6 11 ♕d2 ♖h8 12 a5 ♘bd7 13 ♗g2 h4 14 g4, Korchnoi-Gheorghiu, Baden-Baden 1981. Now 14...♘h7!?, heading for g5, limits White to a modest lead.

d) 6...♘a6 7 ♘g3 h5 8 h4!? ♘c5 (Forintos-Vigh, Hungary 1995, went 8...♘h7 9 ♘ge2 ♗f6 10 g3 ♗g7, when 11 ♗g2!? should offer White something) 9 ♗g5 ♗h6 10 ♗xh6 ♖xh6 11 ♕d2 (also promising is 11 b4!?) 11...♖h8 12 0-0-0 ♔f8 (12...♕e7 followed by ...♗d7 and ...0-0-0 is unclear) 13 f3 a6 14 b4 ♘cd7 15 ♔b2 ♔g7 16 a3 a5 17 ♔b3 axb4 18 axb4, Ermenkov-Spasov, Sofia 1991. In *ECO* Spasov gives 18...♘b6!? 19 ♗e2 ♗d7 20 ♖a1 as a shade preferable for White thanks to the territorial advantage.

7 ♘g3 cxd5

7...a6 8 ♗e2 h5 9 ♗g5 cxd5 10 exd5! gives White an edge (*ECO*), as in Miles-Johansen, Edinburgh 1985.

8 cxd5 a6 9 a4 h5 10 ♗e2

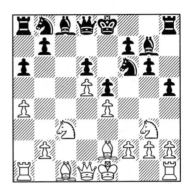

10... a5

10...h4!? 11 ♘f1 ♘h5 12 ♗xh5 ♖xh5 is interesting but we prefer White in this uncommon situation.

11 ♘f1 ♘a6 12 ♗g5 ♗h6 13 ♗b5+

Black is going to play ...♔f8-g7 anyway, so more logical is 13 ♗xh6 ♖xh6 14 ♗xa6!? (this move is also good in the main line) 14...♖xa6 15 ♘e3 with a couple of oddly posted rooks and the more pleasant prospects for White.

13...♔f8 14 ♗xh6+ ♖xh6 15 ♘e3 ♘c5 16 ♕c2 ♘g4 17 ♘c4 f5 18 f3 ♘f6 19 0-0-0

White might consider castling short, which appears to offer chances of an advantage.

19...♔g7 20 b3 ♖h8 21 ♔b2 ♖f8 22 ♖df1 ♕c7 23 ♕e2 fxe4 24 fxe4 ♗g4 25 ♕e3 ♗d7?! 26 ♗xd7 ♘fxd7 27 ♘b5 ♘xa4+ 28 ♔a3 ♕c5+ 29 ♕xc5 ♘axc5 30 ♘cxd6 ♖xf1 31 ♖xf1 ♖f8 32 ♖xf8 ♔xf8 33 b4 axb4+ 34 ♔xb4 ♘d3+?! ½-½

34...♘e7 is more precise, but the game anyway ends peacefully.

Game 5
Korchnoi-Gallagher
Zonal Tournament, Dresden 1998

1 d4 ♘f6 2 c4 g6 3 ♘c3 ♗g7 4 e4 d6 5

②ge2 a6 6 g3!?

White steers the game back to the ♗g2 system, where the early ...a7-a6 could prove to be of little use. If Black insists on executing the plan with ...c7-c6 and ...b7-b5 it will be met with ♗g2 followed by e4-e5 with a nice game for White. On the other hand, the g1-knight is seldom developed on e2 in the fianchetto line. Nevertheless, there is no clear route to equality for Black. Incidentally, 6 f3 makes sense, transposing to the Sämisch variation.

6...0-0

A dubious choice is 6...c5, e.g. 7 dxc5 ♕a5?! (7...dxc5 8 ♕xd8+ ♔xd8 9 e5 ②g4 10 f4 ②c6 11 ♗g2) 8 cxd6 ②xe4 9 ♕d5 ②c5 10 ♗e3 exd6 11 ♕xd6 ②bd7 12 ♗g2 ♗e5 13 ♕d5 0-0 14 0-0 and Black was in trouble in Narciso Dublan-Matamoros Franco, Lanzarote 2003.

7 ♗g2 ②bd7 8 0-0 e5 9 b3

9 dxe5!? ②xe5 10 b3 is enough for a plus according to Korchnoi.

9...exd4 10 ②xd4 ♖e8 11 ♗e3 ♖b8

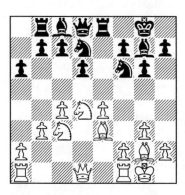

This type of position is quite unpleasant for Black, despite the fact that he has no weak points and faces no direct threats. White's extra space facilitates fluid development and therefore affords him a healthy mobilisation of forces across the board. With this in mind Black is looking to generate counterplay with ...c7-c5 and ...b7-b5.

12 ♖c1 c5

As subsequent events demonstrate, the text

has no tactical justification. Perhaps Black should have decided on a passive move such as 12...c6, or Korchnoi's 12...②e5, when White must consider a knight coming to g4 as well as the 'threatened' ...c7-c5. However, after 13 ♖c2! (Korchnoi) White remains on top, the point being that after ...c7-c5 White's rook will be ready to attack the d6-pawn by switching files to d2 (of course the safety of a rook on d6 should be borne in mind). Black is not sufficiently prepared for the complications that result from 13...b5, e.g. 14 cxb5 axb5 15 f4 ②eg4 16 ②c6 ②xe3 17 ♕c1 ②xc2 18 ♕xc2! ♕d7 19 ②xb8 ♕d8 20 ②c6 ♕d7 21 ②xb5 ♗a6 22 a4 and White has a safe extra pawn. Nor does 13...②fg4 or 13...②eg4 help due to the simple 14 ♗c1. This leaves 14 ②de2 b5 15 cxb5 axb5 16 ♖d2 with decent pressure for White.

13 ②de2 b5

13...②e5 14 ♖c2 b5 15 cxb5 axb5 16 ♖d2 transposes to 12...②e5, above.

14 cxb5 axb5 15 ♕xd6 b4 16 ②a4 ②xe4

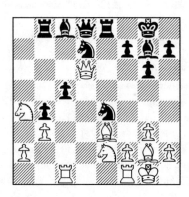

16...♗b7 17 ②xc5 ②xc5 18 ♗xc5 ♗xe4 19 ♕xd8 ♖bxd8 20 ②d4 ♗f8 21 ♗xf8 ♔xf8 22 ♖fd1 does not help Black, who is also without compensation in the event of 16...♗e6 17 ♕d2 ②xe4 18 ♗xe4 ♖xe4 19 ②xc5 ♖e7 20 ②d4.

17 ♕d3?!

17 ♗xe4! ♖xe4 18 ②xc5 improves, when Korchnoi analyses the following: 18...♖e8 (18...♖e7 19 ♗g5 f6 20 ♗f4, 18...♖xe3 19 fxe3

♕e8 20 ♘xd7 ♗xd7 21 ♕f4 and 18...♗f8 19
♕d3 ♖xe3 20 fxe3 ♗xc5 21 ♖xc5 ♗a6 22
♕xa6 ♘xc5 23 ♕a7 are all awful for Black) 19
♖fd1 ♗f8 20 ♕d4 ♗xc5 21 ♖xc5 with a big
advantage.

17...♕e7 18 ♘f4 ♗b7 19 ♘d5 ♕e5?

19...♗xd5 20 ♕xd5 ♘c3 21 ♘xc3 bxc3 22
♖fd1 ♖ed8 23 ♗g5 ♘f6 24 ♕c4 ♖xd1+ 25
♖xd1 h6 26 ♗f4 ♖b4 27 ♕xc3 ♘d5 28 ♕c1
♘xf4 29 gxf4 is a lesser evil that restricts
White to a slight edge according to Korchnoi.

20 ♖fd1 ♖bd8?

Now White is easily winning, although the
improvements still leave Black struggling:
20...♗xd5 21 ♕xd5 ♕xd5 22 ♖xd5 ♘df6 23
♗xe4 ♘xe4 24 ♗xc5 is simple, or 20...♘df6
21 ♘xf6+ ♕xf6 (21...♗xf6 22 ♘xc5 ♘xc5 23
♗xc5 ♖ed8 24 ♕e3 ♖xd1+ 25 ♖xd1 ♗xg2 26
♔xg2) 22 ♘xc5 ♘xc5 23 ♗xc5 ♖ed8 24 ♕c4
♗xg2 25 ♔xg2 ♗h6 26 ♖xd8+ ♖xd8 27 ♖e1
etc.

**21 ♕xe4 ♕xe4 22 ♗xe4 ♖xe4 23 ♘db6
♗d4 24 ♘xd7 ♖xe3 25 fxe3 ♗xe3+ 26
♔f1 ♗a6+ 27 ♖c4 ♗d4 28 ♘dxc5 1-0**

Game 6
Freise-Wiege
Correspondence 1998

**1 d4 ♘f6 2 c4 g6 3 ♘c3 ♗g7 4 e4 d6 5
♘ge2 a6 6 ♘g3 ♘bd7 7 ♗e2**

Rather premature is 7 a4?! when, according
to Kasparov, 7...h5 8 ♗e2 e5 leads to complications that offer Black healthy counterplay: 9
♗e3 (9 d5?! a5) 9...exd4 10 ♗xd4 ♘e5 11 h3?!
(11 0-0 h4 12 ♘h1 c5 13 ♗e3 is unclear) and
now Black has two options:

a) 11...♕e7?! 12 f4 h4 13 ♘f1 ♘c6 14 ♘d5
♕d8 15 ♗c3 0-0 16 ♘d2, Yusupov-
Kasparov, Moscow 1994, favours White.

b) The improvement is 11...♗h6! 12 0-0
(12 ♘d5 h4) 12...♗f4!? (12...♘c6).

7...h5

A typical advance of the h-pawn. Others:

a) The 'Benko' gambit should not worry
White – 7...c5 8 d5 b5 9 cxb5 (Nikolaidis-

Mihelakis, Kavala 1999) is evaluated by Kasparov in *ECO* as slightly better for White.

b) 7...e5, and after 8 d5 0-0 9 0-0 ♘e8 10
♗e3 f5 11 exf5 gxf5 12 f4 Black's ...a7-a6 had
given White a very useful additional tempo in
Kaposztas-Manik, Hlohovec 1996.

8 ♗e3

8 f3 e5 9 d5 h4 10 ♘f1 ♘h5 11 ♘e3 ♗h6
led to excellent counterplay for Black in Corral
Blanco-Pablo Marin, Barcelona 2000.

8...c6 9 f3 b5 10 c5

White wants space on the queenside.

10...h4

10...dxc5 11 dxc5 ♕c7 was not enough for
equality in Serper-Nikolaidis, St Petersburg
1993, which continued 12 0-0 h4 13 ♘h1
♘h5 14 ♕d2 e5 15 ♘f2 ♘f8 16 a4, although
11...h4!? is worth investigating.

11 ♘f1 dxc5 12 dxc5 h3

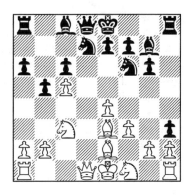

The long march of the h-pawn has its pros
and cons. On the one hand it disrupts White,
while on the other it will require constant protection. 12...♕c7 maintains the balance.

**13 g3 0-0 14 ♘d2 ♘e5 15 ♕c2 ♗e6 16
0-0 ♕c7 17 ♘d1 ♗h7 18 ♘f2 ♗h6?**

Black's method of trading bishops is both
unusual and suspicious. The simple 18...♖ad8
offers Black adequate prospects.

**19 ♗xh6 ♔xh6 20 ♕c3 ♖ad8 21 f4 ♘eg4
22 f5 ♘xf2 23 ♖xf2 gxf5 24 exf5 ♗d5 25
g4 ♖g8 26 ♕xh3+ ♔g7 27 ♕e3 ♔f8 28
h3**

White is simply a safe pawn to the good.

28...⌐h8 29 a4 b4 30 a5

Of course White can never take on a6 in view of ...⌐xg4.

30...⌐h4 31 b3?!

Contributing nothing to the cause. In this sharp position White should consider 31 ⌐a4!?, intending to meet 31...⌐e8 (31...⌐d7 32 ⌐f1) with the strong 32 g5 ⌐e4? (32...⌐d7 33 ⌐f1) 33 ⌐xb4 etc.

31...⌐e8 32 ⌐h2 e6 33 ⌐f2 ⌐h8 34 fxe6 ⌐xe6

Black is gradually generating counterplay.

35 ⌐c4?!

35 ⌐e1 is preferable.

35...⌐xc4 36 ⌐xc4 ⌐e4 37 ⌐e3 ⌐e7 38 ⌐d1 ⌐xc5 39 ⌐g3 ⌐e4 40 ⌐d3 ⌐c3 41 ⌐d8+ ⌐g7 42 ⌐d4+ f6 43 ⌐d6 ⌐e5 44 ⌐f5+

44 ⌐f1 ⌐b5 (44...⌐xa5? 45 ⌐xb4 ⌐a7+ 46 ⌐h1) 45 ⌐xb5 axb5 is level.

44...⌐xf5 45 gxf5 ⌐xd1 46 ⌐xd1 ⌐c5+ 47 ⌐f2 ⌐g8 48 ⌐f3 ⌐f8+ 49 ⌐h2 ⌐xa5 50 ⌐f4 ⌐f7 51 ⌐c4+ ⌐d5 52 ⌐xb4 ⌐e5+ 53 ⌐f4 ⌐b8 54 ⌐xe5 fxe5 55 ⌐c2 ⌐b6 56 ⌐g3 ⌐f6 57 b4 ⌐xf5 58 ⌐c4 ⌐e6 59 ⌐f3

Better is 59 h4.

59...⌐d5 60 ⌐h4 ⌐b8 61 ⌐e3 ⌐f8 62 ⌐e2 ⌐f5 63 ⌐e3 ⌐f1 64 ⌐e2 ⌐g1 65 ⌐d2 ⌐g2+ 66 ⌐d3 ½-½

A surprising decision considering Black's improved prospects.

Game 7
Novikov-Van Wely
Helsinki 1992

---

1 d4 ⌐f6 2 c4 g6 3 ⌐c3 ⌐g7 4 e4 d6 5 ⌐ge2 a6

The actual move order in the game was 5...c6 6 ⌐g3 h5 7 ⌐e2 a6 8 0-0 b5 9 e5 but we have altered the sequence in order to more conveniently look at alternatives.

6 ⌐g3

Black prepares action on the queenside based on a timely push of the b-pawn. Al-

though this plan isn't usually Black's main weapon it is occasionally used in various systems, often being started before castling. Generally White's thematic reaction is e4-e5.

6...c6 7 ⌐e2

Alternatives:

a) 7 h4 h5 8 ⌐g5 ⌐bd7 9 ⌐e2 0-0 10 ⌐d2 b5 11 cxb5 axb5 12 b4 ⌐b6 (Liardet-Gallagher, Geneva 1993) 13 ⌐c1 is given as unclear in *NCO*.

b) 7 f4. The Four Pawns Attack theme appears logical here, with Black having 'lost' two tempi on the queenside. However, White's knight on g3 is not ideally placed, and this has also taken time. Eliet-Petit, Montpellier 1991 saw 7...0-0! (rapid development is paramount) 8 e5 ⌐fd7 (8...dxe5 9 dxe5 ⌐xd1+ 10 ⌐xd1 ⌐e8 11 ⌐e3 f6 12 exf6 ⌐xf6 is equal) 9 ⌐e3 c5 and the challenge in the centre resulted in muddying the water.

c) 7 a4. This advance has more appeal when Black has already played ...⌐bd7. A typical reaction is 7...a5, freeing the a6-square to make way for ...⌐a6-b4. Then 8 ⌐e2 0-0 leads to the following position:

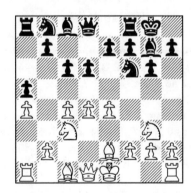

9 f4?! gives the game a Four Pawns flavour that tastes nicer for Black thanks to White's vulnerable queenside dark squares. 9...e5 10 dxe5 dxe5 11 ⌐xd8 ⌐xd8 12 f5 ⌐a6 13 0-0 ⌐d7 14 ⌐e3 ⌐dc5 15 ⌐ad1 ⌐d7 (Flear-Gallagher, Brocco 1991) is a shade favourable for Black according to *NCO*. 9 h4 e5 10 d5 h5 11 ⌐g5 ⌐b6 12 ⌐a3 ⌐bd7! 13 ⌐c2 ⌐c5 14

♗e3 ♗d7 15 ♘f1 ♖ac8 16 ♘d2 ♕b4 17 ♘a2 ♕b6 was balanced in Ionov-Bologan, Moscow 1991. 9 0-0 e5 10 ♗e3 (10 d5 ♘a6 11 ♗e3 ♘c5 12 ♖e1 h5 13 f3 h4 14 ♘h1 ♘h5 15 ♘f2, Verdikhanov-Kruppa, Nikolaev 1993, and now 15...♗f6! continues the fight for the dark squares on the kingside – 16 ♘d3 ♘xd3 17 ♕xd3 ♗g5 18 ♗f1 ♗xe3+ 19 ♕xe3 with an unclear position according to Verdikhanov and Diafarov in *ECO*) 10...♘a6 11 ♕d2 (11 dxe5 dxe5 12 ♕xd8 ♖xd8 13 ♖ad1 ♖xd1 14 ♖xd1 ♗e6 with equality in Andersen-Jaksland, Copenhagen 2004) 11...♘g4 12 ♗xg4 ♗xg4 13 f3 exd4 14 ♗xd4 ♗e6 15 ♖ad1 ♘c5 16 ♗xg7 ♔xg7 17 ♔h1 f6 and Black was okay in Gulko-Benjamin, Los Angeles 1991.

7...h5

Not surprisingly Black is free to adopt another strategy:

a) 7...♘bd7 8 ♗e3 h5 9 f3 b5 10 c5 dxc5 11 dxc5 ♕c7 (11...h4!? 12 ♘f1 transposes to Game 6) 12 0-0 h4 13 ♘h1 ♘h5 14 ♕d2 e5 15 ♘f2 was the continuation of Serper-Nikolaidis, St Petersburg 1993, the position after the subsequent 15...♘f4 16 ♘d3 ♗h6 17 a4 assessed as slightly better for White by Serper in *ECO*.

b) 7...b5!? and now:

b1) 8 cxb5 axb5 9 b4 h5 10 ♗e3 ♘g4 11 ♗xg4 ♗xg4 12 f3 ♗e6 13 ♘ge2 ♗c4 was quite pleasant for Black in Hanks-Fuller, Adelaide 1990.

b2) 8 0-0 bxc4 (8...h5!? 9 e5 dxe5 10 dxe5 ♕xd1 11 ♖xd1 leads to the main game, but 9 a3 is interesting here) 9 ♗xc4 d5 10 ♗b3 dxe4 11 ♘gxe4 (Novikov-Kruppa, Moscow 1991) 11...♘xe4!? 12 ♘xe4 ♕xd4 13 ♕f3 and White has definite compensation for the pawn.

b3) 8 e5 dxe5 9 dxe5 ♕xd1+ 10 ♘xd1 ♘fd7 11 f4 ♘b6 (11...f6!?) 12 ♘e3 ♗e6 13 ♗d2 ♘8d7 14 ♖c1 ♗h6 left much to play for in Goormachtigh-Watson, Brussels 1986.

8 0-0 b5

Also good is 8...♘bd7, monitoring e5. M.Gurevich-Van Wely, Tastrup 1992 continued 9 ♖e1 b5 10 a3 0-0 11 ♗g5 ♘h7 12 ♗e3

♖b8 13 ♕d2 e5 14 d5, when the position after 14...cxd5 15 cxd5 h4!? 16 ♘f1 f5 is far from clear according to Gurevich (*ECO*).

9 e5 dxe5 10 dxe5 ♕xd1 11 ♖xd1 ♘g4 12 f4

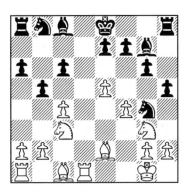

A key position. If Black fails to contest White's strong grip on the centre he will be doomed to passivity.

12...g5!

Now or never. Black exploits the fact that the capture on f4 comes with tempo, ensuring sufficient counterplay.

13 h3 gxf4 14 ♗xf4 ♗xe5?!

With the active 14...h4 15 ♗xg4 ♗xg4 16 hxg4 hxg3 17 ♗xg3 (Novikov) 17...♘d7 18 e6 fxe6 Black would secure decent chances in the ending.

15 ♘xh5 ♗xf4 16 ♘xf4 ♘e3 17 ♖dc1

17 ♖d2 e5 18 ♘h5 ♘xc4 19 ♘f6+ ♔e7 20 ♗xc4 bxc4 (Hurme-Nouro, Finland 1993) with compensation according to Novikov.

17...♘xc4 18 ♗xc4 bxc4 19 ♘a4 ♘d7 20 ♖xc4

The transition to an ending has favoured White. Black has the weaker, vulnerable pawns, while White's are quite safe. Meanwhile, White also has the more active forces. Nevertheless, such endings tend to require accurate play from the attacker, who must consider the possibility of allowing his opponent some kind of counterplay as a result of targeting and winning a pawn.

20...♘e5 21 ♖c5 f6 22 ♘b6 ♖b8 23

♘xc8 ♖xc8 24 ♖a5 ♖a8 25 ♖d1

The apparently active 25 ♘e6 ♔f7 26 ♘c5 is premature, and Black has no problems after the simple 26...♘c4 27 ♖xa6 ♖xa6 28 ♘xa6 ♘xb2, 26...♖ag8!? 27 ♔h1 (27 ♔f1? ♘c4 28 ♖xa6 ♘e3+ 29 ♔f2 ♖xg2+ 30 ♔xe3 ♖xh3+ 31 ♔d4 e5+ 32 ♔c4 ♖c2+ 33 ♔b4 ♖h4+ 34 ♔a5 ♖xc5+ 35 ♔b6 ♖c2 and Black has serious winning chances) 27...♘c4 28 ♖xa6 ♘e3 29 ♖g1 ♖g3 30 ♔h2 ♖hg8 31 b4 f5 or 26...♖h5 27 ♖xa6 ♖g8 (Maki Uuro-Salo, Helsinki 1993).

25...♔f7 26 b3 ♖hb8

26...♖hd8!? (Novikov).

27 ♖d4 ♖d8

27...♖b5 28 ♖da4 improves, with an edge for White.

28 ♖xd8 ♖xd8 29 ♖xa6 ♖d2 30 ♔h2?!

Novikov's 30 a4!? ♖b2 31 ♖b6 ♖a2, with compensation, or 30 ♔f1 offers superior chances, although it is not easy to make the extra pawn tell.

30...♘f3+ 31 ♔g3 ♘e1

Black has counterplay based on the weak g2-pawn.

32 ♖a7 f5 33 h4 ♔f6 34 ♘h5+ ♔f7 35 ♘f4 ♔f6 36 ♘h5+ ♔f7 37 ♘f4 ½-½

Game 8
Yusupov-Shaked
Linares Open 1997

---

1 d4 ♘f6 2 c4 g6 3 ♘c3 ♗g7 4 e4 d6 5 ♘ge2 0-0

While delaying castling is quite reasonable it is nonetheless the most popular continuation.

6 ♗g5 h6

Black can also play 6...a6 7 ♕d2 ♘bd7 8 ♘g3 c6, e.g. 9 ♗e2 (Horvath-Wang Rui, Budapest 2000) 9...b5! 10 0-0 (10 b3 b4 11 ♘a4 c5! with counterplay) 10...b4 11 ♘a4 c5 with chances for both sides. 9 ♗h6 e5 10 d5 cxd5 11 cxd5 ♗xh6 12 ♕xh6 ♘g4 13 ♕d2 ♕h4 14 h3 ♘gf6 15 ♗d3 ♘c5 16 ♗c2 a5 was also unclear in Kogan-Drozdov, Groningen 1994, while 9 a4 weakened the dark squares in

Chernin-Lautier, Paris 1989, both 9...a5 and 9...e5!? 10 d5 ♘c5 appearing fine for Black.

Let us return to 6...h6.

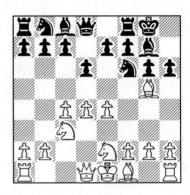

The bishop's arrival on g5 is not unusual for this and Sämisch lines, but here the text puts an awkward question to White in terms of where to put the piece next.

7 ♗f4

Alternatives:

a) 7 ♗h4 does not fit well with any system, e.g. 7...c5 8 f3 ♘c6 9 dxc5 dxc5 10 ♕xd8 ♖xd8 with good play for Black in Edery-Demarre, Paris 1993.

b) After 7 ♗e3 White invites 7...♘g4, e.g. 8 ♗c1 e5 9 h3 (9 d5 f5 10 f3 ♘f6 is a very good Sämisch for Black) 9...♘f6 10 d5 ♘bd7 11 g4 ♘h7 with mutual chances in Breder-Koetterheinrich, 1996 German U18 Championship, or 8...c5 9 d5 e6 10 h3 ♘e5 (Larsen-Gligoric, Leningrad 1973) 11 ♘g3, given as unclear by Gligoric in *ECO*.

7...♘c6

7...c5!? is an interesting option.

8 ♕d2

8 d5!? e5 (also good is 8...♘e5 9 ♘g3 c6 with chances for both sides – *ECO*) 9 ♗e3 ♘e7 10 f3 c6 11 ♕d2 h5 (11...cxd5 12 cxd5 h5 and 12...♔h7 are safer) and now White can try 12 dxc6 bxc6 13 ♖d1 d5 14 cxd5 cxd5 15 exd5 when Black does not have full compensation for the pawn. Instead Kohlweyer-Scalcione, Lido Estensi 2003 went 12 0-0-0 cxd5 13 cxd5 ♗d7 14 ♔b1 b5 15 ♘c1 b4 16

♘3e2 a5 with an interesting struggle ahead .

8...e5

8...♔h7!? comes to mind.

9 ♗xh6

Obviously not 9 dxe5? dxe5 10 ♗xh6? ♗xh6 11 ♕xh6 ♘b4 (Shaked) with a winning position for Black due to the threats of 12...♘c2+ and 12...♘d3.

9...♗xh6

Black cannot play 9...exd4? 10 ♗xg7 dxc3?? due to 11 ♕h6 (Shaked).

10 ♕xh6 ♘xd4

10...exd4 11 ♘d5 ♘xe4 is risky as 12 f3 followed by 0-0-0 and launching the h-pawn looks dangerous.

11 ♕d2

Quite harmless for Black is 11 ♘xd4 exd4 12 ♘d5 ♘g4 13 ♕d2 c6 (Shaked) with the slightly more pleasant prospects for Black.

11...c5

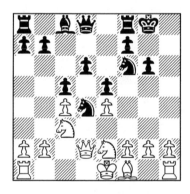

Now Black has a very solid position with a great outpost for the knight on d4.

12 ♘g3 a6 13 ♗d3

Shaked recommends 13 h4!? ♔g7 14 h5 ♖h8 with an unclear game.

13...b5 14 h4?!

One tempo too late! 14 0-0 ♗e6 15 b3, intending f2-f4, is proposed by Shaked.

14...♗e6 15 0-0-0?

The wrong decision. 15 b3!? maintains the balance.

15...bxc4 16 ♗b1 ♘h7 17 ♘f1?!

Again White has better, with 17 ♖df1 ♕f6,

17 h5 ♕g5 and 17 f4 exf4 18 ♕xf4 ♕f6 all limiting Black to an edge according to Shaked.

17...a5

17...♖b8!? followed by ...♕b6 and doubling rooks on the b-file might be preferable.

18 ♗c2 a4 19 a3

19 ♗xa4!? is on here.

19...♕b6 20 ♖e1 ♖fb8 21 ♗d1 ♖a7 22 ♖e3 ♖ab7 23 ♘xa4 ♕c6 24 h5 g5 25 ♘g3

25 h6 c3!?, or 25...f5 (Shaked).

25...c3 26 ♘xc3 ♖xb2 27 ♕xb2 ♖xb2 28 ♔xb2 ♕b6+ 29 ♔c1 ♘f6 30 ♘f1 ♕a5 31 ♔b2 ♕b6+ 32 ♔c1 ♕a5 33 ♔b2 ♘b5 34 ♘xb5 ♕xb5+ 35 ♔c1 ♕c4+ 36 ♗c2 ♘g4 37 ♖f3 ♕d4 38 ♘e3 ♕a1+?!

Shaked gives 38...♘xf2 39 ♖xf2 ♕xe3+ 40 ♖d2 c4 with a decisive lead.

39 ♗b1 ♕xa3+ 40 ♔d2 ♕b4+ 41 ♔c1 ♕a3+?!

41...♘xe3 42 ♖xe3 c4 is simpler.

42 ♔d2 ♕b2+ 43 ♗c2 ♕d4+ 44 ♔e2 ♘xe3 45 ♖xe3 ♗c4+ 46 ♔f3 f5! 47 g4 ♕b2 48 ♗b1 ♗e2+!! 49 ♔g2 f4 50 ♖eh3 c4 51 h6 ♔h7 52 ♖h5 ♕d2 53 ♔h3 ♕c3+ 54 ♔h2 ♕f3 55 ♖g1 ♕xf2+ 56 ♖g2 ♕e1 0-1

Game 9
Kakageldyev-Smirin
2002 Bled Olympiad

---

1 d4 ♘f6 2 c4 g6 3 ♘c3 ♗g7 4 e4 d6 5 ♘ge2 0-0 6 ♘g3

The main choice. The knight might appear awkwardly placed on g3, but it has its uses – both offensive and defensive. Apart from the obvious support of the advance of the h-pawn the knight also monitors f5, facilitating an attack on that point should Black seek to generate activity with ...f7-f5, as well as introducing the possibility of using h5 for the knight in the event of ...f7-f5, e4xf5, g6xf5 etc. On the downside, of course, White needs to keep in mind the implications of the advance ...h7-h5-h4.

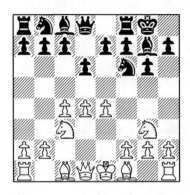

6...h5

As we remarked earlier, this move has both good and bad factors. Sometimes the pawn might prove weak and, consequently, Black's kingside weakened. This brings us to the alternatives:

a) 6...♘fd7 7 ♗e3 e5 8 d5 a5 9 ♗e2 ♘a6 10 0-0 h5 11 ♕d2 ♘ac5 was okay for both sides in Dive-Eid, Moscow 1994, while 9 ♗d3 ♘a6 10 a3 (Kurbetdinov-Golubka, Simferopol 2003) 10...♘ac5 11 ♗c2 ♘b6 is also interesting.

b) 6...♘c6 7 d5 ♘e5 (7...♘b8 8 ♗e2 c6 9 0-0 cxd5 10 cxd5 ♘a6 11 ♗e3 ♗d7 12 h3 ♕b8, Szabo-Westerinen, Leningrad 1967, and now 13 ♖b1 b5 14 b4 is given by Minev in *ECO* as favouring White) 8 ♗e2 e6 (8...c6 9 f4 ♘ed7 10 ♗e3 cxd5 11 cxd5 a6 12 0-0 b5 13 ♖c1 ♘b6 14 b3 was excellent for White in Malaniuk-Zagorskis, Swidnica 1997) 9 f4 ♘ed7 10 dxe6 fxe6 11 0-0 ♕e7 12 ♗e3 left Black still working to equalise in Forintos-Szabo, Hungary 1968.

7 ♗e2 h4

7...e5!? 8 d5 and now:

a) 8...h4 9 ♘f1 ♘h7 (9...♘e8 10 g4 a6 11 ♗e3 c6 12 g5 b5 13 a3 was a shade better for White in M.Ivanov-Mutschnik, Stuttgart 2003) 10 h3 ♘d7 (10...♘a6!? is worth a try) 11 ♘h2 f5 12 ♗e3 ♘df6 13 ♗d3 fxe4 14 ♘xe4 ♘h5 ½-½, Narciso Dublan-Moreno Carnero, Barcelona 2000.

b) 8...♘a6 9 ♗g5 ♕e8 10 ♘f1 ♘c5 11

♘d2 a5 12 0-0 ♗d7 13 b3 ♘h7 14 ♗e3 ♗f6 15 ♗h6 (15 a3!?, intending to expand by pushing the b-pawn, looks good) 15...♗g7 16 ♗e3 (16 ♗xg7 ♔xg7 17 a3 might be preferable) 16...♗f6 17 ♗h6 ♗g7 ½-½, Novikov-Ibragimov, Bled 1996.

c) 8...♘h7 9 ♗e3 ♘d7 (9...h4 10 ♘f1 ♘a6 11 ♘d2 helped White in Shemeakin-Prokhorov, Yalta 1995) 10 0-0 h4 11 ♘h1 f5 12 exf5 gxf5 13 f4 exf4 14 ♗xf4 ♘e5 15 ♘f2 ♘g5 16 ♘b5 ♗f6 17 ♘d4 (Novikov-Gleizerov, Pavlodar 1987) is given as an edge for White in *ECO*.

8 ♘f1

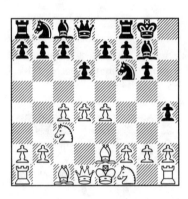

8...c5

a) 8...♘c6 9 d5 (9 ♗e3!?) 9...♘e5 10 h3 ♘h7 (Dive-Smart, London 1994 saw White emerge with the better prospects after 10...c6 11 ♗g5 ♕a5 12 ♘d2) 11 f4 ♘d7 12 ♗e3 e5 ½-½, Dive-De Coverly, Norwich 1994, but 13 f5, with the idea 13...gxf5 14 exf5 ♘c5 15 g4, justifies continuing the struggle.

b) 8...♘h7 9 ♗e3, and now both 9...e6 10 ♘d2 e5 11 ♘f3 exd4 12 ♘xd4, Hort-Bouaziz, Tunis 1985, and 9...♘d7 10 ♕d2 e5 11 d5 f5 12 exf5 gxf5 13 f4, Remlinger-Situru, Honolulu 1996 were easier for White.

c) 8...e5!? and it is not clear whether White has anything better than transposition to 7...e5 8 d5 h4 (see the note to Black's 7th move).

9 d5 b5

An original idea in the spirit of the Benko Gambit. We think, however, that it is a rather inferior version for Black, and instead recommend 7...e5 or 8...e5 (above). Both 9...♕a5!? and 9...♘bd7!? lead to positions that are a touch preferable for White.

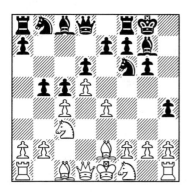

10 cxb5 h3 11 gxh3 a6 12 bxa6 ♗xh3 13 ♖g1 ♘xa6 14 ♖g3 ♕c8

Now the queen will be tied to the h3-bishop, which will have to withdraw sooner or later anyway. Simply dropping to d7 (even on the next move) is sensible.

15 ♘e3 ♘c7 16 f4 ♗d7 17 f5 gxf5 18 ♘xf5

White should play 18 ♘c4, e.g. 18...♕d8 19 ♗h6 ♘ce8 (19...♘fe8 20 ♕d2) 20 ♕d2 with a winning attack, or 18...fxe4 19 ♗h6 ♘ce8 20 ♘b6 ♕b7 21 ♘xa8 ♖xa8 22 ♕d2 etc.

18...♗xf5 19 exf5 ♕xf5 20 ♗h6 ♘ce8 21 ♕d3

White need not exchange queens, and more consistent is 21 ♕d2 intending 0-0-0, ♖dg1 with a winning attack.

21...♕h7 22 ♕e3 ♕c2 23 ♗xg7 ♘xg7 24 ♕h6 ♕h7 25 ♕g5 ♘d7?

Missing the last chance with 25...♕g6.

26 0-0-0 f6 27 ♕e3 ♖f7 28 ♖dg1 f5 29 ♕e6 ♘e5 30 ♖xg7+ ♕xg7 31 ♖xg7+ ♔xg7 32 ♗h5 1-0

Game 10
I.Sokolov-Hjartarson
Chess@iceland-B, Kopavogur 2000

---

1 d4 ♘f6 2 c4 g6 3 ♘c3 ♗g7 4 e4 d6 5

♘ge2 0-0 6 ♘g3 c6 7 ♗e2 a6

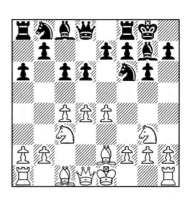

Once again Black elects for action involving ...b7-b5, hoping to have at his disposal both ...b5-b4 and ...b5xc4 followed by ...d6-d5.

8 ♗e3

White has tried several other continuations:

a) 8 h4!? h5 9 ♗e3 (9 ♗g5 b5 10 ♕d2 ♘bd7 11 ♖c1 ♕a5 was Psaras-Szekely, Athens 1997) 9...b5 (9...♘g4!?) 10 ♕d2, Tuchenhagen-Temirbaev, Shenyang 1999, and now Black can maintain the balance with 10...♘g4!?.

b) 8 ♗g5 b5 9 cxb5 axb5 10 a3 ♗b7 11 0-0 ♘bd7 12 ♕d2 ♕b6 13 b4 ♕d8 14 f4 (play on the queenside is another option, e.g. 14 ♖fc1!?, intending a2-a4, or the immediate 14 a4) 14...h6 15 ♗h4 ♘b6 16 ♔h1 ♗c8 17 ♗d3 e5 was seen in Topalov-Spasov, Elenite 1992, when 18 fxe5 dxe5 19 ♗xf6 ♗xf6 20 d5 would have led to an interesting struggle.

c) 8 a4 a5 9 0-0 e5 10 d5 ♘a6 11 ♗e3 (11 ♗g5!? ♖e8 12 ♕d2 ♘c5 13 ♖a3 was interesting in Sale-S.Nikolic, Belgrade 1989) 11...♘c5 12 ♖e1 h5 13 f3 h4 14 ♘h1 ♘h5 15 ♘f2. Thus far we have been following Verdikhanov-Kruppa, Nikolaev 1993, and here Verdikhanov gives 15...♗f6! 16 ♘d3 ♘xd3 17 ♕xd3 ♗g5! 18 ♗f1 ♗xe3+ 19 ♕xe3 as unclear, Black having rid himself of the passive dark-squared bishop.

d) After 8 0-0 ♘bd7 9 ♗e3 b5 White seems to be guaranteed an edge with either 10 cxb5 axb5 11 a3 ♘b6 12 b3 ♗e6 13 f4 b4

(Arkhipov-Schneider, Hungary 1992) 14 axb4 ♖xa1 15 ♕xa1 ♗xb3 or 10 b3 h5 11 f3 (Ratkovich-Kovalev, Minsk 2001) 11...h4 12 ♘h1 b4 13 ♘a4. This leaves the consistent 8...b5, with the following position:

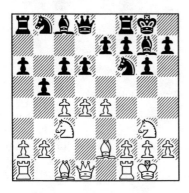

Now Serper-Schroer, Philadelphia 1997 continued 9 cxb5 axb5 10 b4 ♘bd7 11 a4, when Black should have settled for a slight disadvantage with 11...bxa4 12 ♖xa4. 9 f4 ♘bd7 10 e5 ♘e8 11 ♗e3 ♗b7 12 c5 ♘c7 13 cxd6 exd6 14 exd6 ♘d5 15 ♘xd5 cxd5 16 f5 was also good enough for a pull in Miles-Nunn, Amsterdam 1985.

However, the most direct is 9 e5 ♘fd7 (9...dxe5 10 dxe5 ♕xd1 11 ♖xd1 ♘g4 12 f4 f6 13 h3 ♘h6 14 exf6 exf6 15 ♘ge4 ♘f7 as in Tregubov-Hebden, Clichy 2001 when, according to Hazai, White should have played 16 c5!?, e.g. 16...f5 17 ♘d6 ♘xd6 18 cxd6 or 16...♘d7 17 ♗f3 f5 18 ♘d6 ♘xc5 19 ♗xc6 ♖b8 20 ♗e3, with an advantage for White).

After 9...♘fd7 White must decide what to about his e5-pawn:

d1) 10 f4 bxc4 (10...b4 11 ♘ce4) 11 ♗xc4 d5 (11...♘b6 12 ♗b3 a5 13 ♕f3 a4 14 ♗c2 favoured White in Poluljahov-K.Georgiev, Antalya 2002) 12 ♗e2 e6 13 ♗e3 a5 14 ♘a4 ♗a6 15 ♖c1 ♕c7 16 ♖c3 ♖c8 17 ♕c2 ♗xe2 18 ♘xe2 ♘b6 19 ♖c1 ♘xa4 20 ♕xa4 ♖a6 21 ♖1c2 ♗f8 22 ♘c1 ♘d7 23 ♘d3 ♕b7 24 ♖c1 ½-½, Novikov-Wojtkiewicz, New York 1993. White has been in the lead throughout but making progress is another matter.

d2) 10 exd6 exd6 11 ♗f4 ♘b6 12 cxb5 axb5 13 ♕d2 f5 14 a3 (14 ♗f3!?) 14...♗e6 15 ♖fe1 ♗f7 16 ♗g5 ♗f6 17 ♗xf6 ♕xf6 18 ♕f4 ♘d5 led to a level game in Naumkin-Hvenkilde, Copenhagen 1992, but 12 c5!? dxc5 13 dxc5 ♗xc3 14 bxc3 is worth investigating, e.g. 14...♘a4 15 ♗d6 ♘xc3 16 ♕d2 ♘xe2+ 17 ♘xe2 when White has at least enough for the pawn, or 14...♕xd1 15 ♖fxd1 ♘a4 16 ♗h6 ♖e8 17 ♘e4 ♘d7 18 ♗f3 with a definite plus.

8...b5 9 e5 ♘fd7 10 f4 bxc4

Worse are 10...♗b7 11 c5 ♕c7 12 0-0 dxe5 13 dxe5 when Black was in trouble in Goormachtigh-Peelen, Sas van Gent 1990, and 10...c5 11 ♗f3 ♖a7 12 dxc5 dxc5 (Palliser-Ghasi, Halifax 2003), when 13 cxb5 axb5 14 ♘xb5 sees White net both a pawn and the better position.

11 ♗xc4 ♘b6

In general Black should keep the d5-square for his pieces, 11...d5 12 ♗d3 e6 13 h4 f5 14 exf6 ♕xf6 15 h5, Novikov-Kozul, Tbilisi 1988, being a good example of what to avoid.

12 ♗b3 a5

Or if instead 12...♘d5 then 13 ♘xd5 cxd5 14 ♖c1 e6 15 0-0 with better chances for White.

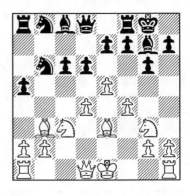

Let us have a look at the position after 12...a5. White certainly stands much better, two important factors being his extra space and attacking chances on the kingside involving the push of the h-pawn. Meanwhile, Black has no genuine prospects of counterplay in the near future. What Black should be concentrating on is White's dark-squared bishop – if he can manage to occupy d5 and block the position with ...f7-f5, thus accentuating the passive bishop, then he can at least make progress awkward.

13 a3?!

13 ♖c1 is more effective.

13...♗a6 14 h4 ♗c4

Right square, wrong piece. 14...♘c4 15 ♗xc4 (15 ♗c1 ♘d7 16 h5 c5) 15...♗xc4 16 ♖c1 f6 is the appropriate course.

15 ♗c2 f5

After 15...♘d5 16 ♘xd5 ♗xd5 17 h5 White gets to work on the kingside.

16 h5?!

White would do better to avoid the closing of the centre with 16 exf6 exf6 17 f5, providing the aforementioned bishop with some breathing space and intending 17...♕e7 (or 17...♖e8) 18 ♔f2.

16...e6

16...♘d5 seems to limit White to an edge.

17 ♕f3 ♘d5 18 hxg6 hxg6 19 ♗f2?!

19 b3! ♗a6 20 ♘ge2 ♗xe2 21 ♘xe2 ♘d7 22 ♗f2 is excellent for White.

19...♘d7

19...a4 makes life more difficult for White.

20 ♘ge2

Again 20 b3 comes to mind, when 20...♗a6 21 ♘ge2 ♘xc3 22 ♘xc3 favours White.

20...♖b8 21 ♖b1 ♔f7 22 ♘g1?!

Too passive. White has missed his chance; 22 ♗h4 and 22 g4 are preferable.

22...♘xc3

The active and consistent 22...dxe5!? 23 dxe5 ♖h8 gives Black good play.

23 ♕xc3 ♗d5 24 ♘f3 ♗xf3?

24...dxe5!? 25 dxe5 ♖h8 is unclear.

25 ♕xf3 d5?!

Taking away a potentially useful square cannot be good, although careless play has seen Black drift back into a poor position, e.g. 25...♖h8 26 ♖xh8 ♗xh8 27 g4! and Black is in trouble. Relatively best is 25...dxe5 26 dxe5

♘b6 27 ♗c5 ♖h8 28 ♖xh8 ♗xh8 29 g3 ♕d5 30 ♕xd5 ♘xd5, with a lead for White.

26 g4 ♖h8

N.B. On both the Internet and ChessBase the game runs 26...♖g8 27 ♖h8 ♖f8 28 ♖h1 ♖h8 but this must be an error, so we have corrected it as follows:

27 ♖g1 ♕e7 28 ♕c3 ♖bc8 29 ♕xa5 c5 30 ♗a4 cxd4 31 gxf5 gxf5 32 ♕a7 ♖hd8 33 ♖d1 ♖a8 34 ♕xd4 ♖h8 35 ♖d3 ♗f8 36 ♖c3 ♕d8 37 ♗c2 ♗e7 38 ♖cg3

38 ♗xf5! wins at once.

38...♗h4 39 ♖g7+ ♔f8 40 ♕b4+ ♗e7 41 ♕b5 ♖b8 42 ♕e2 ♖xb2 43 ♕h5 1-0

> ## Game 11
> ## Vladimirov-Gadjily
> *Dubai 2001*

---

1 d4 ♘f6 2 c4 g6 3 ♘c3 ♗g7 4 e4 d6 5 ♘ge2 0-0 6 ♘g3 ♘bd7 7 ♗e2 c6

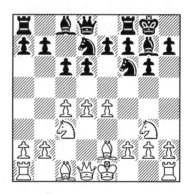

Black prepares ...e7-e5. 7...a6 8 0-0 c5 9 d5 ♖b8 10 f4 ♘e8 helped only White in Rodriguez Castelao-Gonzalez Blanco, Gijon 2002, when 11 ♗e3 secures a definite advantage.

8 0-0

Castling is perfectly natural, but there are alternatives:

a) 8 h4!? h5 9 ♗e3 a5?! 10 ♕d2 ♖e8 11 f4 e5 12 fxe5 dxe5 13 d5 ♘h7 14 0-0-0 ♗f6 was the course of Vasiliou-Exarchos, Ambelokipi 2002, and now 15 ♘f1, intending to launch the g-pawn, spells trouble for Black. An improvement is 9...a6 followed by ...b7-b5.

b) 8 ♗g5 h6 9 ♗e3 a6 10 ♕d2 h5 11 ♗h6 h4 12 ♗xg7 ♔xg7 13 ♘f1, I.Sokolov-Van Wely, Akureyri 1994, is an edge for White according to *ECO*.

c) Corral Blanco-Illescas Cordoba, Cala Galdana 1999 went 8 ♗e3 a6 9 ♕d2 b5 10 ♗h6 (10 f3 and 10 0-0 both favour White) and now 10...♗xh6!? 11 ♕xh6 b4 12 ♘d1 e5 is unclear.

8...e5

8...a6 transposes to Game 10, note to White's 8th move ('d').

9 d5

Also good is 9 ♗e3, e.g. 9...♘e8 10 ♕d2 ♕c7 11 ♖ad1 f5 12 exf5 gxf5 13 dxe5 dxe5 Nickel-Hueneburg, MVP 1996, when 14 f4 is very good for White. Black should play 9...a6 10 d5 cxd5 11 cxd5, transposing to Game 15.

9...c5

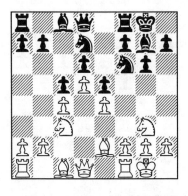

This cannot be recommended. Although Black has closed the position and has no weaknesses, in doing so he has also deprived himself of any counterplay. Consequently White has a modest but long-term advantage on both flanks. With this in mind Black has 9...cxd5, transposing to Game 15.

10 a3

In the event of 10 ♖b1 Black should play 10...♘e8!?, intending ...f7-f5 and limiting White to an edge. This is certainly an improvement on Kaposztas-Kanya, Salgotarjan 1979, where 10...a6 11 a3 ♖b8 12 b4 ♕c7 13

♗e3 b6 14 ♕d2 was awful for Black.

10...♔h8

10...♘e8 11 ♗g4 ♘b6 12 ♗xc8 ♖xc8 was seen in Bakros-Hadorn, Varmdo 1988, and now 13 b3 is enough to secure a small advantage.

11 ♗e3 ♘g8 12 ♕d2 h5 13 ♖ab1 ♔h7

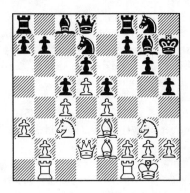

Preparing a trade of the dark-squared bishops, after which White – who will be left with his lesser bishop – will not be so comfortable on the dark squares. There is also another feasible plan available in 13...h4 14 ♘h1 ♘e7 15 f3 f5, when Black should be close to equality.

14 b4 ♗h6 15 ♘b5 h4 16 ♘h1 ♕e7 17 ♖be1 a6 18 ♘c3 a5 19 bxa5

19 b5 is an option.

19...♖xa5 20 ♘b5 ♖a6 21 ♖b1 ♘b6 22 ♖b3 ♗xe3 23 ♕xe3 ♘h6 24 f4

This thrust is connected with some kind of strategic risk, which is why some players might prefer the safer 24 f3 followed by ♘f2.

24...exf4 25 ♕xf4 ♘d7 26 ♘f2 ♘e5 27 ♘h3 ♗xh3 28 ♖xh3 g5 29 ♕f6?

Under no circumstances should White exchange queens, and now White's future begins to look rather bleak. Instead 29 ♕f2 keeps the game well balanced.

29...♕xf6 30 ♖xf6 ♖d8 31 g3 ♔g7 32 ♖f1 hxg3 33 ♖xg3 ♔g6 34 ♔f2 ♖d7 35 ♖fg1 f6 36 ♔e1 ♔g7 37 h4 g4 38 h5 ♔h7 39 ♖f1 ♖f7 40 ♖g2 ♘g8??

It is difficult to understand how Black arrived at this blunder. After the simple 40...f5 41 exf5 (41 ♖gf2 fxe4 42 ♖xf7+ ♘hxf7 43 ♗xg4 ♘g5) 41...♖xf5 White would be seriously regretting his 29th move.

41 ♗xg4 ♘xc4 42 ♔e2?

Why not 42 ♗e6, winning material?

42...♖a5 43 ♗f5+ ♔h8 44 ♖b1 ♘h6 45 ♗e6 ♖e7?

45...♖g7 puts up more resistance.

46 ♖g6 ♘f7 47 ♖bg1 ♘ce5 48 ♖g8+ ♔h7 49 ♗f5+ ♔h6 50 ♖1g7 ♔xh5 51 ♖g1 1-0

Game 12
Poluljahov-Sale
ADCF Masters, Abu Dhabi 2002

---

1 e4 g6 2 d4 ♗g7 3 c4 d6 4 ♘c3 ♘f6 5 ♘ge2 0-0 6 ♘g3 c5

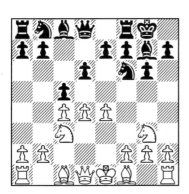

Black prepares to play in the style of Modern Benoni Defence...

7 d5

Unlike Game 1, 7 dxc5 is harmless for Black here as he has already castled, e.g. 7...dxc5 8 ♕xd8 ♖xd8:

a) Black is fine after 9 ♘d5 ♘c6 10 ♗e3 ♘d4 11 0-0-0 ♘xd5 12 exd5, Arbil-Goldfine, San Francisco 2002 – 12...e6 is equal, while 9...♘xd5 and 10...e6 looks nice for Black.

b) Smirnov-Usov, Tula 2001 went 9 e5 ♘e8 10 f4 ♘c6 11 ♗e3 b6 (11...g5!?) 12 ♗e2 ♘d4 13 ♗xd4, when 13...cxd4 is very pleasant for Black. Perhaps even better is 9...♘g4 10 f4

♘c6 11 ♗e2 g5 or 10 ♘d5 ♘c6 11 f4 g5 with excellent counterplay.

7...e6

The standard plan, after which positions often arise that are similar to some lines of the Averbakh or the 5 h3 systems. After exchange on d5 White can play the Modern Benoni or exd5. In the latter case White usually has a small space advantage but Black's position is solid enough. In comparison with the system with h2-h3 White cannot advance his kingside pawns as his knight stands on g3.

7...a6 8 ♗e2 ♕c7 9 0-0 h5 10 a4 b6 11 ♖e1 ♘bd7 12 h3 ♖e8 13 ♗f4 ♘h7 14 ♕d2 ♖b8 15 ♘f1 was an edge for White in Kaposztas-Nowik, Budapest 1998. Takeuchi-Clayton, Correspondence 2001 went 7...e5 8 ♗e2 ♘e8 9 h4 f5 10 exf5 gxf5, when 11 ♘h5! would have secured White a lead. White could also have emerged with the better game after 7...♘bd7 8 ♗e2 a6 9 h4 h5 10 ♗g5 ♖b8 11 ♕d2 ♘e5 in Beheshtaein-Guliev, Fajr 2001 with 12 0-0.

This leaves 7...♘a6 8 ♗e2:

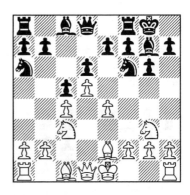

a) 8...e6 9 0-0 ♘c7

a1) 10 ♗f4 exd5 (10...e5 11 ♗e3 ♕e7 12 h3 h6 13 ♕d2 ♔h7 14 ♗d3 b6 15 ♖ae1 favoured White in Hort-Duric, Antwerp 1994) 11 exd5 ♘fe8!? (intending ...f7-f5) 12 ♕d2 f5 13 ♖fe1 (13 a3!?) 13...♗f6 14 ♗h6 ♘g7 15 ♗d3 ♖e8 16 f4 ♗d7 17 ♗g5 saw White earn a slight advantage in Prusikhin-Madl, Rieden 1996, although after 17...♖xe1+ 18 ♖xe1 ♕f8

19 ♗xf6 ♕xf6 20 ♘f1 ♖b8 21 ♕e2 ♖e8 the game was agreed drawn.

a2) 10 h3 exd5 11 exd5 ♖e8 (11...♖b8 12 a4 b6 13 ♗g5 h6 14 ♗e3 ♘h7, Hoffman-Becerra Rivero, Havana 1999 and now 15 ♕d2 h5 16 ♗d3 keeps White just ahead) 12 ♗g5 h6 13 ♗e3 b6 14 ♕d2 ♔h7 was the course of Flear-Botterill, Southampton 1986, and now both 15 ♗d3 and 15 ♗f4 put the onus on Black to work for equality.

b) 8...♘c7 9 0-0 ♖b8 (9...h5 and Black was a shade worse after 10 f3 ♗d7 11 a4 ♖b8 12 ♗e3 b6 13 ♕c2 in Korchnoi-Gonzalez, Las Vegas 1993) 10 ♗e3 ♗d7 11 a4 (11 e5!?) 11...b6 (11...a6 12 a5 b5 13 axb6 ♖xb6, Rudolf-Kirichenko, Orsk 2002, and now 14 ♖a2 retains White's lead) 12 ♕d2 ♘g4?! 13 ♗xg4 ♗xg4 14 ♗h6 with trouble for Black in Bilek-Yanofsky, Stockholm 1962.

8 ♗e2

After 8 dxe6 Black is active, e.g. 8...♗xe6 9 ♗d3 ♘c6 10 0-0 ♘g4 11 ♗e2, Vincent-Guidez, France 1996, when 11...♕h4!? 12 ♗xg4 (12 h3? ♘xf2) 12...♕xg4 13 ♕xg4 ♗xg4 gives Black the bishop pair and the better chances. 8...fxe6 9 ♗e2 ♘c6 10 0-0 ♕e7 11 ♗g5 h6 12 ♗e3 b6 13 ♕d2 ♔h7 14 ♖ad1 ♖d8 15 f4 d5 (Wallis-Littlewood, Sunderland 1966) is given as unclear in *ECO*.

8...exd5 9 exd5

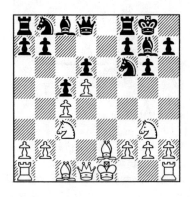

9...♘fd7!?

Now Black has a wide range of continuations.

a) 9...♖e8 10 0-0 ♘bd7 (10...a6 11 ♗f4 ♕e7 12 ♖e1 ♘bd7 13 ♕d2 ♘e5 14 h3 ♕f8 15 ♗e3, Forintos-Zimmerman, Hungary 1998, with an edge for White) 11 ♗f4!? a6 12 ♕d2 ♘e5 13 ♗g5 ♕b6 (13...♕c7 14 a4 is given by Serper in *ECO* as slightly better for White) 14 a4 ♕b4 15 ♖fe1 ♗f5 (not 15...♘xc4? 16 ♗xc4 ♕xc4 17 ♗xf6 ♖xe1+ 18 ♖xe1 ♗xf6 19 ♖e8+ ♔g7 20 ♘ce4 etc.) 16 ♘xf5 gxf5 17 ♕c2 ♘xc4 18 ♗xf6 ♗xf6 19 ♕xf5 and White had managed to retain the lead in Serper-Van Wely, Krumbach 1991.

b) 9...♘bd7 10 ♗f4 (10 0-0 ♘e8!? 11 ♗d2 ♕h4 12 ♘ge4 h6 13 g3 ♕e7 14 f4 f5 15 ♘f2 ♘c7 16 a4 b6 17 ♕c2 ♘f6 18 ♖ae1 a6 with a level game in Hoffmann-Mohr, Elista 1998) 10...♘e8 (10...♘e5 11 0-0 h5 12 ♗g5 ♕b6 13 ♕b3 left Black slightly worse in Flear-Van Wely, Mondorf 1991) 11 ♕d2 f5 (11...a6, Danieli-Cebalo, Bratto 2003, and now 12 a4 ♘e5 13 a5 favours White) 12 ♗h6 ♘e5 (12...♗xh6!? 13 ♕xh6 f4 14 ♘ge4 ♘e5 is interesting) 13 ♗xg7 ♘xg7 14 f4 ♘d7 15 0-0 ♘f6 (Szabo-Ciolcaltea, Hamburg 1965) with equality according to *ECO*.

c) 9...♘a6 10 0-0 (10 ♗f4 ♘c7 11 ♕d2 was played in Serper-Kramer, St Paul 2000, when 11...b5 12 cxb5 ♗b7 13 ♗g5 should secure White an edge) 10...♘c7 11 a4 (11 ♖e1 ♖e8 12 a4 ♗g4 13 f3 ♗c8 14 ♗f4 a6 15 ♕d2 b6 16 ♗g5 is another route to a modest lead) 11...♖e8 12 ♗f4 ♕e7 13 ♕d2 ♕f8 14 ♖a3 (14 ♖fe1!?) 14...♘d7 15 ♘ge4 ½-½, Comas Fabrego-Silva, Elista 1998, although White stands a little better here.

d) After 9...♘e8 10 h4!? White hopes to put the fact that he has not castled to good use, e.g. 10...♘d7 11 h5 f5 12 hxg6 hxg6 13 ♗h6 ♗xh6 14 ♖xh6 ♕g5 15 ♕d2 ♕xd2+ 16 ♔xd2 ♔g7 17 ♖ah1 and White had the easier game in Topalov-Danailov, Candas 1992. Remlinger-Formanek, Philadelphia 1992 saw Black prevent the further advance of White's pawn, but 10...h5 11 ♗g5 f6 12 ♗f4 ♘d7 13 ♘ge4 ♕e7 14 ♕d2 ♘e5 15 0-0-0 still favoured White.

e) 9...a6 10 a4

e1) 10...♘bd7 11 0-0 ♘e8 (11...♘e5 12 h3 ♘e8 13 f4 ♘d7, Teyssou-Garriga Nualart, Monzon 1987, and now 14 a5 favours White) 12 ♗e3 h6 (12...f5 13 ♕d2 ♕h4 14 ♗g5 ♕d4, Hermansson-Hansson, Reykjavik 1988, and here 15 ♕f4!? should keep White ahead) 13 ♕d2 ♔h7 14 f4 (14 a5!?) 14...f5 15 a5 with a minimal pull for White, Malaniuk-Kaminski, Koszalin 1996.

e2) 10...♖e8 11 ♗f4 (11 0-0 ♘bd7 12 ♖e1 ♘e5 was unclear in Kleiser-Manhardt, Austria 2001) 11...♕c7 (11...♗g4?! was tried in Pyrich-Cutillas Ripoll, Correspondence 1999, 12 f3! ♘h5 [12...♗c8 13 a5 is the lesser evil] 13 ♘xh5 ♗xh5 14 ♕d2 f5 15 0-0-0 being great for White) 12 ♕d2 ♘bd7 13 0-0 b6 14 ♗h6 ♗h8 15 h3 ♘e5 16 f4 ♘ed7 17 ♗d3 with an edge for White, Vaughan-Ramsden, Correspondence 1987.

10 ♗f4

10 0-0 f5 11 f4 ♗xc3 (11...♖e8!?) 12 bxc3 ♘f6 13 h3 ♘bd7 14 ♗d3 (14 ♖b1!?) 14...♕a5 15 ♗d2 ♘b6 led to chances for both sides in Hoffman-Barria, Cordoba 1998.

10...♘e5 11 ♕d2 ♖e8

The immediate 11...f5 12 h4 helps White, while 11...♘bd7 12 h4 (12 0-0!?) 12...♖e8 13 ♔f1 (13 0-0-0!?) was the course of Maki Uuro-Carlsson, Copenhagen 1998, when 13...h5 would have been unclear.

12 0-0 f5 13 ♗g5 ♕b6 14 ♖fe1 ♘a6 15 ♗f1 ♗d7

A typical set-up for Black, who has restricted the scope of the g3-knight with ...f7-f5 and achieved harmonious development.

16 ♖ac1 ♘c7 17 b3 ♘f7 18 ♗e3 ♕a5

Black has good play on the queenside.

19 ♘b1?!

19 a4 is better, with a level game.

19...♕xd2 20 ♗xd2 ♔f8 21 ♘c3 ♘e5

21...b5!? is an interesting and active possibility, intending 22 cxb5 ♗xc3 23 ♗xc3 ♘xd5 with advantage to Black.

22 h3 ♖eb8 23 a4 a6 24 f4

After 24 ♖a1 b5 25 axb5 axb5 26 cxb5 ♖xa1 27 ♖xa1 ♗xb5 28 ♘xb5 ♘xb5 29 ♗xb5 ♖xb5 30 ♖a8+ ♔f7 31 ♖a7+ ♔f8 32 ♖a8+ the position is drawn.

24...♘f7 25 ♗d3 b5 26 a5?!

26 ♖b1 improves.

26...♘d8 27 ♖c2 bxc4 28 bxc4 ♖b3

Black has the superior prospects but there is no clear way of making progress.

29 ♖a1 ♖ab8 30 ♖aa2 ♘e8 31 ♘ge2 ♗f6 32 ♘c1 ♖3b4 33 ♗f1 ♗d4+ 34 ♔h2 ♗g7 35 ♘d3 ♖b3 36 ♘c1 ♖3b7 37 ♘d3 ♗f6 38 g3 ♗g7 39 ♔g2 ♘f6 40 ♘f2 ♖b3 ½-½

Game 13

Serper-Becerra Rivero

Foxwoods Open, Connecticut 2000

1 d4 g6 2 e4 ♗g7 3 c4 d6 4 ♘c3 ♘f6 5 ♘ge2 0-0 6 ♘g3 e5

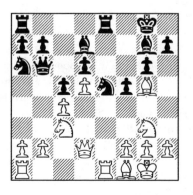

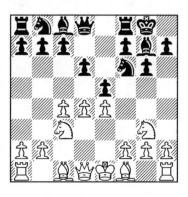

Black simply continues in traditional King's Indian style, effectively forcing White to close the centre. The point is that after d4-d5 Black can employ the thematic thrust of the f-pawn or place a knight on c5. Another plan is to exchange pawns on d5 followed by queenside expansion. Of course these themes are not exclusive to just one strategy.

7 d5 ♘fd7

We should also consider the following, less popular Black's continuations, none of which is enough for equality:

a) 7...h5 8 ♗g5 ♕e8 9 ♗d3 ♘h7 10 ♗e3 h4 11 ♘f1 ♘a6 12 ♘d2 f5 13 f3 with an edge for White in Hort-Uhlmann, Bad Neuenahr 1991.

b) 7...♘g4 8 ♗e2 (8 f3 ♘h6 9 h4 f5 10 h5!? f4 11 hxg6 hxg6 12 ♘ge2 g5 13 ♘g1 g4 was Szekeres-Varga, Hungary 1992, and now 14 g3! is strong) 8...♕h4 9 ♘b5! ♘a6 10 ♗d2 c6 (10...♗h6 11 ♗xh6 ♘xh6 12 0-0 favours White according to *NCO*) 11 ♕c1! (11 dxc6 bxc6 12 ♘xd6 ♘xf2! 13 ♔xf2 ♕f6+) 11...♕d8 12 ♘c3 (Forintos-Sinkovics, Hungary 1986) is given as slightly better for White in *ECO*.

c) 7...♘bd7 8 h4 (8 ♗e2 a6 9 h4 h5 10 ♗g5 ♕e8 11 ♕d2 ♘h7 12 ♗h6 ♘df6 13 ♗xg7 ♔xg7 14 0-0-0 ♗d7 15 ♖dg1 b5 is evaluated as even in *ECO*) 8...h5 9 ♗g5 ♕e8 (9...♖e8 10 ♗e2 ♘f8 11 ♕d2 ♘8h7 12 ♗h6 with a modest plus for White in Serper-Wallach, Oakbrook 1996) 10 ♗e2 ♘c5 (10...a5 11 ♘b5 ♕d8 12 ♕c2 leaves Black slightly worse) 11 b4 ♘a6 12 a3 and Black was struggling in Mitchell-Kornhauser, Lansing 1988.

d) 7...♘e8

d1) 8 ♗d3 f5 (8...a5 9 0-0 ♘a6 10 a3 ♗d7 11 ♗e3 ♗f6 12 ♕d2 keeps White ahead) 9 exf5 gxf5 10 ♕c2 ♕f6 11 0-0 ♕g6 was the course of Krantz-Brzozka, Correspondence 1972/81, when White's best is 12 ♗e2 ♘f6 (12...f4 13 ♗d3 ♕h6 14 ♘f5) 13 f4 with a definite plus.

d2) 8 h4 h5 9 ♗e2 (White enjoyed the easier game after 9 ♗g5 ♗f6 10 ♕d2 ♘g7 11

♗d3 ♘d7 12 ♘ge2 ♘c5 13 ♗c2 a5 14 0-0-0 in Remlinger-Belakovskaia, Philadelphia 1991) 9...♘d7 (9...♗f6 10 ♗h6 ♘g7 11 ♕d2 ♗xh4 12 0-0-0 ♗e7 13 ♔b1 ♘d7 14 ♗xh5! is a typical sacrifice in this system, and one worth remembering – 14...♘xh5 15 ♘xh5 gxh5 16 ♖xh5 and the clouds were gathering around Black's kingside in Kovacs-Haik, Reggio Emilia 1977) 10 ♗g5 ♗f6 11 ♕d2 a5 12 0-0-0 with a nice position for White, De Wachter-Vingerhoets, Huy 1992.

8 ♗e2

Also good is 8 h4, when 8...f5? (Unger-Kugelmann, Bayern 1997) runs into 9 exf5 gxf5 10 ♘h5 ♗h8 11 ♗h6 ♖e8 12 g4 with a strong attack. Instead Burgerhoff-Bakker, Vlissingen 2000 continued 8...h5 9 ♗g5 ♘f6 10 ♗e2 ♕e8 11 ♕d2 ♘h7 12 ♗h6, when Black is still struggling to equalise.

Let us return to 8 ♗e2:

8...a5

Black has also tried:

a) 8...♘a6 9 0-0 (9 h4!?) 9...h5 10 ♗e3 h4 11 ♘h1 f5 12 exf5 gxf5 13 f4 and White stood better in Dive-Britton, London 1994.

b) 8...f5 9 exf5 gxf5 (Mourot-Huisman, France 1999) and now Serper gives 10 f4 as favouring White.

9 h4 f5 10 exf5 gxf5 11 ♗g5 ♘f6

11...♕e8?? 12 ♗h5 (Serper) is final, but 11...♗f6 12 ♕d2 is quite playable, with an edge for White according to Serper.

12 ♘h5 ♗h8

Perhaps 12...♕d7 13 ♘xg7 ♕xg7 14 ♖g1 is an improvement on the game for Black, although this also looks difficult.

13 g4!!

13...♕d7

13...fxg4? loses due to 14 ♘e4 ♘bd7 15 ♗xg4 etc. (Serper), while 13...f4 14 ♗h6 ♖e8 15 g5 ♘xh5 16 ♗xh5 appears hopeless for Black.

14 ♖g1! f4

No better is 14...♘xh5 15 gxh5 ♔f7 16 h6! ♖g8 17 ♗h5+ ♔f8 18 ♕e2 ♘a6 19 0-0-0 (Serper), when Black is doomed to waiting for his execution.

15 ♗xf6 ♗xf6 16 g5 ♗g7 17 ♗g4

White should avoid 17 ♘f6+? ♗xf6 18 gxf6+ ♔h8 19 ♖g7 ♕h3, which Serper judges to be unclear. However, 17 ♗d3 ♔h8 18 ♗xh7 ♔xh7 19 ♘f6+ is nice.

17...♕d8 18 ♘e4 ♔h8

Or 18...♗xg4 19 ♕xg4 ♕c8 20 ♕f3 etc.

19 ♘xg7 ♔xg7 20 ♘f6 ♘a6?

A blunder in a lost position. Better was 20...♗xg4.

21 ♗xc8 ♕xc8 22 ♕b1 ♖h8 23 ♘h5+ ♔f8 24 g6 ♖g8 25 g7+ ♔e7 26 ♕xh7 ♕h3 27 0-0-0

27 ♕g6! (Serper).

27...♘c5 28 ♕g6 a4 29 ♕f6+ ♔e8 30 ♘xf4 ♕f3 31 ♕g6+ ♔e7 32 ♕g5+ ♔d7 33 ♕f5+

33 ♘h5 is simple and effective.

33...♔e8 34 ♕h5+ ♕xh5 35 ♘xh5 ♔f7

36 ♖g4

36 f4!? exf4 37 ♖df1.

36...a3 37 b3 e4 38 ♔c2 ♖ae8 39 ♖f4+ ♔g6 40 ♘f6 ♘d3 41 ♖g1+ ♔f7 42 ♘xg8+ ♔xg8 1-0

Game 14
Lutz-Gelfand
Horgen 1994

1 d4 ♘f6 2 c4 g6 3 ♘c3 ♗g7 4 e4 d6 5 ♘ge2 0-0 6 ♘g3 e5 7 d5 a5

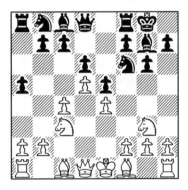

This thematic advance prepares to reinforce Black's control of the c5-square, which is being prepared as an outpost for a knight.

8 ♗e2

White continues with standard development. By now it should also be natural for us to consider starting immediate aggression on the kingside with 8 h4 followed by h4-h5 etc. Black must decide what to do in response to this 'threat' – ignore it or prevent it:

a) 8...♘a6 9 h5 c6 was Black's reply in Serper-Watzka, Eupen 1994, when 10 hxg6 fxg6 11 f3 ♘c5 12 ♗e3 favoured White. This certainly looks better than 9...♘c5 10 ♗e2 ♘e8 11 ♗e3 f5 12 hxg6 hxg6 13 exf5 gxf5 14 ♘h5, which saw Black in trouble in M.Ivanov-Chrz, Schwabisch Gmund 1999.

b) 8...c6 9 h5! cxd5 (Betaneli-Van Delft, Philadelphia 2001) 10 hxg6! is an idea to keep in mind, e.g. 10...fxg6 (10...hxg6 11 cxd5 ♘a6 12 ♗g5 ♕b6 13 ♗b5, 10...dxe4? 11 gxf7+

♖xf7 12 ♘gxe4 and 10...d4 11 gxh7+ ♔h8 12 ♘d5 all fail to help Black) 11 ♘xd5 ♗e6 12 ♗g5 etc.

c) 8...h6 does address White's own h-pawn but the downside is that after h4-h5 Black is forced to play ...g6-g5, thus leaving a gaping hole on f5. Consequently we would suggest that White makes the consistent advance h4-h5, either now or on the next move. White waited a little longer in M.Ivanov-Stiefel, Friedrichrodaer 2003: 9 ♗e2 ♘a6 10 ♗e3 ♔h7 (10...c6 11 ♕d2 ♔h7 12 f3 cxd5 13 cxd5 with an edge, Kaposztas-Bednar, Slovakia 1996) 11 ♕d2 ♘c5 (11...♘g4 12 ♗xg4 ♗xg4 13 h5 g5 leaves Black slightly worse) 12 h5 g5 13 ♗xc5 dxc5 14 ♘d1 ♘e8 15 ♘e3 ♘d6 16 ♕c2 a4 17 ♗g4! and White, who has been methodically fighting for control of the f5-square, had a (well deserved) big lead. There followed 17...♗d7 18 0-0 ♕c8 19 f3 ♖d8 20 b3 ♔h8 21 ♕b2 f6 22 b4 c6?? 1-0 (23 ♗xd7 ♖xd7 24 bxc5).

d) 8...h5 is – perhaps not surprisingly – Black's best. With this preventative measure Black loses some potential influence over g5, so a logical reaction from White is 9 ♗g5. Then 9...♕e8 10 ♗e2 ♘h7 11 ♗e3 ♕e7 12 ♕d2 ♘a6 13 0-0-0 ♗d7 14 ♔b1 ♖fd8 15 ♖dg1 left White with a healthy initiative in Svendsen-Lakat, Budapest 2002, which leaves the immediate 9...♘a6 – 10 ♗e2 ♕e8 (10...♖e8? is careless because 11 ♗xh5! gxh5 12 ♘xh5 ♘c5 13 ♕f3 ♘cd7 14 ♘d1 – intending ♘e3 – is dangerous, as in B.Vigh-Szittar, Hungary 1985, but 10...♕d7 11 ♕d2 ♘c5 is quite playable, with just an edge for White) 11 ♕d2 and here:

d1) 11...♘h7 12 ♗e3 (12 ♗h6!? ♗xh6 13 ♕xh6 ♕e7 14 0-0-0 ♕f6 15 f3 ♗d7 16 ♘f1 ♖ae8 17 g3 ♕g7 18 ♕d2 f5 19 ♘e3 slightly favoured White in Ader Hausman-Bolbochan, Mar del Plata 1952) 12...♗d7 13 a4!? ♕e7 14 ♘b5 f5!? 15 exf5 gxf5 16 ♗g5 ♘xg5 17 ♕xg5 ♕xg5 18 hxg5 e4 19 0-0-0 ♗xb5 20 axb5 ♘c5 21 ♘xh5 a4!? (M.Gurevich-Nijboer, Netherlands 1992) with compensation according to

Gurevich in *ECO*.

d2) 11...♗d7!? 12 0-0-0 ♘c5 13 ♖dg1 (13 ♔b1 ♘h7 14 ♗e3 b6 15 ♗h6 ♗xh6 16 ♕xh6 ♕e7 17 ♘f1 ♕f6 18 ♕e3 ♕f4, Ghaem Maghami-Darban, Mumbai 2003, with chances for both sides) 13...a4 14 f3 ♘h7 15 ♗h6 a3 16 b3 ♕e7 17 ♗xg7 ½-½, Novikov-Tsarev, Tuzla 1989.

8...♘a6 9 h4

The sharpest continuation, preparing an attack on the kingside.

a) 9 ♗g5 h6 10 ♗e3 h5! 11 ♗g5 (11 f3 h4 12 ♘f1 ♘d7 is unclear, as was Novikov-Loginov, Tashkent 1986, which continued 11 ♕d2 ♘g4 12 ♗xg4 ♗xg4 13 f3 ♗d7 14 0-0-0 ♕e7) 11...♕e8 (a standard idea in this structure, to play ...♘h7 followed by ...h5-h4 and ...f7-f5) 12 ♕d2 (Vladimirov-Thipsay, Sangli 2000 saw chances for both sides after 12 h4 ♗d7 13 ♕d2 ♘h7 14 ♗h6 ♗xh6 15 ♕xh6 ♕e7 16 ♘f1 ♕f6) 12...♘h7 13 ♗h6 (13 ♗e3 gives White nothing) 13...h4 14 ♗xg7 ♔xg7 15 ♘f1 ♘c5 16 g3 ♕e7 17 ♕e3 ♗d7 with an interesting battle in prospect, Rohde-J.Polgar, New York 1992.

b) 9 0-0

White settles for a traditional, sober set-up. Now 9...c6 10 ♗g5 h6 11 ♗e3 h5 12 ♗g5 ♕c7 13 ♕d2 ♘h7 14 ♗e3 left White with a modest plus in Efimov-Martinovic, Lido Estensi 2000, while 9...h5 10 ♗g5 ♕e8 11 ♕d2 ♘h7 12 ♗e3 ♕e7 13 ♖ae1 ♗d7 14 ♘h1 ♗f6 15 f3 ♗g5 16 ♘f2 ♘c5 17 ♘d3

♗xe3+ 18 ♕xe3 ♘xd3 19 ♗xd3 also retained the first player's edge in Derjabin-Shulga, Simferopol 2003.

However, Black should be consistent and hop into c5. Giorgadze-Akopian, Tbilisi 1989 continued as follows: 9...♘c5 10 b3 ♗d7 11 ♖b1 h5 12 ♗g5 ♕e8 13 ♕d2 ♘h7 14 ♗h6, when White's decision to trade these bishops doesn't look appropriate (14 ♗e3 is worth considering). White should not exchange his dark-squared bishop unless he has attacking chances, as his piece is clearly superior to its opposite number. After the subsequent 14...h4 15 ♗xg7 ♔xg7 16 ♘h1 ♕e7 17 ♖be1 ♕g5 18 ♕xg5 ♘xg5 19 f3 f5 Black had assumed the advantage .

9...c6

Black should play 9...h5, when 10 ♗g5 transposes to 8 h4.

10 h5 cxd5

Naturally Black can opt for the immediate 10...♘c5, but after 11 ♗e3 he will have to take on d5 sooner or later, transposing to the main game. Chilingirova-Grabics, Timisoara 1993 went 11...♕b6 12 ♕d2 a4 13 ♖b1 cxd5 14 cxd5 with an edge for White, while Black should avoid 11...♗d7 12 dxc6 ♗xc6 13 f3 etc.

11 cxd5

This is the most usual recapture, White intending to complete development and then combine play in the centre with an attack on the kingside. Nevertheless, 11 exd5!? is certainly worth our attention. This approach is known from previous games, but here White has not yet castled, a difference that could be significant in that Black's kingside is more likely to come under attack. In fact Black must be careful here. 11...♕b6 12 ♘a4! ♕c7 13 ♗e3 ♘d7 14 hxg6 hxg6 15 ♕d2 f5 16 ♗h6 (Hazai) is what White is looking for, while 11...♘e8 (intending ...f7-f5) meets with 12 hxg6 hxg6 13 ♗h6 etc. Meanwhile 11...♘c5 12 ♗e3 ♗d7 13 hxg6 fxg6 14 ♗xc5 dxc5 15 ♕b3, with the idea of answering 15...a4 with 16 ♕a3, also favours White, as does 11...♕c7

12 ♗e3 ♘c5 13 ♕d2 a4 14 ♗h6. This leaves 11...♗d7, when 12 hxg6 fxg6 13 ♗e3, as in Kleiser-Müller, Vienna 2002 limits White to a modest lead and looks like the best that Black can achieve. Notice here that the automatic 12...hxg6?! is dangerous due to 13 ♗g5.

11...♘c5

11...♗d7 12 ♗e3 ♖c8 13 f3 left Black slightly worse in Arkhipov-Groszpeter, Kecskemet 1992.

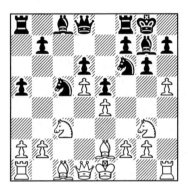

White has a number of ways to meet the arrival of the knight on c5.

12 ♗e3

Monitoring the knight with a view to removing it under favourable circumstances should the opportunity present itself. Alternatively:

a) 12 hxg6 fxg6! 13 ♗e3 ♗d7 14 f3 ♕b6 15 ♕d2 ♖fc8 was handled well by Black in Kleiser-Ragger, Staatsliga 'B' 2000/1.

b) 12 ♗g5 a4 13 ♕d2 ♕a5 14 f3 (14 0-0 ♗d7 is balanced) 14...♗d7 15 ♔f2 (15 h6!? ♗h8 16 0-0 – intending f3-f4 – is interesting, 16...b5 providing Black with counterplay) 15...b5 16 b4 axb3 17 axb3 ♕b6 18 ♗e3 b4 with excellent play for Black, Novikov-J.Polgar, Pamplona 1990.

c) 12 h6 ♗h8 13 ♗g5 with a further branch:

c1) 13...♗d7 14 0-0 (White wants to play ♔h1 followed by launching the f-pawn in order to organise a kingside offensive) 14...♕b6 15 ♖b1 a4 (15...♖fc8!? 16 ♔h1 ♘e8,

Kaposztas-Groszpeter, Szekszard 1994, might be worth another try) 16 ♕d2 (16 ♔h1 was White's choice in Kaposztas-Kerek, Eger 1995, and now 16...♖fc8 looks like the best way for Black to maintain the balance) 16...♖fc8 17 ♔h1, Jakab-Berkes, Paks 1998, and now 17...♘e8 18 f4 f6 leaves Black fairly solid.

c2) Also fine is 13...♕b6 14 ♕d2 ♗d7 15 0-0 a4!, e.g. 16 ♔h1 (Jakab-Schumi, Budapest 1999) 16...♘g4! 17 ♖ab1 (17 f3 f6!) 17...f6 18 ♗xg4 ♗xg4 19 ♗e3 with equality, or 16 ♔h2 ♘g4+ 17 ♔h1, Jakab-Flumbort, Paks 1996, when 17...f6 secures Black decent counterplay.

d) 12 a4!? voluntarily weakens b4 and b3 but this advance could still prove awkward for Black. White gets control over the important b5-square! Novikov-Cvitan, Forli 1993 is a good example of how play might unfold: 12...♗d7 13 ♖a3 (13 ♗e3 ♕b6!? 14 ♘b5 ♖fc8 was tried in Poluljahov-Nadyrhanov, Krasnodar 2002, but then 15 hxg6 hxg6 16 ♖c1 is excellent for White) 13...♖c8 (13...♕b6, intending 14 ♗e3 ♕b4, is another candidate) 14 ♗e3 ♕b6 15 hxg6 fxg6 16 f3 (this position is assessed as slightly better for White in *ECO*, while 16 ♘b5 could improve) 16...♕xb2!? 17 ♗xc5 ♖xc5 18 ♖b3 ♕xc3+ 19 ♖xc3 ♖xc3 20 ♕a1 (20 ♗b5!?; 20 ♕b1!?) 20...♖fc8 21 ♔f2 h5 22 ♖b1 ♗h6 23 ♘f1 ½-½.

12...♕b6

White has a small edge after both 12...a4 13 ♗xc5 dxc5 14 ♘xa4 ♗d7 15 ♘c3 and 12...♗d7 – Nunn (*ECO*).

13 ♖b1

Once again White is not without choice:

a) 13 0-0!? ♗d7! is unclear according to Nunn in *ECO*, but 13...♕xb2? 14 ♗xc5 dxc5 15 ♘a4 spells trouble for Black.

b) 13 b3 ♗d7 14 0-0 ♖fc8 prompts another unclear assessment from Nunn in *ECO*, which leaves 14...♕b4!? and a further decision from White:

b1) 15 ♗d2!? ♕d4?! (repeating the position with 15...♕b6 16 ♗e3 ♕b4 is preferable) 16 ♕c2 and Black has problems in all variations,

e.g. 16...a4 (16...b5 17 ♗e3 ♕b4 18 ♖fb1, or 16...♘g4 17 ♗xg4 ♗xg4 18 ♘b5 ♕d3 19 ♕xd3 ♘xd3 20 ♘xd6) 17 b4 ♘a6 18 a3.

b2) 15 ♕d2 ♖fc8 16 a3! ♕b6 17 ♖ab1 ♕d8, Korchnoi-Nunn, Wijk aan Zee 1992 (Nunn's evaluation in *ECO* being unclear).

c) 13 ♕d2 ♗d7 14 ♖b1 a4 15 f3 ♕a5 (15...♖fc8, Herzog-Bucher, Switzerland 1997, and now 16 b4!? axb3 17 axb3 earns White a plus) 16 h6 (16 ♗h6 b5 17 hxg6 fxg6 18 ♗xg7 ♔xg7 19 ♕h6+ ♔g8 favours Black according to Hazai) 16...♗h8 17 ♘f5!? (this appears rather cavalier but is in fact a typical motif in this situation) 17...♗xf5 18 exf5 e4! 19 fxg6 (19 ♗xc5 ♕xc5 20 fxe4 ♖fe8 with initiative – Hazai) 19...fxg6 20 0-0 exf3 21 ♖xf3, Bauer-Degraeve, Marseilles 2001. After 21...♘fd7 Black gets control over both c5 and e5 and does not stand not badly, though with 22 ♘b5 ♕xd2 23 ♗xd2 ♗e5 24 ♗e3 White is able to obtain a minimal advantage.

13...♗d7 14 ♘f1

White sets in motion the transfer of the knight to c4, via d2. Alternatively:

a) 14 0-0 ♖ac8 (Hazai) with chances for both sides.

b) 14 h6 ♗h8 15 0-0 ♖fc8 and there was no reason for Black to feel uncomfortable in Williams-Doggers, Hoogeveen 2003.

14...a4 15 ♘d2 ♕a5

16 hxg6

Not 16 a3 ♘fxe4!, but 16 ♔f1 (Gelfand) is interesting.

16...hxg6

16...fxg6 also looks pleasant for Black.

17 f3

Gelfand's proposed 17 ♔f1 is better, or 17 ♘c4.

17...b5 18 a3 ♘h5!

Black is gradually taking over the initiative.

19 g4?

Gelfand offers 19 ♔f2 ♘f4 20 g3 ♘fd3+ (wrong knight – after 20...♘cd3+ White is forced to capture with 21 ♗xd3 as 21 ♔f1? loses to 21...♘xb2 22 ♕c2 ♖fc8) 21 ♗xd3 (missing 21 ♔g2, e.g. 21...♘xb2 22 ♕c2, which is no problem for White, or 21...f5 22 ♘f1 with an excellent position for White) 21...♘xd3+ 22 ♔g2 (Gelfand gives 22 ♔e2 ♘xb2 23 ♕c2 b4 24 axb4 ♕a6+) 22...♖fc8 23 ♕c2 b4 and White is in dire straits.

19...♘f4 20 ♔f2 ♗f6

Black wants control of the h-file. Another plan is 20...♘cd3+!? (after 20...♘fd3+ 21 ♔g2 the position is far from clear) 21 ♗xd3 ♘xd3+ 22 ♔e2 ♘f4+ 23 ♔f2 ♖fc8, intending ...b5-b4, or at once 23...b4.

21 ♕g1 ♗g5

Obviously not 21...♔g7?? 22 g5 ♗e7 23 ♗xf4 exf4 24 ♖h7+! (Gelfand) 24...♔g8 25 ♕h2 ♗xg5 26 e5 dxe5 27 ♘ce4 ♘xe4+ 28 ♘xe4 with mate to follow.

22 ♕h2 ♔g7 23 ♕h7+?

23 ♗xf4 ♗xf4 24 ♕h7+ ♔f6 is a lesser evil, with a very big advantage for Black.

23...♔f6 24 ♘a2?

24 ♔f1 postpones the end, leaving Black with a strong enough initiative.

24...♘fd3+ 25 ♗xd3 ♘xd3+ 26 ♔e2 ♗xe3 27 ♔xe3 ♘f4 28 ♕h4+ g5 29 ♕h6+ ♔e7 30 ♕xg5+ f6 31 ♖h7+ ♖f7 32 ♖xf7+ ♔xf7 0-1

Game 15
Munschi-S.Farago
Budapest 1994

1 d4 ♘f6 2 c4 g6 3 ♘c3 ♗g7 4 e4 d6 5 ♘ge2 0-0 6 ♘g3 e5 7 d5 c6 8 ♗e2 cxd5

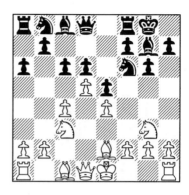

Concentrating on the queenside. The main alternative is 8...a6, and now:

a) 9 a4?! a5! is a textbook positional theme. Then play can continue 10 h4 h5 11 ♗g5 (11 ♗e3 ♘a6 12 ♕d2 ♕c7 was dynamically balanced in Storhaug-Wuerth, Norway-Switzerland Correspondence Match 1994) 11...♕b6 12 ♖a3 (12 ♕c2 ♘a6, Jacob-Sikiric, Hiddenhausen 1996, and now 13 0-0!? – intending ♖ad1 – is interesting, with chances for both sides, while 12 dxc6 also deserves attention, e.g. 12...♘xc6 13 ♘b5 or 12...bxc6 13 ♕xd6 ♕xb2 14 0-0) 12...♘bd7 (Ionov-Bologan, Moscow 1991) 13 0-0!? (Black cannot take the b2-pawn anyway) 13...♘c5 14 ♗e3 with an interesting middlegame in prospect.

b) 9 ♗g5!? h6 10 ♗e3 cxd5 11 cxd5 h5 (11...b5 12 ♕d2 ♔h7 13 h4 h5 14 f3 ♘g8 was Plachetka-Hausner, Marianske Lazne 1978, with 15 b4 securing White an edge) 12 ♗g5 ♕e8 13 ♕d2 ♘bd7 14 a4 (14 ♖c1!?) 14...♘h7 15 ♗h6 ♗xh6 16 ♕xh6 ♕d8 17 h4 with a slight plus for White, Comas Fabrego-Xie Jun, Pamplona 1999.

c) 9 h4, and now 9...b5 10 h5! cxd5 11 cxd5 ♘bd7 12 ♗e3 ♘b6 13 b3 (Ermenkov-Topalov, Sumen 1991) is given as slightly better for White in *ECO*, and 9...h5 10 ♗g5 ♕c7 (Tuchenhagen-Eitel, Germany 1995) also leaves White with an edge in the case of 11 ♕d2.

9 cxd5

9 exd5 proved quite harmless for Black in

Aldag-Heck, Hermannen 1997 after 9...♘e8 10 0-0 f5 11 f4 ♘d7 12 ♔h1 ♘ef6 13 ♗e3 a6, although recapturing with the c-pawn looks like the most appropriate course anyway, giving us the following position:

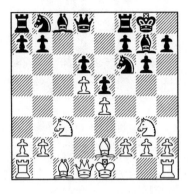

An important situation has arisen which requires rather careful handling by Black. The exchange on d5 is usually followed by ...a7-a6 and ...b7-b5, or ...a7-a5 and ...♘d7/a6-c5 with counterplay on the queenside. However, Black occasionally combines this with play on the opposite flank.

9...♘bd7

a) 9...h5?! looks out of place here – 10 ♗g5 ♕b6 (10...a6 11 0-0 ♕e8 12 ♕d2 ♘h7 13 ♗e3 h4 14 ♘h1 f5 15 exf5 gxf5 16 f4 was poor for Black in Kaposztas-Szieberth, Budapest 1994) 11 0-0 (11 ♕d2 ♘h7 12 ♗e3 ♕d8 13 0-0 h4 14 ♘h1 ♘d7 15 f3 f5 16 exf5 gxf5 17 f4 and Kaposztas had another victim, this time Gazik, Slovakia 2000) 11...♘h7 (not 11...♕xb2? 12 ♘b5!) 12 ♗e3 ♕d8 13 ♖c1 and Black was already in trouble in Paehtz-Bastian, Bad Wildbad 1993.

b) 9...♘e8 10 0-0 h5 11 h3 (11 ♗d3!? h4 12 ♘ge2 ♘d7 13 ♗e3 f5 14 exf5 gxf5 15 f4 with a plus for White, Carbone-Szmetan, Buenos Aires 1973) 11...♘d7 (11...h4!? 12 ♘h1 ♘d7, intending ...f7-f5, is worth investigating) 12 ♖e1 ♗f6 (12...h4 is still a preferable option, although the knight can now retreat to f1, 13 ♘f1 f5 leaving Black slightly worse) 13 ♗h6 ♘g7 14 ♕d2 ♔h7 15 ♖ec1 with a clear edge

(*ECO*) in Forintos-Suer, Athens 1969.

c) 9...a5

c1) 10 ♗e3 ♘a6 11 0-0 ♘c5 (11...h5 12 ♗g5 ♗d7 13 ♖e1 ♕b6 14 ♕d2 ♘g4 15 ♘h1 ♘c5, as in Forintos-Byrne, Monte Carlo 1968, is equal according to *ECO*) 12 f3 h5 13 ♕d2 h4 14 ♘h1 ♘h5 saw a lot of knight moves in Jakab-Horvath, Budapest 1998, when 15 ♘f2 would have led to a complicated position favourable to White.

c2) Matulovic-Bednarski, Palma de Mallorca 1967 went 10 h4 ♘a6 11 h5 ♘c5 12 ♗g5 (12 ♗e3!? ♗d7 13 a4! ♘e8 14 ♖a3 ♘c7 15 ♕d2 was enough for a slight pull in Hort-Schoene, Bad Neuenahr 1991, and this might be White's best) 12...♗d7 (12...a4 13 ♕d2 ♕a5 14 f3 ♗d7, Novikov-J.Polgar, Pamplona 1990, and now 15 h6!? ♗h8 16 0-0 b5 is unclear) 13 ♕d2 a4 14 0-0-0 ♕a5 15 ♔b1 b5 with an assessment of unclear in *ECO*.

d) 9...a6

d1) 10 0-0 b5?! might seem like a logical follow-up to 9...a6, but White seems to be able to steer the game to his advantage, e.g. 11 b4!? ♘bd7 12 a4! bxa4 13 ♕xa4 ♗b7 14 ♗d2 h5 15 ♖fc1, Yurtaev-Monin, St Petersburg 1997 with a similar lead for White to that seen in the main game. Black does better to forget about his b-pawn for the time being, 10...♘bd7!? 11 ♖e1 h5 12 ♗g5 ♕e8 13 ♕d2 ♘h7 14 ♗e3 leaving him only a little worse in Kaposztas-Neuschmied, Budapest 1993.

d2) 10 a4

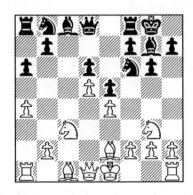

Pushing the a-pawn rules out ...b7-b5 but the main purpose is to gain space on the queenside. 10...♘bd7 11 h4 (only Black's h-pawn saw service in Inarkiev-Agopov, Elista 1998, which went 11 0-0 ♘e8 12 ♗e3 h5 13 ♕d2 h4 14 ♘h1 f5 15 exf5 gxf5 16 ♗g5 ♗f6 17 ♗xf6 ♕xf6 18 f4 with the better game for White) 11...h5 (11...a5 weakens the b5-square and after 12 h5 ♘c5 13 ♗e3 ♕b6 14 ♘b5 ♗d7 15 ♖c1 ♖ac8 16 ♖c3 White had a secure lead in Remlinger-Dannevig, Gausdal 1992) 12 ♗g5 and then:

d21) 12...♕b6 13 a5 ♕c7 (13...♕xb2 14 ♗d2 ♗h6 15 ♗xh6 ♕xc3+ 16 ♗d2 ♕c7 17 0-0 and White had more than enough compensation for the pawn in Robbiani-Bigini, e-mail 1998) 14 ♕d2 b6 (Black must be careful here – 14...♔h7 15 0-0 ♘c5 16 ♖a3 b6 17 b4 ♘cd7 18 ♖c1, Gradl-Klimek, Augsburg 1995, and 14...♘c5 15 ♖a3 b6 16 b4, Forintos-Udovcic, Uzice 1966, are both to be avoided) 15 axb6 ♕xb6 16 0-0 with an edge for White, Munoz Sotomayor-Garcia, ECU 1999.

d22) 12...♘e8!? (intending ...♘h7, ...♕e7 and ...♗f6) 13 ♕d2 (13 ♖a3 ♘h7 14 ♗e3 ♘df6 15 ♕b3 ♕e7, Forintos-Borocz, Hungary 1993, and 16 a5 keeps White just in front) 13...♘h7 14 ♗xh5 (14 ♗e3!?) 14...gxh5 (14...♘xg5 15 ♕xg5 ♗f6 16 ♕h6 ♗g7 17 ♕g5 ♗f6 forces a draw and is therefore an improvement) 15 ♘xh5 and White had a strong attack for the piece in Soman-Saravanan, India 1994.

10 ♗e3

An alternative is 10 ♗g5 h6 11 ♗e3 (note that if Black decides to push to h5 the game will transpose to 11...h5 in the note to Black's 11th move) 11...a6 12 0-0 b5 13 b4 ♘b6 14 a4 ♘xa4 15 ♘xa4 bxa4 16 ♖xa4 h5!, Szabo-Yanofsky, Winnipeg 1967, and now 17 ♗g5 seems to benefit White. 12 ♕d2 h5 13 ♗g5 b5 14 0-0 ♕e8 15 ♖fc1 ♘h7 16 ♗e3 favoured White in Cavril-Renaud, Correspondence 1996, while 12 h4 ♘e8 13 ♕d2 h5 14 ♖c1 ♗f6 15 ♗g5 ♗xg5 16 hxg5 b5 17 b4 was another postal game, Freise-Bellmann, Corre-

spondence 1996, when 17...♘g7 18 a4 bxa4 19 ♘xa4 a5 20 b5 ♗b7 21 ♕e3 would have left both sides with chances according to Bellmann.

10...a6 11 0-0

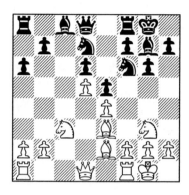

Castling is the most accurate continuation. 11 b4, on the other hand, is premature, 11...h5 12 0-0 (12 ♗g5!?) 12...h4 13 ♘h1 ♘h7 14 f3 ♗f6 (Forintos-Sznapik, Ljubljana 1981) given as preferable for Black in *ECO*. Nor does 11 a4 furnish White an advantage, 11...h5 12 ♘f1 ♘c5 13 ♘d2 ♘g4 14 ♗xc5 dxc5 15 ♘c4 b6 giving Black as much to smile about as White in Rodriguez-Vogt, Thessaloniki 1988. 11 ♕d2 b5 12 f3 transposes to the Sämisch System.

11...b5

This thrust looks natural but is not without a downside. Consequently Black should consider 11...h5, e.g.

a) 12 ♗g5 ♕e8 13 ♕d2 (13 a4 ♘h7 14 ♗e3 h4 15 ♘h1 f5 16 exf5 gxf5 17 f4 and White had a modest advantage in Poluljahov-Gasanov, Krasnodar 2002) 13...♘h7 14 ♗h6 h4 15 ♗xg7 (15 ♘h1 ♕e7 16 ♗xg7 ♔xg7 was unclear in Z.Polgar-Brustman, Thessaloniki 1988) 15...♔xg7 16 ♘h1 f5 (16...♕e7!?) 17 exf5 gxf5 18 f4 and the trade on f5 followed by pushing the f-pawn again afforded White a definite plus, this time in Shemeakin-Gaponenko, Alushta 1998.

b) 12 ♖e1 allows 12...h4, when 13 ♘f1 ♘h7 14 ♕d2 f5 15 exf5 gxf5 16 f4 saw

White's now familiar better game in Avrukh-Van den Doel, Duisburg 1992. Black has also played the deliberate but lengthy 12...♘h7 13 ♘f1 ♗f6 14 a4! ♗g5, when in Chekhov-Ye Jiangchuan, Beijing 1991 White pressed on with 15 a5 h4 16 b4!? f5. Then Ye Jiangchuan gives 17 exf5 gxf5 as unclear in *ECO* but, in our opinion, White has an advantage.

12 b4 ♘b6 13 a4

The point. Rather than allow Black freedom on the queenside White has taken aggressive action of his own there, blockading and then challenging the enemy duo.

13...♘xa4!

Not 13...♘c4?! 14 axb5 ♘xe3 15 fxe3 ♕b6 16 ♕d3 (Szabo-Byrne, Havana Olympiad 1966) with a clear lead for White according to *ECO*.

14 ♘xa4 bxa4

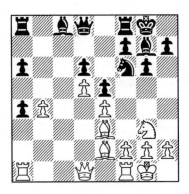

Black's position appears fairly solid (the two potential weaknesses on a6 and d6 are quite easy to defend) but as far as the future is concerned there is nothing positive to look forward to. If White plays correctly there should be no counterplay. However, it is not easy to actually engineer a decisive advantage from White's pluses.

15 ♕xa4

15 ♖xa4 is similar: 15...h5! and now 16 b5 lets Black achieve counterplay, e.g. 16...♗d7

17 ♖xa6 h4 18 ♘h1 ♘xe4 19 ♕c2 f5 with chances for both sides in Hansson-Modig, Correspondence 1988/90. This leaves 16 ♗g5, and now:

a) 16...♖b8?! 17 ♗xh5 (17 ♗xa6 ♗d7 18 b5 ♖xb5 19 ♗xb5 ♗xb5 should end in a draw) 17...♗d7 (after 17...gxh5 18 ♘xh5 Black has no good defence against ♕f3 and f2-f4) 18 ♖a3 ♖xb4 19 ♗e2 a5 20 ♕e1 ♕b6 (20...♖b8!? 21 ♗xf6 ♗xf6 22 ♖xa5 and Black has some compensation for the pawn) 21 ♗e3 ♕b8, Derjabin-Maximov, Dnepropetrovsk 2002, and now White could have won a pawn with 22 ♖xa5! as after 22...♘xe4 23 ♗a7 ♕b7 24 ♗a6 ♕xa7 25 ♕xb4 he wins.

b) 16...♕b6 17 b5 was Eber-Polster, Correspondence 1989. Then 17...♘d7!? is interesting, e.g. 18 ♗e3 ♘c5 19 ♗xc5!? dxc5 (19...♕xc5 20 ♕d2 a5 21 ♖c1 ♕b6 22 ♖c6 ♕d8 23 b6 is awful for Black) 20 ♗c4 h4 21 ♘e2 ♖a7 22 bxa6 ♗xa6 and Black is only slightly worse.

c) 16...♗d7 17 ♖a3 (after 17 ♖xa6 ♖xa6 18 ♗xa6 ♕b6 19 ♕d3 ♕xb4 20 ♖b1 ♕a5 Black exchanges queenside pawns) 17...♕b6 18 ♕d2 with something for White in Derjabin-Egorov, Ukraine 2002.

15...♗d7

Suba, in *ECO*, prefers 15...h5!, with an assessment of unclear, e.g. 16 f3 ♗d7 17 ♕c2 h4 18 ♘h1 a5 19 bxa5 (19 b5 ♘h5) 19...♖xa5 20 ♕d2 ♖xa1 21 ♖xa1 with only a symbolic advantage for White.

16 ♕a5

16 ♕c2!? deserves a look.

16...♕xa5 17 ♖xa5 ♖fb8 18 ♖xa6?!

This leads to an immediate draw. Obviously White can hang onto b4 and a6, and after 18 ♖b1 ♗c8 remains with some extra space and the better dark-squared bishop. Nevertheless, it is very difficult to make progress in this position.

18...♖xa6 19 ♗xa6 ♖xb4 20 f3 ½-½

Summary

Black has a few interesting ideas in this variation but, in our opinion, two in particular merit special attention. The first is ...c7-c5 followed by exchanging on d5 with ...e7-e6xd5, leading to a middlegame in which Black's chances are certainly not worse (Game 12). The second concerns development with ...e7-e5, ...a7-a5, ...♘a6-c5 and ...c7-c6xd5. Note that if White begins active play on the kingside with h4 Black should take measures to block with ...h7-h5. The best example of this is Game 14.

1 d4 ♘f6 2 c4 g6 3 ♘c3 ♗g7 4 e4 d6 5 ♘ge2 (D)
5...0-0

> 5...c5 6 dxc5 dxc5 7 ♕xd8+ (*Game 1*)
> 5...c6 6 ♘g3 ♘bd7 7 ♗e2 h5 (*Game 2*)
> 5...♘bd7 6 ♘g3 e5 7 d5 h5 (*Game 3*)
> 5...e5 6 d5 c6 7 ♘g3 cxd5 8 cxd5 (*Game 4*)
> 5...a6 (D)
>> 6 g3 (*Game 5*)
>> 6 ♘g3 ♘bd7 (*Game 6*)
>> 6 ♘g3 c6 (*Game 7*)

6 ♘g3

> 6 ♗g5 (*Game 8*)

6...e5

> 6...h5 (*Game 9*)
> 6...c6 7 ♗e2 a6 (*Game 10*)
> 6...♘bd7 (*Game 11*)
> 6...c5 (*Game 12*)

7 d5 (D)
7...♘fd7 (*Game 13*)

> 7...a5 8 ♗e2 ♘a6 (*Game 14*)
> 7...c6 8 ♗e2 cxd5 (*Game 15*)

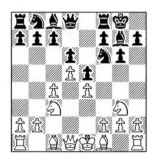

5 ♘ge2   5...a6   7 d5

CHAPTER TWO

5 ♗d3

1 d4 ♘f6 2 c4 g6 3 ♘c3 ♗g7 4 e4 d6 5 ♗d3

5 ♗d3 was played for the first time in Schwarz-L.Paulsen, Leipzig 1879, although there White developed the g1-knight to f3. The idea of following up with 6 ♘ge2 was found by F.Sämisch and played in his game against Wagner (Wroclaw 1925).

5 ♗d3 has obvious advantages, both developing the bishop and affording White some flexibility. White plans to develop the king's knight on e2 (which is, in this scenario, more convenient than f3) and, depending on how Black reacts, adopt either a Sämisch approach with f2-f3 or the Makogonov with h2-h3.

The most well-known grandmaster playing this variation regularly is Yasser Seirawan (perhaps it would be a good idea to name this variation after him...), while other followers of this variation are Pinter, Skembris, Sagalchik and Misanovich (occasionally this system appears in the games of Bareev and Krasenkow).

Let's see what attracts these strong players to 5 ♗d3.

Game 16
Hort-Kaplan
San Antonio 1972

1 c4 g6 2 d4 ♗g7 3 ♘c3 d6 4 e4 ♘f6 5

♗d3 0-0 6 ♘ge2 ♘c6

One of the most logical moves. Black immediately attacks the weakened d4-pawn.
7 f3

More flexible is 7 0-0, retaining the option of going with the f-pawn or the h-pawn until later. After the text we have an original position which, at first glance, very closely resembles the Sämisch. However, here White has played ♗d3 and ♘ge2 instead of ♗e3 and ♕d2. One advantage of this version for White is that Black cannot employ the typical plan involving ...a7-a6, ...♖b8 and ...b7-b5. On the other hand, Black can rather easily generate counterplay in the centre and on the kingside...
7...e5 8 d5 ♘d4 9 ♗e3

One drawback to 7 f3 is demonstrated in the variation 9 ♘xd4 exd4 10 ♘e2 ♘d7 as in such a position White often plays something along the lines of 11 0-0 c5 12 f4, but here this simply loses a tempo compared with 7 0-0.
9...♘h5 10 ♕d2 c5 11 dxc6

The only way to undermine the support of Black's knight.
11...bxc6 12 b4 f5

A very committal advance with which Black seems to be trying drum up counterplay at any price. The result is a weakening of his position. A safer option is 12...♗e6 with a playable position.

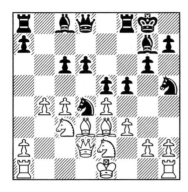

13 exf5 gxf5

Consistent and equally committal. A very interesting alternative is 13...&f4, e.g. 14 &xf4 (14 &xf4 exf4 15 fxg6 Wh4+ 16 &d1 hxg6 with an unclear position) 14...exf4 15 &xd4 (15 &f2 &xf5 16 &xf5 &xf5 17 &d4 &xd4 18 Wxd4 Wh4+ 19 &f1 &e6 is equal, while after 15 &xf4?! &xf5 16 &xf5 &xf5 17 &d1 Wh4+ 18 g3 Wh3 Black has a strong initiative) 15...&xd4 16 fxg6 hxg6 17 &d1 &e3 with more than sufficient compensation.

Additionally, if Black is feeling more peacefully inclined, there are 13...&xf5 14 &g5 Wc7 15 &c1 &f6 16 b5 &b8 17 h4 &b7 18 h5 &xh5 19 &xf5 and 13...&xf5 14 &xf5 &xf5 with a playable position in both cases.

14 0-0 &xe2+

14...&e6 15 &ad1 We8 16 &fe1 Wf7 looks effective, exerting pressure on White's centre.

15 &xe2 &f4 16 &fd1

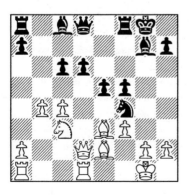

Although 16 &xf4 (now or on the 17th move) 16...exf4 splits Black's pawns it would be an error because Black's dark-squared bishop would then come alive, while ...Wb6 is an example of how Black might exploit the trade. How should Black continue after the arrival of the rook on d1? Some accuracy is required.

16...&f6

There is no clear route to equality.

a) 16...Wg5 17 &f1 &h3+ 18 &h1 f4 19 &g1 &xg1 20 &xg1 and White is ready to assume control of key light squares, e.g. 20...&f5 21 &d3 (21 Wxd6 e4 presents Black with counterplay) 21...&ad8 22 &ab1 &e6 23 &e4 &xc4 24 &xc6 Wg6 25 &d5+ etc.

b) 16...&xe2+ might be Black's best attempt. 17 Wxe2 We7 18 &ac1 &e6 19 b5 is good enough only for equality, which leaves 17 &xe2, when 17...&e6 18 &ac1 d5 19 cxd5 Wxd5 (19...cxd5 20 f4!) 20 a3 (20 We1 Wxa2 21 &xc6 &fd8) leaves White having to settle for an edge after either 20...&fe8 or 20...Wxd2 21 &xd2 &fc8.

17 &f1

The immediate 17 b5 &xe2+ 18 Wxe2 looks very good, e.g. 18...cxb5 (18...f4 19 &f2 is similar) 19 &g5 Wb6+ 20 &h1 &e6 21 &d5 Wb7 22 cxb5 and Black has problems.

17...&g6 18 &h1 &h5

White's defensive resources are too sound to justify a full offensive from Black. With this in mind, before stepping up a gear on the kingside, Black should concentrate on developing the light-squared bishop in order to protect important squares:

a) 18...&b7 19 &ab1 &h5 (19...Wh4 leads to an advantage for White after 20 g3 Wh5 21 gxf4 exf4 22 &xf4 Wxf3+ 23 &g2 Wxc3 24 Wxc3 &xc3 25 &xd6) 20 g4! fxg4 21 &d3 Wf6 22 &xg6 hxg6 23 fxg4 Wf3+ 24 Wg2 &g3+ 25 hxg3 Wxe3 26 &e4 &f7 27 Wf1+ &e7 28 &e1 with a clear advantage for White.

b) 18...&d7 is different in that this time the f5-square is protected. However, 19 b5 gives White a clear lead, e.g. 19...Wh4 20 g3 Wh5 21 gxf4 exf4 22 ♗xf4 ♕xf3+ 23 ♗g2 ♕xc3 24 ♕xc3 ♗xc3 25 ♖ac1 etc. Note here that after 19...♘h5 20 c5! we can see a serious drawback to 18...♗d7 – although it defends the c6-square the bishop now finds itself unprotected!

19 b5 f4 20 ♗f2

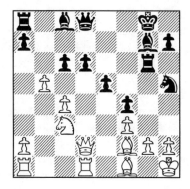

20...♘g3+

Onward. Black could keep the 'score' level with 20...cxb5 but after the simple 21 cxb5 ♔h8 22 ♘e4 ♗f8 23 ♗c4 ♕e7 24 ♗d5 ♗b7 25 ♖ac1 White has a clear advantage.

White can also take control of the light squares after 20...♗b7 (or 20...♗d7), e.g. 21 ♗d3 (21 ♘e4 ♕c7 22 ♗d3 ♘f6 23 ♗c2 ♘xe4 24 ♗xe4 ♖f6 25 ♕d3 cxb5 26 cxb5 is also good) 21...♖h6 22 bxc6 ♗xc6 23 ♗e4 ♘g3+ 24 ♗xg3 fxg3 25 h3 ♕d7 26 ♖ac1 etc.

An attempt to activate Black's dark-squared bishop with 20...e4 works only after 21 fxe4 in view of a well timed ....♗e5, e.g. 21...♘g3+ 22 ♗xg3 fxg3 23 bxc6 ♕h4 24 h3 ♗xh3 25 gxh3 g2+ 26 ♗xg2 ♕g3 and Black is having all the fun. However, White has a strong response to 20...e4 in 21 ♘xe4! ♗xa1 22 ♖xa1 ♗e6 23 bxc6 with a big advantage.

21 ♗xg3

21 hxg3!? fxg3 22 ♗xg3 ♖xg3 23 ♕xd6 ♕h4+ 24 ♔g1 and White wins with ease.

21...fxg3 22 bxc6 ♕h4

Perhaps 22...♗e6, hoping for 23 ♕xd6?? ♕h4 24 h3 ♗xh3 25 gxh3 ♖xd6 26 ♖xd6 e4, but after 23 ♘e4 ♕h4 24 h3! (24 ♘xg3?? ♖h6

25 ♕xh6 ♕xh6) White enjoys similar play to the main game.

23 h3 ♗f5 24 ♘e4 ♖c8?

The only way to put up some sort of resistance is with 24...♗f8, although after 25 ♖ab1 ♖c8 26 ♖b7 White should win.

25 ♖ab1

Why not 25 ♘xd6 ♖xd6 26 ♕xd6 with a winning position?

25...♗xe4

25...♗f8 26 ♖b7 leads us back to the note to Black's 24th move.

26 fxe4 ♕e7 27 ♖b7 ♕e8 28 ♕d5+ ♔h8 29 c5 ♗f8 30 c7

30 ♖d7 ♖d8 31 ♖xa7 is more accurate.

30...♕d7 31 ♗b5 ♕e7 32 ♖f1 ♖f6 33 ♖xf6 ♕xf6 34 ♗c4 ♕g5 35 ♕d1 ♕e7 36 ♕g4 1-0

Game 17
I.Sokolov-Smirin
Dos Hermanas 2001

---

1 d4 ♘f6 2 c4 g6 3 ♘c3 ♗g7 4 e4 d6 5 ♗d3 ♘c6 6 ♘ge2 0-0 7 0-0 ♗d7

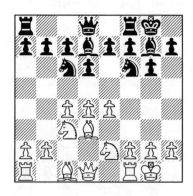

A very interesting position, Black electing to make a flexible move before embarking on any adventure in the centre. White must now decide on action of his own after taking into consideration that Black, after 8...e5 9 d5, has a few possibilities – namely 9...♘b4, 9...♘e7 and 9...♘d4 (although we must remember here that on d7 the bishop occupies a potentially useful square for the f6-knight).

Incidentally Black can also consider 7...a5, e.g. 8 h3 e5 9 d5 ♘b4 10 ♗b1 ♗d7 11 ♗e3 ♘h5 12 a3 ♘a6 13 ♗c2 ♕e8 14 ♖b1 f5 with chances for both sides in Sagalchik-Wojtkiewicz, Boston 2001.

8 ♗c2

Reconnecting the queen's communication with d4 at the cost of a tempo (note that White find himself moving this piece yet again in the event of ...♘b4). The text has been seen only a few times in tournament practice, so expect theory to develop along with the increasing number of high-level games.

A logical move is 8 f3, when play can continue 8...e5 9 d5 ♘b4 10 ♗b1 (intending a2-a3 followed by b2-b4) 10...a5 11 a3 (11 ♗e3 ♕e7 12 a3 ♘a6 13 ♗c2 c5 14 ♗a4! is a theme specific to the posting of White's bishop on d3, the exchange of light-squared bishops working in White's favour with this structure, while the awkward 14...♗c8 leaves White with an edge after 15 ♕d2) 11...♘a6 12 ♗c2 ♘e8 13 ♗e3 and now:

a) In the case of 13...f5 White should make sure to trade with 14 exf5, which is the thematic response in this kind of position. Otherwise Black can generate an initiative on the kingside by simply advancing with ...f5-f4 and ...g6-g5 etc. After 14...gxf5 15 ♕d2 c5 16 ♗g5 ♗f6 17 ♗h6 ♗g7 18 ♗g5 ♗f6 19 ♗h6 ♗g7 20 ♗g5 Dokutchaev-I.Zaitsev, Cherepovets 1993 ended peacefully thanks to a threefold repetition, but White has a definite improvement in 19 f4!?, e.g. 19...♖f7 (19...e4 20 g4) 20 ♗xf6 ♕xf6 21 fxe5 dxe5 22 ♘g3 ♘d6 23 ♘ce4 ♘xe4 24 ♘xe4 ♕g6 25 ♘g3.

b) 13...c5 and White stands better due to his extra space, the poor a6-knight and Black's potential problems on the light squares. Matamoros Franco-Glavina Rossi, Ceuta 1995 continued 14 g4 ♗f6 15 ♕d2 ♘g7 16 ♘g3 ♔h8 17 ♔h1 ♗e7 18 ♗h6 ♘g8 19 ♖g1 with a comfortable advantage for White, although the subsequent 19...♘c7 20 a4 ♘ce8 saw the players agree a draw.

8...e5 9 d5 ♘b4 10 ♗b1 a5

Black must prevent a2-a3 and b2-b4, when White would have too big a share of the queenside and Black's knight would be out of play.

11 f3

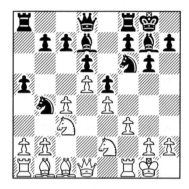

Compared with 8 f3, above, White has lost a tempo. However, the significant factors of the position remain the same, and White should be the happier of the two. The plan is to continue with ♗e3 and c4-c5xd6, controlling the weakened g1-a7 diagonal – in particular the b6-square.

11...♔h8

Preparing the not uncommon idea of ...♘g8 and ...♗h6 with a view to a trade of bishops that is favourable to Black. Unfortunately the operation is time-consuming, and Black might do better to look for an alternative strategy. Hazai's recommendation 11...♘e8, unleashing the f-pawn, seems more direct and therefore fits the bill. After 12 ♗e3 Black can address the 'threat' of c4-c5 with 12...♘a6!? or get on with business on the kingside with 12...f5: 13 c5 dxc5 (13...f4 14 ♗f2 is a little better for White) 14 ♗xc5 ♘d6 and Black puts his hopes in the blockade on d6. Play might continue 15 a3 ♘a6 16 ♗f2 (Hazai gives only 16 ♗e3 ♘c4 17 ♗f2, when Black has an excellent game after 17...♕g5 18 ♗a2 ♘e3 19 ♗xe3 ♕xe3+) 16...f4 17 ♗d3 and in our opinion White has chances of obtaining a small advantage, e.g. 17...♕g5 18

♔h1 h6 19 ♜c1 ♜fc8 20 ♜g1 ♕f6 21 g3 fxg3 22 ♜xg3.

12 ♗e3 ♞g8 13 c5

Also good is 13 ♕d2, directed against 13...♗h6. Hazai gives 13...♕h4 with the forcing variation 14 ♗g5 ♗h6 15 ♗xh4 ♗xd2 16 ♗f2 b6 17 ♜d1 ♗g5 18 a3 ♞a6 19 ♗c2, evaluating the position as slightly better for White. In general Black should avoid exchanging queens in this kind of position because the strength of his potential counterplay decreases. White has a very clear and effective plan in ♗a4 (assuming control of key light squares), ♜ab1 and b2-b4, preparing c4-c5. Indeed Black has nothing constructive in reply. With this in mind we prefer to choose from one of the following, although none guarantees Black equality: 13...f5 14 c5, 13...b6 14 a3 ♞a6 15 ♗c2 and 13...♞a6 14 ♗c2.

13...♗h6 14 ♗f2 ♕e7 15 cxd6 cxd6 16 ♞a4 f5 17 ♞b6

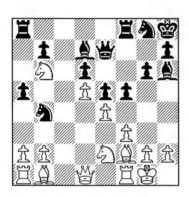

17...fxe4!?

White has a clear advantage, and after 'normal' moves Black's weakened queenside anyway confers White a clear lead (the a5-pawn and the b6-square are the most obvious, but White's 'control' of c8 is equally annoying for Black). Furthermore the hoped for counterplay with the f-pawn might result in a new weak f5-pawn, e.g. 17...♜ae8 (or 17...♜ad8) 18 a3 ♞a6 19 exf5 gxf5 20 ♜e1 ♞f6 21 ♞d4. Consequently Black decides to sacrifice an exchange.

18 ♗xe4

Obviously White declines the offer. After 18 ♞xa8 Hazai mentions 18...exf3 19 ♞b6 fxe2 20 ♕xe2 ♞f6 with compensation for the exchange. In our opinion White's chances are better after 21 ♗h4 but it is always wise to play a position with a stable centre when the opponent has no counterplay.

18...♜ae8 19 ♞xd7

Black would have had serious problems after 19 a3 ♞a6 20 ♕e1 ♗b5 21 a4 ♗xe2 22 ♕xe2 ♞f6 23 ♞c4.

19...♕xd7 20 a3 ♞a6 21 ♕e1! ♕d8 22 ♞c3 ♞f6 23 ♜d1 ♞d7?!

According to Hazai this move is weak and allows White to exploit the light squares. He recommends 23...♞c5 24 ♗xc5 dxc5 25 d6 ♕b6 26 ♕e2, although White still retains an edge.

24 ♗d3

White has a big lead.

24...♞ac5 25 ♗b5 ♜e7 26 b4 axb4 27 axb4 ♞b3

After 27...♞a6 White has a clear advantage after both 28 ♗xa6 bxa6 29 ♜a1 and 28 ♞e4 ♞f6 29 ♗xa6 bxa6 30 ♗h4 ♕b6+ 31 ♔h1 ♗g7 32 ♗xf6. The text simply aims for d4, which Black is interested in even at the price of pawn, hoping for drawing chances in view of the ending with opposite-coloured bishops.

28 ♞e4

Not bad, but two other continuations are better – 28 ♞e2!? (in order to take a pawn while avoiding opposite-coloured bishops) 28...♗g7 29 ♗xd7 ♕xd7 30 ♕c3 ♞d4 31 ♞xd4 exd4 32 ♗xd4 ♗xd4+ 33 ♕xd4+ with a pure extra pawn, or 28 ♗xd7!?, securing the e4-square for the knight – 28...♜xd7 29 ♞e4 and Black has problems.

28...♞f6

Black should have decided on 28...♞d4!? 29 ♗xd7 ♜xd7 30 ♗xd4 exd4 31 ♜xd4 ♕b6 32 ♕f2 ♜c7 with some compensation for the pawn.

29 ♞xf6 ♜xf6 30 ♕c3 ♞d4 31 ♜xd4! exd4 32 ♗xd4 ♜e5 33 ♗xe5 dxe5 34

♕xe5

Despite collecting two pawns, winning this ending is still problematic due to the opposite-coloured bishops. Moreover, what is worse from White's point of view is that Black's bishop is more active, and the prospect of activity on the dark squares is quite real.

34...♗f8 35 ♖b1 ♗d6 36 ♕c3?!

Hazai rightly recommends 36 ♕d4! here.

36...♔g7 37 ♗f1?

Again White has better, this time with the prophylactic 37 ♔h1.

37...♕b6+ 38 ♔h1 ♕f2 39 ♕e1 ½-½

After 39 ♖e1 ♕h4 Black also has to lose a pawn: 40 g3 ♗xg3 41 ♖e7+ ♔h6 42 ♕d2+ ♗f4 with equality. The final position is drawn, the simplest being 39...♖xf3 etc.

Game 18
Christiansen-Yermolinsky
USA Championships, Parsippany 1996

---

1 c4 ♘f6 2 ♘c3 g6 3 e4 d6 4 d4 ♗g7 5 ♗d3 ♘c6

Black usually plays ...0-0 first, which makes sense as castling tends to be almost mandatory in this line, and doing so early at least keeps Black's options open.

6 ♘ge2

A reasonable alternative is 6 d5, e.g. 6...♘e5 (6...♘d4 7 ♘ge2 e5 8 ♘xd4 exd4 leads back to the text). Notice that an albeit minor difference here is that, with the usual move order of 5...0-0 6 ♘ge2 ♘c6, White could not now retreat the bishop, but here 7 ♗e2 is possible, as in Ramseier-Milov, Baden 1998. The game continued 7...c6 8 ♘f3 (8 f4 ♘ed7 9 ♘f3 looks more logical, causing Black some inconvenience) 8...♘ed7 (8...♘xf3+!? 9 ♗xf3 ♘d7 10 0-0 0-0 avoids the loss of a tempo) 9 ♗e3 0-0 10 h3 ♘c5 11 ♕c2 ♗d7 12 ♗xc5 dxc5 13 g4 (13 0-0!? Hazai) 13...♗c8 14 ♖d1 ♘d7 15 ♔f1 ♕c7 16 ♔g2 ♘e5 17 ♘xe5 ♗xe5 and, according to Hazai, the position is unclear.

6...e5

An original idea is 6...♘d7 7 ♗e3 e5 8 d5

♘d4 with the following position:

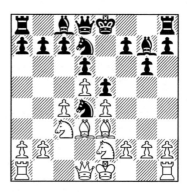

Of course White cannot play ♘xd4, but there is a way to address the new arrival, namely 9 ♘b5!, which is White's best chance of fighting for an advantage.

a) 9...♘xe2 gives White the better game after both 10 ♕xe2 a6 11 ♘c3 0-0 12 0-0-0! f5 13 exf5 gxf5 14 g4 (14 f4!? also looks enough to retain a pull) and 10 ♗xe2 0-0 11 0-0 f5 12 f3 a6 13 ♘c3 a5 14 a3 b6 15 b4 ♘f6 16 c5, Glek-A.Kuzmin, Moscow 1991.

b) 9...♘xb5 10 cxb5 0-0 (10...♘c5!?) 11 0-0 f5 12 f3 f4 13 ♗f2 g5 14 ♖c1 ♖f7 15 ♖c3 is slightly favourable for White due to the weakness of c7.

7 d5

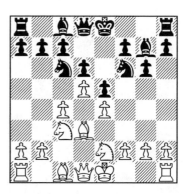

7...♘d4 8 ♗g5

Other ideas are 8 ♘xd4 exd4 9 ♘e2 ♘d7!? 10 b4!? a5 11 b5 ♘c5 12 ♗b2, and 8 f3 c5 9 ♗g5 h6 10 ♗e3 a6 11 0-0 (11 ♖b1!?)

11...♘h5?! (11...0-0) 12 ♖b1 ♗f6 13 b4, with a small advantage for White (Hort), Hort-Uhlmann, Thessaloniki 1988.

8...h6

Yermolinsky's 8...c6! deserves attention – 9 0-0 h6 10 ♗xf6 ♕xf6 (10...♗xf6!?) 11 ♘xd4 exd4 12 ♘e2 0-0 is level but White has chances to fight for an advantage after 10 ♗e3!? ♘g4 11 ♗c1 0-0 12 f3. Perhaps 11...♕h4!? is the solution for Black, e.g. 12 h3 ♘f6 13 ♘xd4 exd4 14 ♘e2 ♘d7.

9 ♗xf6

Alternatively:

a) 9 ♗e3? makes no sense here as it invites 9...♘g4, when White is made to regret the bishop sortie. 10 0-0 ♕h4 11 h3 ♘xe3 12 fxe3 ♘xe2+ 13 ♕xe2 seems to be White's most tenable continuation, with a slight edge to Black. This is certainly better than 10 ♗d2 ♕h4 11 ♘g3 0-0 and White has problems with development because 12 h3? is met by 12...♘xf2 13 ♔xf2 f5 14 exf5 ♗xf5 etc. Nor does 10 ♘g3 offer any respite, as 10...0-0-0 followed by ...f7-f5 is very nice for Black. Note here that 11 h3? walks into 11...♘xe3 12 fxe3 ♕h4 13 ♔f2 f5 and Black wins (Yermolinsky).

b) 9 ♗h4 0-0 10 0-0 c5 11 ♘xd4 exd4 12 ♘e2 ♕e8 13 ♗xf6 ♗xf6 14 ♕d2 ♗g7 was equal in Seirawan-Nunn, Cannes 1992.

9...♕xf6

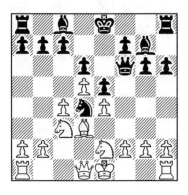

Also good is 9...♗xf6 10 ♘xd4 exd4 11 ♘e2 c5, and Black stands well.

10 ♘xd4

Yermolinsky gives 10 ♘b5! ♕d8 11 ♘bxd4 exd4 12 0-0 but in our opinion Black does not have any problems here. White could count on an advantage only if he managed to win the d4-pawn, but this is impossible, e.g. 12...0-0 13 ♗c2 c5 14 dxc6 bxc6 15 ♘xd4 ♕b6 16 ♘b3 ♗xb2 17 ♖b1 ♗e5.

10...exd4 11 ♘e2 h5 12 0-0 0-0-0

Inserting 12...h4 before castling is logical. Then White can try 13 h3 with the idea of meeting 13...♗xh3 with 14 gxh3 ♕f3 15 ♗c2! (any other moves lead – at least – to a perpetual check due to attacking possibilities ...♕h3, ...♖h5 and ...♗e5 etc.) 15...♖h5 16 ♘g3 ♕xd1 17 ♗xd1 ♖g5 18 ♗g4 hxg3 19 f4 ♖h5 20 ♗xh5 gxh5 21 h4. Instead after 13 f4 h3 14 g3 0-0 White has weak light squares in his camp, although the situation is rather unclear.

13 ♕b3 c6 14 ♖ae1 ♕d8

The game is well balanced.

15 ♕a3

Both 15 ♕a4!? c5 16 b4 and 15 f4 can also be considered.

15...♖e8 16 f4 cxd5 17 cxd5 ♕b6 18 ♔h1 ♗d7 19 ♘g1 a5 20 ♘f3 ♕b4 21 ♕xb4 axb4 22 e5 ♖e7

22...♖xa2 23 e6 ♗a4 is interesting, with chances for both sides.

23 e6

23 exd6!? ♖xe1 24 ♖xe1 ♗f8 25 ♘e5 ♖d8 26 ♖e4 should be enough to keep White just in front.

23...fxe6 24 dxe6 ♗e8 25 ♘g5?

25 ♘h4! is the correct move, 25...♖xa2 26 ♘xg6! ♗xg6 27 ♗xg6 ♖xb2 28 ♗xh5 d3 29 g4 leaving White with the more threatening pawns.

25...♖xa2 26 ♖f2 ♖a5 27 h4 ♗f6 28 ♖c2?!

28 ♔h2 with the idea of continuing to h3 and g4 is level.

28...♔g7 29 ♖ec1 ♗c6 30 ♖e2 b3 31 ♔h2 ♗b5 32 ♖d1 d5

Yermolinsky gives 32...♖a1!? 33 ♖xa1 ♗xd3 34 ♖d2 ♗c2 35 ♖ad1 d3 36 ♖xd3 ♗xb2 37 ♖xb3! ♗xb3 38 ♖b1 ♗xe6 39

♘xe6+ ♖xe6 40 ♖xb2 and White should draw the ending. However, in our opinion 35...♗xd1!? 36 ♖xd1 ♖c7 deserves attention as it seems to present Black with winning chances, e.g. 37 ♘e4 d5 38 ♘d2 (38 ♘xf6 ♚xf6 39 ♖xd4 ♚xe6 40 ♖d3 ♖d7 41 ♚g3 d4 42 ♚f3 ♚d5) 38...♚f8 39 ♘xb3 ♚e7 40 ♘xd4 ♖c4 41 ♘e2 ♚xe6.

33 g4 hxg4 34 ♚g3 ♗c4

34...♗a6! is the last chance to press for more than a draw.

35 ♚xg4 ♖a8 36 ♘f7 ♖ae8 37 ♘d6 ♖h8 38 ♘xc4 dxc4 39 ♗xc4 ♖xh4+ 40 ♚f3 ♖h3+ 41 ♚e4 b5 42 ♗d5 ♖e3+ 43 ♖xe3 dxe3 44 ♚xe3 ♗xb2 45 ♗xb3 ½-½

1 d4 ♘f6 2 c4 g6 3 ♘c3 ♗g7 4 e4 d6 5 ♗d3 e5

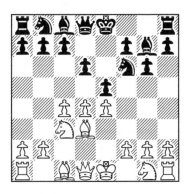

As in the previous game Black latches onto a plan of action before castling, although in this particular case the push of the e-pawn is justified in that the d3-bishop prevents a trade of queens on the d-file.

Another possibility is 5...c5, e.g. 6 d5 e6 (6...♘a6 7 h3 ♘c7 8 ♗e3 0-0 9 ♘f3 a6 10 a4 b6 11 0-0 e5 12 dxe6 ♘xe6 13 ♕d2 ½-½, Dorfman-Vasiukov, Volgodonsk 1981, but White must be a little better) 7 h3 ♘a6 8 ♘f3 ♘c7 9 ♗g5 h6 10 ♗e3 exd5 (10...0-0 11 0-0

♖e8 12 ♕d2 with an edge for White) 11 exd5 b5? (according to Hazai 11...0-0 has to be played) 12 ♕d2! and Black has serious problems with his king. For example 12...bxc4 13 ♗xc4 g5 (13...♚f8 14 0-0 ♚g8 15 ♖fe1 ♚h7 limits White to an albeit comfortable advantage) 14 h4! g4 15 ♘g1 ♘d7 16 ♘ge2 ♘e5 17 b3 ♖b8 18 ♘g3 ♗f6?! (after 18...♘xc4 19 bxc4 ♖b4 20 0-0! Hazai gives only 20...♖xc4 21 ♕e2! and White wins, but 20...♚f8 – despite White's obvious superiority – at least keeps Black in the game) 19 ♖c1 ♗xh4 20 ♘ce4 ♗xg3? (20...♗e7 21 ♖xh6 ♖xh6 22 ♗xh6) 21 ♗g5! 1-0, Azmaiparashvili-Ehlvest, Pula 1997.

6 d5 a5 7 ♘ge2

In Panczyk-Nowak, Poznan 1985 White tried 7 h3, securing in some variations the e3-square for his bishop. 7...♘a6 8 ♘ge2 ♘c5 9 ♗c2 c6 10 ♗g5 h6 11 ♗e3 ♗d7 (11...cxd5 improves) and now White should have played 12 dxc6 ♗xc6 13 f3 with better chances in view of the weak d6-pawn.

7...♘a6

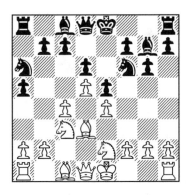

7...♘fd7 8 ♗e3 0-0 9 0-0 ♘a6 10 ♖c1 ♘dc5 11 ♗b1 ♗d7 12 ♕d2 f5 13 exf5 gxf5 14 f4 e4 15 ♗d4 was a shade preferable for White in Ionescu-Socko, Istanbul 2000, while 7...♘h5 8 ♗e3 ♘a6 9 f3 ♘c5 10 ♗c2 f5 11 exf5 gxf5 12 ♕d2 ♗d7 13 0-0-0, Misanovic-Petrovic, Zlatibor 1989, would have been only slight worse for Black after 13...0-0.

8 0-0

Preparing a Sämisch set-up of ♗e3 and ♕d2 requires White to first address the possibility of ...♘g4. Thus after 8 f3 ♘d7 we have:

a) 9 ♗e3 ♗h6 10 ♕d2 (10 ♗xh6 ♕h4+) 10...♗xe3 11 ♕xe3 0-0!? (Black was less careful in Seirawan-Ivanchuk, Groningen 1997, 11...c6?! 12 ♕h6 ♘dc5 13 ♖d1 ♕b6 14 ♗b1 ♔e7 15 f4! giving White a very big lead according to *NCO*) 12 0-0 ♘ac5 with chances for both sides.

b) With 'a' in mind there is the more ambitious looking 9 0-0 0-0 10 ♗e3 ♘b6 11 b3 c6 (11...f5!?) 12 ♕e1 f5 13 ♕f2 c5 14 exf5 gxf5 with an unclear game, Seirawan-I.Ivanov, Los Angeles 1991.

Finally, Seirawan's new idea of 8 a3! deserves further investigation and is assessed by him in *ECO* as slightly better for White. The point is simply to expand on the queenside with ♖b1 and b2-b4 etc.

8...♘d7 9 a3 ♘ac5 10 ♗c2 ♘b6 11 b3 0-0 12 ♖b1 f5 13 exf5 gxf5 14 ♗e3

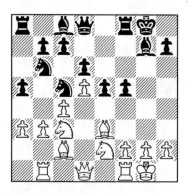

14...♘cd7

Black should try for counterplay with 14...f4!? 15 ♗xc5 dxc5 16 f3 ♖f6 and ...♖h6.

15 f4

15 ♘g3 e4 16 ♘b5 a4 17 ♘h5 axb3 18 ♗xb3 ♗e5 19 ♗h6 ♖f7 20 f4 with a modest plus for White.

15...a4 16 fxe5 axb3 17 ♗xb3 ♗xe5 18 ♘b5 ♘c5 19 ♘f4 ♗d7 20 ♖f3

20 ♗xc5 dxc5 21 ♘d3 also looks awkward for Black.

20...♖f7 21 ♘d4

Both 21 ♕e2 and 21 ♗xc5 come into consideration.

21...♕h4 22 ♖h3 ♕e7 23 ♘de6 ♖xa3?

23...♗xe6 24 ♘xe6 ♖xa3 was imperative.

24 ♖g3+♔h8 25 ♕h5 ♖f6 26 ♕h4 ♗e8 27 ♖g7 ♕xg7 28 ♘xg7 ♔xg7 29 ♗xc5 dxc5 30 ♘e6+ ♔g8 31 ♘xc5 ♗f7 32 ♘d3 ♗c3 33 ♕g3+ ♗g6 34 c5 ♗d4+ 35 ♔h1 f4 36 d6+??

White replaces the very strong 36 ♕g4! with a blunder.

36...♖xb3! 37 ♕e1 ♖xb1 38 ♕xb1 ♗xc5

Black has better in 38...f3! 39 gxf3 (39 cxb6 ♗e4) 39...♖xf3 40 ♕a2+ ♔h8 41 cxb6 ♗e4.

39 ♕a2+ ♗f7 40 ♕a1 ♖xd6?! 41 ♘xc5 ♘d5 42 ♘xb7 ♖b6 43 ♘c5 ♗g6?! 44 ♕a8+ ♔g7 45 ♔g1 ♘f6?! 46 ♕d8 ♖c6 47 ♕e7+ ♗f7 48 ♕e5 h6 49 ♘d3 ♖c4 50 ♘xf4 c5 51 ♘d3 ♖d4 52 ♘xc5 ♖d1+ 53 ♔f2 ♖d2+ 54 ♔e1 ♖xg2 55 ♘e4 ♖g6 56 h4 h5 57 ♔d2 ♖g2+ 58 ♔c1 ♖g6 59 ♘g5 ♗g8 60 ♕e7+ ♔h8 61 ♕e5 ♗g7 62 ♔b2 ♗f8 63 ♕d6+ ♔e8 64 ♔a3 ♗d5? 65 ♘h7 ♔f7 66 ♕c7+ ♔e6 67 ♘f8+ ♔f5 68 ♕c8+ 1-0

Game 20
Sturua-Gutman
5th Wichern Open 1999

1 d4 ♘f6 2 c4 g6 3 ♘c3 ♗g7 4 e4 0-0 5 ♗d3 d6 6 ♘ge2 ♘fd7

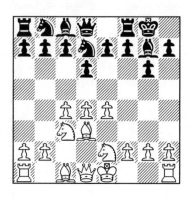

An interesting idea. Black wants to play ...c7-c5, the point being that after a subsequent d4-d5 there is ...♘e5, forcing the exchange of White's bishop, while the text also serves to generally increase the scope of the g7-bishop.

Others:

a) 6...c6 7 0-0 (White can also steer the game into Sämisch waters with 7 f3, e.g. 7...a6 8 0-0 b5 9 a3 ♘bd7 10 ♔h1 e5 11 cxb5 axb5 12 ♗e3 ♖b8 13 b4 ♗b7 and White had the easier of it in Eslon-Mednis, Amsterdam 1986) 7...a6?! (7...♘a6!?) 8 f4! b5 9 e5! ♘g4? (9...♘e8!?) 10 h3 ♘h6 11 g4 bxc4 12 ♗xc4 ♔h8 13 ♘g3 f6 14 ♗e3 and Black was already in trouble in Krasenkow-Kaminski, Poland 1996.

b) 6...a6 7 0-0 (7 f3!? transposes to a version of the Sämisch that is to White's benefit) 7...♘bd7 (7...♘fd7 8 ♗c2 c5 9 ♗e3 ♘c6 10 h3 ♖b8 11 a4 ♕a5 was unclear in I.Farago-Lanka, Regensburg 1996) 8 f3 c6 9 ♗g5 (9 ♗e3!?) 9...b5 10 ♔h1 (10 a3) 10...♘b6 (10...b4!? 11 ♘a4 c5 is equal) 11 b3 bxc4 12 bxc4 ♘fd7 13 f4 c5 14 d5 with an edge for White, Christiansen-Babula, Germany 1995.

7 0-0 c5 8 dxc5 dxc5

After 8...♘xc5!? Black has a perfectly playable Maróczy position.

9 f4 ♘c6 10 e5 f6

Black must do something about White's centre before the space advantage is converted into something concrete after ♗e3, ♕d2, ♗e4 and ♖ad1 etc.

11 e6

11 exf6 ♘xf6 is nice for Black, while 11 ♘g3 fxe5 12 f5 ♘f6 13 fxg6 ♕d4+ 14 ♔h1 hxg6 15 ♗xg6 ♗e6 and 11 ♗e3 fxe5 12 f5 gxf5 13 ♗xf5 ♘d4 fail to cause Black any inconvenience.

11...♘b6 12 f5 ♘e5

White's advanced pawns look very strong and seriously cramp Black, whose king is in danger of coming under fire, too. On the other hand White's pawns might prove vulnerable should Black succeed in attacking them. Consequently it is imperative that both sides conduct the next phase of the game accurately in order to maximise their potential advantages, and our analysis shows that White is, in fact, in the driving seat.

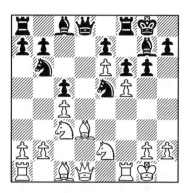

13 ♗c2 ♘bxc4

13...gxf5 14 ♘f4 ♕xd1 (14...♘c6 15 ♕h5 ♘d4 16 ♗d3 ♘xe6 17 ♗xf5 ♘g5 18 ♗c2) 15 ♖xd1 ♘c6 16 ♘cd5 ♘xd5 17 ♖xd5 ♗h6 18 ♗xf5 with an advantage for White.

14 ♘f4 b6

Trading queens does not help Black, e.g. 14...♕xd1 15 ♖xd1 ♘c6 16 ♘cd5 gxf5 (16...♘4e5 17 ♗e3 b6 18 ♗a4 ♗h6 19 fxg6 ♗xf4 20 ♘xf4) 17 ♗a4 ♘4e5 18 ♗e3 b6 19 b4 ♗h6 20 bxc5 ♗xf4 21 ♘xf4 and White maintains a lead.

15 ♕e2 g5

Now Black has absolutely no counterchances, although after 15...gxf5 16 ♖d1 ♘d6 17 ♗xf5 White nevertheless has a strong initiative on the kingside.

16 ♖d1 ♘d6 17 ♘h5 ♘c6 18 ♗e3 ♕e8 19 ♘d5 ♖b8 20 a4

Attacking with 20 h4 looks interesting.

20...♔h8 21 ♕g4 ♘e5 22 ♕h3 h6 23 ♗xg5 fxg5 24 ♘xg7 ♔xg7 25 ♕c3 ♘dc4 26 b3 ♔g8 27 bxc4 ♘c6 28 ♕h3 1-0

Game 21
Seirawan-Ivanchuk
World Cup, Reykjavik 1991

1 d4 ♘f6 2 c4 g6 3 ♘c3 ♗g7 4 e4 d6 5

♗d3 0-0 6 ♘ge2 ♘bd7 7 ♗c2

After 7 d5 ♘e5 White cannot avoid exchanging his light-squared bishop. Panczyk-Zhigadlo, Warsaw (rapidplay) 2003 continued 7 0-0 c5 8 b3 a6 9 ♗b2 ♕a5 10 ♘d5 e6 11 ♘e7+ ♔h8 12 ♘xc8 ♖axc8 13 ♕e1 ♕c7 14 ♖d1 b6 15 ♕d2 ♕b7 16 e5 dxe5 17 dxe5 ♘g4 18 f4 ♖cd8 19 ♘g3 with a clear advantage to White. Black could have taken on d4 numerous times and should have done so.

Instead of 8 b3 White has 8 d5, when 8...♘e5 9 f4 ♘xd3 10 ♕xd3 leads to the following position:

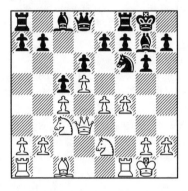

This position is difficult to assess. Black has managed to remove the bishop but White enjoys a territorial superiority, an imposing centre and prospects of an initiative on the kingside. Moreover, after ...e7-e6 (which looks like the only possibility of generating any kind of play) and dxe6 Black will face a serious dilemma – after ...♗xe6 White has the aggressive f4-f5 followed by stepping up the pressure with ♗g5, while ...f7xe6 leaves the d6-pawn susceptible to attack. Therefore Black has to play accurately to emerge with a playable game.

a) In the event of 10...a6 White should throw in 11 a4 because Black is happy to play along the lines of the Benko Gambit now that White's light-squared bishop has left the arena. Seirawan-Kamsky, Monte Carlo 1994 went 11...b6 12 h3 ♖a7 13 ♗e3 e6 (now Black is well prepared for the critical challenge in the

centre) 14 dxe6 fxe6 15 a5 bxa5 16 e5 and now 16...dxe5! gives Black an attractive game, e.g. 17 ♕xd8 ♖xd8 18 ♗xc5 ♖b7 19 fxe5 ♘d7.

b) The immediate 10...e6 fails to deliver in our opinion: 11 dxe6 fxe6 (11...♗xe6? 12 f5 was terrible for Black in Skembris-Bellia, Arco 1999) 12 ♖d1 ♘e8 13 e5 ♖f7 14 exd6 ♖d7 15 ♘e4 b6 and although Seirawan (in *ECO*) estimates this position as unclear we believe that Black has problems, e.g. 16 ♖b1 ♕h4 (16...♗b7 17 ♕h3 ♗e4 18 ♕xe6+ ♔h8 19 ♕xe4) 17 ♗d2 ♗b7 18 ♗c3 etc.

7...a6

Black is not without alternatives:

a) 7...e5 8 d5 a5 9 h3 ♘c5 10 ♗g5 h6 11 ♗e3 ♗d7 12 ♕d2 ♔h7 13 g4 (13 0-0!?) 13...♘g8 14 ♘g3 ♗f6 15 0-0-0 ♗g5 16 ♘f1 ♔g7 17 ♔b1 ♕f6 with a level game in Hauchard-Ferreira, Porto 2000.

b) 7...c5 8 d5 ♘e5 and now White has 9 b3 when, according to Hazai, the sacrifice 9...b5 is not entirely correct – 10 cxb5 a6 11 f4 (11 0-0!? axb5?! 12 ♘xb5, intending a2-a4 and ♘ec3, favoured White in Matamoros Franco-Pecorelli Garcia, Santa Clara 1996) 11...♘ed7 12 ♗d3 axb5 13 ♗xb5 ♘b8 14 ♗d2 e6 15 0-0 exd5 16 exd5 ♘a6, Semkov-Georgiev, Bulgaria 1992, and now 17 a3!? ♘c7!? 18 ♗c6 ♖a6 19 ♗e1 ♗d7 20 ♗xd7 ♕xd7 gives Black some compensation for the pawn.

Let us return to the position after 7...a6:

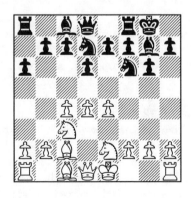

8 a4

After 8 0-0 c6 9 a4 a5 10 h3 e5 11 ♗e3 (11 d5!?) 11...exd4 12 ♗xd4 White might have problems with b4 and c5, which are ideal spots for Black's pieces. On the other hand White has a strong centre and prospects of a kingside attack with f2-f4, as well as pressure against the weak d6-pawn. Chances are equal. 12...♖e8 13 f4 b6 was the course of Georgiev-Dimitrov, Pamporovo 2001, when 14 ♕d3!? looks interesting.

8...e5 9 d5 a5! 10 h3

10 ♘g3 ♘c5 11 h4 h5 12 ♖a3 c6 with excellent play for Black, Godard-Glek, Clermont-Ferrand 2003.

10...♘c5 11 ♗e3 ♘fd7 12 0-0

12 ♕d2 f5 13 exf5 gxf5 14 f4 exf4 15 ♗xf4!? is unclear according to Seirawan.

12...♘a6

12...f5 13 exf5 gxf5 14 f4 with an edge for White (Seirawan).

13 ♘a2 ♘dc5 14 ♕d2

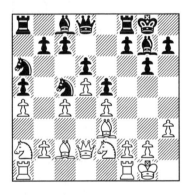

14...♗d7

14...b6! is given as equal by Ivanchuk in *ECO*.

15 ♕xa5!?

15 b3 b6 is level.

15...♘xe4 16 ♕e1 ♘f6

Seirawan gives 16...♘g5?! 17 h4 (17 ♕d2! ♘ec5!?) ♘f3+ 18 gxf3 ♕xh4 with compensation. In our opinion 17...♘h3!+ is an improvement.

17 b4 ♘h5 18 f3 f5 19 ♖b1 b6 20 ♘ac3 ♗f6 21 ♕d2 ♗h4?! 22 f4 ♗f6 23 fxe5

dxe5 24 d6 c6! 25 ♔h1 ½-½

The final position is rather messy and both sides have strengths and weaknesses to consider, but they were probably not in a fighting mood...

Game 22
Agdestein-Dolmatov
Tilburg 1993

---

1 d4 ♘f6 2 c4 g6 3 ♘c3 ♗g7 4 e4 d6 5 ♗d3 0-0 6 ♘ge2 ♘c6 7 0-0 ♘d7

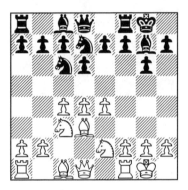

An interesting idea. Black refrains from an immediate 7...e5, opting instead to exert further pressure on d4. White has three methods of defence but each has its disadvantages. First there is 8 d5, allowing the exchange of his light-squared bishop after 8...♘ce5. Secondly, after 8 ♗e3 e5 9 d5 ♘d4 White cannot take on d4 with his e2-knight in view of the fork. Finally, dropping the bishop back to c2 doesn't look appropriate in some variations.

8 ♗e3

Others:

a) 8 d5 ♘ce5 9 f4 ♘xd3 10 ♕xd3 and Black's price for eliminating the bishop is in the form of White's extra space and presence in the centre, which makes counterplay awkward to engineer. Unfortunately this position is very rare in tournament practice, but play can continue as follows: 10...♘c5 (Kleissl-Neumeier, Austrian League 1999 saw Black fail to equalise after 10...c6 11 ♗e3 ♕a5 12

♗d4 ♘c5 13 ♕e3 ♗xd4 14 ♘xd4 e5 15 fxe5 dxe5 16 ♘f3) 11 ♕f3 e6 (11...c6!?) 12 ♗e3 ♘d3 13 b3 exd5 14 cxd5 f5 ½-½, Chatalbashev-Georgiev, French League 2003 but in our opinion after 15 ♖ad1 White would have stood better.

b) 8 ♗c2 e5

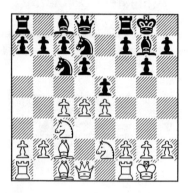

b1) 9 dxe5 ♘dxe5!? (9...dxe5 10 ♗e3 was Nutu Gajic-Grigorian, Moscow 1994, when 10...f5!? 11 exf5 gxf5 12 f3 ♘b6 13 ♕xd8 ♖xd8 14 ♗g5 ♖f8 15 c5 ♘d7 16 ♘d5 ♘xc5 17 ♘xc7 ♖b8 looks equal) and White has to deal with potential activity from the enemy forces, 10 b3 f5 11 f4 ♘g4 12 exf5 ♗xf5 (12...gxf5!?) 13 ♗xf5 gxf5 (13...♖xf5!?) 14 ♕d5+ ♔h8 15 h3 ♘h6 16 ♗e3 securing him an edge in Piskov-Atalik, Romania 1993.
b2) 9 d5 ♘d4 (9...♘e7 10 ♘g3 a5 11 ♗e3, Pinter-Dolmatov, Lyon 1994, and now 11...f5!? offers Black counterplay) 10 ♘xd4 exd4 11 ♘b5 ♘e5 with a further branch.

b21) 12 ♗b3 is interesting, e.g. 12...c5 13 dxc6 and here Black should play 13...bxc6 14 ♘xd4 ♗a6, transposing to 'b22', below

b22) 12 ♘xd4 ♘xc4 (12...c5 13 dxc6 bxc6 14 ♗b3 ♗a6 15 ♖e1 ♕b6 16 ♗e3 c5 17 ♘b5 ♘xc4 with equality, Hort-Xie Jun, Roquebrune 1998) 13 ♖b1 ♖e8 14 b3 ♘e5 15 ♗b2 c6 16 dxc6 bxc6 was unclear in Haik-Groszpeter, Cannes 1996.

8...e5 9 d5

9 ♗c2 exd4 10 ♘xd4 ♘de5 leaves White's pieces rather awkwardly placed, e.g. 11 ♗b3

♘a5 12 ♕e2 c5 13 ♘db5 a6 14 ♘a3 ♘ec6 15 ♕d2 ♗e6 and Black assumed the lead in Seirawan-J.Polgar, Monte Carlo 1993.

9...♘d4

Less promising is 9...♘e7 10 ♕d2 f5 11 exf5 gxf5 12 f4 ♘g6 (12...e4!? 13 ♗c2 ♘f6 is a shade preferable for White) 13 ♖ae1 ♖f7, Lorscheid-Kozul, Munich 1992/3, and now 14 fxe5!? ♘dxe5 15 ♗g5 ♗f6 16 ♗xf6 ♕xf6 17 ♘g3 should keep White's advantage intact. Anyway, it makes sense to send the knight into d4 after so much preparation.

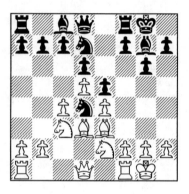

10 ♖c1

Not surprisingly this is one of numerous options.

a) 10 ♘b5?! is inadvisable in this specific situation. 10...♘xb5! 11 cxb5 f5 12 f3 and now instead of 12...♘f6 13 ♔h1 ♗d7 14 ♕c2 fxe4 15 fxe4 ♘g4 16 ♗g1 with a plus for White in Ehlvest-Xie Jun, Tallinn 1998, Black should play 12...f4 13 ♗f2 ♘f6 14 ♖c1 g5, when the kingside was looking rosy for Black in Illescas Cordoba-Romero Holmes, Leon 1993.

b) 10 ♗c2 is harmless in view of 10...♘xc2 11 ♕xc2 f5 12 exf5 gxf5 13 f4 ♘f6 14 h3 ♗d7 15 ♕d2 ♕e8 16 a4 a6 17 ♘g3 ♕g6 with an excellent game for Black, Olafsson-Khalifman, Wijk aan Zee 1991.

c) 10 ♔h1 c5 11 ♕d2 a6 12 ♖ab1, Christiansen-Xie Jun, San Francisco 1995, and now 12...f5!? 13 exf5 gxf5 is unclear.

d) 10 ♗b1 is interesting. For the price of a tempo (or even two) White wants to force

Black to exchange his well-placed knight. 10...♘xe2+ 11 ♕xe2 f5 (11...a5 12 ♗c2 ♘c5 13 a3 f5 14 exf5 gxf5 15 f4 e4 with chances for both sides in Arbakov-Belov, Katowice 1990) 12 exf5 gxf5 13 f3 ♔h8 14 ♗c2 ♘f6 15 c5 ♘h5 16 cxd6 cxd6 17 ♕c4 ♖g8 18 ♔h1 ♗f8 19 f4 ♕h4 20 ♖f3 ♕g4 21 ♕f1 e4 22 ½-½, Lastin-Galkin, Volgodonsk 1993.

10...c5 11 dxc6 bxc6 12 b4 f5

Another idea is 12...♗b7 13 ♗b1 c5 14 bxc5 dxc5 15 ♘d5, when both sides have outstanding outposts for their knights. In Pinter-Sepp, Yerevan 1996 Black played 15...♘b6. Here *ECO* gives 16 f4!? (instead of 16 ♗d3, as played by Sepp) 16...exf4 17 ♖xf4!? as favouring White. We suggest that Black should play 16...♘xd5!? 17 cxd5 (17 exd5 ♕c7) 17...exf4 18 ♘xf4 ♕e7 with sufficient counterplay. Also interesting is the immediate 15...f5, e.g. 16 f3 (16 exf5 gxf5 is equal) 16...f4 17 ♘xd4 cxd4 18 ♗d2 ♖f7 19 ♗d3 ♘c5 20 ♗b4 ♗f8 with equality, or 16 f4 ♗xd5 17 exd5 ♖e8 with good play for Black.

13 exf5 gxf5 14 ♗xd4

In our opinion after 14 f4!?, combining threats of b4-b5, c4-c5 and in some variations fxe5 to hit the f5-pawn, White has the advantage, e.g. 14...♖b8 (14...♘e6 15 b5) 15 ♕d2 (or 15 a3 a5 16 b5) 15...♖xb4 (15...a5 16 b5) 16 ♘b5 ♘c5 17 ♘bxd4 exd4 18 ♗xd4 ♖b7 19 ♖b1 with the better game.

14...exd4 15 ♘a4 ♕g5 16 f4 ♕g6 17 c5

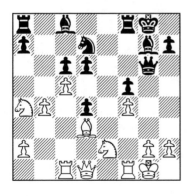

According to Belov White has a clear ad-

vantage in the diagram position but in our opinion Black is not doing too badly.

17...♔h8 18 ♘g3

Attacking the isolated pawn on f5. According to Agdestein (*ECO*) after 18 ♖f3 White has a clear advantage due to two threats: ♗b1 followed by ♘xd4, and ♖f1-f3-g3-g5. Nevertheless, 18...a5 looks effective, and earns Black counterplay, e.g. 19 a3 (19 cxd6 axb4 20 ♖xc6? ♗b7) 19...axb4 20 axb4 ♗a6 etc. 18 cxd6 is worth testing.

18...♘f6 19 ♕f3

19 cxd6!? ♘d5 20 ♕d2 ♕xd6 21 ♖c5, intending ♘h5, ♖fc1 (Agdestein).

19...d5 20 ♖fe1 ♗d7 21 ♖e7 ♖ae8 22 ♖ce1 h5

Agdestein gives 22...♖xe7 23 ♖xe7 ♖e8 24 ♕e2 as unclear but we like 23...♖d8 with the idea of following up with 24...♘e4.

23 ♖xe8 ♖xe8 24 ♖xe8+ ♕xe8 25 ♕e2 ♕b8

25...♕g6!? 26 ♕e5!? ♘e4 27 ♕b8+ ♔h7 28 ♘e2 (Agdestein) is unclear.

26 ♘xh5 ♕xb4 27 ♘xg7

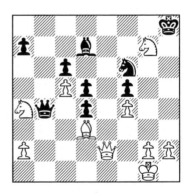

27...♔xg7??

The only move is 27...♘e4!! with a draw in all variations – 28 ♘xf5 (28 ♘h5 ♕xa4 29 ♘f6 ♘xf6 30 ♕e7 ♕d1+ 31 ♗f1 ♘g8 32 ♕xd7 d3 33 ♕xf5 d2 34 ♕e5+, or 28 ♗xe4 fxe4 29 ♕h5+) 28...♗xf5 29 g4 (29 ♗xe4 dxe4 30 ♕h5+ ♗h7 31 ♕e5+) 29...♗xg4 30 ♕xg4 ♕e1+ etc.

28 ♕e7+ ♔g6 29 h4!!

Effectively sealing Black's fate.

29...♕xa4 30 ♗e2! ♕a3 31 h5+ ♔h6 32 ♕xf6+ ♔h7 33 ♕e7+ ♔h6 34 ♕d6+ 1-0

Game 23

Nenashev-Yermolinsky

Pavlodar 1987

---

1 d4 ♘f6 2 c4 g6 3 ♘c3 ♗g7 4 e4 d6 5 ♗d3 0-0

N.B. The game actually went 5...♘c6 6 ♘ge2 e5 7 d5 ♘d4 8 ♘xd4 exd4 9 ♘e2 0-0 10 0-0 ♖e8 but we have tweaked the move order in order to more conveniently feature alternatives.

6 ♘ge2 ♘c6 7 0-0 e5

One of the most common and direct methods of concentrating on the slightly weakened d4-point.

8 d5

White is forced to close the centre as 8 dxe5 ♘xe5 is good for Black, while attempts to retain the tension in the centre cannot be recommended for White, e.g. 8 ♗c2 exd4 9 ♘xd4 ♘xe4, or 8 ♗e3 ♘g4.

8...♘d4

After the inconsistent 8...♘e7 White has two good replies.

a) 9 ♘g3 h5 (9...♘d7 10 ♗e3 f5 11 exf5 ♘xf5 12 ♘xf5 gxf5 13 f4 with the better chances for White in Racasan-Petcoiu, Eforie Nord 1998) 10 f3 ♘h7 11 f4 exf4 12 ♗xf4 ♘f6 13 e5! ♘g4 14 exd6 cxd6 15 ♕d2! (Albrecht-Adam, Correspondence 1992) is evaluated by Korchnoi in *ECO* as favouring White.

b) 9 ♗c2 a5 10 ♗g5 (10 ♘g3!?) 10...♘h5 11 ♘g3, Aleksandrov-Ovsejevitsch, Nikolaev 1995, and now 11...♘xg3!? 12 hxg3 f6 13 ♗e3 h5 provides Black with counterplay according to Dolmatov. However, we prefer 12 fxg3, e.g. 12...f6 13 ♗e3 f5 14 ♕d2 ♖f7 15 exf5.

9 ♘xd4

White does not want to see the intruder stay rooted to d4. Other continuations fail to offer the first player anything concrete.

a) 9 ♗g5 h6 (9...c5 10 ♕d2 a6 11 ♘xd4 exd4 12 ♘e2 ♕c7 13 ♗xf6 ♗xf6 14 b4 b6 with equality in Seirawan-Nunn, Monte Carlo 1994) 10 ♗h4 c5 11 f3 (11 dxc6 bxc6 12 b4 ♖e8 13 b5, Dzindzichashvili-Benjamin, Los Angeles 1991, when 13...♕a5 would have guaranteed Black counterplay) 11...g5 12 ♗e1 ♘h5 13 ♘xd4 exd4 14 ♘e2 ♘f4 15 g4 ♗e5 ½-½, Ionescu-Sofronie, Bucharest 2002.

b) 9 ♗c2. Despite its passive appearance the light-squared bishop performs an important function, so its removal can, in fact, help Black: 9...♘xc2 10 ♕xc2 ♘h5 11 ♗e3 f5 12 exf5 gxf5 13 f4 ♗d7 14 ♖ae1 ♕h4 with chances for both sides in Christiansen-Nunn, San Francisco 1995. It is worth noting that 9 ♗b1 deserves attention, the point being to eliminate Black's unruly knight with the inferior version on e2.

c) 9 f3 c5 10 ♘xd4 cxd4 11 ♘a4 sees White start operations on the queenside. 11...♗d7 12 b4 a5 was the continuation of Tunik-Kempinski, Karvina 1994, 13 a3!? ♗xa4 14 ♕xa4 ♘d7 looking nice for Black.

9...exd4

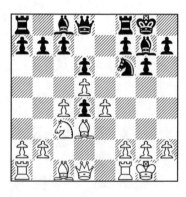

A key position that has its pros and cons whichever side of the board we are sitting on. Black's pawn has managed to cross into enemy territory, which is quite a rarity in the King's Indian. Consequently there is a semi-open file on which to plant a rook and perhaps pressure the e4-pawn. Even the occasionally passive g7-bishop enjoys considerable freedom, with the e5-square within range should the square play a part as the game unfolds. However, if Black finds himself having to come to the aid of the lone d4-pawn with ...c7-c5, then his structure will be static and therefore susceptible to attack, while there is no guaranteed counterplay available in the shape of ...b7-b5. Meanwhile, over on the other flank, pushing the f-pawn won't achieve anything useful.

10 ♘e2

In addressing the attention being paid to d4 Black nearly always adopts the formation with pawns on d4, c5 and d6 against White's on c4, d5 and e4. Depending on further play White can try to make things happen on both wings, but Black's position tends to be rather solid.

10...♖e8

A sound alternative is 10...♘d7!? 11 ♖b1 ♖e8 12 f3 c5 13 b4 b6 (13...♘e5 14 bxc5 dxc5 is equal, but the subsequent 15 f4? ♘xd3 16 ♕xd3 ♖xe4 left White with insufficient compensation for the pawn in Yrjola-Rantanen, Finland 1992, although a draw was now agreed) 14 f4 ♘f6 15 ♘g3 (Piskov-Nunn, Germany 1992) 15...cxb4!? 16 ♖xb4 ♘d7 17 ♖b1 ♘c5 with a good game for Black. Note that 15 bxc5 is equal here.

11 f3 c5

Others:

a) 11...c6 12 b3 (12 ♗f4!?, or 12 dxc6 with a transposition to 11...c5 12 dxc6, below) 12...♕b6 ½-½, Panczyk-Schmidt, Cetniewo 1991. Yermolinsky and Livshitz give 13 ♗b2 ♘d7 14 ♔h1 as a slight edge to White.

b) 11...♘d7 12 b3 ♘c5 13 ♗b2

b1) 13...f5 14 ♗xd4 fxe4 15 fxe4 ♘xe4 is given as equal by Yermolinsky and Livshitz but after the forcing 16 ♗xg7 ♔xg7 17 ♗xe4 ♖xe4 18 ♘g3 ♖e5 19 ♕d4 ♗d7 20 ♖f4 c5 21 ♕f2 White has a big advantage.

b2) 13...♕g5 is interesting. After 14 f4 ♕g4 15 ♕c2 f5 16 ♘xd4 ♘xd3 17 ♕xd3 fxe4 18 ♕e3 a6 19 ♗c3 and 14...♕h6 15 ♘xd4 ♘xe4 16 ♕e2 ♗d7 17 ♗xe4 f5 18 ♘e6 ♗xe6 19 ♗xg7 ♕xg7 20 ♗f3 ♗f7 21 ♕d2 Black is

only slightly worse.

The text is quite different in that Black is willing to fix his centre pawns.

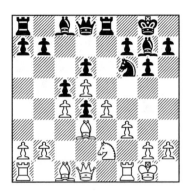

12 ♗g5

a) 12 dxc6 bxc6 13 b4 c5 14 ♖b1 (14 a3!? at least keeps White's pawns intact) 14...♘d7 15 ♘g3 cxb4 16 ♖xb4 ♘c5 was awful for White in Marcinkowski-Sarwinski, Warsaw 1989.

b) With 12 ♘g3!? White wants to get to work on a kingside offensive with a build-up along the lines of ♗d2, h2-h3, f3-f4, ♕c2/f3, ♖ae1 and a well timed e4-e5. 12...b5 13 b3 bxc4 14 bxc4 ♖b8 15 ♗d2 h5 16 ♕c2 h4 17 ♘h1 ♘h5 18 f4 h3 was far from clear in Nikolaidis-Makropoulou, Hania 1994, which leaves 12...♖b8. Then 13 ♗d2 ♗d7 14 b3 b5 15 ♕c2 bxc4 16 bxc4 ♕c7 17 ♖ae1 ♖b7 18 h3 ♖eb8 19 ♗c1 ♗c8 20 f4 ♘d7 21 ♕f2 ♖b4 22 e5 dxe5 23 fxe5 ♘xe5 24 ♗f4 was the course of Sek-Gregorczyk, Correspondence 2000, and now 24...f6! 25 ♗xe5 fxe5 26 d6 ♕d8 is critical, when after both 27 ♕f7+ and 27 ♘h5 Black can defend with 'only' moves.

12...♕c7

Less natural is 12...♕b6 13 ♖b1 ♗d7 14 ♕d2 ♖e5, Khalifman-Shirov, Moscow 1993, when White should have played 15 b4! with a big advantage.

13 ♕d2

13 ♘g3 ♘d7 14 f4 h6 15 ♗h4 b5! was equal in Yudasin-Temirbaev, Kujbyshev 1986.

13...♘d7!?

This is an improvement on a game between

the same players a year earlier (USSR): 13...a6 14 ♘g3 b5 15 b3 ♖b8 16 ♖ae1 ♕b6 17 ♗h6 and Black was in trouble.

14 f4 b5

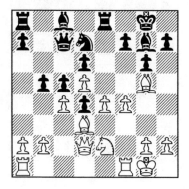

Tempting White, who tends to politely refuse the offer with the next modest nudge of the b-pawn.

15 b3

After taking on b5 White merely invites his opponent to undermine the support of the e4-pawn with, for example, a well timed ...c5-c4. There is no need to entertain such possibilities when White is able to maintain his presence in the centre.

15...bxc4 16 bxc4 ♖b8

Black's pieces have found decent posts in relation to the pawn configuration. The d7-knight protects e5 (guarding against e4-e5) and the b8-rook is playing a part. Note that the light-squared bishop must be ready to go to a6. This is another reason why Black should push the b-pawn without preparation (in other words leaving out ...a7-a6), thus keeping the a6-square free, as well as saving a tempo. There is also an argument for executing the same queenside strategy with the rook still on f8 rather than moving it to e8. This is because White's thematic e4-e5 d6xe5, f4-f5 plan is less of a problem for Black because the f7-pawn would then be more secure.

Yermolinsky and Livshitz give 16...♘f6 with the idea of sending the knight into e3 via g4. Consequently 17 ♗xf6! is necessary, when

after 17...♗xf6 18 ♘g3 White continues to toy with e4-e5, although we believe that after 18...♖b8 Black has sufficient defensive resources thanks to the bishop pair, the facility to defend with ...♖b6 and the general activity on the queenside.

17 ♘g3 ♖b4

17...♘f6 once again deserves attention.

18 e5 dxe5 19 f5 ♕b6 20 ♘e4?!

Although the attraction of 19...♕b6 is that it defends along the rank while simultaneously introducing the possibility of ...♖b2 White might be able to exploit the former factor with 20 ♖ab1!?, taking charge of the b-file and preparing for aggressive action on either side of the board. For example c5 is a target, while after the trade on b4 White's centre pawns grow in strength, e.g. 20...f6 21 ♗h6! ♘f8 22 ♖xb4 ♕xb4 23 ♕xb4 cxb4 24 ♗d2 etc.

20...f6 21 d6

21 fxg6? hxg6 and White will regret releasing Black's f-pawn. After 21 ♗h6 Black enjoys an edge.

21...♖b2 22 ♕c1

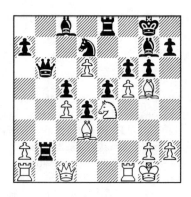

22...♗b7

Of course the game is becoming rather complex and, with it, the decision making process. However, with 22...gxf5! Black can find a route to a considerable advantage: 23 ♖xf5 fxg5 24 ♕xg5 ♕d8 25 ♕h5 ♗b7 and the onus is on White to demonstrate compensation for the lost piece.

23 fxg6?

The lesser evil is 23 &d2!? gxf5 24 ♖xf5 &xe4 25 &xe4 ♖b8 with a messy situation that holds more worries for White than Black.

23...hxg6 24 &xf6 ♘xf6

Why not 24...&xe4! 25 &xe4 ♘xf6 with a big advantage?

25 ♖xf6 &xf6

25...&xe4! is again strong.

26 ♕h6 ♖f8

Yet again 26...&xe4! should net Black the full point – 27 &xe4 ♕xd6 28 &d5+ ♖e6 29 ♖f1 ♔f7, e.g. 30 g4 ♔e7 31 g5 &xg5 32 ♕g7+ (32 ♕xg5+ ♖f6) 32...♔d8 33 &xe6 &f4 34 ♕g8+ ♔c7 and the king easily finds sanctuary on the queenside, leaving Black to push his centre pawns or even construct an attack against the enemy king. Note that the opposite-coloured bishops only help the aggressor in this kind of scenario.

27 ♕xg6+ &g7 28 ♕e6+ ♔h8 29 ♕h3+ ♔g8 30 ♕e6+ 1-0

Game 24
Krasenkow-Kempinski
Polish League, Lubniewice 1995

---

1 d4 ♘f6 2 c4 g6 3 ♘c3 &g7 4 e4 d6 5 &d3 0-0 6 ♘ge2 ♘c6 7 0-0 e5 8 d5 ♘d4 9 ♘xd4 exd4 10 ♘b5

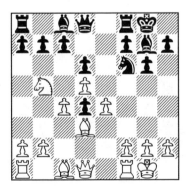

This move is much more forcing (and risky) than 10 ♘e2. White threatens to win the d4-pawn without obstructing the e-file, thus enabling him to protect the e4-pawn with

♖e1. On the downside, if White fails to achieve his objective the knight will be forced to retreat to the poor post on a3.

10...♖e8

Others:

a) 10...♕e7 11 ♖e1 ♘g4 12 h3 and Black was already in trouble in Seirawan-Gelfand, Wijk aan Zee 1992.

b) 10...♘d7 11 &c2 ♘e5 12 ♘xd4 (12 &b3 c5 13 dxc6 bxc6 14 ♘xd4 &a6 transposes to Hort-Xie Jun – see Game 22, note to White's 8th move, 'b22') 12...♘xc4 13 ♖b1 &d7 14 b3 ♘b6 15 &e3 ♖e8 (15...c5!? 16 dxc6 bxc6 17 ♕d2 d5 gains a tempo) 16 ♕d2 c5 17 dxc6 bxc6 18 ♖fd1 d5 19 ♘e2!?, Wu Shaobin-Wang Pin, Beijing 2001, with an edge for White.

c) 10...♘e8 has not been sufficiently tested in tournament practice but is undoubtedly worth a look. White has a few continuations.

c1) 11 b4 a5 (11...c6!? 12 dxc6 bxc6 13 ♘a3 f5 gives Black counterplay) 12 bxa5 c6 13 ♘a3 ♖xa5 14 ♕b3 (Hazai prefers 14 ♘c2 ♘c7 15 a4 ♖a7) 14...♘c7 15 &d2 ♖a8 16 ♘c2 ♘a6 and Black emerged from the run-around with a slight advantage in Bareev-Tkachiev, Cap d'Agde 2002.

c2) 11 &b1 ♕f6 12 a4 a6 13 ♘a3 ♕h4 14 ♕d3 ♘f6 15 ♕g3 ♕xg3 16 hxg3 ♖e8 17 f3 ♘d7 18 b4 ♘b6 19 a5 ♘a4 20 &d3 f5 led to a level game in Knaak, Arkhipov-Yurtaev, Oberwart 1991.

c3) 11 &c2 ♕f6 12 f4 a6 13 e5 dxe5 14 fxe5 ♕b6 15 ♘xd4 &xe5 with chances for both sides, Gofshtein-Ballmann, Zurich 2000.

11 ♖e1 a6

11...&g4?! 12 f3 &d7 13 &g5 ♕b8 14 &f1 c5 15 a4 a6 16 ♘a3 h6 17 &d2 and, according to *ECO*, White has a big advantage. However, Marin-Raul Garcia, Andorra 1992 went 17...b6 18 b4 ♖a7 19 a5, when Black could have played 19...bxa5!? 20 bxa5 ♕c7 21 ♕c1 ♔h7 with an equal position. But there is an interesting alternative for White in 15 dxc6!? bxc6 16 ♘xd4 ♕xb2 17 ♘b3, when Black has problems with the d6-pawn.

Black can also send his knight to g4 – 11...♘g4 12 h3 with the following position:

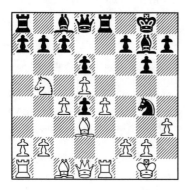

In order to avoid losing the d4-pawn Black now has to make a threat of his own and attack White's knight. In Milov-Sutovsky, Struga 1995 Black chose to use the a-pawn, but after 12...a6 13 hxg4 axb5 14 cxb5 ♕h4 15 ♗f4! ♗xg4 16 ♕d2 had a poor position.

This brings us to 12...c6.

a) 13 dxc6 bxc6 14 hxg4 cxb5 15 cxb5 (15 g5!?) 15...♕h4 16 ♗e2 (16 ♕d2!? ♗xg4 17 ♕g5 ♕xg5 18 ♗xg5 seems to favour White) 16...d5 (16...♗e5 17 f4 d3? [17...♗g7!?] 18 ♗f3 ♗d4+ 19 ♗e3 ♗xb2 20 ♖b1 ♗c3 21 ♗f2 ♕e7 22 ♖e3 Korchnoi-Ligterink, Amsterdam 1976 and, according to Knaak, White has a clear advantage) 17 g3! ♕h3 18 ♗f3 (18 exd5 ♗xg4 19 ♗xg4 ♖xe1+ 20 ♕xe1 ♕xg4 21 d6! looks good) 18...dxe4 19 ♖xe4 ♖xe4 20 ♗xe4 ♗xg4 21 ♕f1! and *ECO* evaluates this position as very good for White. We cannot agree with this, for after 21...♕xf1+ 22 ♔xf1 ♖e8 23 f3 (Olafsson-Mortensen, Espoo Zonal 1989) 23...♗e6! 24 ♗d3 ♗d5 the ending is balanced.

b) It is surprising that the analogous line to 12...a6 has gone practically untested – 13 hxg4!? cxb5 14 cxb5 (14 g5 bxc4 15 ♗xc4 also looks pleasant for White) 14...♕h4 and now White has better chances after both 15 ♗f4 ♗e5 16 ♗xe5 dxe5 17 ♗e2 and 15 g3 ♕xg4 16 ♕xg4 ♗xg4 17 ♔g2 (17 ♗f4 ♗e5 18 ♗d2 f5 19 ♖ac1 fxe4 20 ♗xe4) 17...f5 18 f3 fxe4 (Etchegaray-Weindl, Cannes 1996) 19 ♗xe4.

12 ♘xd4 ♘xd5 13 cxd5

Only this move, which gives White valuable extra space, offers chances of fighting for an advantage. 13 ♘c2?! is harmless: 13...♘b6 14 ♘e3 ♘d7 15 f3 ♘c5 16 ♗c2 ♗e6 left Black active in Sulyok-Freitag, Austria 1996.

13...♗xd4 14 ♕c2

14 ♕a4 ♗e5 15 ♖b1 (15 ♕b3 c5 16 dxc6 bxc6 with equality, V.Georgiev-Szelag, Cappelle la Grande 1999) 15...♗d7 16 ♕b4 c5 17 dxc6 (17 ♕xb7? ♗a4! 18 b3 ♖e7) 17...♗xc6 was unclear in Damljanovic-Kozul, Pula 1990. Black also has 14...c5!? 15 dxc6 ♕b6 16 ♗e3 ♗xe3 17 ♖xe3. These positions tend to look a little better for White in view of the superior pawn structure, but tournament practice in recent years does not confirm this, perhaps because Black is sufficiently active – especially the bishops on open diagonals – and there are no knights with which to fully exploit weak squares. Play has continued 17...bxc6 18 ♕c2 ♗e6 19 b3 a5 20 ♖ae1 a4 21 ♗c4 ½-½, Zaja-Stevic, Istanbul 2003. Finally 14...♗f6 15 ♕c2 ♗d7 16 ♗e3 c5 17 dxc6 ♗xc6 18 ♖ad1 produced another early draw in the game Stern-Gruenenwald, Germany 1995.

14...♗d7

Not 14...♕f6?! 15 ♗e3 ♗xb2 16 ♖ab1, e.g. 16...♗e5 17 ♕xc7, spoiling the pawn structure, or 16...♗c3 17 ♖ec1 ♗d4? 18 ♕a4 and White won in Nutu Gajic-Bobrowska, Timisoara Women's Zonal 1993 .

15 ♗e3

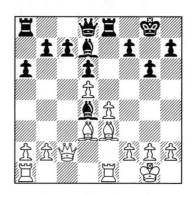

15...♗e5!?

Black should avoid the bishop trade for a couple of reasons – his bishop is the more active and, secondly, Black's pawns would prove more vulnerable in its absence.

a) 15...♗xe3 16 ♖xe3 c5 17 ♕c3 (Marin-Timoshchenko, Calimanesti 1992) 17...b5!? 18 b3 b4 19 ♕b2 ♗b5 20 ♖ae1 ♕g5 is level. 17 dxc6 improves, with better chances for White.

b) 15...♗g7 16 ♖ad1 c5 17 dxc6 was equal and agreed drawn in Seirawan-Benjamin, Los Angeles 1991.

16 ♕b3

If your opponent has weaknesses, attack them. Comfortably defending b7 appears to be a problem for Black as both 16...b6 and 16...b5 compromise the queenside, while 16...♕c8 and 16...♕b8 look awkward.

16...♖b8?

Now Black has to play a difficult ending. Kempinski must have overlooked a tactical trick because he could have played 16...c5! with the following position:

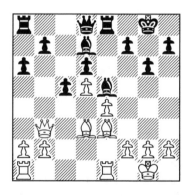

Now 17 ♕xb7?? ♗a4! traps the queen(!), so it is time for the sober 17 dxc6. Then 17...bxc6 18 ♕c2 a5 is equal, which leaves 17...♗xc6. Again this is level after 18 ♖ad1. Anyway, if White cannot take the b7-pawn, then 16 ♕b3 is best avoided as the queen is worse on b3 than c2. With this in mind 16 ♖ac1 would have been preferable.

17 f4

Avoiding complications that follow 17 ♗a7

♖a8 18 ♕xb7 ♕h4 19 g3 ♕f6 20 ♖e3 ♗b5.

17...♗g7 18 ♗a7 ♖a8 19 ♕xb7 ♕c8

Perhaps Black should look for counterplay with 19...♗b5 20 ♗xb5 axb5 21 ♖e2 f5.

20 ♕xc8 ♖exc8 21 ♗f2 ♗xb2 22 ♖ab1 ♗c3

Chekhov recommends 22...♖cb8!? 23 ♖e2 ♗c3, but after 24 ♖xb8+ (24 ♖c1!?) 24...♖xb8 25 ♗a7 ♖a8 26 ♖c2 ♗f6 27 ♗e3 White has an undeniable advantage in the ending.

23 ♖e2 c6 24 ♖b7 ♗g4 25 ♖c2 cxd5 26 exd5 a5 27 h3 ♗d1 28 ♖c1 ♗a4 29 g3 ♗d2 30 ♖cc7 ♖xc7 31 ♖xc7 ♖e8 32 ♖a7 ♖c8 33 ♖a6 ♗d7

33...♗b4 34 a3 ♖c1+ 35 ♔h2 ♗c5 36 ♗xc5 ♖xc5 37 ♗e4 gives White too much according to Chekhov.

34 ♖xd6 ♗xh3 35 ♖b6 ♗b4 36 ♖c6 ♖d8?!

Chekhov gives 36...♗d7!? as better.

37 ♗c4 ♗f5 38 ♗b6 ♖e8 39 ♗d4 ♗f8 40 d6 ♖c8 41 ♖xc8 ♗xc8 42 ♗e5 ♗d7 43 ♔f2 ♗g7 44 ♗xg7 ♔xg7 45 ♔e3 ♔f6

45...f6 puts up stiffer resistance.

46 ♔d4 ♗e6 47 ♗d5 1-0

47 ♗d5 ♗d7 48 ♔c5.

Game 25
Korchnoi-Radjabov
Najdorf Memorial, Buenos Aires 2001

---

1 c4 g6 2 e4 ♗g7 3 d4 d6 4 ♘c3 ♘f6 5 ♗d3 0-0 6 ♘ge2 ♘c6 7 0-0 ♘h5

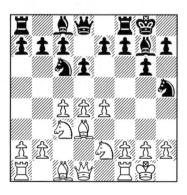

Continuing the now familiar theme with a different recipe, this time Black increases the pressure against d4 by sending his knight to h5. The point in lodging the knight on the edge of the board is to accelerate any offensive action in the event of the traditional ...e7-e5, d4-d5 when f4 is better monitored, the knight is closer to White's king and – no less important – Black is free to continue with a more fluid development.

8 ♗c2

White has a number of perfectly satisfactory alternatives:

a) 8 d5 is another example of gaining more space in the centre in return for allowing the exchange of the d3-bishop. However, in this case Black's h5-knight might prove to be out of play, although White constantly has to contend with ...f7-f5. A typical continuation is 8...♘e5 9 f4 ♘xd3 10 ♕xd3, e.g. 10...c6 11 ♗e3 ♗d7 12 ♗d4 ♖c8 13 dxc6 bxc6 14 ♗xg7 ♘xg7 15 b3 with an edge for White in Bönsch-Maiwald, Cologne 2003, while the aggressive 10...f5!? 11 ♘d4 c5 12 dxc6 bxc6 13 ♗e3 ♗d7 14 exf5 gxf5 15 c5 was not enough to deny White a lead in Van der Werf- Gallagher, Cannes 1997.

b) 8 ♗e3 allows the knight to reach d4, e.g. 8...e5 9 d5 ♘d4. Then 10 ♗c2 ♘xc2 11 ♕xc2 f5 12 exf5 (B.Kovacevic-Zelenika, Pula 1999) 12...gxf5!? is unclear, while 10 ♕d2!? c5 11 dxc6 bxc6 12 b4 ♗e6 13 b5 f5 14 ♗g5 ♕d7 15 bxc6 ♘xc6 16 ♘d5 f4 17 f3 ♔h8 18 ♔h1 h6 19 ♗h4 left White with a pull in Seirawan-Kasimdzhanov, Bled 2002. Meanwhile 10 ♘b5 ♘xb5! 11 cxb5 f5 12 f3 f4 13 ♗f2 g5 14 ♘c3 ♘f6 15 ♗e2 ♕e8 (15...h5!?, intending ...g5-g4) 16 a4 ♕h5 was the course of Skembris-Dimitrov, Kavala 2001, when 17 ♕e1!? and 17 ♖c1 offer White chances of obtaining an advantage. Perhaps Black might try 16...♕g6!? here.

8...e5 9 d5

After 9 dxe5 ♘xe5 10 b3 ♕h4 Black was active in Aleksandrov-Golubev, Nikolaev 1993.

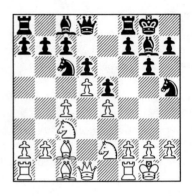

9...♘e7

Now that White has a little more influence over d4 than in some earlier examples Black does better to avoid temptation as 9...♘d4 runs into 10 ♘xd4 exd4 11 ♘b5 c5 12 dxc6 bxc6 13 ♘xd4 ♕b6 14 ♘b3 (or 14 ♘f5) 14...♗e6 15 ♕xd6 ♗xc4 16 ♗e3 with a very big advantage for White according to Piket. However, 9...♘b4 10 ♗b1 a5 is quite playable.

10 a4

This thrust is a good example of a dual-purpose move – White hopes that the a4-pawn will contribute to the cause on the queenside while the advance has also introduced the possibility of ♖a3 followed by swinging over to the kingside. The only disadvantage of the text is that after 10...a5 the pawn structure on the queenside is less dynamic. However, White has the inviting b5-square for his knight.

Others:

a) 10 ♔h1 f5 (10...c5 11 f4 f5 12 exf5 ♗xf5 13 ♗xf5 gxf5 14 fxe5 dxe5 15 ♘g1, as in Conquest-Hebden, Clichy 1997 is assessed as a shade better for White in *NCO*) 11 exf5 gxf5, Atalik-Polzin, Kallithea Halkidiki 2003, and now 12 ♘g3!? ♘f6 13 ♘h5 ♘xh5 14 ♕xh5 secures White a nagging pull.

b) 10 ♖b1 f5 11 exf5 and White should emerge with the better prospects regardless of how Black recaptures, e.g. 11...♘xf5 12 ♘e4 ♗h6 13 ♗xh6 ♘xh6 14 ♕d2, Delchev-Rutkowski, Bad Wildbad 2002, or 11...gxf5 12 f4 ♘g6 13 fxe5 dxe5 14 c5 ♔h8 (14...f4 15 ♘e4! ♘f6 16 ♘2c3) 15 b4 f4 16 ♘e4 ♗g4 (Feletar-Gallagher, Pula 2000), when 17 h3 ♗f5 18 d6 ♘f6 19 ♘2c3 favours White according to Hazai.

10...f5

Black wastes no time.

a) 10...♔h8 11 a5 (11 ♖a3 f5 12 exf5 gxf5 13 ♘g3 ♘xg3 14 fxg3 ♘g6 15 ♘e2 ♗d7 16 ♗e3 looked better for White in I.Sokolov-David, Bordeaux 2003) 11...f5 12 exf5 gxf5 13 ♘g3 ♘f4 (13...♘xg3 14 fxg3!) 14 ♘h5 ♘xh5 15 ♕xh5 and White was already fully in charge in Piket-Fedorov, Wijk aan Zee 2001.

b) 10...a5 11 ♖a3 f5 12 exf5 ♘xf5 13 ♘e4 ♘f6 14 ♗g5 ♕e8 15 ♘2c3 ♘xe4 16 ♗xe4 ♗f6 17 ♗c1 ♕e7 18 ♘b5 (Bareev-Dolmatov, Elista 1997) with the better chances for White according to *ECO*.

11 exf5 gxf5 12 ♘g3

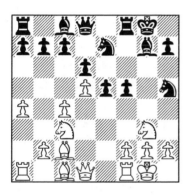

12...♘f4

12...♘xg3 13 fxg3 ♕e8 14 ♘b5 ♕d7 15 ♗e3 a6 16 ♘c3 ♕e8 17 c5 ♗d7 was unclear in Palliser-Nunn, England 2001. White might try 16 ♘a7!? here instead of retreating to c3.

13 ♘h5!?

13 ♖a3 ♘eg6 14 ♘ce2 was Pinter-Nataf, Batumi 1999, and now 14...♘xe2+ 15 ♕xe2 maintains the balance.

13...♘xh5 14 ♕xh5 ♘g6 15 f4 exf4

Black can also permit the trade on e5, the point being to generate piece play (dark squares) and use the e5-square as a knight

outpost. However, perhaps 15...e4!? is the best of the available options.

16 ♗xf4

Chatalbashev-Isonzo, Cutro 2002 demonstrated White's most promising course: 16 ♘e2!? ♗d7 17 ♖a3 ♗e5 (17...♕f6!? should be tried, restricting White to a slight advantage) 18 ♘xf4 ♘xf4 19 ♗xf4 ♕f6 20 ♗xe5 ♕xe5 (20...dxe5 21 ♖b3 is a lesser evil) 21 ♖h3 etc.

16...♕f6 17 ♖ad1 ♘xf4 18 ♖xf4 ♕h6 19 ♖h4 ♕xh5 20 ♖xh5 ♗xc3 21 bxc3 ♗d7

Black's weak f5-pawn is easy to defend. A means of making progress for White is problematic indeed, particularly in view of the fact that White's bishop longs for better times and the c4-pawn could be a juicy target for Black to aim at.

22 ♔f2 ♖ae8 23 a5 ♖e5 24 ♖b1 b6 25 axb6 axb6 26 ♖a1 ♗e8 27 ♖g5+ ♗g6 28 ♖a7 ♖e7 29 ♔f3 ♔g7 30 ♔f4 h6 31 ♖g3 ♔f6 32 ♗d3 ♖fe8 33 ♖f3 ♔g7 34 ♖h3 ♖f7 35 ♖g3 ♔f6 36 ♖f3 ♖fe7 37 ♔g3 ♖f7 38 ♔h4 ♔g7 39 ♖a1 f4 40 ♖af1 ♗e4 41 ♖e1 ♖fe7 42 ♖xe4 ♖xe4 43 ♗xe4 ♖xe4 44 ♔g4 ♖xc4 45 ♔f5 b5 46 ♖d3 ♖a4 47 ♖d2 ♖c4 48 ♖d3 ♖a4 49 ♖d2 ♖c4 ½-½

Game 26
Sagalchik-Graf
Kemerovo 1995

1 d4 ♘f6 2 c4 g6 3 ♘c3 ♗g7 4 e4 d6 5 ♗d3 0-0 6 ♘ge2 e5 7 d5 c6

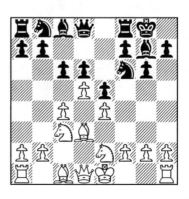

Black decides to make an early challenge on White's centre, the point being to open the c-file, facilitate counterplay involving ...b7-b5 and then secure a stable knight outpost on c5 by placing the a-pawn on a5. Of course opening the c-file is a double-edged strategy as White might seek to control it. Meanwhile, with ...f7-f5 in the air, White's light-squared bishop might come to life.

8 0-0

White can also stake a claim for queenside territory immediately with 8 ♖b1. Then 8...a5 9 a3 cxd5 10 cxd5 ♘h5 11 0-0 ♘d7 12 ♗e3 f5 13 exf5 gxf5 14 ♘g3! ♕xg3 15 fxg3 e4 16 ♗e2 (Piskov-Hermesmann, Dortmund 1992) favours White according to Piskov in *ECO*, as did 8...cxd5 9 cxd5 ♘bd7 10 ♘g3 h5 11 ♗g5 ♘c5 12 ♗c2 a5 13 a3 ♗g4 14 f3 ♗d7 15 b4 axb4 16 axb4 ♘a6 17 ♕d2 in Pinter-Kozul, Pula 1996. Black's best seems 8...♘bd7 9 b4 (Hedman-Shtyrenkov, Pardubice 2000) 9...a5!? with chances for both sides.

8...♘bd7

Retaining the tension in the centre has its advantages for Black, but by not trading immediately he must take into account the possibility that White might recapture on d5 with the knight, or alter the flavour of the game by throwing in d5xc6.

a) 8...cxd5 9 cxd5 ♘bd7 (9...♘h5 10 ♗e3 f5 11 exf5 gxf5, Franz-Boca, Bayern 1998 and now 12 ♘g3!? seems to keep White slightly ahead) 10 f3 ♘c5 11 ♗c2 a5 12 ♗e3 ♗d7 13 a3 ♘h5 14 ♗xc5 dxc5 15 ♗a4 (Rozentalis-Yrloja, Voronez 1987) and, according to Rozentalis, White has an advantage due to weakness of the b5-square.

b) 8...a5 9 a3 (9 f3!? is interesting, while 9 ♗g5 h6 10 ♗d2 ♘a6 11 a3 ♗d7 12 dxc6 bxc6 13 ♘a4 d5 was unclear in Skembris-Collutiis, Cesenatico 2000) 9...♘h5 10 ♗e3 f5 11 exf5 gxf5 12 f3 (12 ♘g3!?) 12...c5 13 ♔h1 ♘a6 (Ehlvest-Cvitan, Biel Open 1997) 14 ♕c2! with an advantage to White according to Ehlvest.

9 ♗c2

Now White is able to occupy d5 with a piece rather than a pawn.

9...cxd5

Black can also defend the d6-pawn with 9...♕e7, although in Matamoros Franco-Perdomo Abad, Las Palmas 1995 White engineered an advantage after 10 f3 a5 11 ♗e3 ♘e8 12 ♕d2 f5 13 exf5 gxf5 14 f4.

10 ♘xd5

10 cxd5 a5 11 f3 tends to lead to similar positions to those after 8...cxd5 9 cxd5 ♘bd7 10 f3, but White can leave his f-pawn alone and instead try 11 ♘g3, e.g. 11...♘c5 12 a3 (12 ♖b1 ♗d7 13 ♕e2 ♕b6 14 ♗g5 ♖fc8 15 ♕d2 ♘g4 16 ♗d1 f6 17 ♗xg4 ♗xg4 18 ♗h6 ♗d7 19 ♗xg7 ♔xg7 led to a level game in Illescas Cordoba-Matamoros Franco, Lanzarote 2003) 12...♗d7 13 ♗e3 ♘g4 14 ♗xc5 dxc5 15 ♗a4 f5 16 ♗xd7 ♕xd7 (Meleghegyi-Redolfi, Correspondence 1995) 17 ♘a4!? with an edge for White.

10...♘xd5 11 ♕xd5

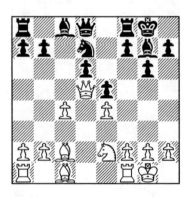

11...♘c5

A surprising idea is 11...♘b6 12 ♕d3 ♕c7 13 b3 d5, when 14 cxd5 ♘xd5 15 ♗a3 ♖d8 16 ♖ad1 ♗g4 17 exd5 ♗f5 18 ♕e3 ♕xc2 secured White a minimal edge in Akhmadeev-Chuprov, Novgorod 1999, but 15...♖e8!? 16 ♖ad1 ♘f6 17 ♗b1 ♗g4 appears to solve all Black's problems. White can avoid this with 13 ♘c3, which is certainly worthy of further tests as 13...♕xc4 14 ♕xd6 ♗e6 15 ♗b3 ♕d4 16 ♘b5 ♕xd6 17 ♘xd6 ♗xb3 18 axb3 looks quite awkward for Black.

12 b3 ♗e6 13 ♕d2 f5 14 ♖d1

Attacking the backward d6-pawn, but Black has a simple defence. Therefore White should consider 14 ♘c3 followed by ♗b2 and ♖ad1 etc.

14...♖f7 15 ♗b2

After 15 ♕xd6?? Black always has 15...♖d7.

15...♖c8 16 exf5 gxf5 17 f4?!

White unnecessarily allows tactics to develop in the shape of the g1-a7 diagonal. 17 ♘c3 is the correct course, with the superior pawn structure and the easier game for White.

17...♗xc4

Movsziszian gives 17...♕b6 18 ♕xd6 ♖c6 19 ♕d8+ but Black can try 17...♘e4!, e.g. 18 ♗xe4 (18 ♕e3 exf4 19 ♘xf4 ♗xb2 20 ♘xe6 ♕f6 21 ♗xe4 ♗xa1 is nice for Black) 18...♕b6+ After 19 ♔h1 fxe4 20 h3 (20 ♕xd6 ♗g4 21 ♕xb6 axb6 22 ♖e1 exf4 23 ♗xg7 ♔xg7) 20...♖e8 Black has an excellent game.

18 ♗xe5!

Also quite playable is 18 bxc4 (or, in another move order, 18 fxe5 ♕b6 19 bxc4) 18...♕b6 19 fxe5! (Movsziszian gives only 19 ♕xd6 ♕xb2 20 ♖ac1? ♖d7 etc.) 19...♕xb2 (19...dxe5 20 ♗a3 ♘e4+ 21 c5!, or 19...♘b3+ 20 ♗d4) 20 exd6 ♕b6 21 ♖ab1 with a forcing variation that leads to a drawn ending – 21...♘b3+ 22 ♔h1 ♘xd2 23 ♖xb6 ♘xc4 24 d7 ♖d8 25 ♖xb7 ♘e3 26 ♖b8 ♗f6 27 ♖xd8+ ♗xd8 28 ♖d2 ♘xc2 29 ♖xc2 ♖xd7.

18...♗xe5

18...♗xe2 19 ♕xe2 ♕e8 20 ♖xd6 ♘d7 21 ♖ad1 ♘xe5 22 fxe5 ♗xe5 23 ♖6d2 with a level game is fine for Black, but the best continuation here is the unexpected 18...♕b6 19 ♗xg7 ♗xe2 20 ♕xe2 (or 20 ♗d4 ♗xd1 21 ♕xd1 d5 with a plus for Black) 20...♘d3+ 21 ♔f1 ♘xf4 22 ♗d4 ♕xd4 23 ♖xd4 ♘xe2 24 ♖d2 ♘f4 25 b4 ♔f8 26 ♖ad1 ♘d5, when Black is on top.

19 fxe5 ♕b6 20 ♔h1 ♗xe2 21 ♕xe2 ♖e8 22 ♗xf5 ♖xe5 23 ♕g4+ ♖g7 24 ♕h3 d5?

24...♕d8!? is only a shade worse for Black.

25 ♖ac1

25 ♗xh7+ ♖xh7? 26 ♕g3+ improves.

25...♕d6 26 b4 ♘e6 27 ♗xe6+ ♖xe6??

28 ♖c8+ ♔f7 29 ♖f1+

29 ♕f5+ ♖f6 30 ♕h5+ ♖fg6 31 ♖xd5 is simple and very strong.

29...♔g6? 30 ♕f5+ ♔h6 31 ♖c3 1-0

Game 27
Reinderman-Movsesian
Dutch League (play-off) Breda 2001

1 c4 g6 2 ♘c3 ♗g7 3 d4 d6 4 e4 ♘f6 5 ♗d3 0-0 6 ♘ge2 e5 7 d5 a5

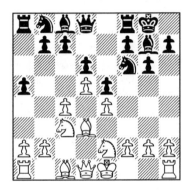

Black secures the c5-square for his knight. The immediate 7...♘a6 is also possible, e.g. 8 0-0 (8 f3!? ♘c5 9 ♗c2 a5 10 ♗e3 ♘h5 11 0-0 f5 12 exf5 gxf5 13 f4 with an edge for White, Farago-Knoll, Aschach 1994) and a crossroads:

a) 8...♘h5 9 a3 (9 ♗e3 f5 10 exf5 gxf5 11 f4 e4 12 ♗c2 ♘f6 13 h3 c5 14 a3 ♗d7 with chances for both sides, Chatalbashev-Janev, Opatija 2003) 9...c5 10 dxc6 bxc6 11 ♗e3 (Happe-Poetzsch, Correspondence 1993) and now 11...f5 12 ♕a4 ♕c7 13 exf5 gxf5 sets up a balanced middlegame. 11 b4 ♘c7 12 ♖b1 f5 gives Black counterplay.

b) 8...♘c5 9 ♗c2 a5 10 b3 ♘h5 11 ♗e3 f5 12 exf5 gxf5 with much to play for in J.Christiansen-Josephsen, Denmark 1995.

c) 8...♘d7 9 ♗e3 f5 10 exf5 gxf5 11 f4 (Summerscale-Coleman, Norwich 1994) and now 11...♘f6 12 fxe5 ♘g4 13 ♗c1 ♕h4 14 h3 ♘xe5 leads to a double-edged position.

d) 8...c6 9 a3 ♘c5 10 ♗c2 cxd5 11 cxd5 a5 12 ♗g5 h6 13 ♗e3 ♘g4 14 ♗d2 f5 with counterplay, Arkhipov-Gallagher, Kecskemet 1990 .

8 a3

A natural alternative is 8 0-0 ♘a6 (8...♘bd7 9 f3 ♘e8 10 ♗e3 f5 11 exf5 gxf5 12 f4 ♘df6 13 h3 ♘h5 14 ♕d2 e4 15 ♗c2, Ionescu-Vajda, Bucharest 1997, favours White) 9 f3

a) 9...♘h5 10 ♗e3 f5 11 exf5 gxf5 12 a3 (12 f4 ♘f6 13 h3 e4 14 ♗c2 c5 15 dxc6 bxc6 16 ♕d2 ♖b8 and Black enjoyed counterplay in Kiselev-Bragin, Podolsk 1992) 12...♗d7 13 ♗c2 ♕e8 (Terron Elena-Rubio Doblas, Malaga 2000) 14 ♗a4!? is good for White.

b) 9...c6 10 ♗e3 ♘h5 (10...♗d7 11 ♘a4 c5 12 a3 ♖b8 13 ♖b1 with an edge, Lalic-Cheparinov, Lausanne 2001) 11 ♕d2 f5 12 exf5 gxf5 and now 13 f4! e4 14 ♗c2 (Marin-Bologan, Calimanesti 1992) is a standard route to an advantage.

8...♘a6 9 ♗c2 ♘c5 10 f3

If 10 ♖b1 Black must advance with 10...a4 in order to address the threatened b2-b4, but now the a4-pawn is vulnerable. This was seen in Heinimaki-Johansson, Turku 1997 – 11 0-0 ♗d7 12 f3 ♘e8 13 ♗e3 f5 14 exf5 gxf5 15 ♗xc5 dxc5 16 ♗xa4 etc. However, Black has a possible improvement in 12...♕e8.

10...♘fd7!?

This looks superior to 10...♗d7, which failed badly in Feletar-Bilobrk, Pula 1999 after 11 ♗e3 ♘e8 12 0-0 h5 13 b4 axb4 14 axb4 ♘a6 15 ♖b1 etc. 12...f5!? looks like an improvement.

11 0-0 f5

11...♘b6!? exploits the pin on the a-file and thus after 12 b3 f5 13 exf5 gxf5 effectively gains a tempo should play then follow the same course as the main game.

12 exf5

After 12 ♖b1 f4 13 b4 ♘a6 14 ♗d2 (No-vikov-Belov, Volgograd 1996) 14...♘b6!? 15 ♗d3 axb4 16 axb4 c5 Black has a good position.

12...gxf5 13 ♖b1 ♘b6

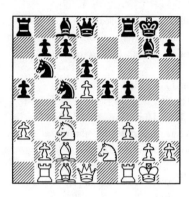

The key position. Black switches wings so that the queenside is currently the main arena, exerting pressure on White's pawns.

14 b4 axb4 15 axb4 ♘a6 16 ♗d3 c5

The point – Black's play thus far has been geared to executing this thematic break-through.

17 bxc5

17 dxc6 bxc6 merely frees the excellent e6-square for Black's bishop.

17...♘xc5 18 ♗e3

Both sides have weaknesses and, consequently, targets.

18...♗d7

18...♘bd7!? denies White his next possibility.

19 ♗xc5 dxc5 20 ♕c2 ♖a6 21 ♖b3

The immediate 21 ♘g3!? looks fine for White, meeting a subsequent 21...♕g5 with 22 ♘b5.

21...♕h4

Attacking the c4-pawn and preparing offensive operations on the kingside with ...♖f6-h6. White must also keep an eye on another standard theme here, namely the activation of Black's dark-squared bishop with ...e5-e4 followed by ...♗e5 or ...♗d4 (should the e2-knight move).

22 ♖fb1

White could address Black's plan with 22 ♕b1 ♖f6 23 ♕e1.

22...♖f6 23 ♘g3 e4!

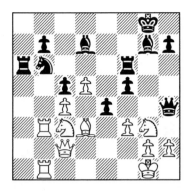

A typical idea in the King's Indian. Black kills two birds with one stone, increasing the scope of the dark-squared bishop while simultaneously denying White's pieces access to the potentially useful e4-square.

24 fxe4 f4

The point, putting a difficult question to the knight. The rather blunt looking 24...♖h6 is also effective, when 25 ♘f1 f4 transposes to 24...f4 25 ♘f1 ♖h6 (below) and 25...fxe4 26 ♘xe4 ♗a4 keeps enough fuel in the tank for both players.

25 ♘f1 f3?

This time 25...♖h6 is the correct move, e.g. 26 ♘b5 ♗e5 with chances for both sides, or 26 ♔h1 ♗e5 followed by ...f4-f3 etc.

26 e5! ♕d4+ 27 ♔h1

27 ♕f2 ♕xe5 28 ♘e4 ♖g6 29 ♕xf3 looks simpler.

27...fxg2+ 28 ♕xg2 ♕xe5 29 ♘e4 ♖g6 30 ♘fg3 ♕d4 31 ♘d2 ♖a2 32 ♘f3

After the simple 32 ♗xg6 ♖xd2 33 ♕g1 ♕xc4 34 ♗e4 White should have won.

32...♕xd3

After 32...♕f4 White has a forcing variation in 33 ♕xa2 ♕xf3+ 34 ♕g2 ♖xg3 35 ♗xh7+ ♔xh7 36 ♖xf3 ♖xg2 37 ♔xg2 ♘xc4 38 ♖xb7 etc.

33 ♖xd3 ♖xg2 34 ♔xg2 ♗f5 35 ♖db3?

Missing 35 ♖xb6 ♗xd3 36 ♖xb7 or 36 d6, with winning chances for White.

35...♗xb1 36 ♖xb1 ♘xc4 37 ♖xb7 ♘e3+ 38 ♔f2 ♘xd5 39 ♘f5 ♗f8 40 ♘e3 ♘c3

41 ♘c4 ♖e6 42 ♘fe5 h6 43 ♔e3 ♗g7 44 ♔d3 ♘d5 45 ♔e4 ♘e7 46 ♖c7 ♘g6 47 ♖xc5 ♘xe5 48 ♘xe5 ♖xe5+ 49 ♖xe5 ♗xe5 ½-½

Game 28
Panczyk-Kempys
Polish Championship, Cetniewo 1991

Many of the notes to this game are from our survey in *NIC Yearbook No. 66.*

1 d4 ♘f6 2 c4 g6 3 ♘c3 ♗g7 4 e4 d6 5 ♗d3 0-0 6 ♘ge2 e5 7 d5 ♘h5

This move looks logical, Black wasting no time preparing an offensive on the kingside.

8 h3!?

This the idea of Polish correspondence master Zbigniew Sek. If Black fails to react energetically he will lose two tempi after White advances g2-g4.

8 ♗e3 f5 9 f3 ♘f4!? 10 0-0 ♘xd3 11 ♕xd3 f4 12 ♗f2 ♘d7 13 ♖fc1 (Yakovich-Temirbaev, Pinsk 1986) 13...♘c5 14 ♕d2 a5 is quite pleasant for Black, but 8 0-0 is (obviously) a feasible alternative. Then 8...c5 9 ♗e3 f5 10 exf5 gxf5 (Bouaziz-Spisak, Cappelle la Grande 1995) 11 ♘g3!? and 8...♘d7 9 ♗e3 f5 10 exf5 gxf5 11 ♘g3 (Marin, Aleksandrov-Shchekachev, Jurmala 1991) leave White with the easier game, and 8...♘a6 9 a3 ♘c5 10 ♗c2 a5 11 ♖b1 f5 12 exf5 ♗xf5 13 b4 axb4 14 axb4 ♘d7 15 ♗xf5 gxf5 16 f4 also favoured White in Basagic-Spaete, Baden Baden 1988.

Most interest has been in 8...f5, when 9 ♘g3 ♘f4 10 ♗c2 (Braumann-Kilic, Magdeburg 1997) walks into 10...♘xg2!! and Black has all the fun, e.g. 11 ♔xg2 f4 12 ♗d3 ♕h4 etc.

This leaves 9 exf5:

a) 9...♗xf5 10 ♗xf5 gxf5 11 ♘g3!? ♘xg3 12 fxg3 (V.Georgiev-Rama, Durres 2001) and now 12...♘d7!? 13 ♗e3 a6 14 ♕b3 b6 15 ♕c2 ♕f6 16 ♖f2 ♕g6 is a promising continuation for Black, the idea being 17 ♖af1 ♖f6 18 ♖xf5 ♖af8 19 g4 ♕xg4 20 ♖xf6 ♖xf6.

b) 9...gxf5

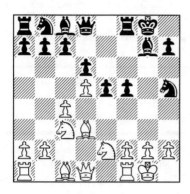

Recapturing with the pawn is the more consistent choice, affording Black a rather intimidating presence on the kingside. Consequently White must address the situation accordingly, otherwise Black will continue the build-up. In fact White has three typical approaches in the diagram position. Occasionally we see 10 f3, directed against ...e5-e4, while 10 f4 is another candidate. With this more aggressive thrust White achieves two goals with one move – blockading the f5-pawn and introducing the threat to take on e5 in order to bring unwelcome attention to the potentially vulnerable f5-pawn. Thus after 10 f4 Black sometimes captures or allows f4xe5 so as to use the dark squares (such as e5 and g5) and take his chances in an open position, but in most cases 10...e4 is played, e.g. 11 ♗c2 ♖f6 12 ♗e3 ♖h6 13 ♕e1 ♘f6 with chances for both sides in Sjoberg-Ziegler, Gothenburg 1997.

White's strongest is 10 ♘g3!, in reply to which Black has two typical responses.

b1) After 10...♘xg3 11 fxg3 White monitors the f5-pawn. 11...♖e8 12 ♗e3 a5 13 ♕d2 ♘a6 14 ♖f2 ♗d7 15 ♖af1 ♕g6 16 ♗c2 led to an edge for White in Sagalchik-Luchan, Mineola 1993, while 13 g4!? is possible.

b2) With 10...♘f4 Black is prepared to accept a weakness on f4, putting the onus on White to find a route to an advantage. 11 ♘h5 is often played but the real test has to be 11 ♗xf4 exf4 12 ♘h5 ♗e5 13 ♕f3 ♕g5 14 ♖ab1 ♘d7 (14...♕g4!? 15 ♗e2) 15 ♘e2 ♗xb2

(Sagalchik-Shirazi, New York 1992) 16 ♖xb2 ♘e5 17 ♕h3 f3 18 ♘ef4 ♘xd3 19 ♘xd3 with a clear advantage for White. Note that after 15...♕g4!? 16 ♘hxf4 ♕xf3 17 gxf3 ♘c5 18 ♗c2 a5 the extra pawn would be difficult to convert.

Let's get back to 8 h3:

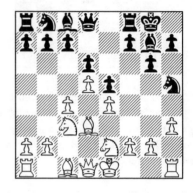

8...f5

8...♕f6?! attempts to secure f4 but the idea falls short:

a) The immediate 9 g4!? looks simplest, when 9...♕f3 is a serious error due to 10 ♖h2, e.g. 10...♘f6 11 ♕c2 ♘fd7 12 ♘f4 exf4 13 ♗e2 ♘e5 14 ♔f1 and Black's queen is trapped in all variations, or 10...♘f4 11 ♗xf4 exf4 12 ♕c2 ♘a6 13 ♘g1 ♘b4 14 ♘xf3 ♘xc2+ 15 ♗xc2 etc. Therefore Black has to play 9...♘f4 10 ♘xf4 exf4 11 ♕f3 ♘d7 12 ♕xf4, when there is no compensation for the pawn.

b) 9 g3 ♘a6 (9...♕f3 is again poor, as was demonstrated in Seirawan-Fishbein, Seattle 2002 after 10 ♖h2 ♘a6 11 ♗e3 f5 12 exf5 ♗xf5 13 ♗xf5 gxf5 14 ♕b1!? ♘f6 15 g4 ♘e4 16 ♘xe4 ♕xe4 17 ♕xe4 fxe4 18 ♘c3 ♘b4 19 ♔d2, intending ♘xe4) 10 ♗e3!? ♘c5 11 ♗c2 ♗d7 12 ♕d2 a5 13 g4 ♘f4 14 ♘xf4 exf4 15 ♗xf4 favours White.

From these examples we can see that Black must either play a position a pawn down for insufficient compensation or withdraw his queen and subsequently lose additional time with the h5-knight.

9 exf5 gxf5

9...&xf5?! (Sek-Adamski, Warsaw 1987) and now 10 &xf5! gxf5 11 g4 is very strong, e.g. 11...fxg4 12 hxg4 ♘f4 13 ♕c2 h6 14 &xf4 exf4 15 0-0-0, or 11...♘f6 12 gxf5 ♘bd7 13 ♖g1 ♔h8 14 &g5 ♕e8 15 ♕d3 ♘c5 16 ♕e3 etc.

10 g4

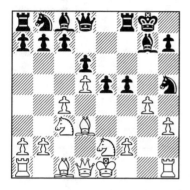

This is the main idea behind 8 h3, White sacrificing a pawn in return for two open files (on which White aims to place both rooks). Notice also that the text opens the b1-h7 diagonal, with particular attention on the h7-pawn.

10...fxg4

If Black declines the sacrifice the prospect of earning anything approaching equality are slim indeed, e.g. 10...♘f4 11 &xf4 exf4 12 &xf5 &xf5 13 gxf5 and now

a) 13...♖xf5 (Panczyk-Gullaksen, London 1997) 14 ♕c2!? (14 ♖g1!? ♘d7 15 ♕c2 ♖g5 16 0-0-0 f3 17 ♘f4 ♘c5 18 ♘e6 ♘xe6 19 dxe6 is excellent for White) 14...♖f7 15 ♖g1 ♕h4 16 ♘d4 ♘d7 17 0-0-0 ♔h8 18 ♘e6 &xc3 19 ♕xc3+ ♘e5 20 ♖de1 and Black is in trouble.

b) 13...f3 14 ♘d4 (Panczyk-Buckley, Monmouth 2000) 14...♕g5!? 15 ♘e6 ♕g2 16 ♔d2 ♕xf2+ 17 ♔c1 ♘d7 18 ♕g1 ♕xg1+ 19 ♖xg1 ♖f7 20 ♘e4 ♖e8 21 ♔c2 ♔h8 22 ♖af1 and White is in a commanding lead.

11 hxg4 &xg4 12 ♕c2 h6 13 &e3

The key position.

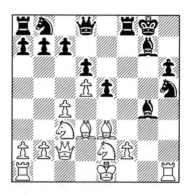

13...♘f4

In our opinion the most consistent move is 13...♘a6!?, an interesting line being 14 0-0-0 ♘b4 15 &h7+ ♔h8 16 ♕g6 ♘xa2+ etc. White should prefer 14 &h7+! ♔h8 15 &e4 ♘c5! 16 f3 ♖xf3! 17 &xf3 &xf3 18 ♖h2 e4 19 ♘d4 (19 ♔d2 ♘f6 20 &xh6 ♘g4 21 &g5+ ♘xh2 22 &xd8 &h6+ 23 ♔e1 ♘d3+ is unclear) 19...&xd4 20 &xd4+ ♔h7 21 &e3 ♕g8 22 ♘e2 ♕g7 23 &xc5 dxc5 24 0-0-0 ♕e5 25 ♖f2 with much still to play for.

14 0-0-0 ♘a6 15 &xf4

Missing 15 ♘xf4! exf4 16 &d4 &xd4 17 &h7+ ♔h8 18 ♖xh6! ♕g5 19 ♖dh1 f3+ 20 ♔d1 &g7 21 ♖g6 with a menacing attack.

15...exf4

15...♖xf4 16 ♖dg1 &xe2 17 &h7+! (17 &xe2 ♔h8 18 ♘e4 offers some compensation) 17...♔h8 18 ♖xg7!! is a nice variation.

16 ♖dg1 ♘b4?

Losing by force. Black is in serious danger anyway, but 16...♕d7 at least puts up more resistance, when play might continue 17 ♕d2 (17 f3!?) 17...♘b4 18 &b1 h5 19 &g6 &f5 (19...f3 20 ♘d4) 20 &xf5 ♖xf5 21 ♘d4 ♕h7 22 ♘e6 and the party is almost over.

17 &h7+ ♔h8 18 ♕g6 ♕d7 19 ♖xg4 ♘d3+ 20 ♕xd3 ♕xg4 21 &e4 f3 22 ♘g3 ♖ae8 23 ♔b1 ♖e5 24 &g6 ♖g5 25 &e4 a6 26 ♘d1 ♕f4 27 ♘h5 ♕e5 28 &xf3 ♕d4 29 &e2 ♕xd3+ 30 &xd3 &e5 31 ♔c1 &d4 32 ♘g3 &g7 33 ♔d2 ♖e8 34 b3 ♔g8 35 ♘f5 ♖g2 36 ♘g3 1-0

Game 29
Gulko-A.Ivanov
Moscow Rapidplay 1992

1 c4 g6 2 d4 ♗g7 3 e4 d6 4 ♘c3 c5 5 d5 e6 6 ♗d3 ♘f6 7 h3 0-0

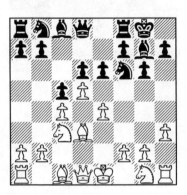

The Modern Benoni treatment with ...e7-e6 is designed to offer Black some kind of activity, rather than drift into passivity or close the centre with the solid but rather lifeless ...e7-e5. Black usually follows ...e7-e6 with ...e6xd5, and after e4xd5 White has a bit more space and an advantage that can be confusing because Black, despite the ostensibly cramped situation, has practically no weaknesses to worry about. Therefore on both wings it is far from easy for White to engineer anything positive. Note also that the existence of a sole open file tends to induce the trade of heavy pieces.

8 ♘ge2 ♘bd7

8...exd5!? 9 exd5 is quite typical. White wants to increase his presence in the centre, control important squares – especially e5 – and, after developing his pieces (usually along the lines of ♗e3/d2, ♕d2/c2, ♖ae1 and f2-f4), step up a gear – often on the kingside but occasionally on the other flank, too.

a) 9...♖e8 10 ♗g5 transposes to Chapter 3.

b) 9...♘fd7!? is interesting. White took control of g4 but why not jump into e5 via d7? The point is that 10 f4 can be met with 10...♕h4+ 11 g3 ♕e7 (11...♗xc3+?! 12 ♔f2!).

Therefore White has to play 10 b3 ♖e8 11 ♗d2 (11 ♗e3?! ♖xe3!? – P.Cramling) 11...♘a6 12 a3 ♕h4, when 13 0-0!? ♘e5 is equal and 13 ♕c1 (Sarmiento Alfonso-Danailov, Las Palmas 1993) 13...♘e5! unclear .

9 f4 exd5 10 exd5 ♘h5

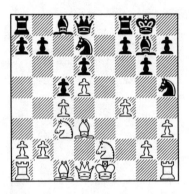

Wisely refusing to hang around while White completes development and uncorks g2-g4 to leave Black lacking counterplay. Positive action is called for, and the best recipe features the f7-pawn. The other way to clear the path is 10...♘e8 11 0-0 f5, e.g. 12 ♗e3 (12 ♗d2 ♘df6 13 ♕c2 ♘c7 14 ♔h2 a6 15 a4 b6 16 ♘g1 ♖b8 17 ♘f3 ♗d7 18 ♖ab1 ♖e8, Forintos-Matulovic, Sochi 1964, and now 19 ♖fe1 is equal) 12...♘df6 13 ♕d2 ♘c7 14 ♖ab1 and now both 14...♖e8!? 15 a3 a5 16 ♖be1 a4 17 ♗f2 ♗d7 and 14...♗d7 15 a3 ♔h8 16 b4 b6, Ivanov-Timoshenko, USSR 1976, leave much to play for.

11 0-0

Of course Black's previous move seems to add weight to g2-g4, but in this particular position the attack is premature – 11 g4 ♗xc3+! bxc3 ♕h4+ 13 ♔d2 ♘g7 14 ♔c2 (B.Schmidt-Kassebaum, Germany 1994) and now 14...a6!? gives Black an excellent game.

11...f5 12 ♗e3 ♖e8

12...♘df6 13 ♕d2 ♗d7 14 ♖ae1 ♕c7 with a level game, makes sense.

13 ♗f2 ♘f8 14 ♕d2 ♗d7 15 a3 ♕c7 16 b4 b6 17 ♖ab1 cxb4 18 axb4 a5 19 bxa5 bxa5 20 ♘b5 ♗xb5 21 cxb5 ♕b7 22 b6

Wxd5 23 ᗢc3?

23 ᙆb5 Wf7 24 ᙆfb1 and White is winning.

23...&xc3 24 Wxc3 ᙆac8 25 Wd4 Wb7?

Missing the much less obliging 25...Wxd4 26 &xd4 ᗢe6 27 &e3 ✿f7 (not 27...ᙆc3? 28 ᙆfc1 ᙆxd3 29 b7 ᗢf6 30 ᙆc8 ᗢd7 31 ᙆxe8+ ✿f7 32 ᙆxe6 ✿xe6 33 b8W ᗢxb8 34 ᙆxb8 etc.) 28 &b5 ᙆe7 29 &a6 ᙆb8 when White has good compensation for the pawn but nothing like the fun he has in the game.

26 &c4+ ᗢe6 27 &d5 Wf7 28 &xe6 ᙆxe6 29 b7 ᙆb8 30 ᙆfc1 ᙆee8 31 Wc4 d5 32 Wc7 ᗢf6 33 Wxf7+ ✿xf7 34 &a7 ᗢd7 35 &xb8 ᙆxb8 36 ᙆc8 a4 37 ᙆxb8 ᗢxb8 38 ᙆa1 ✿e6 39 ᙆxa4 ✿d6 40 ✿f2 ✿c7 41 ᙆd4 ✿c6 42 ✿f3 ✿xb7 43 ᙆxd5 ✿c6 44 ᙆd8 1-0

Game 30
Haik-Gheorghiu
Thessaloniki Olympiad 1984

---

1 d4 ᗢf6 2 c4 c5 3 d5 d6 4 ᗢc3 g6 5 e4 &g7 6 &d3 0-0 7 ᗢge2 e6

Note that Black can transpose to the Old Benoni with 7...e5, e.g. 8 a3 ᗢa6 9 0-0 ᗢc7 10 ᙆb1 ᗢd7 11 Wc2 b6 12 &e3 &a6 13 ᗢb5 ᗢxb5 14 cxb5 and White had a definite pull in B.Kovacevic-Kuljasevic, Zadar 2000.

8 0-0

Compared with the previous game White has saved time in not playing h2-h3, but this means that Black's knight can jump in to g4.

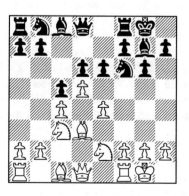

8...exd5

Others:

a) 8...ᙆe8!? 9 h3 exd5 10 exd5 ᗢfd7 11 f4 ᗢa6 12 f5 ᗢe5 13 fxg6 hxg6 14 ᗢg3 (Oster-gaard-Christensen, Festuge 1991) and now 14...f5 gives Black a good game.

b) 8...ᗢa6 9 f3 ᗢc7 10 &g5 exd5 11 exd5 h6 (Arlamowski-Plater, Wroclaw 1955) 12 &f4!? ᙆb8 13 Wd2 ✿h7 14 ᗢg3 b5 15 ᙆae1 favours White.

c) 8...ᗢg4 9 &c2 Wh4 (9...ᗢe5 10 b3 exd5 11 exd5 was seen in Seirawan-Dimitrov, Moscow 1994, when 11...f5 12 f4 would have restricted White to a slight edge) 10 h3 ᗢe5 11 dxe6 (11 &b3!?) 11...&xe6 (11...fxe6!? 12 f4 ᗢf7 13 &e3 ᗢc6 is interesting, although perhaps not enough to deny White a modest lead) 12 f4 ᗢxc4, Knaak-Marin, Dresden 1988. Knaak evaluates the position after 13 &b3 as clearly better for White but after 13...We7 14 f5 gxf5 15 exf5 ᗢe3 16 &xe3 &xb3 17 Wd2 &c4 the position is unclear. In our opinion after the best 13 f5! and Wxd6 White has a clear advantage.

9 exd5 ᗢg4

Others:

a) In the case of 9...ᗢe8 White achieved nothing special with 10 &e3 ᗢd7 11 ᗢg3 ᗢe5 12 &e2 f5 13 Wd2 ᗢf6 14 h3 ᙆe8 15 ᙆfe1 in Yoffie-Matulovic, Skopje 1969, while 10 h3 ᗢd7 11 f4 f5 12 &d2 ᗢdf6 13 Wc2 ᗢc7 was equal in Forintos-Matulovic, Sochi 1964.

b) 9...ᗢa6 10 h3 ᗢc7 seems to favour White, e.g. 11 &g5 Wd7 12 a4 ᙆe8 13 Wd2 ✿h8 (Willenborg-Unrath, Baunatal 1996) 14 ᗢg3, or 11 &f4 a6 12 ᙆb1 ᙆb8 13 ᗢg3 b5 14 Wc2 bxc4 15 &xc4, Marcondes Cesar-Batezelli, Sao Paulo 1997.

c) 9...ᗢbd7 10 b3 ᗢe5 11 &c2 ᙆe8 12 ᙆb1 a6 13 &g5 h6 14 &h4 (Betke-Illgen, Rostock 2002) 14...b5! gives Black counter-play, and 10 h3 ᗢe5 11 &e3?! ᗢh5 was excellent for Black in Staeblein-Karcevski, Bayern 1995. Perhaps White should consider 10 f4!? here.

Now back to the position after 9...♘g4:

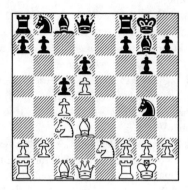

Sending the knight forward exploits the fact that after 10 f4 Black will be able to focus on the e3-square.

10 h3

Others:

a) 10 f4 is clearly the most principled response but, unfortunately for White, he is not able to keep control over e3. For example after 10...♖e8 White cannot be too stubborn, e.g. 11 ♖f3? ♕h4 12 h3 ♗d4+ 13 ♘xd4 and White has to lose material, 13...♖e1+ 14 ♕xe1 ♕xe1+ 15 ♖f1 ♕e7 16 ♘c2 ♘h6 spelling doom for White in S.Kasparov-Berger, Pardubice 2000 (White has little to show for the lost material, although it is not a trivial win). Instead 11 h3 ♘e3 12 ♗xe3 ♖xe3 13 ♕d2 ♖e8, as in Seirawan-Wojtkiewicz, Tilburg 1992, has been assessed as a little better for Black by Seirawan.

b) 10 b3!? is given as inaccurate in *ECO* – 10...♘d7 11 h3 ♘h6 (11...♘ge5!? is unclear) 12 ♗e3 ♘e5 13 ♕d2 ♗f5 and *ECO* prefers Black. However, 14 ♗e4!? ♗xe4 15 ♘xe4 ♘f5 16 ♗g5 seems to leave White with a small advantage, while 14 ♗g5 ♕a5 (Borges Mateos-Wojtkiewicz, Polanica Zdroj 1988) 15 ♗e4!? also appears favourable.

c) 10 ♗f4 ♘e5 11 ♕d2 ♘bd7 12 b3 f5 (intending ...♘f7, ...♘de5, ...g6-g5 – Tal) 13 ♗g5 ♘f6 and now instead of 14 f4?! ♘xd3 15 ♕xd3 ♗d7 with advantage to Black in Wiedenkeller-Tal, Rockaden-Trud 1986, thanks to

thanks to the weak points on e3 and e4, White should have played 14 f3 h6 15 ♗e3 ♗d7 with chances for both sides (14 ♘f4 h6 15 ♗xf6 ♕xf6 is excellent for Black).

d) 10 ♗c2 is another way to avoid parting with the light-squared bishop. 10...♘a6 11 a3 (11 ♗f4!? ♘b4 12 ♗b1 ♖e8 13 ♕d2 is less clear) 11...♘c7 12 ♖b1 a5?! (Hazai gives 12...f5 13 f4 ♖e8 with counterplay) 13 h3 ♘e5 14 b3 f5 (Larsen-Hoffman, Pinamar 2001) 15 f4!? with a minimal advantage for White.

10...♘e5 11 ♘g3

11 f4 ♘xd3 12 ♕xd3 ♘a6 13 a3 f5 14 ♖b1 (14 b3!? ♗d7 15 ♗b2) 14...♖e8 left both players with decent prospects in Karafidis-Tringov, Ano Liosia 1997.

11...f5

Or 11...♘bd7 12 f4 ♘xd3 13 ♕xd3 a6 as in Plachetka-Abramovic, Champigny sur Marne 1984, with equality according to *NCO*.

12 f4 ♘xd3 13 ♕xd3 ♖e8

Another attractive plan is 13...♘a6!? intending ...♗d7, ...♘c7 and ...b7-b5, with good play for Black.

14 ♗d2 ♘a6 15 a3 ♗d7 16 ♔h2 ♕f6 17 ♗e3

White must play 17 ♘ce2 in order to neutralise Black's strong dark-squared bishop. Black should then avoid 17...♕xb2? 18 ♖ab1 ♕f6 19 ♗c3 in favour of the sound 17...♖e7 18 ♗c3 ♕f7 19 ♖ae1 with a level game.

17...♘c7 18 ♗f2 b5

Black's play, in the spirit of the Benko Gambit, is fully justified as he must win back the pawn sooner or later.

19 cxb5 ♖eb8 20 a4 a6 21 ♘ge2 axb5 22 axb5 ♖xa1 23 ♖xa1 ♘xb5 24 ♖a5 ♘c7 25 ♖a7 ♕d8 26 ♕b1 ♕c8 27 ♕a2 ♖b7 28 ♗h4 ♗f8 29 ♘g1 ♕b8 30 ♖xb7 ♕xb7 31 ♘f3 h6 32 ♗d8 ♘b5 33 ♕b3 ♕b8 34 ♗f6 ♕e8 35 ♘xb5 ♗xb5 36 ♗c3 ♕e2 37 ♘h4?!

37 ♘d2 is better.

37...♔f7 38 ♕a3 ♗c4?

38...♕e4! wraps up the game.

39 ♕a7+ ♕e7 40 ♕a4 ♗xd5 0-1

Summary

Black can try to play ...c7-c5 followed by ...e7-e6 and ...exd5, the best examples being Games 29 & 30. However, a simpler and more original method involves counterplay with ...♘c6, ...e7-e5 and, after closing the centre, ...♘d4 in order to exploit the weakness of the d4-square. This plan can be used both with (Games 23, & 24 are particularly good examples) or without (earlier) castling.

1 d4 ♘f6 2 c4 g6 3 ♘c3 ♗g7 4 e4 d6 5 ♗d3 (D)

5...0-0

    5...♘c6 6 ♘ge2

        6...0-0 *(Games 16 & 17)*

        6...e5 *(Game 18)*

    5...e5 6 d5 a5 *(Game 19)*

6 ♘ge2 e5

    6...♘fd7 *(Game 20)*

    6...♘bd7 *(Game 21)*

    6...♘c6 7 0-0

        7...♘d7 *(Game 22)*

        7...e5 8 d5 ♘d4 9 ♘xd4 exd4 (D) *(Games 23 & 24)*

        7...♘h5 *(Game 25)*

    6...c5 7 d5 *(Games 29 & 30)*

7 d5 (D)

7...c6 *(Game 26)*

7...a5 *(Game 27)*

7...♘h5 *(Game 28)*

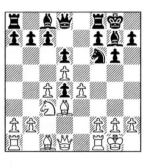

    5 ♗d3   *9...exd4*   *7 d5*

CHAPTER THREE

The Makogonov System: 5 h3

1 d4 ♘f6 2 c4 g6 3 ♘c3 ♗g7 4 e4 d6 5 h3

Despite its rather 'inactive' appearance this system is very flexible. 5 h3 was proposed by Réti and analysed by HGM V.Makogonov, the first known game being Tartakower-Teichmann, Ostend 1907. The system was also tried by Sämisch and Tarrasch.

White prepares to secure the e3-square as an outpost for his bishop by ruling out the potentially annoying ...♘g4. There is also the bonus of facilitating active operations on the kingside involving g2-g4. Ironically, White very often develops his dark-squared bishop on g5, tempting Black into the automatic hit with ...h7-h6, after which the bishop drops back to e3, when Black can consequently pay the price for slightly compromising his kingside because White is able to further development with ♕d2, simultaneously hitting the h6-pawn. Not surprisingly, then, Black should resist the urge to chase the enemy bishop away from g5.

Adherents of the Makogonov system in recent years include Suba, Lazarev, P.Varga, Ksieski, Avrukh and Chernin. Top players who have included it in their opening repertoire are Bareev and Beliavsky, while it has also been tried by I.Sokolov, Dreev and even Kasparov...

Game 31
Nikolaidis-Kotronias
Peristeri 1996

---

1 d4 ♘f6 2 c4 g6 3 ♘c3 ♗g7 4 e4 d6 5 h3 0-0

The most natural move. Black must castle anyway, so it makes sense to do so immediately and await developments before deciding on the next step. However, there are alternatives. 5...c5 6 d5 e5 7 ♗d3 ♘h5 8 ♘ge2 (Zsu.Polgar-Uhlmann, Aruba 1992) 8...♘a6!? is a shade better for White, and 6 dxc5 ♕a5 7 ♗d3 ♘fd7 8 ♘ge2 ♘xc5 9 0-0 (Dzindzichashvili-Byrne, Berkeley 1984) 9...♘xd3 10 ♕xd3 is given by Suba in *ECO* as favouring White.

5...e5 can have independent significance, Black being willing to see his king displaced, as in 'a', below.

a) 6 dxe5 dxe5 7 ♕xd8+ ♔xd8 8 ♘f3 ♘bd7 9 ♗e3! c6 10 c5!? ♘e8 11 0-0-0 left White with a nagging edge in Costa-Hug, Switzerland 1992. In fact this position looks better for White than a typical ending in the King's Indian, with more than his usual (early) share of the queenside and an excellent post for the bishop in the shape of the c4-square. Black is also a little passive and rather cramped, unable to jump into d4 with his knight or exchange dark-squared bishops. Nevertheless, the symmetrical pawn structure and lack of weaknesses in Black's camp, combined with the closed character of the position, at least make White's task of finding something tangible somewhat problematic.

b) 6 d5 ♘bd7 (6...a5 7 ♗d3 ♘a6 8 ♘ge2 0-0 9 ♗g5!? ♗d7 10 0-0 and now White emerges with a plus after 10...♕e8 11 ♖c1 ♘c5 12 ♗b1, Chernin-Brunner, Buenos Aires 1992 or 10...♘c5!? 11 ♗c2). In Suba-Zapata, New York 1988 White's 7 ♗g5 h6 8 ♗e3 worked out well after 8...♘c5 9 f3 a5 10 ♘ge2 ♘h7 11 ♕d2 ♗f6 12 g3! with a definite advantage, but here 9 f3 does not fit well with h2-h3, and Black seems to have improvements in 10...♘fd7!? and 10...0-0!?.

7 ♗d3 transposes to the 5 ♗d3 system, h2-h3 here looking a little premature as well as inflexible (it is not always necessary in this system). Suba in *ECO* evaluates the position after 7...♘c5 8 ♗c2 as slightly better for White, but Black's situation is, in fact, not that bad, e.g. 8...a5 (8...0-0!?) 9 ♘ge2 0-0 10 ♗g5 h6 11 ♗e3 ♘fd7 12 ♕d2 ♔h7 13 g4 ♘b6 with good play for Black, Moranda-Lubczynski, Zagan 2002.

The main move is 7 ♗e3 ♘c5 8 ♕c2 with the following position:

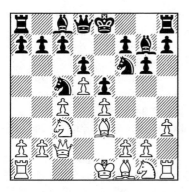

b1) 8...a5 'secures' the post of the c5-knight. 9 ♘ge2 ♗d7 10 f3 (notice the transpositional possibilities of which White should be

aware – for example White could try 10 g3!? and ♗g2 here, with decent chances of finding an advantage) 10...h5 11 ♕d2 h4 12 ♗g5 (12 0-0-0!? ♘g8 13 ♔b1 ♗h6 is equal) 12...♖h5 13 ♘c1 (13 ♗e3 ♘g8 followed by ...♗h6), Shabalov-Kveinys, USSR 1987, and now 13...♘fxe4! 14 ♗xd8 ♘xd2 15 ♗xc7 ♘xf1 16 ♔xf1! ♔e7 17 ♘b3 ♖c8 is given by Shabalov, with the better game for Black in all variations, e.g. 18 ♘xc5 (18 ♗b6 ♘d3! 19 ♘xa5 ♘xb2 20 c5 e4; 18 ♗xa5 ♘d3 19 ♘d2 ♗h6 20 ♘de4 f5 21 g4 hxg3 22 ♘xg3 ♖g5 etc.) 18...♖xc7 19 ♘xd7 ♔xd7 20 ♘a4 e4! etc.

b2) 8...0-0 is the riskier option, and now:

b21) 9 g4 c6 10 ♘ge2 cxd5 11 cxd5 ♗d7 12 ♘g3 (12 b4!? might well favour White) 12...♖c8 13 g5 ♘h5 (there is no reason to voluntarily damage the kingside structure, and after the simple 13...♘e8!? 14 ♕d2 f5 15 gxf6 ♘xf6 Black could generate good counterplay without any risk, although the move chosen is, nevertheless, probably the correct one) 14 ♘xh5 gxh5 15 ♕d2 (15 ♗e2 f5 16 gxf6 ♕xf6 with good counterplay for Black as 17 ♗xh5 ♕h4 18 ♗e2 b5 offers sufficient compensation) 15...♕a5! 16 ♖b1 ♕b4 17 a3 ♕b3 18 ♗e2 f5 19 gxf6 ♖xf6 20 ♗xh5, Grivas-Nunn, Athens 1991, and now 20...♕c4! 21 ♗e2 (21 ♗xc5 ♕xc5 22 ♗g4 ♗h6 gives Black enough play) 21...♘xe4 22 ♕c2 ♕a2 23 ♕xe4 ♖xc3 24 bxc3 ♗f5 25 ♕b4 ♕xb1+ 26 ♕xb1 ♗xb1 27 c4 b6 is equal (Grivas & Nunn).

b22) 9 b4 is awarded a '!' in *ECO*. Retreating the knight loses Black two tempi, but the tempting – and typically King's Indian – 9...♘xe4? is definitely incorrect, e.g. 10 ♘xe4 ♘xe4 11 ♕xe4 f5 12 ♕c2 e4 13 0-0-0! f4 14 ♗d4 ♗xd4 15 ♖xd4 ♗f5 16 ♕c3 (Bagirov-Casper, Berlin 1979) is very good, whereas after 9...♘cd7 the situation is by no means simple. Black wants to play ...a7-a5 and regain the outpost on c5 for the d7-knight. Moreover, White's forces are not well developed, and he is not guaranteed to maintain his space advantage on the queenside, with a concession such as the c5-square or the a-file likely.

White's most ambitious continuation is 10 a3 (10 c5 a5 11 c6 does not look dangerous for Black, e.g. 11...bxc6 12 dxc6 ♘b6 13 b5 d5 14 ♗xb6 cxb6 15 exd5 ♘xd5 16 ♖d1 ♘b4) 10...a5, and now 11 ♖d1 axb4 12 axb4 ♘h5 13 ♗e2 ♘f4 and 11 ♖b1 c5 (11...♘h5!?) 12 dxc6 bxc6 13 b5 cxb5 are unclear. If White wants to hang on to the a-file he must return the two tempi with 11 ♕d1 or 11 ♕c1.

6 ♘ge2

6 ♗d3 c5 7 d5 e6 8 ♘ge2 ♘bd7 9 f4 exd5 10 exd5 ♘e8 11 0-0 f5 was the interesting course of Matisons-Euwe, Karlsbad 1929, while 8 ♗g5 exd5 9 exd5 h6 10 ♗h4 ♖e8+ 11 ♘ge2 ♘bd7 was also unclear in Martins-Guimaraes, Bello Horizonte 1997. The aggressive 8 g4 was tried in Milov-Gheorghiu, Switzerland 1999, when after 8...exd5 9 exd5 ♘fd7 10 f4 Black could have secured an early lead with 10...♘a6!? 11 ♘f3 ♖e8+.

6...c6

6...c5!? 7 d5 e6 8 ♘g3 exd5 9 cxd5 leads to the Modern Benoni, and 6...e5 usually steers us to positions that will be discussed later, e.g. 7 d5 c6 8 ♗e3 cxd5 9 cxd5 ♘bd7 10 g4 ♘c5 11 ♘g3 with a transposition to Game 33 (7...c6 8 g4).

7 g4 d5?!

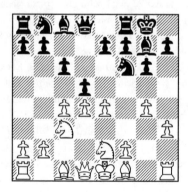

Yet another in the increasing number of Black's unorthodox treatments of the King's Indian. Is this a hypermodern mixture of the King's Indian and the Grünfeld? It is true that White's two flank moves could provoke a

reaction in the centre (the thematic response in such a situation) but here White's influence over the e4-square (♗g2!) makes the text rather doubtful. Worse still is 7...b5? 8 cxb5 cxb5 9 e5 because the threat to quickly exploit the freshly opened long diagonal with ♗g2 is decisive, e.g. 9...dxe5 10 dxe5 ♕xd1+ 11 ♔xd1 ♖d8+ 12 ♔c2 ♗b7 13 exf6 ♗xh1 14 fxg7 b4 15 ♘g3, with ♘ce4 coming. However, Black does have a worthy possibility in 7...♘fd7!? followed by ...e7-e5 or perhaps ...c6-c5 with chances of generating counterplay.

8 cxd5 cxd5 9 e5 ♘e4 10 ♘xe4 dxe4 11 ♗g2 ♗e6 12 ♗xe4 ♗d5 13 ♗xd5 ♕xd5 14 0-0 ♘c6 15 ♕b3 ♕e4 16 ♕e3 ♕c2

16...♕d5!? – Kotronias.

17 ♗d2?!

Kotronias recommends 17 ♘c3! ♖ad8 18 ♖d1 (threatening to capture the queen after 19 ♖d2) 18...g5 19 b3! f6 20 d5! (20 ♗a3 fxe5 21 ♖ac1 ♕g6 22 d5 ♘d4 23 ♗xe7 ♖f3 24 ♗xd8 ♖xe3 25 fxe3 ♘f3+ 26 ♔g2 ♘h4+ with counterplay) 20...♘xe5 21 ♗a3 and White has an initiative.

17...♕xb2 18 ♖fb1 ♕c2 19 ♖xb7 ♖ab8 20 ♖xb8

20 ♖c7!? ♖b2 21 ♗c3 ♕xe2 22 ♕xe2 ♖xe2 23 ♖xc6 ♖c2 24 f4 f6!? with counterplay – Kotronias.

20...♖xb8 21 ♖c1 ♖b1 22 ♔g2 ♖xc1 23 ♘xc1 e6

Black has compensation for the pawn due to the weaknesses on a2 and d4, as well as the light squares.

24 ♕d3 ♕xd3 25 ♘xd3 ♘xd4 26 ♗e3 ♘c6 27 f4 f6 28 exf6 ♗xf6 29 ♔f3 ♔f7 30 ♔e4 h5 31 gxh5 gxh5 32 f5 exf5+ 33 ♔xf5 ♗d8 34 ♘e5+

After the superior 34 ♘f4 h4 Black still has problems to solve.

34...♘xe5 35 ♔xe5 a6 36 ♔f5 ♗h4 37 ♗g5 ♗e1 38 ♗f6 ♗d2 39 ♗h4 ♗e3 40 a4 ♗d2 41 ♔e5 ♔g6 42 ♔d5 ♔f5 43 ♔c6 ♔f4 44 ♔b6 ♗f3 45 ♗d8 ♔g2 46 h4 a5 47 ♔a6 ♗e1 48 ♔b5 ♔f3 49 ♗xa5 ♗xh4 50 ♗c7 ½-½

Game 32
Akopian-Temirbaev
USSR Championship, Uzhgorod 1988

1 d4 ♘f6 2 c4 g6 3 ♘c3 ♗g7 4 e4 d6 5 h3 0-0 6 ♗e3

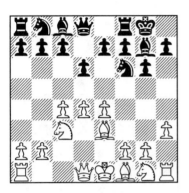

Not surprisingly this posting fits in well h2-h3. Remember that the modest looking nudge of the h-pawn affords White some flexibility, preventing ...♘g4 on the one hand while introducing – usually after closing the centre – the possibility of going on the offensive with g2-g4, often followed by ♘e2-g3 in order to clamp down on the f5-square as well as assuming a menacing stance (h3-h4-h5 etc.).

6...c5

Instead:

a) 6...c6 7 ♗d3 ♘bd7 (7...a6 8 e5 ♘fd7 9 exd6 exd6 10 ♘f3 b5 11 0-0 ♘b6 12 b3 ♘8d7 13 a4 bxc4 14 bxc4 a5 15 ♗g5 ♘f6 16 ♘e4 with an edge for White in Osnos-Polugaevsky, Leningrad 1963) 8 ♘ge2 c5!? (Black can also push the e-pawn, e.g. 8...♖e8 9 0-0 e5 10 d5 cxd5 11 cxd5 ♘c5 12 ♗c2 a5 13 a3 ♘h5 14 b4 axb4 15 axb4 ♖xa1 16 ♕xa1 ♘a6 ½-½, Eroglu-Kugic, Rimavska Sobota 1996, although Black was still slightly worse in the final position) 9 0-0 b6 10 ♖c1 (10 f4!? and 10 ♕d2!? are worth a thought) 10...cxd4 11 ♗xd4 (11 ♘xd4 ♗b7 is given as equal in *ECO*) 11...♗h6! (Grivas-Smirin, Tel Aviv 1991) and now Smirin gives 12 f4 e5 13 ♗e3

exf4 14 ♗xf4 ♗xf4 15 ♘xf4 as level in *ECO*.

b) The flexible 6...♘bd7 usually transposes to one of the positions discussed in Game 33, but occasionally has independent significance, e.g. 7 ♗d3 c5 8 ♘f3 b6 9 0-0 cxd4 10 ♗xd4 and Black has won a tempo compared with Grivas-Smirin, above – after the subsequent 10...♘c5 11 ♗c2 ♗b7 12 ♖e1 ♖c8 Black was doing well in the game Osnos-Stein, Kiev 1964.

7 dxc5

Quite different but equally sound is 7 d5, e.g. 7...a6 (7...e6 8 dxe6 ♗xe6 9 ♘f3 ♕a5 10 ♘d2 ♘c6 11 ♗e2 a6 12 0-0 ♖fe8 13 a3 ♖ab8 14 ♘d5 ♕d8 with chances for both sides, Averbakh-Tal, Kislovodsk 1964) 8 ♕d2 (8 a4 e6 9 ♘f3 exd5 10 cxd5 ♘bd7 11 ♗e2 b6 12 0-0 ♕e7 13 ♘d2 ♘e8 14 ♖e1 ♖b8 15 ♗f1 ♘c7 was balanced in Taimanov-Suetin, Budva 1967) 8...♕a5 and now 9 ♗d3 b5 10 ♘ge2 (Johannessen-Bednarski, Havana Olympiad 1966) 10...bxc4 is equal while 10...b4!? is unclear. White can try his luck with 9 a4!? ♘bd7 10 ♘f3 (10 ♗e2 b5 11 cxb5 ♕b4 12 f3 c4 gives Black compensation) 10...b5 11 cxb5 axb5 12 ♗xb5 ♘xe4 13 ♘xe4 ♕xb5 14 axb5 ♖xa1+ 15 ♔e2 ♖xh1 with an interesting struggle in prospect.

7...♕a5 8 ♗d3 dxc5 9 e5 ♘fd7

9...♘e8 is believed to be inaccurate due to 10 f4 f6 11 exf6 (11 ♘f3!?) 11...exf6 12 ♕a4! ♕b6 13 ♘ge2 f5 14 ♘d5 ♕d6 15 0-0-0 (Bagirov-Sibarevic, Vrnjacka Banja 1974) with a sizeable lead for White according to *ECO*, but Black can try 11...♖xf6! with chances for both sides, e.g. 12 ♘f3 ♖d6! 13 ♕c2 ♘c6 or 12 ♕a4 ♕xa4 13 ♘xa4 ♖e6 14 ♔f2 b6; 12 ♕d2 ♘c6 13 ♘e4 ♕xd2+ 14 ♗xd2 ♖f8 15 0-0-0 b6.

10 f4 ♖d8

Black prepares to cause trouble on the d-file with a view to pinning the bishop, thus introducing a couple of 'tricks' for White to mull over. For example White must check out not only ...♘xe5 followed by ...♗f5 but also ...♘b6 with the threat of ...♘xc4 or ...♘a4.

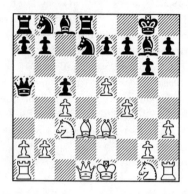

If Black manages to break White's strong centre he will have an excellent position. Otherwise White simply develops his pieces before going on to exploit the extra space. Note that we do not recommend 10...f6 11 e6 ♘b6 12 ♗d2 ♕a6 (12...♘c6 13 a3! followed by ♘d5 or ♘b5 spells trouble for Black), and now instead of 13 f5 ♖d8 (unclear in *ECO*), Chernin-Chiburdanidze, USSR 1982, White has the simple 13 ♘b5, forcing a favourable gain of material, e.g. 13...♘a4 14 ♗e2! ♗xe6 (14...♘xb2 15 ♕b3) 15 b3 (or 15 ♘c7 ♕c6 16 ♘xe6 ♘xb2 17 ♕b3 ♕xe6 18 ♕xb2 f5 19 ♗c3) 15...f5 16 ♖b1 ♕c6 17 ♗f3 ♕d7 18 bxa4.

11 ♕e2

Another way to address White's problems is 11 ♔f2, e.g. 11...♘c6 (11...♘b6!? 12 ♕e2 ♘c6) 12 ♕e2 (12 ♘d5 ♘b6 13 ♗d2 ♘b4 14 ♗xb4 cxb4 15 ♘xe7+ ♔f8 16 ♘xc8 ♖axc8 with compensation) 12...♘b6 13 a3, Ivanov-Cherniaev, Vladivostok 1995, although Black should be quite content with his lot after 13...f6. Also 13 ♘f3 f6 is possible.

White can ignore Black's threats with 11 ♘f3, with a choice for Black.

a) 11...♘c6 12 0-0 (12 ♕e2 transposes to the main line; 12 ♕b1!?) 12...♘b4! 13 ♘d5 ♘xd5 14 cxd5 ♘b6 leaves much to play for.

b) 11...♘b6, intending ...♘a4.

c) Finally Black has 11...♘xe5 12 ♘xe5 ♗xe5 (12...♗f5 13 0-0 ♗xe5 14 fxe5 is a different move order) 13 fxe5 ♗f5 14 0-0 ♗xd3?

(Reicher-Ardeleanu, Romania 1984) 15 ♘d5! etc. Black should prefer 14...♗xd3 15 ♕e2 ♘c6!, which keeps White to a slight edge.

If these lines are not for you, then the safety oriented 11 ♕b1 deserves serious consideration, after which Black has no tactical tricks. In fact in our opinion this gives White chances of obtaining an advantage.

11...♘c6

Passive play leads to a cramped position for Black, e.g. 11...♘b6 12 ♗d2 ♘c6 13 ♘f3.

12 ♘f3 ♘d4!

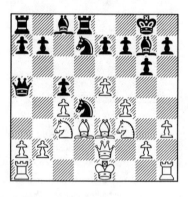

Excellent counterplay!

13 ♘xd4

After 13 ♕f1 f6 Black shatters White's centre and immediately assumes the advantage.

13...cxd4?

For some reason missing 13...♘xe5! and White's pieces in the centre are hanging, e.g. 14 fxe5 cxd4 15 ♗d2 dxc3 16 ♗xc3 ♕b6 17 ♖d1 ♗e6 and Black holds the aces.

14 ♗xd4 ♘c5 15 ♗xc5

The threat of 15...♘b3 forces this exchange, with which White effectively surrenders the dark squares.

15...♕xc5

Black undoubtedly has counterplay in view of the bishop pair, the potential targets on c4 and f4 and the dark squares. White, on the other hand, has strong pawns in the centre that help close out the g7-bishop.

16 0-0-0

It is natural to want to find a haven for the

king, but White might consider leaving his king in the centre a little while longer in order to castle short after evicting the enemy queen. Therefore 16 ♖d1!? comes to mind, with the following position:

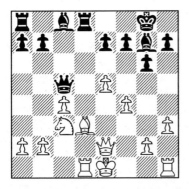

16...♗h6 (16...♗e6!?) 17 g3 (after 17 ♘d5 ♖xd5! 18 cxd5 ♗xf4 Black is doing fine) 17...♗e6 18 b3 a6 19 ♗e4? (19 ♘a4! ♕c7 20 ♕e3 b5 21 ♘c5 and Black does not have enough for the pawn, while 19 ♘e4 and 19 ♕f2 are also possible) 19...♖xd1+ 20 ♘xd1 ♖d8 21 ♔f1 b5 22 ♘e3 bxc4 23 bxc4 ♖d4 24 ♗d5 ♗xd5 25 cxd5 ♕c3 26 ♖h2? (26 ♕e1) 26...♖d3 27 ♘g4? ♕c1+ 0-1, Uznanski-Szczesniak, Correspondence 1995.

16...♗e6 17 ♔b1 ♖d4

Attacking two pawns, but 17...♖ac8, simply introducing another piece, also looks good.

18 ♖hf1 ♖xd3 19 ♖xd3 ♗xc4 20 ♖fd1 ♗xd3+ 21 ♕xd3

Black has regained the pawn but White controls the d-file and has – for the moment, at least – the superior minor piece. Moreover, he now threatens to take the 7th rank. Consequently White's chances are better.

21...♗f8 22 g4 ♖c8 23 ♕e4 b5 24 e6 fxe6 25 ♕xe6+ ♔h8 26 ♖d5 ♕c4 27 ♕e5+ ♗g7 28 ♕xe7 ♗xc3 29 ♖d8+ ♖xd8 30 ♕xd8+ ♔g7 31 ♕e7+ ♔g8 32 ♕e8+ ♔g7 33 ♕e7+ ♔g8 34 ♕e8+ ♔g7 35 ♕d7+ ♔g8 36 bxc3 ♕xc3 37 ♕xb5

After the stronger 37 ♕d5+ ♔f8 38 ♕a8+ ♔e7 39 ♕xa7+ ♔f6 40 ♕b6+ ♔g7 41 ♕xb5

♕e1+ 42 ♔c2 ♕f2+ 43 ♔b3 ♕f3+ 44 ♔a4 ♕xf4+ 45 ♕b4 White has a passed a-pawn.

37...♕xh3

A more stubborn defence results from 37...♕e1+!? 38 ♔c2 ♕f2+ 39 ♔b3 ♕e3+ 40 ♔b4 ♕d2+, trying to take the a2-pawn.

38 ♕b8+ ♔f7 39 ♕xa7+ ♔e6 40 ♕a6+ ♔d5 41 ♕b5+ ♔d4 42 ♕b4+ ♔d5 43 g5 ♕d3+ 44 ♔c1 ♕f1+ 45 ♔c2 ♔c6 46 ♕e4+ ♔b6 47 a3 ♕f2+ 48 ♔b3 ♕g3+ 49 ♔b4 ♕f2 50 ♕e6+ ♔b7 51 ♕d5+ ♔b8 52 ♕g8+ ♔b7 53 ♕xh7+ ♔b8 54 ♕g8+ ♔b7 55 ♕d5+ ♔b8 56 ♕b5+ ♔a8 57 ♕c6+ ♔b8 58 ♕d6+ ♔b7 59 ♔c4 1-0

Game 33
Knaak-Piket
SKA Hamburg 1991

---

1 d4 ♘f6 2 c4 g6 3 ♘c3 ♗g7 4 e4 d6 5 h3 0-0 6 ♗e3 e5

N.B. The actual move order was 6... ♘a6 7 ♗d3 e5 8 d5 but we have made alterations in order to accommodate the examination of additional variations.

7 d5 ♘a6

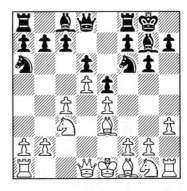

This flexible flank development has become part of numerous systems in the modern treatment of the King's Indian. From a6 the knight is ready to go to c5 but – as opposed to d7 – does not obstruct the other pieces. Apart from the obvious improvement of the c8-bishop we should also note that with the knight on a6 Black can play ...c7-c6 because the d6-pawn is protected by the queen.

Let's take a look at the alternatives:

a) 7...♘e8 8 g4 c6 9 ♘ge2 cxd5 10 cxd5 ♘d7 11 ♘g3 a5 12 ♕d2 ♘c5 13 ♗e2 ♗d7 14 h4, as in Sokolsky-Geller, USSR 1949, is given as slightly better for White in *ECO*.

b) 7...♘bd7 is obviously similar to main line but without the flexibility of 7...♘a6. Play might continue 8 ♗d3 (8 ♕c2 ♘c5 9 ♗e2 a5 10 g4 c6 11 g5 ♘e8 12 0-0-0 with an edge for White in Vorontsevich-Grokhotov, Orel 1974) 8...♘e8 9 g4 ♘c5 10 ♗c2 f5 (10...a5!? 11 ♘ge2 ♗d7 12 ♘g3, Benesch-Hadorn, World Team Championship 1994, and now 12...♗f6 maintains the balance) 11 gxf5 gxf5 12 ♘f3 ♕f6 13 h4 h6 14 ♕e2 is given in *ECO* as favouring White, 14...a6 15 0-0-0 b5 16 cxb5 axb5 17 ♗xc5 dxc5 18 ♕xb5 ending in a draw in Grivas-Nunn, Novi Sad 1990.

c) 7...c6 8 g4 (8 ♗d3 cxd5 9 cxd5 ♘h5 10 ♘ge2 f5 11 exf5 ♗xf5 12 g3 ♘d7 with chances for both sides, Gerusel-Schubert, Germany 1982) 8...cxd5 9 cxd5 ♘a6 (9...♘bd7 10 ♗d3 ♘c5!? 11 ♗c2 a5 is fine for Black) 10 ♘ge2 ♘c5 11 ♘g3 ♕a5 12 ♗d2 ♗d7 13 a3 ♕d8 14 b4 ♘a6 15 ♗d3 ♕e7 16 ♕e2 ♖fc8, Brinck Claussen-Tukmakov, Ybbs 1968, and now 17 g5 ♘e8 18 h4 puts Black in serious trouble.

d) 7...a5 is standard, preparing to place the knight on a6 now that b2-b4 has been prevented.

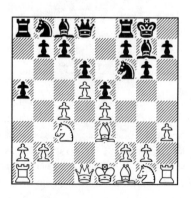

d1) With 8 g4 White wants to restrict Black's counterplay on both sides of the board. 8...♘a6 (8...c6 9 a4 ♘a6 10 ♘ge2 h5 11 f3, Shabalov-Lanka, Riga 1988 and 11...♘c5!? secures Black a level playing field) 9 ♘ge2 h5 (Black won't be dictated to, avoiding, for instance, 9...♘c5 10 ♘g3 ♘e8 11 ♕c2, when Dinstuhl-Hoffmann, Castrop-Rauxel 1990 saw 11...♗f6!? 12 ♕d2 ♗h4 13 ♖g1 ♘g7 14 0-0-0 f6 15 ♗e2 ♗d7 with a somewhat passive but solid position) 10 f3 ♘h7 (Black must hurry with this plan – 10...♘c5 11 ♕d2 ♘h7 12 0-0-0 h4 13 ♖g1 a4 14 ♔b1 ♗d7 15 ♘c1 ♗f6 16 g5 ♗e7 17 ♘d3 ♘xd3 18 ♗xd3 c5 19 f4 exf4 20 ♗xf4 with a plus for White in Shabalov-Kozul, Belgrade 1988) 11 ♕d2 ♕h4+ 12 ♗f2 ♕f6 13 ♗g2 h4 14 0-0 with a slight advantage to White in Aleksandrov-El Taher, New Delhi/Tehran 2000.

d2) 8 ♗d3 ♘a6 9 ♘ge2 ♘c5 (9...c6 10 a3 ♗d7 11 ♗c2! cxd5 12 cxd5 b5!? 13 0-0 ♕c7 14 ♕d2 ♖fc8 15 ♖fc1, Chernin-Beliavsky, Portoroz 1997, is given as better for White in *ECO*) 10 ♗c2 c6 (10...♘fd7!?, intending ...♘b6 with counterplay) 11 a3 cxd5 12 cxd5 ♗d7 13 b4 ♘a6 (13...axb4 14 axb4 ♖xa1 15 ♕xa1 ♘a6 16 ♕a3, Todorovic-Antic, Tivat 1995 is assessed by I.Sokolov in *ECO* as slightly better for White) 14 ♖b1 axb4 15 axb4 ♘h5 16 ♘a4! (White's knight is going to b6, a more effective continuation than 16 ♕d2 ♖c8 17 0-0 ♘f4 18 ♖fc1 ♕h4 19 ♗d1 ♘xg2 20 ♔xg2 ♕xh3+ 21 ♔g1 f5 22 f4?, when P.Cramling-Kindermann, Dortmund 1986 went 22...g5! 23 fxg5 f4 24 ♘xf4 exf4 25 ♗d4 ♕g3+ 26 ♔h1 ♗xd4 27 ♕xd4 f3 0-1, while 16 0-0 ♘f4 17 ♘a4 ♗b5 18 ♘ac3 ♗d7 19 ♘a4 ♗b5 20 ♘ac3 was agreed drawn in Kuprijanov-Zhuravlev, Cherepovets 2002) 16...♘f4!? (16...f5 17 exf5, I.Sokolov-Thipsay, Moscow 1994 and here 17...gxf5!? is unclear) 17 ♘xf4 exf4 18 ♗xf4 ♗b5 with compensation, B.Kovacevic-Zufic, Nova Gorica 2001.

8 ♗d3 ♘h5

Heading for f4. Others:

a) 8...♘c5 9 ♗c2 a5 10 ♕d2 ♗d7

(10...♕e8!?, intending 11 ♘f3 ♘fxe4 12 ♘xe4 ♘xe4 13 ♗xe4 f5 14 ♘g5 f4 with chances for both sides) 11 ♘f3 ♘e8 12 g4 ♕b8 13 a4 b6 was unclear in Pribula-Helbich, Slovakia 1997.

b) 8...♘d7!? 9 g4 (9 ♘f3 f5 10 0-0 f4 11 ♗d2 ♘ac5 12 ♗c2 ♘b6 with counterplay) 9...♘dc5 10 ♗b1 c6 11 a3 cxd5 12 cxd5 f5 13 b4 ♘xe4 14 ♘xe4 fxe4 15 ♗xe4 ♘c7 and Black was fine in Hirt-Schenk, Rhein 1998.

c) 8...c6 9 ♘ge2 cxd5 10 cxd5 ♘c5 11 ♗c2 a5 (11...♘h5 12 0-0 h6, Lipnitsky-Geller, Moscow 1950 and now 13 ♕d2 is very strong) 12 a3 ♗d7 13 0-0 ♖c8 14 ♕d2 ♘h5, Romero Holmes-Stellwagen, Groningen 2002, when 15 b4 secures White a lead.

9 g3

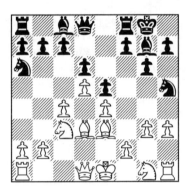

Or 9 ♘ge2 ♘c5 10 ♗c2 f5 11 exf5 gxf5 12 b4 ♘a6 13 ♖b1 ♕h4 14 g3 ♕e7 15 ♕d3 ♗d7 16 g4 ♘f4 17 ♗xf4 exf4 with chances for both sides, Rivas Pastor-Z.Polgar, Salamanca 1989.

9...♘c5

9...c5 is less active and seems inconsistent with Black's play thus far. Play can develop as follows: 10 ♗e2 ♘c7 (10...♘f6!? 11 ♕d2 with a slight advantage to White) 11 ♗xh5 gxh5 12 ♕xh5 f5 13 ♘f3 is poor for Black, but interesting is 9...♕e8 10 ♗e2 ♘f6 11 ♘f3 (11 h4!?) 11...♗d7 12 ♘d2 c6 13 ♔f1 (13 g4!?) 13...♕e7 14 g4 ♘c7 15 ♔g2 c5! 16 ♖b1 ♘fe8 17 b4 b6 18 bxc5 dxc5 19 a4 ♘d6 20 a5 ♖fb8!, Vilela-Moreno, Havana 1997 – both players give this position as unclear in *ECO*.

10 ♗e2

Forcing the knight's retreat, and more logical than 10 ♗c2 a5 11 ♕e2 (11 ♘f3 ♗d7 12 a3 ♕c8 13 ♘h4 ♘f6 14 g4 c6 was fine for Black in Grishchenko-Alekseev, Korolev 2000) 11...♗d7 12 0-0-0 a4 13 ♘f3 ♕c8 14 ♖dg1 a3 15 b3 ♘a6, Wade-Olafsson, Hastings 1953, when White was not better.

10...♘f6

Black lost two tempi but White made two moves with his light-squared bishop and placed his pawn on g3. However, White's game is the easier to play.

11 ♕c2 a5 12 0-0-0 a4 13 g4 ♘e8

13...♘fd7!? 14 ♔b1 a3 15 b3 with a slight advantage to White, or 13...♗d7 14 g5 ♘e8 15 h4 with initiative.

14 h4

The prophylactic 14 ♔b1 a3 15 b3 is good, when White follows up with h3-h4.

14...f5 15 gxf5 gxf5 16 ♘f3 a3

16...fxe4 17 ♘g5 ♘d3+ 18 ♗xd3 exd3 19 ♕xd3 ♗f5 20 ♘ge4 with the more pleasant game for White.

17 b4

17 b3!? looks more solid, with a slight advantage to White.

17...fxe4

17...♘xe4 18 ♘xe4 fxe4 19 ♘d2 (19 ♘g5?! ♘f6 20 ♖hg1 ♔h8 21 h5 ♗h6 with a good game for Black) 19...c6 (19...♘f6 20 ♖dg1 ♔h8 21 h5 with a plus for White) 20 ♘xe4 cxd5 21 ♖xd5 with a pull for White.

18 ♘e1

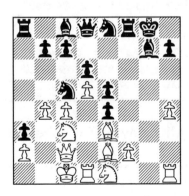

White wants to win the a3-pawn but the successful execution of this plan takes considerable time, and Black can generate strong counterplay. The sober 18 ♘g5 ♘d3+ 19 ♗xd3! (19 ♖xd3 exd3 20 ♗xd3 h6 is tempting but leaves White with insufficient compensation for the exchange) 19...exd3 20 ♕xd3 ♗f5 21 ♘ge4 ♘f6 22 h5 ♗xe4 23 ♘xe4, intending f2-f3 followed by doubling rooks on the g-file, offers White better chances.

18...♘a6 19 ♕b3 ♗f5 20 ♘c2 ♔h8 21 ♘xa3 ♘f6

21...c5!? is a candidate.

22 ♖hg1 ♕d7 23 ♘ab1

After 23 ♘c2? ♘g4 Black has strong counterplay, 24 ♘xe4 ♘xe3 25 ♕xe3 ♕a4 26 a3 ♗xe4 27 ♕xe4 ♗h6+ a good example of what White has to cope with.

23...♘g4

23...c5! is more consistent and is good for Black.

24 ♗xg4 ♗xg4 25 ♖de1 c5 26 dxc6?

Missing 26 bxc5! with a guaranteed advantage, e.g. 26...♘xc5 (26...dxc5 27 a3 ♗f5 28 ♘d2 ♗g6 29 ♘dxe4) 27 ♗xc5 dxc5 28 ♘xe4 with an effective presence in the centre.

26...bxc6 27 ♘xe4

Now Black's central pawn duo plays a crucial role.

27...d5 28 ♘c5 ♘xc5 29 ♗xc5 ♖f3 30 ♕c2 d4 31 ♖g3 ♗f5

31...♗h6+ 32 ♔b2 d3! 33 ♕c3 d2 wraps up the full point immediately.

32 ♕e2 ♖xg3 33 fxg3 d3 34 ♕d2?

34 ♕b2 e4 35 ♕b3 ♕c7! 36 ♗f2 ♕e5 intending ....♗h6 (Piket).

34...♕e6 35 g4 ♕xc4+ 36 ♕c3 d2+ 0-1

A possible finish is 37 ♔xd2 ♖xa2+ 38 ♔d1 ♕xg4+ 39 ♔c1 ♗h6+ 40 ♗e3 ♕e4 etc.

Game 34
Mikhalevski-Timoshenko
Paris Championship 2000

1 d4 ♘f6 2 c4 g6 3 ♘c3 ♗g7 4 e4 d6 5 h3 0-0 6 ♗g5

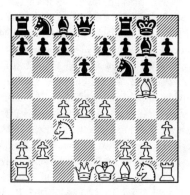

This bishop's sally is directed against 6...e5 (7 dxe5 dxe5 8 ♕xd8 ♖xd8 9 ♘d5), but the posting on g5 is anyway more active than 6 ♗e3 because after the typical ...e7-e5 advance the f6-knight will be pinned. If Black decides to play ...h7-h6, then after ♗e3 the same position will arise as with 6 ♗e3 but with a potential target on h6 that White can exploit with ♕d2 (not forgetting the general structural implications of ...h7-h6).

6...♘bd7

We don't recommend 6...♘c6, when 7 ♘f3 h6 8 ♗e3 e5 9 d5 ♘e7 10 g4!? h5!? 11 ♘h2 c6 12 ♗e2 gave White a slight advantage in Lazarev-Kummerow, Recklinghausen 1997. However, 6...c6 is playable, e.g. 7 ♗d3 e5 (7...♘a6 proved unconvincing in Solumunovic-Reschke, Griesheim 2000 after 8 ♘ge2 ♘c7 9 0-0 d5 10 cxd5 cxd5 11 e5 ♘fe8 12 ♗e3 f6 13 f4 ♗h6 14 ♕d2, while 7...♕b6 8 ♘ge2 ♘bd7 9 ♖b1 e5, Lazarev-Kozul, Bled 1994, should favour White after 10 d5) 8 d5 a5 (8...♘a6, transposing to 6...♘a6, is best) 9 ♘ge2 ♘a6 10 0-0 ♗d7 11 ♗c2 ♘c5 12 a3 ♕b6, Neidhardt-Kachiani Gersinska, Germany 2001, and now 13 ♗e3!? cxd5 (13...♕xb2?? 14 ♗xc5 dxc5 15 ♘a4) 14 cxd5 ♖fc8 (14...♕xb2?? 15 ♗xc5 dxc5 16 ♖b1 ♕xa3 17 ♖b3) 15 ♖b1 is an edge for White.

7 ♗d3

7 g4 e5 8 d5 was Suba-Lane, London 1988, when 8...h6 9 ♗e3 ♘c5 10 ♕c2 a5 is given as unclear by Suba in *ECO*. 7 ♕d2 c6 8 ♘ge2 b5

9 cxb5 cxb5 10 f3 b4 11 ♘d1 a5 was also interesting in Suba-Martinez Martin, Dos Hermanas 2002.

7...c5

The other plan features 7...e5 (or 7...h6 8 ♗e3 e5 9 d5 a5 10 ♘ge2 ♘c5 11 ♗c2 ♗d7 [11...♘fd7!?, intending ...♘b6] 12 ♕d2 ♔h7 13 0-0-0 a4 with play for both sides, Yermolinsky-Treger, Washington DC 1997) 8 d5 with a branch:

a) 8...c6 9 ♘ge2 cxd5 (9...♕b6 10 ♘a4 ♕a5+ 11 ♗d2 ♕c7 12 ♖c1 ♕b8 13 b4 a6 14 0-0 with a slight advantage to White in Bareev-Morovic Fernandez, Cap d'Agde 2002) 10 ♘xd5 h6 11 ♘xf6+ ♘xf6 12 ♗e3 b5 13 ♘c3 b4 14 ♘e2 ♗b7 15 f3 a5 16 ♕d2 ♘h7 17 ♗c2 (17 0-0 secures an edge) 17...♕h4+ (17...f5!?) 18 ♗f2 ♕g5 19 ♕xg5 ♘xg5 20 0-0-0 with a plus for White, Chernin-Kasimdzhanov, Bad Godesberg 1999.

b) 8...♘c5 9 ♗c2

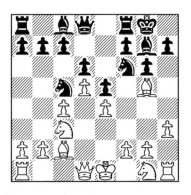

9...a5 (9...c6 10 ♘ge2 cxd5 11 exd5 ♕b6 12 b3 ♗d7 13 ♖b1 a5 was unclear in Christiansen-Gallagher, Reykjavik 1998)

b1) 10 g4 c6 11 ♕d2 (11 a3 cxd5 12 cxd5 ♕b6 13 ♘ge2 ♗d7 14 f3 ♖fc8 15 ♔f1 a4 with an edge for Black, Mikhalevski-Maes, Gent 2001) 11...cxd5 12 cxd5 a4 13 ♘ge2 ♕a5 14 f3 b5 (14...a3 15 bxa3 ♕xa3 16 0-0 ♗d7 17 ♖ab1 ♖fb8 ½-½, Vucicevici-Har-Zvi, Agios Nikolaos 1995) 15 ♘d1 (15 a3!?) 15...b4 16 ♘f2 ♕b5 (16...♗a6!?) 17 0-0 ♗a6 with an excellent position for Black, Spraggett-Sion

Castro, Seville 1993.

b2) 10 ♕d2 c6 11 ♘ge2 cxd5 12 exd5 (12 ♗xf6 ♗xf6 13 ♘xd5 ♗g5 is unclear, 12 cxd5 ♗d7, intending ...b7-b5, gives Black good counterplay, 12 ♘xd5 ♘cxe4! 13 ♗xe4 ♘xe4 14 ♗xd8 ♘xd2 15 ♗e7 ♘xc4 16 ♗xf8 ♔xf8 provides sufficient compensation and 12...♗d7 13 0-0 ♕b6, Bazin-Fedorov, Kstovo 1994 is unclear according to *ECO*.

b3) 10 a3 c6 11 ♖b1 a4 12 ♘f3 (12 ♘ge2 cxd5 13 cxd5 ♗d7 with chances for both sides, Budde-Stoeber, Germany 1992, and 12 ♗xf6 ♗xf6 13 ♗xa4 b5! looks pleasant for Black) 12...h6 13 ♗e3 cxd5 14 cxd5 ♗d7 15 ♕d2 ♔h7 16 g4, Bareev-Voitsekhovsky, St Petersburg 1998, and now 16...♘e8! followed by ...f7-f5 offers Black counterplay (Bareev).

8 d5

Black has a good game after 8 ♘f3 (or 8 ♘ge2) 8...cxd4 9 ♘xd4 ♕a5 10 ♗d2 ♘e5 (10...♕b6 11 ♘b3 ♘e5 12 ♗e2 ♗e6 is also good, while 10...♘c5!? is interesting) 11 ♗e2 ♕c5 12 ♘b3 (Avrukh-Smirin, Israel 1999) 12...♕c7!? 13 ♖c1 (13 ♘d5 ♕d8 is unclear) 13...a5 with a double-edged struggle in prospect.

8...♘e5

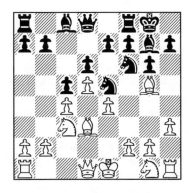

9 ♘f3

After 9 ♗e2 Black should play in the spirit of the Benko Gambit or find himself severely cramped (and losing a tempo) after f2-f4. In fact after 9...b5 10 cxb5 a6 Black has a more comfortable position than in the normal

Benko, White having lost time in making two moves with his bishop and another one on h2-h3. Additionally the position of the g5-bishop might well prove inappropriate, e.g. 11 bxa6 (11 ♘f3 ♘xf3+ 12 gxf3 axb5 13 ♗xb5 h6 14 ♗e3 e6 15 dxe6 ♗xe6 16 ♕d2 ♔h7 17 ♖d1 ♕a5 with compensation in Costa-Nemet, Switzerland 1993, or 11 a4 ♕a5 12 ♗d2 ♕b4 13 ♕c2 axb5 14 ♘f3, Slipak-R.Garcia, Trelew 1995, when 14...♘c4 is promising for Black) 11...♕a5 12 ♗d2 ♗xa6 13 ♕c2 ♖fb8 14 ♖b1 ♘fd7 and the investment looked sound in Pinter-Tkachiev, Porec 1998.

9...♘xd3+ 10 ♕xd3 a6 11 a4 ♘h5

Better than 11...e6 (or 11...e5) 12 dxe6! ♗xe6 13 0-0 h6 14 ♗f4 and White had a comfortable lead in Bareev-Svidler, Russian Championship 1997.

12 0-0

12 ♕d2!? looks good, after which White stabilises the position of the g5-bishop and introduces ♗h6 as a viable possibility.

12...h6 13 ♗d2

13 ♗e3 f5 14 exf5 ♗xf5 15 ♕e2 ♗d7 16 ♖fe1 ♘f4 17 ♗xf4 ♖xf4 and both sides could be fairly optimistic in Beliavsky-Smirin, Belgrade 1998.

13...e5 14 dxe6 ♗xe6 15 ♖ad1

Others:

a) 15 ♘d5 ♖e8 16 ♖ad1 ♗xd5 17 exd5 ♕d7 18 b3 (18 a5!?) 18...b5 19 axb5 axb5 20 cxb5 ♖ab8 21 b4 ♖xb5 with an excellent position for Black as the d5-pawn is weaker than the d6-pawn. Nevertheless a draw was agreed here in Mikhalevski-Smirin, Rishon Le Ziyyon 1997.

b) 15 a5!? is directed against Black's standard means of counterplay (...♕b6).

15...♕b6 16 ♘d5 ♗xd5

Not 16...♕xb2? 17 g4 ♗xd5 18 exd5 ♘f6? (Black is in trouble, but this hastens the end) 19 ♖b1 ♕a2 20 ♖a1 ♕b2 21 ♖fb1 etc.

17 exd5 ♖ae8

17...♖fe8 looks more natural.

18 a5 ♕c7 19 ♖b1 ♘f6 20 b4 ½-½

White has a modest but definite initiative on the queenside.

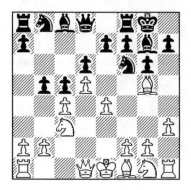

Game 35
Rogozenko-Ardeleanu
Cupa Dinamo, Brasov 1998

1 d4 ♘f6 2 c4 g6 3 ♘c3 ♗g7 4 e4 0-0 5 ♗g5 d6 6 h3 c5 7 d5 b5

Black's Benko approach is partly justified by White's 'wasted' h2-h3, although 4 e4 works in White's favour as the light-squared bishop is ready to join the battle. If we compare this game with Farago-Zaitsev (Chapter 5, Game 68), h2-h3 has here replaced ♗e2, but in our opinion Black still has difficulty solving the usual opening problems.

7...h6 8 ♗e3 e6 9 ♗d3 exd5 10 exd5 is dealt with in the next main game, but 7...a6 has been played: 8 a4 ♕a5 (8...e6!? 9 ♗d3 exd5 10 exd5 ♖e8+ 11 ♘ge2 ♘bd7 12 0-0 h6 13 ♗f4 ♘e5 14 ♘g3 ♘fd7 15 ♖e1 ♘xd3 16 ♖xe8+ ♕xe8 17 ♕xd3 ♘e5 18 ♕e2 ♗d7 19 ♘ge4 Ghitescu-Kviatkovsky, Romania-Bulgaria Match 1956, and now 19...♕e7 20 ♖e1 ♖e8 favours Black) 9 ♗d2 e6 10 ♗d3 ♖e8 11 ♘ge2 (11 ♘f3 exd5 12 ♘xd5 ♕d8 13 ♘xf6+ ♗xf6 14 ♕b3 ♘c6 15 0-0 ♖b8 with chances for both sides, Caselas Cabanas-Herraiz Lopez, Canete 1994) 11...♕c7 12 0-0 exd5?! (12...b6!? is given by Skembris in *ECO*) 13 exd5 ♘bd7 14 f4 b6 (Dokhoian-Skembris, Igalo 1994) 15 g4 with an edge for White according to Suba in *ECO*.

8 cxb5 a6 9 a4

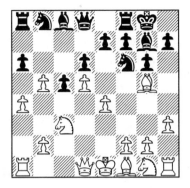

After 9 bxa6 Black has good compensation for the pawn in all variations: 9...♕a5 10 ♗d2 (10 ♕d2 ♗xa6 11 ♗xa6 ♘xa6 12 ♘ge2 ♖fb8 13 f3 c4 14 ♗e3 ♕b4 15 ♖b1 ♘c5, Skembris-Kostic, Vrnjacka Banja 1982, with compensation in *ECO*) 10...♗xa6 (10...♕b4 11 ♕c2 ♗xa6 12 ♗xa6 ♘xa6, Rashkovsky-Geller, Sochi 1977, and then 13 ♘ge2 ♕c4 14 0-0 ♖fb8 with enough play according to Geller) 11 ♗xa6 ♘xa6 12 ♘f3 (12 ♘ge2 ♕b4 13 ♕b1 ♖fb8 14 b3 c4, Skembris-Sznapik, Vrnjacka Banja 1981, is given as good for Black in *ECO*) 12...♖fb8 13 0-0 ♖xb2 14 ♘a4 ♖xd2 15 ♘xd2 ♘xe4 16 ♘c4 ♕b4 and once again Black was happy in Shepherd-Bentley, Port Erin 2003.

9...h6

Over the next few moves a number of scenarios resemble those encountered in Farago-Zaitsev in Chapter 5 (Game 68), where various themes are discussed.

9...♕a5 10 ♗d2 and now 10...axb5 is best avoided, e.g. 11 ♗xb5 ♗a6 12 ♖a3! ♘bd7 13 ♘f3 ♗xb5 14 ♘xb5 ♕b6 15 ♕c2 with a big lead for White (*ECO*) in Suba-Plachetka, Moscow 1977. 10...♕b4 is correct – 11 ♗d3 (11 f3 ♘fd7 12 ♕c2 c4 13 ♘d1 ♘c5 14 ♕xc4 axb5 15 ♕xb5 ♗a6 16 ♕xc5 ♘xc5 17 ♗c3, Foisor-Ghitescu, Baile Herculane 1984 with the more pleasant game for White according to *ECO*) and we have another similar position to Farago-Zaitsev, the only difference being

White's h-pawn (h2). Play has continued 11...c4 12 ♗c2 ♘fd7 (12...♕xb2 13 ♖b1 ♕a3 14 b6 ♗b7 15 ♘ge2 ♕c5 16 a5 with a pull for White, Peskov-Kruglyakov, Simferopol 2003) 13 ♘f3! axb5 (13...♘c5 14 0-0 ♘b3 15 ♗xb3 cxb3 16 ♕e2, Marin-Ardeleanu, Bucharest 1994, and 13...♕xb2 14 ♖b1 ♕a3 15 ♘e2 ♗b2 16 ♘ed4 ♘c5 17 0-0 ♖e8 18 ♖e1, Shaw-Vujadinovic, E-mail 1998, are both excellent for White) 14 ♘xb5 ♕xb2 15 ♖b1 ♕a2 16 0-0 ♗a6 17 ♘fd4 ♗xb5 18 ♘xb5 ♘a6 19 ♕c1 and White was doing very well in Glek-Shchekachev, Moscow 1989.

10 ♗e3 ♕a5 11 ♗d2 e6

After 11...♕b4 the position differs from Game 68 only with the inserted moves h2-h3 and ...h7-h6.

12 ♗c4

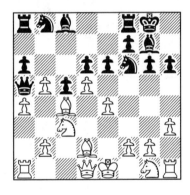

12 ♗d3 axb5 (Bates-Gufeld, London 1994) 13 ♗xb5 ♘a6!? gives Black sufficient play according to Gufeld in *ECO*.

12...♕d8

Rogozenko gives 12...exd5 13 ♘xd5 ♕d8 14 ♘xf6+ ♕xf6 15 ♗d5 ♖a7 16 b6 ♖e7 17 ♗c3 ♕g5 18 ♗xg7 ♔xg7 19 ♘f3 and in our opinion White has a winning position. Better is 12...axb5! 13 ♘xb5 (13 ♗xb5 transposes to 12 ♗d3) 13...♕d8 14 dxe6 fxe6 15 e5 ♘e4 16 ♘f3 d5.

13 dxe6 ♗xe6

After 13...fxe6 14 e5! dxe5 15 ♘ge2 (Rogozenko) Black is seriously struggling in view of the poor c8-bishop.

14 &xe6 fxe6 15 e5!

The most active and consistent move.

15...&d5

15...dxe5 16 &ge2 &d5 17 0-0 certainly doesn't help Black, who is in big trouble according to Rogozenko. After 17...axb5 18 &xb5 &c6 19 ♕c2 Black's pawn structure is scandalous.

16 &f3

After 16 &xd5?! exd5 17 &xh6 dxe5 Rogozenko evaluates the position as unclear. However, 16 exd6 &xc3 17 &xc3 &xc3+ 18 bxc3 ♕f6 19 &f3 ♕xc3+ 20 &f1 axb5 21 &c1 ♕f6 22 axb5 is worthy of further investigation, White appearing to have a slight lead.

16...axb5

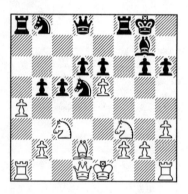

In his efforts to restore material equilibrium Black pays the price in the (terrible) shape of his pawn structure, thus affording White a definite advantage. With this in mind Black should prefer 16...&xc3 17 &xc3 d5 with some counterplay for the pawn.

17 &xb5 dxe5 18 ♕c2 &f5 19 0-0

Obviously not 19 ♕xc5? e4 20 ♕d6 (20 &fd4 &f4) 20...♕xd6 21 &xd6 exf3 and Black has the upper hand.

19...&c6

19...&a6 20 &e3 &ab4 21 ♕c4 with a slight advantage to White (Marin).

20 ♕xc5 e4 21 ♕xc6

This move guarantees White an advantage but in doing so unnecessarily sharpens the play. One to avoid is 21 &h2 &e5! 22 &g4

&f4 with a menacing concentration of Black's forces on the kingside, e.g. 23 &xe5 ♕xd2 24 ♕c6 &af8 25 &g4 e3 26 &xe3 &e2+ 27 &h2 (27 &h1 ♕xe3!) 27...&e5+ 28 &h1 ♕xe3 29 ♕xe6+ &h8 30 ♕xf5 &g3+ 31 &g1 &e2+ with perpetual check. After the simple 21 &h4 ♕xh4 22 ♕xc6 &af8 23 ♕xe6+ &h7 Black is in dire straits.

21...exf3 22 g4?

Marin points out the effective 22 ♕xe6+ &h7 23 g3.

22...♕h4! 23 ♕xe6+

23 gxf5 ♕xh3 24 ♕xe6+ &h8 25 ♕xg6 transposes to the main line.

23...&h8 24 gxf5

Now 24 &h2 meets with 24...&e5+ (Marin).

24...♕xh3 25 ♕xg6 &e5!

25...&g8 26 &d6 &e5 27 &f7 mate (Marin).

26 ♕xh6+♕xh6 27 &xh6 &g8+ 28 &h1 &g4 29 &fd1 &h4+ 30 &g1 &h2+ 31 &f1 &f4 32 &g1 &h2+ 33 &f1 &f4 0-1

Game 36
Suba-Nunn
Dubai Olympiad 1986

---

1 d4 &f6 2 c4 g6 3 &c3 &g7 4 e4 d6 5 h3 0-0 6 &g5 c5 7 d5 e6

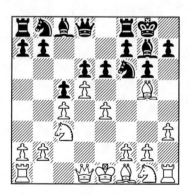

A standard, thematic strategy with this structure, Black hoping to point to h2-h3 as a concession of some kind.

8 ♗d3 exd5

Black can also insert 8...h6, e.g. 9 ♗e3 (9 ♗h4 exd5 10 cxd5 ♗d7 11 a4 ♘a6 12 ♘f3, Goldin-Minasian, Paris 1994, and now 12...♕b6! 13 ♕d2 ♘b4 14 0-0! ♘xd3 15 ♕xd3 g5 16 ♗g3 ♘h5, intending ...♕xb2, is unclear – Goldin) 9...exd5 (9...♖e8 10 ♘f3 a6 11 a4 exd5 12 exd5 ♘bd7 13 0-0 ♘e5 14 ♘xe5 ♖xe5 15 ♕d2 ♕f8 16 ♗f4 ♖e8 17 ♖fe1 ♗d7 18 ♗h2 ♖xe1+ 19 ♖xe1 with a small edge for White, Mititelu-Marsalek, Leningrad 1960) 10 exd5 a6 (10...♘bd7 11 ♘f3 ♖e8 12 ♕d2 ♔h7 13 0-0 favoured White in Gaertner-Wildi, Zurich 1989) 11 ♕d2 ♔h7 12 a4 ♘bd7 13 ♘f3 ♖e8 14 g4 ♘e5 15 ♘xe5 ♖xe5 16 0-0 ♖e8 17 ♔g2 ♘d7 18 f4 ♘f6?! 19 ♖ac1 (19 g5!) 19...♔g8 20 ♗f2 ½-½, Bengtson-Fenster, Philadelphia 1996.

9 exd5

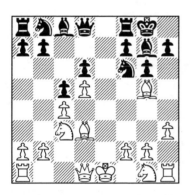

White's decision is not easy because 9 cxd5 leads to a variation of the Benoni where h2-h3 simply does not fit in with the set-up. Nor does 9 ♘xd5 achieve anything, e.g. 9...♗e6 10 ♘e2 ♘c6 11 0-0 ♗xd5 12 exd5 ♘e5 13 f4 ♘xd3 14 ♕xd3 ♕b6 with equality, Wiese-Froehner, Correspondence 1991.

9...♘bd7

A sharp alternative is 9...♖e8+, when 10 ♔f1 h6 11 ♗f4 ♘h5 12 ♗h2 (Dobosz-Pikula, Zurich 1997) 12...♘a6 is good for Black. Instead after 10 ♘ge2 h6 11 ♗h4 (11 ♗d2 ♘bd7 12 f4 ♘h7 13 g4 ♘df8 14 ♔f1, Smirin-Mohr, Pula 2000 and now 14...b5!? 15 ♘xb5

♗xb2 16 ♖b1 ♗g7 is tricky) 11...♘bd7 12 f4 a6 13 a4 b6 (13...♕c7 14 0-0 ♘h7 15 ♕d2 f5 with chances for both sides in Steinhoff-Garber, Duisburg 1992) 14 0-0 ♖a7 (14...♕c7!?, intending ...♗b7, ...♖e7, ...♖ae8) 15 ♖f3 ♘f8 16 ♕d2 ♘8h7 17 ♖af1 ♖ae7 and both sides had to keep their eyes peeled in Panno-Rossetto, Buenos Aires 1996.

10 ♘f3

Once again White has to make a difficult strategic decision, the text surrendering castling rights. The ambitious 10 f4, taking charge of the important e5-square, leads to intense complications:

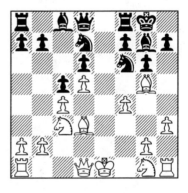

a) 10...♕a5 11 ♕d2 (11 ♔f2 ♘h5 12 ♘ge2 f6 13 ♗h4 ♘h6! 14 f5 ♘e5 with chances for both sides, Salceanu-Kazoks, Correspondence 1990, or 11 a4 ♕b4 12 ♕d2 ♘b6 13 ♘b5 ♖e8+ 14 ♘e2 ♕xd2+ 15 ♔xd2 ♘e4+ 16 ♔c2 ♘f2 17 ♘xd6 ♖e3 with compensation, Melikhov-Bazhin, Podolsk 1993) 11...a6 12 ♘ge2 ♖b8 (12...b5 13 cxb5 axb5 14 ♗xb5 ♖b8 15 a4 ♘xd5 16 0-0 ♘7b6 17 ♖fd1 ♘xc3 18 bxc3 f6 19 ♗h4 ♖d8 20 ♕e3 with a plus for White, 20...♔f7?? 21 ♖xd6 ♗f5 22 ♕xc5 1-0 ending in disaster for Black in Roze-Bakulin, Correspondence 1994) 13 0-0 (13 a4 ♖e8 14 0-0 h6 15 ♗h4 ♘f8 16 g4 ♘6h7 17 f5 g5 18 ♗e1, Pohla-Leluashvili, Correspondence 1988, and now 18...♕c7 leaves both sides with chances) 13...b5 14 b3, Ksieski-Wolf, Bayern 1999, and now 14...b4!? is unclear.

b) 10...a6 11 a4 ♕e8+ and Black unpins with tempo. 12 ♘ge2 ♘h5 13 ♘e4 (13 0-0 ♕e3+ 14 ♔h1 ♘e5! is a typical tactical motif, 15 fxe5 ♕xg5 16 exd6 f5 as in Rapoport-Mittelman, Rishon Le Ziyyon 1997 being exactly what Black is hoping for here; 13 ♔d2 f6 14 ♗h4 ♗h6 15 ♖f1 f5 16 ♔c2 ♘df6 17 ♖e1 ♕f7 with chances for both sides, F.Andersen-Quist, Correspondence 1986) 13...f6 14 ♗h4 (14 ♘xd6 ♕e3 15 ♖a3 ♕e7 16 ♘xc8 ♖axc8 17 ♗h4 ♘xf4 18 0-0 ♘xd3 19 ♖xd3 ♖ce8 is unclear) 14...♘xf4 15 ♘xf4 f5 16 ♘e6 fxe4 17 ♘xf8 ♘xf8 (17...exd3+ 18 ♘e6 ♘b6, Tacu-Marin, Predeal 1989 is given as unclear in *ECO*, while 17...♗xb2!? was seen in Haeussler-Lueues, Correspondence 1993, 18 0-0! ♘xf8 leaving both sides with resources) 18 ♕e2, Partos-Ostojic, Bucharest 1973, and now 18...♗xb2!? 19 ♖a2 ♗c3+ 20 ♔d1 ♘d7 21 ♗xe4 ♘e5 is finely balanced.

10...♖e8+ 11 ♔f1 h6

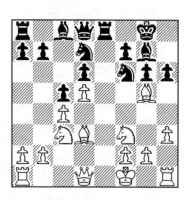

11...a6 12 a4 ♘e5 13 ♘xe5 ♖xe5 14 ♕d2 (14 ♗f4 ♖e8 15 ♕d2 ♘h5 16 ♗g5 f6 [16...♗f6!?] 17 ♗e3 f5 18 g3 ♕e7 19 ♔g2 ♗d7 20 ♖he1 ♕f8 21 f4 ♖e7 ½-½, I.Botvinnik-Hristodorescu, Drobeta 1993) 14...♗f5 (14...♕c7!?) 15 ♗xf5 gxf5 16 ♕c2 (16 f3 ♕b6 with counterplay) 16...♕d7 17 g3, Kustanovich-Mittelman, Beer Sheva 1997, with 17...♘e4 18 ♗f4 ♖e7 19 ♔g2 ♗e5 securing equality according to Mittelman in *ECO*.

12 ♗f4

White does not achieve anything after ei-

ther 12 ♗e3 a6 13 a4 (Dumitrescu-Negulescu, Odorheiu Secuiesc 1993) 13...♘e5 14 ♘xe5 ♖xe5 15 ♕d2 ♕f8 16 ♗f4 ♖e8, intending ...♘d7 (evaluated as equal by Nunn in *ECO*), or 12 ♗h4 ♕b6 13 ♕d2 (Rufener-Antognini, Biel 2001) 13...♘h5, which is unclear.

12...♘e5 13 ♘xe5 dxe5 14 ♗e3 b6 15 ♕d2

15 a4 fails to trouble Black, e.g. 15...♗d7 (15...a5 16 ♔e1 ♘h5 17 g4 ♘f4 with advantage to Black in Avrukh-Krakops, Bratislava 1993) 16 ♕d2 (16 ♔g1!?) 16...♔h7 (16...e4!? 17 ♗e2 ♔h7 18 ♔g1 ♘g8 19 a5 ♘e7 20 ♘xe4 ♘f5 with an edge for Black) 17 g4 ♘g8 18 ♔e2 f5 19 gxf5 ♗xf5 with a pull for Black, Suba-Spasov, Debrecen 1992.

15...h5

Interesting was 15...e4 16 ♗e2 (16 ♗c2? ♗a6 17 b3? ♘xd5) 16...♔h7 with an excellent game for Black.

16 a4 a5?!

After 16...♘h7!?, intending ...f7-f5, Black can be content with his lot.

17 ♔e1 e4

17...♘h7 18 ♔d1 f5 19 f3 with an edge for White (Nunn).

18 ♗e2

18 ♗c2?! meets with 18...♗a6! followed by ...♘d7-e5.

18...♘d7 19 ♔d1

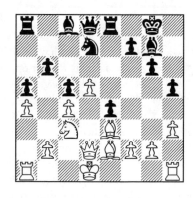

Black now pays the price for closing the queenside with his 16th move, as White now has an excellent refuge for his king on b3.

19...♘e5 20 ♔c2 ♗f5

Nunn recommends 20...f5, intending ...♘f7 and ...♖a7 with chances for both sides. However, after 21 f4! exf3 22 gxf3 ♗a6 23 b3 ♘f7 24 ♖ae1 White stands better.

21 ♔b3 ♖a7

21...♕d7 22 ♗h6 ♗h8 23 ♖af1 h4 (23...♗f6!? with a slight advantage to White) 24 ♖e1 (now or on the next move White should play 24 ♗g5 with a very big lead) 24...♖ad8 (24...f6!?) 25 ♗f4 b5 (definitely too optimistic!) was Suba-Cheparinov, Dos Hermanas 2002, 26 ♘xb5! netting White a pawn.

22 ♖ag1 h4 23 ♗g5

23 g4 hxg3 24 fxg3 ♘f3 25 ♗xf3 exf3 is given as unclear by Nunn.

23...♗f6 24 ♗xf6 ♕xf6 25 ♕h6?!

An improvement is 25 g4 hxg3 26 fxg3 ♘f3 27 ♗xf3 exf3 28 g4 ♗c8 29 g5 ♕f5 30 h4 with advantage (Nunn).

25...♘d3 26 ♗xd3 exd3 27 ♖e1 ♖ae7 28 ♖xe7 ♖xe7 29 ♖d1 ♕d4 30 ♕d2 ♖e8 31 ♘b5 ♕f6 32 ♕c3 ♕d8 33 ♖d2 f6 34 d6 ♔f7 35 g4 hxg3 36 fxg3 ♖e3 37 g4 ♗e4 38 h4 ♖h3 39 g5 ♗f5 40 d7 fxg5 41 hxg5 41...♕e7 42 ♘c7

Taking no risks, although after 42 ♕e5!? ♕xe5 (42...♕xd7?! 43 ♕f6+ ♔g8 44 ♕xb6) 43 d8♕ ♖e3 44 ♘d6+ ♔e6 45 ♘e8 ♖e2 46 ♘f6 ♕d6 47 ♕e8+ ♕e7 48 ♕c6 White has something.

42...♕xg5 43 ♘d5

Nunn gives 43 ♕e5? ♕xd2 44 d8♘+ ♔g8 45 ♕e8+ ♔h7 46 ♕e7+ ♔h6 47 ♘f7+ ♔h5 etc.

43...♗xd7 44 ♖xd3?!

44 ♘xb6 followed by ♕xa5 is unclear (Nunn).

44...♖xd3 45 ♕xd3 ♕d8?

Missing 45...♕g4!, when the ending after 46 ♘xb6 (46 ♔a2 ♗f5 47 ♕b3 ♕e4 48 ♕b5 ♕b1+ 49 ♔b3 ♕d3+ 50 ♔a2 g5) 46...♕h3 is difficult for White, e.g. 47 ♔c3 (47 ♕xh3 ♗xh3 48 ♘d5 g5) 47...♕xd3+ 48 ♔xd3 ♗c6 49 b3 ♔e6 50 ♔e3 ♔e5 51 ♘c8 g5.

46 ♕f3+?!

46 ♘f4 with advantage to White (Nunn).

46...♗f5 47 ♕f4 ♕d7 48 ♕e5 ♕e6 49 ♕c7+ ♔g8 50 ♔a2

50 ♕d8+ (Nunn) here on the next move leads to a quick draw. Instead the game took a while longer to reach the same result:

50...♗d3 51 ♘xb6 ♗xc4+ 52 ♘xc4 ♕xc4+ 53 b3 ♕c2+ 54 ♔a3 ♕c1+ 55 ♔a2 ♕d2+ 56 ♔b1 g5 57 ♕xc5 ♔f7 58 ♕f5+ ♔e7 59 ♕c5+ ♔e6 60 ♕c8+ ♔e5 61 ♕e8+ ♔f4 62 ♕b8+ ♔e4 63 ♕e8+ ♔f3 64 ♕c6+ ♔g3 65 ♕c7+ ♔h3 66 ♕h7+ ♔g4 67 ♕e4+ ♔g3 68 ♕e5+ ♔h3 69 ♕h8+ ♔g2 70 ♕b2 ♕xb2+ 71 ♔xb2 g4 72 b4 axb4 ½-½

Game 37
Yermolinsky-Barcenilla
Chicago 2000

---

1 d4 ♘f6 2 c4 g6 3 ♘c3 ♗g7 4 e4 d6 5 h3 0-0 6 ♗g5 h6?!

For what should become the loss of a tempo later thanks to ♕d2 Black is able to play ...e7-e5.

7 ♗e3 e5 8 d5

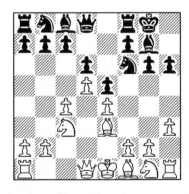

An early assessment here should give White the advantage. The 'extra' moves with the h-pawns favour White because his pawn prevents an often annoying ...♘g4 whereas ...h7-h6 serves only to weaken the kingside as well as invite the natural and effective ♕d2.

8...a5

8...♘e8 (8...c6 9 ♕d2 cxd5 10 cxd5 ♔h7 was Lazarev-Kuntzig, Hamburg 1993, and now 11 g4 favours White according to *NCO*) 9 ♕d2 ♔h7 10 ♗d3 a5 (10...f5 11 exf5 ♗xf5 12 ♘ge2 ♘d7 13 ♘g3 ♗xd3 14 ♕xd3 with the more pleasant game for White in Sulyok-Meier, Vienna 2003) 11 ♘ge2 ♘a6 12 g4 ♘c5 13 ♗c2 b6 14 0-0-0 (14 ♘g3 ♗a6 15 b3 ♗c8 16 ♗d1 ♗d7 17 h4 ♖c8 18 f3 ♕d8 19 h5 g5 20 0-0 ♕e7 21 ♗e2 with a pull for White, Praszak-Diek, Prague 1990) 14...♕d7 (14...♕h4!?) 15 g5 h5 16 ♘b5 ♗a6 17 ♘ec3 and Black was in trouble in Minogina-Malashenko, Elista 1997.

9 ♕d2

The most logical, although White has also played 9 c5 ♘a6 10 cxd6 cxd6 11 ♗xa6 ♖xa6 12 ♕d2 b5 (unclear), Goehler-Kucypera, Germany 1997 and 9 ♗d3. Then 9...♘fd7!? 10 ♘ge2 ♘c5 11 ♗c2 ♘bd7 (intending ...♘b6) provides counterplay, while 9...♘h5 10 ♘ge2 f5 (Dybowski-Pedzich, Bydgoszcz 1990) 11 exf5! gxf5 12 g4 f4 13 ♗c1 ♘f6 14 f3 is slightly better for White. This leaves 9...♘a6 10 ♘ge2 ♘d7!? 11 ♕d2 ♘dc5 12 ♗b1 ♔h7 13 g4 ♕h4 with equal chances in Kachur-Dobrowolski, Krakow 1998.

9...♔h7

Others:

a) 9...h5?! 10 f3 (10 c5!?) 10...♘a6 11 ♗d3 ♘d7 12 g4 ♘dc5 13 0-0-0 (Ksieski gives 13 ♗c2!? ♘b4 14 0-0-0 f5 15 gxf5 gxf5 16 ♘ge2 with a slight advantage to White, but 14...h4 deserves attention) 13...f5 (13...h4!?) 14 exf5 ♘xd3+ 15 ♕xd3 gxf5 16 ♘ge2 (Ksieski-Zesch, Leipzig 1998) 16...♘c5!? 17 ♕d2 e4 18 fxe4 fxg4 19 ♘f4 ♕e8 20 hxg4 ♗xg4 21 ♖dg1 is unclear according to Ksieski, but White's play can be improved here, e.g. 17 ♗xc5 dxc5 18 gxh5 followed by ♖g1, when Black has problems.

b) Black can try 9...♘a6!? with the idea 10 ♗xh6 ♘xe4 11 ♘xe4 ♕h4 with chances for both sides. After other replies Black plays ...♘c5 and wins a tempo, e.g. 10 f3 ♘c5 with the same idea! 11 0-0-0 ♔h7 (f2-f3 looks out

of place here), or 10 ♘ge2 ♘c5 and White has to block his g-pawn with 11 ♘g3, or again play 11 f3.

10 g4

For 10 ♗d3 ♘a6 see 6...♘a6.

10...♘g8

Yermolinsky gives the deadly variation 10...♘a6 11 g5! ♘g8 12 ♘f3 f6 13 gxh6 ♗xh6 14 h4 ♗g4 15 ♘g5+, but Black has 11...hxg5 12 ♘f3 ♖h8 13 ♘xg5+ ♔g8 which restricts White to a more modest lead.

11 ♗d3 ♘a6

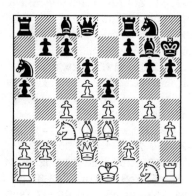

Black has a very passive position.

12 0-0-0

12 ♘ge2 ♘e7 13 ♖g1 (13 ♘g3 c6 14 f3 ♗d7 15 h4 with advantage, Mikhalevski-Ionica, Biel 2001) 13...♘b4 14 ♗b1 c6 15 a3 ♘a6 16 ♘a4 with advantage to White in Potapov-Stoumbos, Agios Kyrikos 2000.

12...b6?!

12...♘c5 13 ♗c2 ♗d7 14 ♗xc5?! dxc5 15 d6 c6 16 ♕e3 b6 is unclear according to Yermolinsky but White should play 14 ♘ge2.

13 f3 ♗d7 14 h4 ♘c5 15 ♗c2 ♘e7 16 ♘ge2 a4 17 g5

White wants to get to work on the kingside. Another option is 17 h5 g5 18 ♘g3 when White has an advantage across the whole board, the logical follow-up being to regroup and gradually prepare action on the queenside.

17...h5 18 f4 exf4 19 ♘xf4 ♗e5 20 ♗d4 ♘c8 21 ♖df1 ♕e8 22 ♖f2 b5?!

After 22...♗xd4 23 ♕xd4 ♕e5 24 ♕xe5

dxe5 25 ♘d3 ♘xd3+ 26 ♗xd3 White has a better ending (Yermolinsky).

23 cxb5 ♗xb5?

23...♘b6 24 ♗xe5 ♘c4 (24...dxe5 25 ♘d3) 25 ♕e2 ♘xe5 26 ♘xh5! gxh5 27 ♕xh5+ with a dangerous attack – Yermolinsky.

24 ♗xe5 dxe5 25 ♘e6?

White has an easy win with 25 ♘xh5! (this was also possible on the previous move) 25...gxh5 26 ♘xb5 ♖b8 (26...♕xb5 27 g6+! with a winning attack) 27 ♘a3 ♕e7 28 ♕e2 ♖h8 29 ♘c4 ♘d6 30 ♖hf1 etc.

25...♘xe6 26 dxe6 ♗c4

26...♘d6 27 ♘d5 ♕c6 28 e7 ♖fe8 29 ♔b1 fails to save Black, but 26...♗c6 is worth a try.

27 ♘d5 ♗xd5 28 exd5 fxe6 29 ♖xf8 ♕xf8 30 ♕e2! ♕g7 31 dxe6 ♘e7 32 ♖e1 e4 33 ♕xe4 ♖a5 34 ♗xa4 ♕f8 35 ♔b1 ♖f5 36 ♗c2 ♖f4 37 ♕e5 c6 38 ♖d1 ♖xh4? 39 ♕f6 ♔g8 40 ♗xg6 ♕xf6 41 gxf6 ♘xg6 42 ♖d8+ ♔h7 43 e7 1-0

Game 38
Chernin-Cebalo
Slovenian League, Bled 1999

---

1 d4 ♘f6 2 c4 g6 3 ♘c3 ♗g7 4 e4 d6 5 h3 0-0 6 ♗g5 ♕e8

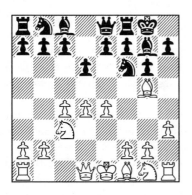

This move unpins the knight and prepares ...e7-e5. Its good point is that it does not weaken Black's kingside and may be used in conjunction with different plans.

7 ♗e2

7 g4 c5 8 d5 e6 9 ♕f3 ♘bd7 10 0-0-0 a6 11 ♕f4 e5 12 ♕e3 b5 saw Black generate counterplay in Renet-Nataf, Clichy 2001. Another option that ...♕e8 even appears to invite is 7 e5 dxe5 8 dxe5 ♘fd7 9 ♘d5, when after 9...♘a6 the complications favour Black, e.g. 10 c5 ♘xe5 11 f4 f6 12 ♗xa6 fxg5 13 fxe5 e6 14 ♘f6+ ♗xf6 15 exf6 bxa6 with an edge, or 10 ♗xe7 c6 11 ♗xf8 ♗xf8 12 ♘c3 ♘xe5 13 ♗e2 ♗f5 with excellent compensation.

7 ♗d3 is popular, when play tends to develop 7...e5 8 d5 ♘h5!? 9 ♘ge2 and now:

a) 9...f5 looks premature after 10 exf5 gxf5, when White can hope for an advantage with 11 ♕d2 e4 12 ♗c2 ♘d7?! (12...♘a6!?) 13 ♘b5!, e.g. 13...♕e5 14 ♘xc7 ♖b8 15 ♘f4 ♘xf4 16 ♗xf4 ♕xb2 17 ♖b1 ♕xa2 18 ♘e6 and Black was in trouble in Wimmer-Aleshnia, E-mail 1998.

However, a more thematic and consistent treatment is 11 g4!?:

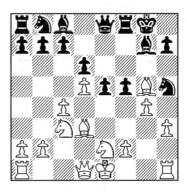

Notice that the diagram position resembles Panczyk-Kempys (Chapter 2, Game 28) and the strategic plans and ideas are indeed similar. 11...h6 12 ♗e3 and a further crossroads.

a1) 12...f4 chronically weakens the light-squares, and after 13 ♗d2 ♘f6 14 ♘e4 ♘xe4 15 ♗xe4 ♘d7 16 ♘c3 ♘f6 17 ♕f3 White stands better.

a2) 12...fxg4 13 hxg4 ♗xg4 14 ♕c2 highlights an important difference with Panczyk-Kempys in that here 14...♘a6??, which would be best with the queen still at home on d8, runs into 15 ♗h7+ ♔h8 16 ♗g6 etc. Thus Black must settle for 14...♘f4, when 15 0-0-0 ♘xd3+ 16 ♕xd3 e4 17 ♕d2 h5 18 ♗d4! ♗xd4 19 ♘xd4 gives White a dangerous attack and 15...♗f3 16 ♖h2 ♘a6 (16...♘xd3+ 17 ♕xd3 e4 18 ♕d2 looks promising for White) 17 ♗xf4 ♖xf4 18 ♘xf4 ♗xd1 19 ♕xd1 exf4 20 ♕g4 is pretty awful.

a3) After 12...♘f4 we can again compare with the aforementioned game. There are two differences – White's bishop stands on e3 (instead of c1) and Black's queen is on e8 (instead of d8) – which are to White's advantage, and after 13 ♗xf5 ♗xf5 14 gxf5 ♖xf5 15 ♕c2! White had already built up a big lead in Tyomkin-Sasikiran, Biel 1999.

b) The best, and rather cunning continuation is 9...♘a6!?, developing the knight. Now White gets less than nothing after 10 g4?! ♘f4 11 ♘xf4 exf4 12 ♗xf4 f5 when Black's queen comes to life. Instead 10 0-0 f5 11 exf5 gxf5 is interesting, when Black had his play on the kingside in Conquest-Moreno Carnero, Pamplona 2002.

7...e5 8 d5

8 dxe5 dxe5 9 ♘f3 poses Black no problems, e.g. 9...c6 10 ♕d6 ♘bd7 11 0-0 h6 12 ♗h4 ♔h7 13 ♖ad1 ♖g8 14 ♖d2 ♘h5 15 ♖fd1 ♘f4 16 ♕e7 ½-½, Dydyshko-Shulman, Ostrava 1998, or 9...♘bd7 10 0-0 ♘c5 11 ♕c2 ♘e6 12 ♗e3 ♘h5 with chances for both sides, Cramling-Jonsson, Sweden 1994.

8...a5

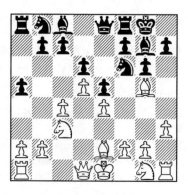

The standard push of the a-pawn in such positions, preparing to send a knight to c5. An alternative is 8...♘a6 9 g4 and now:

a) 9...♔h8!? is interesting, making way for ...♘g8 followed by ...f7-f5.

b) 9...♘c5 10 ♕c2 c6 (10...a5!?) 11 b4 ♘a6 12 a3 cxd5 (12...c5!? is unclear) 13 cxd5 ♗d7 14 ♘f3 ♖c8 15 ♘d2 with advantage to White, Poluljahov-Zulfugarli, Swidnica 1999.

c) 9...♗d7 10 ♘f3 c6 (10...♘c5!? 11 ♕c2 a5) 11 ♕d2 cxd5 12 cxd5 (12 ♗xf6!? ♗xf6 13 ♘xd5) 12...♘c5 with equality, Agrest-Arizmendi Martinez, Reykjavik 2000.

9 ♗f3

9 h4 might seem like an odd choice as White has made a point of introducing a line that partly revolves around placing the pawn on h3. However, it is not clear whether Black's queen stands better on e8 or d8. Moreover, the 8...a5 might prove irrelevant. Let's take a look at how the game might continue – 9...♘a6 10 h5 ♘c5 and now opening the h-file is premature due to 11 hxg6 fxg6 12 ♕c2 ♕f7 with counterplay on the f-file. White's queen should also keep an eye on h5 as Black might otherwise just take the pawn, 11 ♕c2 ♘xh5! 12 ♗xh5 gxh5 (intending ...f7-f5) 13 ♗e3 ♘a6 14 ♘ge2 f5 being a good example, when Black has counterplay.

The appropriate follow-up is 11 ♗f3, e.g.

a) 11...c6 12 ♘ge2!? (12 hxg6 fxg6 13 ♘ge2, Kozul-Stevic, Solin/Split 2001, and now 13...b5! 14 dxc6 bxc4 15 ♕xd6 ♘d3+ 16 ♔f1 ♖a6 with healthy compensation) 12...cxd5 (12...b5!? with similar ideas) 13 ♗xf6 ♗xf6 14 ♘xd5 ♕d8 and the character of the position is similar to that of Farago-Rotstein (Chapter Four, Game 62), although this scenario might be easier for White. Black is not yet without prospects of counterplay as there are chances on the dark squares, and the f3-bishop is pretty poor.

b) More timid but perhaps playable is 11...♗d7, e.g. 12 ♘ge2 (12 ♗e3!?) 12...♘xh5! 13 ♗xh5 gxh5 14 ♗e3 (14 ♘g3 f5 15 exf5 e4! with counterplay according to Hazai) 14...f5

15 ♗xc5 dxc5 16 ♘g3 with the easier game for White.

9...♘a6 10 ♘ge2 ♚h8

Black prepares ...♘g8 and ...f7-f5 or ...♗h6, exchanging dark-squared bishops. Another plan involves 10...♘c5.

11 g4 ♘g8 12 ♗e3

Again White might consider 12 h4!? despite the lost tempo.

12...f5 13 gxf5 gxf5 14 exf5 ♘e7

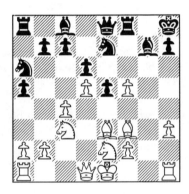

Black has good counterplay.

**15 f6 ♗xf6 16 ♘g3 ♘f5 17 ♘xf5 ♗xf5
18 ♗e4 ♕g6 19 ♗xf5**

No better is 19 ♕b1 ♗h4 (Cebalo).

19...♕xf5 20 ♕b1 e4

An ambitious move. An equal position results after both 20...♗g5 21 ♕xf5 ♖xf5 22 ♔e2 ♗xe3 23 fxe3 ♘c5 and 20...♕h5 21 ♕e4 ♖g8 22 ♘e2 ♖af8.

21 ♘xe4 ♖ae8

21...♗g7 22 ♘g5 and White intends to hop into e6 (Cebalo).

22 ♘xf6 ♕xf6 23 ♔d2??

Losing. The only move is 23 ♕c2:

a) 23...♘b4 24 ♕c3! ♖e4 (24...♕xc3+ 25 bxc3 ♘c2+ 26 ♔d2 ♘xa1 27 ♗d4+ ♖e5 28 ♖xa1 – Cebalo – is decisive, but 26...♘xe3 27 fxe3 is just an edge for White) 25 ♕xf6+ ♖xf6 26 0-0-0 ♖xc4+ 27 ♔b1 ♔g8 (favouring Black according to Cebalo) 28 a3 ♘a6 29 ♗d4 with an edge to White. Cebalo also gives 27...♘c2 as better for Black, but 28 ♗d2 ♖xf2 29 ♖hg1 h6 30 ♖g6 ♔h7 31 ♖dg1 is good for White.

b) Better is 23...b5 24 ♕e2 (24 cxb5 ♘b4 25 ♕c3 ♖e5 with initiative) 24...♘b4 (planning ...♘d3+) 25 0-0-0 (25 ♖d1? ♖xe3!! 26 fxe3 ♕h4+ 27 ♔d2 ♕f2 is decisive) 25...♘xa2+ 26 ♔b1 ♘b4 with equal chances.

**23...♖xe3! 24 fxe3 ♕f2+ 25 ♔d1 ♕xe3
26 ♕c2 ♕f3+ 27 ♔d2 ♕g2+ 0-1**

Game 39
Gyimesi-I.Botvinnik
Tel Aviv 2001

1 d4 ♘f6 2 c4 g6 3 ♘c3 ♗g7 4 e4 d6 5 h3 0-0 6 ♗g5 ♘a6

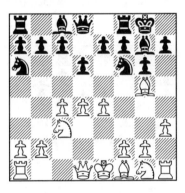

This move is very popular nowadays in many systems of the King's Indian. Black's trump card is flexibility, the a6-knight always able to find a good posting when the situation in the centre stabilises.

7 g4

This does not work properly with ♗g5. Nor does adopting a Four Pawns Attack approach bother Black now that White has lost a tempo on h2-h3. After 7 f4 ♕e8 8 ♗d3 (8 e5? ♘h5 9 ♘ce2 f6 is definitely one that should avoid, while 8 ♘f3 e5 9 fxe5 dxe5 10 dxe5!? ♘d7 11 ♘d5 ♘xe5! 12 ♗e7 c6 13 ♗xf8 ♕xf8 14 ♘c3 ♗e6 offers Black decent compensation) 8...e5 9 fxe5 dxe5 10 d5 ♘h5 11 ♘ge2 f5 12 ♕d2 ♘c5 with chances for both sides, Arbakov-Kurnosov, Alushta 2000.

7...c5

Black seeks to exploit White's awkwardly

placed pieces. Standard counterplay in the centre with ...e7-e5 leads, not surprisingly, to standard positions via a different move order, e.g. 7...c6 (7...e5 8 d5 ♕e8 9 ♘ge2 – see 7 ♘ge2) 8 ♕d2 (8 ♘ge2 e5 9 d5 cxd5 10 cxd5 ♕b6 11 ♕d2 ♘c5 ½-½, Gyimesi-El Taher, Tanta 2000) 8...e5 9 d5 ♘c5 10 f3 cxd5 11 cxd5 a5 12 ♘ge2 a4 13 ♘g3 ♗d7 14 ♗e2 ♕a5 15 ♘d1! ♗b5 16 ♕xa5 ♖xa5 17 ♗d2 ♗xe2 18 ♔xe2 with advantage to White, Suba-Ubilava, Spain 1993.

8 d5 e6

Or 8...♕a5 9 ♗d2 e6 10 ♘ge2 exd5 11 ♘xd5 ♕d8 12 ♘dc3 ♘d7 with an unclear situation in Agrest-Laveryd, Sweden 1998.

9 ♗d3

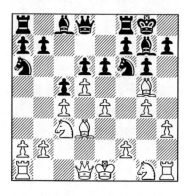

9...exd5

Also good are:

a) 9...♘b4!? 10 ♗e2 (10 ♗b1 exd5 11 exd5 ♖e8+ 12 ♘ge2 with an excellent position for Black) 10...exd5 11 cxd5 ♕e8 12 f3 ♗d7 13 a3 ♘a6 14 ♗f4 ♕e7 with chances for both sides, Suba-Kindl, Hospitalet 1994.

b) 9...♘c7 10 a4 h6 11 ♗e3 exd5 12 exd5 ♘a6 13 ♖c1 ♘b4 14 ♗b1 ♖e8 with good play for Black, Gyimesi-M.Ivanov, Germany 1999.

10 exd5

This position is similar to those discussed earlier but instead of ♘ge2 White has weakened his kingside by pushing the g-pawn. After 10 ♘xd5 ♗e6 Black is slightly better.

10...♕e8+ 11 ♕e2

After 11 ♘ge2 Black has the manoeuvre

11...♘d7 12 f4 ♘b4 13 ♗b1 ♕e3 with initiative (Hazai).

11...♘c7 12 0-0-0 b5 13 cxb5?

13 ♕xe8 ♖xe8 14 ♘f3 bxc4 is the accurate course, although Black's position is nicer.

13...♗b7?

Hazai gives the superior 13...♘fxd5! 14 ♘xd5 ♘xd5 15 ♗e4 ♗xb2+! 16 ♔xb2 ♕e5+ 17 ♔c2 ♘c3 and 16 ♕xb2 ♕xe4 17 ♗h6 ♕c4+ 18 ♔d2 f6 19 ♖c1 ♘b6 20 ♗xf8 ♕d5+, with a practically winning lead in both cases.

14 ♗c4 a6?

14...♖b8 15 ♕e3 a6 (Hazai) improves.

15 b6 ♘b5 16 ♕xe8 ♖fxe8 17 ♘xb5 axb5 18 ♗xb5 ♖ec8

Black should try 18...♘xd5 19 ♗xe8 ♖xe8 20 f3 ♗e5 with some compensation because White has problems developing the kingside.

19 ♗xf6 ♗xf6 20 a4 ♖a5

20...♗d8 21 ♘e2 ♗xb6 22 ♘c3 (Hazai) is a lesser, albeit ugly evil.

21 ♘f3 ♗a6 22 ♗c6 ♖b8 23 g5 ♗d8 24 ♖he1 ♗xb6 25 ♘d2 c4 26 b4! cxb3 27 ♘xb3 ♔g7 28 ♘xa5 ♗xa5 29 ♖e8 ♖b6 30 ♔c2 ♗c4 31 ♖e3 1-0

1 d4 ♘f6 2 c4 g6 3 ♘c3 ♗g7 4 e4 d6 5 h3 0-0 6 ♗g5 ♘a6 7 ♘ge2!?

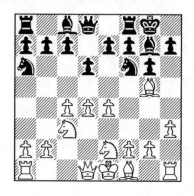

A hybrid, combining different set-ups.

7...c6

Others:

a) As usual White's strange set-up justifies steering the game to Modern Benoni territory, e.g. 7...c5 8 d5 e6 9 ♘g3 h6 10 ♗e3 exd5 11 cxd5 (11 exd5 ♖e8) 11...♖b8 12 ♗e2 ♘c7 with an interesting struggle ahead, Agrest-Sandstrom, Swedish Championship, Haninge 1997.

b) 7...♕e8 8 ♘g3 e5 9 d5 h5 10 ♗e2 ♘h7 11 ♗e3 h4 12 ♘f1 f5 13 a3 ♘c5 14 ♘d2 ♗d7 15 ♕c2 ♘a4 16 ♘db1 a6 17 ♘xa4 ♗xa4 18 b3 ♗d7 19 ♘c3 ♕e7, as in Van Wely-Damljanovic, Elista 1998 is unclear according to Hazai.

c) 7...e5 8 d5 h6!? (8...c6 9 ♕d2 ♘c5 10 ♘g3 cxd5 11 cxd5 a5 12 ♗e2 a4 13 0-0 ♕a5 14 ♖fc1 ♗d7 15 f3 ♖fc8 16 ♘d1 ♕xd2 17 ♗xd2 h5 18 ♘f1 h4 19 ♗g5 ♘h5 20 ♘d2, Suba-Nisipeanu, Tusnad 1997, and now 20...♗f6 21 ♗xf6 ♘xf6 secures equality) 9 ♗e3 ♘c5 10 f3 (10 ♘g3 a5 11 ♗e2 h5 12 ♗g5 ♕e8 13 ♕d2 ♘h7 14 ♗e3 ♕e7, Gabriel-Jenni, Zurich 1999, leads to unclear play) 10...a5 (10...c6 11 ♕d2 cxd5 12 cxd5 ♗d7 13 g4, Agrest-Laveryd, Stockholm 1997, and now Hazai recommends 13...a5 with chances for both sides) 11 ♕d2 c6!? 12 dxc6 bxc6 13 0-0-0 ♗e6, Agrest-Schmaltz, Harplinge 1998, and now 14 ♕xd6 ♘cd7! 15 ♕xc6 ♖c8 16 ♕a4 ♗xc4 is enough compensation according to Hazai.

8 g4

Of course this is not the only option available to White.

a) 8 ♘g3 h6 9 ♗e3 h5 10 ♗e2 ♕a5 11 a3 c5 (given as unclear in *ECO*) 12 ♗f3 cxd4 13 ♗xd4 ♗e6 14 b4 ♕c7 15 ♘d5 ♗xd5 ½-½, Atalik-Van Wely, New York 1997.

b) 8 ♕d2 e5 9 f3 ♕a5 10 d5 cxd5 11 ♘xd5 ♕xd2+ 12 ♔xd2 ♘xd5 13 cxd5 f6 14 ♗e3 ♗d7 15 ♘c3 ♘c7 16 a4 with a plus for White, Chernin-Zimmerman, Hungary 1997.

8...e5 9 d5 cxd5

9...♗d7 10 ♘g3 ♕b6 11 ♖b1 cxd5 12 exd5

♕a5 13 ♗d2 ♘e8?! 14 h4! f5 15 h5 fxg4 16 hxg6 hxg6 17 ♗d3 and White held all the aces in Atalik-Relange, Cappelle la Grande 1999.

10 cxd5

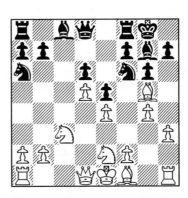

10...♗d7

Alternatively:

a) 10...♕e8 11 ♘g3 ♗d7 (11...♘c7 – the c7-square is usually not the best place for the knight with this set-up – 12 ♕f3 ♘d7 13 h4 b5? 14 ♘xb5 ♘xb5 15 ♗xb5 ♖b8 16 ♗c6 ♖xb2 17 ♕a3 ♖c2 18 ♕xd6 with a big advantage in Suba-Arakhamia Grant, Seville 1994) 12 ♗e3!? ♕d8 13 a3 ♘c7 14 ♖c1 ♕e7 15 ♗e2 ♖fc8 16 h4, Suba-Salamero Pelay, Zaragoza 1997, with an initiative for White.

b) 10...b5 11 ♘g3 (11 ♘xb5? ♕a5+) 11...b4 12 ♘a4 ♕a5 13 b3 ♗d7 (13...♘c5 14 ♘xc5 ♕xc5 15 ♖c1 ♕a5 16 ♕f3! was great for White in Suba-Foisor, Rumania 1992) 14 ♘b2 Atalik-Peng, Wijk aan Zee 1997, and now 14...♘c5!? is unclear.

11 ♘g3

Both sides have announced their plans. White has gone to great lengths to clamp down on ...f7-f5 and he has built a very strong position in the centre, while Black's chances are on the queenside.

11...♕b6

11...♖c8 12 ♕d2 ♘c5 13 b4 ♘a4 14 ♘xa4 ♗xa4 15 ♗d3 ♕e8 16 0-0 ♗b5 17 ♖fc1 ♕d7 18 ♔g2 a6 19 a3 ♗xd3 20 ♕xd3 ♖xc1 21 ♖xc1 ♖c8 ½-½, Varga-Manik, Slovakia 1998.

12 ♕d2 ♘c5 13 ♗e2 a5 14 0-0?!

Black has an excellent position. The more flexible and superior 14 ♗e3 is called for, the point being that White can sometimes use the rook on the h-file. Gyimesi-J.Ivanov, Andorra 2001 continued 14...♖fc8 15 ♖c1 (15 g5!? ♘e8 16 h4 with an initiative) 15...a4 16 f3 ♕a5 17 ♔f2 b5 with chances for both sides .

14...♖fc8 15 ♗e3 a4 16 ♖fc1 ♕a5 17 f3 b5 18 ♘d1 ♕xd2 19 ♗xd2 ♘e8 20 ♘f2 ♘c7 21 ♖c2 ♖ab8 22 ♖ac1 b4 23 ♘d3 b3 24 axb3 axb3 25 ♘xc5?

25 ♖c3 ♘b5 26 ♖c4 ♗f8 is unclear according to Motylev.

25...bxc2 26 ♘xd7 ♖xb2 27 g5

Motylev gives 27 ♗e3 ♖b1 28 ♗f1 ♖xc1 29 ♗xc1 ♖d8 30 ♘b6 ♖b8 31 ♘c4 ♖b1 32 ♘e2 ♘b5 with a big advantage for Black, who plans ...♘d4 .

27...♘e8 28 ♔f1

28 ♘f1 ♖c7 29 ♘f6+ ♘xf6 30 gxf6 ♗xf6 31 ♗d3 with an edge for Black (Motylev).

28...♖c7 29 ♘f6+ ♘xf6 30 gxf6 ♗xf6 31 ♗d3 ♗h4 32 ♘e2 ♖b3 33 ♗c3 ♖bxc3 34 ♘xc3 ♖xc3 35 ♔e2 ♖a3 36 ♖xc2 h5 37 ♖c6 ♖a2+ 38 ♗c2 ♔g7 39 ♔d3 ♖a3+ 40 ♔e2 ♖a2 41 ♔d3 ♖a3+ 42 ♔e2 ♗e7 43 ♖c7 ♗g5 44 ♖c6 ♗e7 45 ♖c7 ♔f6 46 h4 ♖a2 47 ♔f2 ♗d8 48 ♖c6 ♔g7 49 ♔g3 ♗a5 50 ♗d1 ♗e1+ 51 ♔h3 ♗b4 52 ♖c4 ♗c5 53 ♖c2 ♖a1 54 ♗e2 ♖h1+ 55 ♔g3 ♗b4? 56 ♖c6 ♖b1 57 ♔h3 ♗c5 58 ♖a6 ♖e1

58...♖g1 59 ♔h2 ♖c1 60 ♖a2 ♗f2 61 ♔h3 ♗e3 62 ♔g2 is another very good suggestion from Motylev.

59 ♖a2 ♖h1+ 60 ♔g3 ♗e3 61 ♖a6 ♗f4+ 62 ♔f2 ♖h2+ 63 ♔f1 ♖xh4 64 ♖xd6? ♖h1+ 65 ♔g2 ♖h2+ 66 ♔f1 h4 67 ♖d7 h3 68 d6 ♖xe2 0-1

Game 41
Psakhis-Hrbolka
Czech Open, Pardubice 2002

1 c4 ♘f6 2 ♘c3 g6 3 e4 d6 4 d4 ♗g7 5 h3 0-0 6 ♗g5 ♘a6 7 ♗d3

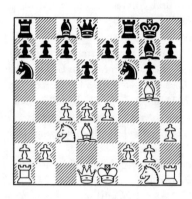

White's most natural and flexible move, against which Black has a choice of plans.

7...♕e8

7...e5 is the subject of the remaining games in this chapter.

8 g4

Employing the stronghold on the kingside, bringing to three the number of guards over f5. However, White usually plays the text after the inclusion of ...e7-e5 and d4-d5, when at least the situation in the centre is more stabile.

8...e5

With this particular move order Black can seriously consider switching to 8...c5 9 d5, when the g4-pawn appears somewhat inappropriate. Play can continue 9...e6 10 ♘ge2 exd5 11 exd5 ♘d7 12 f4 as in Tyomkin-Vouldis, European Junior Championship 1995, and now 12...h6 13 ♗h4 ♘b4 gives Black an excellent position.

9 d5 c6

Black wants to exchange pawns on d5, place his knight on c5 and get the ball rolling on the queenside with ...a7-a5 and ...b7-b5.

Of course, there are other moves here.

a) With 9...♔h8 Black plans ...♘g8 followed by ...♗h6 and ...f7-f5: 10 ♘ge2 ♘g8 11 ♘g3 (White should definitely keep the dark-squared bishops on the board, 11 ♕d2 being enough to give White the more pleasant game) 11...f6!? 12 ♗e3 ♗h6 13 ♗xh6 ♘xh6 and Black's position is very difficult to break. The extra space does not play a big part here, and

White must be careful as far as the dark squares are concerned. 14 ♗e2 ♕e7 15 ♕d2 ♔g7 16 0-0-0 ♗d7 17 ♖dg1 ♘f7 was unclear in Avrukh-Mohr, Pula 2000, while 14 ♕d2 ♘g8 15 ♘b5 ♕e7 16 f3 c6 17 ♘c3 ♘b4 18 ♗b1 cxd5 19 cxd5 a5 20 h4 ♕d8 21 h5 g5 22 0-0 ♘e7 was equally interesting in Potapov-Isupov, Russian League, Orel 1996.

b) 9...♘d7 10 ♘f3 f5! 11 gxf5 gxf5 12 ♖g1 ♔h8 13 ♘h4 ♘dc5 was fine for Black in Paunovic-Kupreichik, Cetinje 1992, while 10 a3 ♘dc5 11 ♗c2 f5 12 b4 ♘xe4 13 ♘xe4 fxe4 14 ♗xe4 ♘b8!, as in Shaw-Cherrington, E-mail 1998 is unclear according to *NCO*. White should play 10 ♘ge2, when 10...♘dc5 gives rise to the following options:

b1) 11 ♘g3 f5 12 gxf5 gxf5 13 ♗b1 (13 exf5 e4! or 13 ♘xf5 ♗xf5 14 exf5 e4, Kustanovich-Moskovic, Witley 1999, with an initiative for Black in either case) 13...♕g6 14 ♗e7 ♖f7 15 exf5 ♕h6 16 f6 ♗xf6 17 ♗xf6 ♖xf6, Chernin-Tratar, Feldbach 1997, with chances for both sides.

b2) 11 ♗c2 f5 12 gxf5 gxf5 13 ♖g1 ♔h8 14 ♗e3 ♕f7 with chances for both sides, Shepherd-Stubberud, Port Erin 2003.

b3) Hazai's recommendation of 11 ♗b1!? looks good, when White's plan is to follow up with a2-a3 and b2-b4 etc. After 11...f5 12 exf5!? gxf5 13 ♖g1 ♕f7 an interesting middle-game is developing.

10 ♘ge2

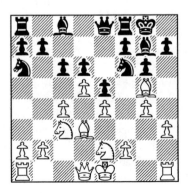

10...♘c5

An early trade on d5 affords White more possibilities, e.g. 10...cxd5 11 cxd5

a) Now after 11...♘c5 White has 12 ♗b5!? (12 ♗c2 a5 transposes to the main line), when 12...♕e7!?, re-entering the pin is probably the most circumspect reply. Instead 12...♗d7 13 ♗xd7 was the course of Sotnikov-Gelman, Russian Junior Championship, Moscow 1995, when recapturing with the queen looks the most promising, e.g. 13...♕xd7!? 14 f3 (14 ♘g3 a5 is fine for Black) 14...♖ac8 15 ♕d2 ♕c7 (followed by ...♕a5) 16 b4 ♘cd7 and the knight is coming to b6.

b) 11...♗d7 12 ♘g3 (12 ♗xa6!?) 12...♘c5 13 ♗c2 a5 14 a4 ♕d8 15 ♖b1 ♖c8 was unclear in Cramling-Gallagher, Biel 1994.

11 ♗c2 cxd5 12 cxd5 a5 13 ♘g3

An alternative is 13 a3 ♗d7 14 b4 axb4 15 axb4 ♘a6 16 ♖b1 ♖c8 17 0-0 (17 ♗d3!?) 17...h6 18 ♗e3 ♖c4 with chances for both sides, Soln-Bratovic, Bled 2002.

13...b5

13...h6 is safer, and after 14 ♗e3 (Sotnikov-Provkin, Voronezh 1997) Black can then push 14...b5!?, with counterplay and similar play to the main line.

14 ♕f3!

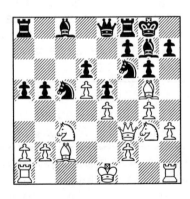

The point behind this blunt attack is that Black has no good retreat available for his knight as 14...♘fd7 leaves the b5-pawn unprotected.

14...b4 15 ♗xf6 bxc3 16 ♘h5

After 16 bxc3 Black has some compensation for the pawn, e.g. 16...♕b5 17 ♗xg7 ♔xg7 18 ♖b1 ♕c4 19 ♘b3 ♕a6 20 ♕e2 ♖b8 21 ♕xa6 ♗xa6.

16...cxb2 17 ♖b1 ♘e6?

A mistake in a complex position in which Black should be doing okay.

a) 17...♗h6, and now 18 g5 (18 ♖xb2 ♗a6 19 ♘g3 ♕c8 20 g5 ♗g7 21 ♗xg7 ♔xg7) 18...♕b5 19 gxh6 ♕b4+ 20 ♔f1 (20 ♔d1 ♗a6 with an initiative for Black) 20...♕c4+ 21 ♕e2 ♗a6 22 ♕xc4 ♗xc4+ 23 ♔g2 ♖fb8 provides enough compensation.

b) 17...♕b5 is also effective, e.g. 18 ♗xg7 ♕b4+ 19 ♔d1 (19 ♔f1 ♕c4+ 20 ♔g2 ♕xc2 21 ♗xf8 ♔xf8 and the investment is justified) 19...♕d4+ 20 ♔e1 ♗a6 21 ♗xf8 ♕b4+ 22 ♔d1 ♕d4+ etc.

18 ♗xg7

18 dxe6! fxe6 19 ♘xg7 is simple and strong.

18...gxh5 19 ♗h6

White has a very strong alternative in 19 ♗xf8 ♘d4 20 ♕f6 ♘xc2+ 21 ♔d2 ♔xf8 22 ♕h8+ ♔e7 23 ♕xe8+ ♔xe8 24 ♖xc2 etc.

19...♘f4 20 gxh5 ♔h8 21 ♖g1 ♖g8 22 ♔d2 ♗a6 23 ♖xg8+ ♕xg8 24 ♗xf4 exf4 25 ♕c3+ ♕g7 26 h6 ♕xc3+ 27 ♔xc3 ♖c8+ 28 ♔xb2 ♖b8+ 29 ♔c3 ♖xb1 30 ♗xb1 ♗b5 31 e5 dxe5 32 ♗f5 ♔g8 33 d6 ♔f8 34 h4 ♗c6 35 ♔c4 e4 36 ♗xh7 e3 37 fxe3 f3 38 ♗d3 f2 39 ♔d4 f5 40 ♔e5 ♗a4 41 ♔f6 1-0

Game 42
Yermolinsky-Radjabov
FIDE World Cup, Hyderabad 2002

---

1 d4 ♘f6 2 c4 g6 3 ♘c3 ♗g7 4 e4 d6 5 h3 0-0 6 ♗g5 ♘a6 7 ♗d3 e5

Normal and popular. By now it is clear that the challenge to the d4-pawn is designed to gain control of the c5-square for the knight, while the possibility of seeking activity on the other flank with ...f7-f5 is another ingredient to add to the mix.

Other continuations are:

a) White should emerge with an edge after 7...h6 8 ♗e3 e5 9 d5 ♘c5 10 ♗c2 a5 11 ♕d2 ♔h7 12 g4 c6 13 ♘f3 ♘g8 14 ♖g1 ♘e7 15 h4, Averbakh-Bondarevsky, USSR Championship 1951.

b) Again the Modern Benoni approach is also possible, e.g. 7...c5 8 d5 e6 9 ♘f3 h6 10 ♗e3 ♘c7 11 a4 ♖e8, which was unclear in Chernin-Barbero, San Bernardino 1994.

8 d5 ♕e8 9 ♕d2

N.B. The actual order of moves was 9 g4 ♘c5 10 ♗c2 a5 11 ♕d2 ♗d7 12 ♘ge2 but we have made alterations in order to accommodate analysis of variations.

9 a3 is too slow, 9...♘h5 10 ♘ge2 f5 11 exf5 gxf5 12 0-0 ♔h8 seeing Black achieve equality in Rapoport-Solleveld, Apeldoorn 1999.

Instead White has 9 ♘ge2, when Black has three knight moves.

a) 9...♘c5 10 ♗c2 a5 11 g4 (11 ♕d2!?) 11...♘fd7 12 ♘g3 ♘b6 13 ♕e2 ♗d7 was unclear in Agrest-Milov, Frankfurt 2000.

b) 9...♘h5 and now instead of 10 g3 ♗d7 11 a3 f5 12 exf5 gxf5 (unclear), Potapov-Stoumbos, Korinthos 2001 and 10 g4 ♘f4 (with compensation) White played 10 ♕d2 in Kozul-Tratar, Portoroz 1997. There followed 10...f5 11 exf5 (11 f3 ♗d7 12 0-0-0 ♘c5 13 ♗c2 f4 with mutual chances, Turna-Maslik, Slovakia 1999) 11...♗xf5 12 0-0 ♘c5 13 ♗b1 a5 14 ♗e3 b6 15 g4 ♗xb1 16 ♖axb1 ♘f4 17 ♘xf4 exf4 18 ♗xf4 ♗xc3 19 bxc3 ♘e4 20 ♕e3 ♖xf4 21 ♕xf4 ♘xc3 22 ♕e3 ♘xb1 23 ♖xb1 ♕xe3 24 fxe3 and the ending should have led to a draw.

c) 9...♘d7

c1) 10 0-0 is inaccurate, e.g. 10...f5 11 exf5 gxf5 12 f4 e4 13 ♗c2 ♕h5! and White had problems with the bishop and Black homed in on d3 in Cramling-Gallagher, Bern 1992, 14 ♘d4 ♕xd1 15 ♖axd1 ♘b4 16 ♗b1 ♘c5 leaving Black with an excellent position. Perhaps 14 ♕d2 h6 15 ♘g3 ♕g6 16 ♗h4 is better.

c2) 10 a3 f5 11 b4 (11 f3 ♘ac5 12 ♗c2 fxe4 13 fxe4 a5 14 b4 axb4 15 axb4 ♖xa1 16

♕xa1 ♘a6 with chances for both sides, Kazhgaleyev-Sande Edreira, Lisbon 2000) 11...f4 (11...♘f6 12 ♕c2 c5 13 ♖b1, Ivanisevic-Xie Jun, Belgrade 2000, and now 13...h6!? 14 ♗d2 f4 is unclear; 12 c5 merits attention) 12 f3 ♗f6 13 ♗xf6 ♘xf6 14 ♕d2 ♕e7 (14...♘b8!?) 15 ♖c1 (15 0-0-0, Ungureanu-Nevednichy, Curtea de Arges 2002, should have met with 15...♘b8 intending ...♘bd7 and ...a7-a5 with active play that guarantees at least equality) 15...♗d7 16 ♘b5 (16 ♘d1 followed by c4-c5 looks better) 16...♘e8 17 ♖c2 c5 (17...c6 might be preferable) 18 dxc6?! bxc6 19 ♘bc3 ♕h4+ 20 ♔f1 ♘ac7 with an edge for Black, Kazhgaleyev-Saravanan, Linares 1999.

Let's return to 9 ♕d2

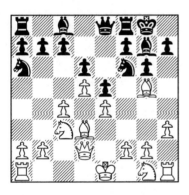

9...♗d7

9...♘d7 is also quite playable. Then 10 0-0-0 ♘dc5 11 ♘ge2 f5 was unclear in Caselas Canabas-Del Rey, Corunha 2000. This leaves 10 g4 ♘dc5 11 ♗b1 ♗d7 12 ♘ge2 b5 13 cxb5 ♗xb5 14 ♘xb5 ♕xb5 15 ♘c3 with an edge for Black in Lehmann-Nowicki, Ruhrgebiet 1998/99. Note that 12...f5 13 exf5 gxf5 14 ♘g3 here is dubious for Black but 12...♘b4 followed by ...a7-a5 with a further ...f7-f5 could be the way to go as the knight would be difficult to drive away from b4.

10 ♘ge2 ♘c5 11 ♗c2 a5 12 g4

This position can also arise after 9 g4, the difference being that Black must also consider ♕f3 instead of ♕d2.

12...b5

A theme that is characteristic of this set-up with ...♕e8 and ...♗d7. After 12...♔h8 13 f3 ♘g8 14 ♘g3 ♘e7 15 0-0-0 b5 16 cxb5 f6 17 ♗e3 ♗xb5 18 h4 ♘a4 19 ♘xa4 ♗xa4 20 h5 ♗xc2 21 ♕xc2 White achieved a slight edge in Steinbacher-Piket, Ostend 1990.

13 cxb5 ♗xb5 14 ♘g3

Others:

a) 14 ♗e3 ♗a6 15 ♗xc5 dxc5 16 ♗a4 ♕e7 (Hazai) is unclear.

b) 14 ♘xb5 ♕xb5 15 ♘c3 ♕xb2 16 ♖b1 ♕a3 17 ♗e3 ♖ab8 and again Hazai believes both sides are doing okay.

14...♗a6!?

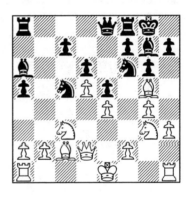

15 0-0-0 ♘fd7

Now White must address ...♘b6-c4.

16 ♗h6 f6

Hazai points out that 16...♘b6? is a blunder due to 17 ♗xg7 ♔xg7 18 ♘h5+! etc.

17 ♗xg7 ♔xg7 18 h4 ♘b6 19 g5 fxg5 20 ♕xg5 ♕d8

20...♖xf2 21 h5 is dangerous for Black.

21 ♖h2

Hazai recommends 21 ♘f5+!, activating the passive g3-knight – 21...♔h8 22 ♘e7 ♖f7 23 ♘c6.

21...♕xg5+ 22 hxg5 ♖f3 23 ♖dh1 h5

Black parts with a pawn but all his pieces will be very active and his rooks will exert a pressure on the f-file.

24 gxh6+ ♔h7 25 ♖g1 ♖af8 26 ♘d1 ♗b5 27 ♘f1 ♖3f4 28 ♘d2 ♘c4 29 ♘b1 ♘b6 30 ♘d2 ♗e2 31 ♖gg2 ♘c4 32 ♘c3

♗d3 33 ♘xc4?!

After the superior 33 ♘b3 Black can retain his slight edge with 33...♗f1! 34 ♘xc5 dxc5 35 ♖g1 ♖xf2 36 ♖xf2 ♖xf2 37 ♘d1 ♖f4 etc.

33...♗xc4 34 ♔d2 ♗f1-+ 35 ♖g1 ♖xf2+ 36 ♖xf2 ♖xf2+ 37 ♔e3 ♖xc2 38 ♖xf1 ♔xh6 39 ♖f2 ♖xf2 40 ♔xf2 ♔h5 41 ♔e3 g5 42 a3 a4 43 ♘b5 g4 44 ♘xc7 g3 45 ♔f3 ♘xe4 46 ♘a8 ♔h4 47 ♔g2 ♘f6 48 ♘b6 ♔g4 0-1

Game 43
Ivanchuk-Kasparov
Novgorod 1994

---

1 d4 ♘f6 2 c4 g6 3 ♘c3 ♗g7 4 e4 d6 5 h3 0-0 6 ♗g5 c6 7 ♗d3 e5 8 d5 ♘a6

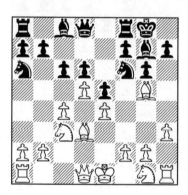

Black has concentrated on the centre and now prepares the standard queenside counterplay consisting of exchanging on d5 followed by ...♘c5 and ...a7-a5 etc.

9 ♘ge2

9 a3 is designed to inconvenience the a6-knight by expanding with b2-b4. Chernin-Kasparov, Munich 1994 continued 9...♘c5 10 ♗c2 cxd5 11 ♘xd5 ♘e6 12 ♗e3 (12 ♘xf6+ ♗xf6 13 ♗h6 ♗g7 14 ♗xg7 ♘xg7 15 ♘e2 ♗e6 with equality) 12...♘xd5 13 cxd5 ♘f4 14 ♕f3? f5 15 exf5 ♗xf5 16 ♗xf5 ♖xf5 (White is already in trouble here) 17 ♗xf4?! ♖xf4 18 ♕b3 ♕a5+ 19 ♔f1 ♖af8 20 f3 e4 21 ♖e1 ♗d4 22 ♘e2 ♕a6 0-1. Perhaps the best move here is 14 ♖h2 but, if White has to go to such

lengths, then he might have to consider playing another variation.

9...♘c5

Black has a wide range of continuations, leading to some instructive 'typical' situations:

a) 9...♘b4 10 ♗b1 cxd5 11 cxd5 a5 12 a3 ♘a6 13 ♗c2 with a slight advantage to White, who is ready to push the b-pawn.

b) 9...cxd5 10 ♘xd5 is of independent significance, 10 cxd5 ♘c5 11 ♗c2 a5 transposing to Kasparov-Kramnik, Game 45. After 10 ♘xd5 ♕a5+ 11 ♗d2 ♕d8 12 ♘xf6+ ♗xf6 13 ♘c3 ♗g7 (Schulze-Loukanov, E-mail 2000) 14 0-0 White has a pull, which leaves 10...♘c5, when 11 ♗c2 ♘e6 12 ♗e3 ♘xd5 13 cxd5 ♘f4 14 ♘xf4 exf4 15 ♗xf4 ♗xb2 was equal in the game Chernin-Zueger, Bern 1995.

c) 9...h6 10 ♗e3 cxd5 (10...♗d7 11 ♕d2 ♔h7 12 0-0 ♘h5 13 ♘g3 ♘f4 14 ♗xf4 exf4 15 ♕xf4 ♗e5 as in Jovanovic-Watanabe, Budapest 1996 provides enough compensation according to Kramnik) 11 exd5. The asymmetric recapture deserves attention and leads to less tested and unclear positions. White can play both on the queenside, trying to put the pawn majority to full use, and on the other flank in order to generate an offensive against Black's king. Now 11...♘d7!? once again deserves attention, but Ksieski-Goemann, Baunatal 2001 saw instead 11...♗d7 12 ♕d2 ♔h7 13 0-0 ♘c5 14 ♗c2 a5 15 f4 with the superior prospects for White.

d) 9...♕b6

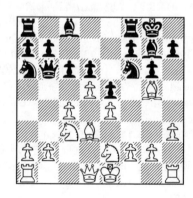

d1) 10 ♘a4 ♕a5+ 11 ♗d2 ♕d8 12 0-0 b5!? 13 cxb5 cxb5 14 ♗xb5 ♘xe4 15 ♗e3 ♖b8 16 ♘ec3 (16 ♗d3 ♘ec5 17 ♗xa6 ♗xa6 18 ♘xc5 dxc5 with excellent play for Black) 16...♘xc3 17 ♘xc3 ♘c7 with a good game for Black, Navrotescu-Motylev, Bucharest 2001. White has also done without castling, e.g. 12 ♗g5 h6 13 ♗e3 (Avrukh-Herraiz Hidalgo, Cala Galdana 1996) 13...cxd5!? 14 cxd5 ♘d7 with chances for both sides (...♘ac5 is coming) or 12 b4 ♘c7 13 g4 b5 14 g5 bxa4 15 gxf6 ♕xf6 16 ♘c3 cxd5 17 cxd5 ♗d7, Porat-Grigore, Budapest 2003, with a similar evaluation.

d2) 10 ♖b1 ♘b4 11 0-0 cxd5 12 cxd5 ♗d7 13 ♗c4 ♖fc8 14 b3 ♕a5 15 a4 a6 16 ♖a1 ♕d8 17 ♕d2 with a pull for White, Potapov-Zakharevich, Perm 1997.

d3) 10 b3 cxd5 11 cxd5 ♘c5 12 ♗c2 ♗d7 13 0-0 a5 14 a3 ♖fc8 (Chernin-Poluljahov, New York 1996) and now Poluljahov gives 15 ♖b1! with an edge for White. Black also has 14...♕c7 15 ♕d2 a4 16 bxa4 ♗xa4, again with a slight plus for White.

10 ♗c2 ♕b6

10...a5 transposes to Bazhin-Fedorov, below (Game 44). 10...cxd5 11 exd5 (11 cxd5 steers us back to Kasparov-Kramnik) and it seems that this asymmetrical structure might again hold some promise (see the comments to Ksieski-Goemann in note 'c' to 9...h6, above).

a) 11...a5 12 0-0 ♗d7 (12...♕b6 13 ♖b1 ♔h8 14 a3 ♗d7 15 b4 axb4 16 axb4 ♘a6 17 c5 with a slight advantage to White, whose pawn majority was starting to work in Kazhgaleyev-Relange, Clermont-Ferrand 2003; 12...h6!? 13 ♗e3 ♘fd7, intending ...f7-f5, is unclear) 13 ♘g3 ♕b6 (Kazhgaleyev-Zhang Zhong, Shenyang 1999) 14 ♕f3!? with the easier game for White. Instead 13...h6!? 14 ♗e3 ♘e8, unleashing the f-pawn, looks like an improvement.

b) 11...♕b6 12 b3 ♗d7 (12...a5!? 13 a3 ♘fd7 14 ♖b1 f5 15 b4 ♘a6 and Black is doing fine) 13 ♖b1 a5 14 0-0 and now 14...♖fc8 15 ♗e3 ♕d8 16 ♕d2 ♕e8 17 a4 favoured

White in Dziuba-Blehm, Lubniewice 1998, while 14...♕a6 was Christiansen-Gallagher, Reykjavik 1998. Then 15 a3!? a4 16 b4 ♘b3 17 ♘xa4 ♗xa4 18 ♗xb3 ♗xb3 19 ♕xb3 ♖fc8 20 ♗xf6 ♗xf6 21 ♖fc1 ♕xa3 22 c5 is a plus for White, with Christiansen evaluating 17 f4 exf4 18 ♖xf4 ♘h5 19 ♖h4 as balanced.

11 0-0 cxd5

Not 11...♕xb2? 12 ♖b1 ♕a3 13 dxc6 etc.

12 cxd5

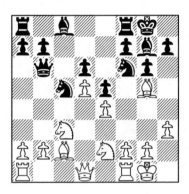

12 ♗xf6 ♗xf6 13 ♘xd5 ♕d8 14 b4 (14 ♘xf6+ ♕xf6 15 ♘c3 a5 with a level game) 14...♘e6 15 ♘xf6+ ♕xf6 16 ♕d3 (Kasparov gives 16 ♕d2 b6! with equality in *ECO*, but 16 ♕xd6?? ♖d8 spells disaster) 16...♖d8 17 ♗a4! ♕h4 (17...♗d7 18 ♗xd7 ♖xd7 19 ♖fd1 ♖ad8 20 ♖d2 ♕e7 21 ♖ad1 b6 with a very slight advantage to White) 18 a3 a6 19 ♖ad1 b5! 20 ♗b3 (20 cxb5 ♗b7 followed by ...d6-d5 and Black achieves counterplay) 20...♗b7 21 f3 ♗c6 with chances for both sides in Sotnikov-Motylev, Ekaterinburg 1996.

12...♗d7

12...♕xb2!? 13 ♖b1 ♕a3 14 ♘b5 ♕xa2 15 ♖a1 (15 ♘xd6 ♕a6! 16 ♘b5 ♕a5 and White does not have full compensation for the pawn) 15...♕b2 16 ♖b1 with equality (Kasparov).

13 ♖b1 a5 14 ♕d2

Despite the numerous options the character of the position does not change:

a) 14 a3 (Gaertner-Neumeier, Graz 2002) 14...a4 is unclear.

b) 14 ♔h2 ♖fc8 15 ♕d2 ♕d8 16 a3 a4 17 f3 ♕f8 18 g4 ♘e8 19 ♘g3 ♘c7 20 ♖g1 ♘b5 with excellent play for Black, Parker-Timoscenko, Werfen 1995.

c) 14 b3 ♖fc8 15 a3 ♕d8 16 b4 axb4 17 axb4 ♘a6 18 ♗d3 ♕e8 19 ♕d2 ♘h5 20 ♖fc1 f5 21 f3 f4 22 ♗h4 g5 23 ♗f2 ½-½, Flear-Apicella, Clichy 1995.

d) 14 ♗e3 ♖fc8 15 f3 ♕d8 16 a4 (16 a3 a4!? keeps White on his toes) 16...♕e8 17 g4 b5 18 axb5 ♗xb5 19 ♖f2 ♗d7 20 ♘g3 ♕d8 with good play for Black, Petursson-Zueger, Horgen 1994.

14...♖fc8 15 ♔h1 ♕d8

Black wants to push the b-pawn. Others:

a) 15...♗e8!? 16 f4?! exf4 17 ♘xf4 ♘fd7 with advantage to Black (Kasparov), but 16 f3 looks safer, with a level game.

b) 15...a4!? is interesting, when Black stands no worse.

16 a3 a4 17 ♖be1 ♖a6 18 ♘c1 ♕a5 19 ♗b1

19 ♘1a2 ♖b6! 20 ♘b4 ♖xb4 21 axb4 ♕xb4 with compensation according to Kasparov.

19...♘h5

19...♗b5 20 ♘xb5 (20 ♘d3!?) 20...♕xb5 21 ♗d3 ♘xd3 22 ♘xd3 ♖aa8 is assessed as unclear by Kasparov.

20 ♘d3 ♘b3 21 ♕e3 f6 22 ♗h6 g5 23 ♗xg7 ♔xg7 24 ♔h2 ♘f4 25 h4 h6 26 ♘b4 ♖aa8 27 g3 ♘g6 28 f4 ♕c5 29 f5 ½-½

White could also try 29 ♕e2!?, when Kasparov gives the position after 29...exf4 30 gxf4 ♘xf4! 31 ♖xf4 gxf4 32 ♖g1+ ♔f8 33 ♕h5 ♘d2 34 ♕xh6+ ♔e7 35 ♖g7+ ♔d8 36 ♕xf6+ ♔c7 as unclear, while he considers 29 f5 ♕xe3 30 ♖xe3 ♘e7 to be level.

Game 44
Bazhin-Fedorov
Kstovo 1994

---

1 d4 ♘f6 2 c4 g6 3 ♘c3 ♗g7 4 e4 d6 5 h3 0-0 6 ♗g5 ♘a6 7 ♗d3 e5 8 d5 c6

N.B. The actual move order was 8...♘c5 9 ♗c2 a5 10 ♕d2 c6 11 ♘ge2.

9 ♘ge2 ♘c5 10 ♗c2 a5

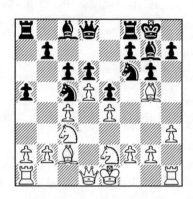

Black reinforces the position of the c5-knight, retaining the tension in the centre.

11 ♕d2

Or 11 a3!? cxd5 12 cxd5 (this time 12 ♘xd5 is harmless, e.g. 12...♘e6 13 ♗e3 ♘xd5 14 cxd5 ♘f4 15 ♗xf4 exf4 16 ♗xf4 ♗xb2 as in Neff-Seeman, Tallinn 1997, when 17 ♖a2 would have maintained the balance) 12...a4 13 ♗xf6?! (13 0-0 transposes to the next main game) 13...♕xf6 14 ♘xa4 ♘xa4 15 ♗xa4 (Mikhalevski-Gulko, Beersheba 1993) 15...♕g5 16 g3 f5 17 ♘c3 fxe4! 18 ♘xe4 ♕d8! 19 ♗c2 ♕b6! 20 ♖b1 ♗f5 21 ♕e2 ♖ac8! 22 ♗d3 ♕d4 23 0-0 ♗xh3 24 ♖fd1 ♕b6 25 ♘g5 with chances for both sides according to Mikhalevski in *ECO*. However, 22...♕a5+!? wins a pawn and looks better.

11...cxd5

Other lines are also okay for Black.

a) 11...♕b6 12 0-0 ♗d7 13 ♗e3 cxd5 14 cxd5 a4 15 ♖ab1 ♖fc8 16 f3 ♘h5 17 ♔h2 ♕d8 18 a3 ♗f6 19 g4 ♘g7 20 g5 ♗e7 21 ♘g3 ½-½, Johansen-Lanka, Adelaide 1990.

b) 11...♗d7 12 ♘g3 cxd5 13 ♘xd5 ♘e6 14 ♘xf6+ ♗xf6 15 ♗xf6 ♕xf6 16 ♕xd6 ♖fd8 17 ♕b6 ♕e7 18 ♕b3 b5 with more than sufficient compensation for the pawn, Geldyeva-Kachiani Gersinska, Istanbul 2000.

12 exd5!?

This decision to avoid symmetry is certainly

an interesting one. Let's have a look at the plans available with this structure. As was mentioned earlier White has two strategies here, namely queenside expansion or aggression on the other flank with f2-f4.

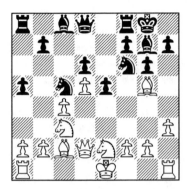

Note that 12 cxd5 ♗d7 13 0-0 transposes to the next main game, Kasparov-Kramnik, and 12 ♗xf6 ♗xf6 13 ♘xd5 ♗g5 14 ♕c3 ♗e6 causes Black no problems. 12 ♘xd5 is simply wrong in view of 12...♘fxe4 13 ♗xe4 ♘xe4 14 ♗xd8 ♘xd2 15 ♔xd2 (15 ♗e7 ♘xc4 16 ♗xf8 ♔xf8 with attractive compensation) 15...♖xd8 16 ♖he1 f5 with an edge for Black.

12...♗d7 13 0-0 ♕b6 14 ♔h1

White can also try:

a) 14 ♘g3?! ♖fc8 15 ♗e3 ♕a6 (15...a4!?) 16 ♕e2 ♘e8 17 f4 f5 18 ♘b5 (Bareev-Gelfand, Linares 1994) and now 18...e4! 19 ♘d4 ♘d3! 20 b3 (20 ♗xd3 exd3 21 ♕xd3 ♕xc4 favours Black) 20...♘b4!? with the idea of 21...♘d5! 22 cxd5 ♗d4 or 21...a4, Gelfand preferring Black.

b) 14 ♖ab1 ♕a6 followed by ...b7-b5.

c) Gelfand gives 14 ♗e3 ♕a6 15 b3 ♖fc8 and the b-pawn is again ready for action.

14...♘h5

Black wants to play ...f7-f5 with a strong centre. Obviously he cannot take on b2 as 14...♕xb2?? loses to 15 ♖ab1 ♕a3 16 ♕e1 ♘a6 17 ♗xf6 ♗xf6 18 ♖b3 ♕c5 19 ♘e4.

15 ♗e3

15 g4 ♘f4 gave Black counterplay in Parker-Bjornsson, London 1994.

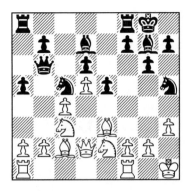

15...♕a6?!

15...♕b4 16 b3 f5 deserves a try, with an excellent position for Black.

16 b3?!

White misses his chance, which comes in the form of 16 ♗xc5! dxc5 17 ♗a4 with a pleasant position, e.g. 17...♗xa4 18 ♘xa4 ♖ac8 19 ♖ad1 with advantage to White.

16...f5 17 f3 ♖ac8 18 a4

18 g4 is preferable (on the next move, too), e.g. 18...♘f6 19 gxf5 gxf5 20 f4 and the battle continues with approximately equal prospects.

18...b6

Right square, wrong piece – 18...♕b6 is correct.

19 ♖ab1 ♖ce8

Perhaps 19...f4 is an improvement, when Black's game looks the more comfortable.

20 g4 ♘f6 21 gxf5 gxf5 22 f4 ♕c8 23 ♖g1 ♔h8 24 ♖g2 ♘fe4 25 ♘xe4 ♘xe4?

Helping only White. Black should play 25...fxe4 26 ♖xg7 ♔xg7 27 fxe5 ♖xe5 (not 27...dxe5 28 ♗h6+ ♔h8 29 ♕g5 ♖f7 30 ♖g1 ♗f5 31 ♗g7+ ♔g8 32 ♕h6) 28 ♗d4, limiting White to a modest but definite lead.

26 ♗xe4

The exchange of the passive light-squared bishop for the c5-knight is advantageous to White. Moreover the c5-knight defended the d7-bishop, which is important in some variations.

26...fxe4 27 ♖bg1?

After 27 ♖xg7! ♔xg7 28 fxe5 ♖xe5

(28...dxe5 29 ♗h6+ ♔h8 30 ♕g5 ♖f7 31 ♖g1)
29 ♗d4 White regains the exchange and keeps the initiative.

27...♖g8 28 f5?!

White is in danger of paying the price for his numerous inaccuracies. This time both 28 ♖g3 and 28 ♗xb6 retain the dynamic equilibrium.

28...♗xf5 29 ♗xb6 ♗xh3 30 ♖g3 ♖ef8 31 ♘c3 ♖f4 32 ♗e3?

After 32 ♘b5 Black cannot play 32...♖h4 because 33 ♕g5 ♖h6 34 ♕xh6 ♗xh6 35 ♖xg8+ ♕xg8 36 ♖xg8+ ♔xg8 37 ♗xa5 is terrible, but 32...♕d7 is a big improvement, when White still has work to do.

32...♖h4-+ 33 ♗g5 ♖h5 34 ♖1g2??

Hastening the end, although 34 ♕h2 e3 followed by ...e3-e2 should be enough to decide in Black's favour.

34...♗xg2+ 35 ♔xg2 ♕f5 36 ♕e3 ♗h6 0-1

Game 45
Kasparov-Kramnik
Las Palmas 1996

---

1 d4 ♘f6 2 c4 g6 3 ♘c3 ♗g7 4 e4 d6 5 h3 0-0 6 ♗g5 ♘a6 7 ♗d3 e5 8 d5 c6 9 ♘ge2 ♘c5 10 ♗c2 a5

N.B. The game actually went 10...cxd5 11 cxd5 a5 12 0-0.

11 0-0 cxd5

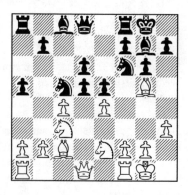

Remember that White can recapture in

three quite different ways from the diagram.

12 cxd5

The most popular and principled response, the chief aim being to retain what stability there is in the centre by keeping the symmetrical structure, thus denying Black unnecessary counterplay. White maintains his territorial advantage and, by keeping his pawn on e4, makes Black's often desirable ...f7-f5 difficult to successfully achieve. On the other hand, Black has no weak points and can now look to the queenside for ideas.

a) After 12 ♘xd5 ♘e6 Black seeks to unpin and to gain immediate counterplay. Winning the d6-pawn promises White nothing, e.g. 13 ♘xf6+ ♗xf6 14 ♗xf6 ♕xf6 15 ♕xd6 ♖a6 16 ♕a3 ♘f4!? 17 ♘xf4 exf4 with compensation according to Hazai. Instead White should drop back to e3: 13 ♗e3 ♘xd5 and now 14 cxd5 ♘c5 15 ♘c3 b6 16 ♖c1 ♗d7 17 ♖e1 f5 was unclear in Socha-Novacek, E-mail 1999, while 14 exd5 ♘c5 15 ♕d2 f5 16 f3 b6 17 ♘c3 f4 was good for Black in Caselas Cabanas-Baron Rodriguez, La Coruna 1996.

b) 12 exd5 ♗d7 13 ♘g3 ♕b6 14 b3 (14 ♖b1 ♖fc8 15 ♕f3 ♘e8 is about even) 14...♖fc8 15 ♖b1 ♘e8 16 ♕d2 f5 17 ♗h6 ♘f6 18 ♗xg7 ♔xg7 with excellent play for Black, Seel-Djukic, Oropesa del Mar 2001.

12...♗d7

Black is looking to step up the pace on the queenside with ...b5-b4. Other continuations:

a) 12...♕b6 13 ♗e3 (13 ♖b1 – or 14 ♖b1 – leads us back to Ivanchuk-Kasparov, Game 43, above) 13...♗d7 (not 13...♕xb2?? 14 ♗xc5 dxc5 15 ♖b1 ♕a3 16 ♖b3) 14 a3 ♖fc8 (Craig-Raijmaekers, Correspondence 1994/98) 15 ♖b1!? ♕d8 16 b4 axb4 17 axb4 ♘a6 18 ♗d3 ♕e8 19 ♕d2 ♘h5 20 ♖fc1 f5 and Black has counterplay. This is the same idea as in Flear-Apicella in Ivanchuk-Kasparov (Game 43), note 'c' to White's 14th move, but White's dark-squared bishop stands on e3, not the g5-square.

b) 12...b5!? 13 ♘xb5 (13 a3 a4 14 ♕d2 ♗d7 with chances for both sides) 13...h6 14

♗e3 (14 ♗xf6 ♕xf6 with compensation) 14...♘fxe4 15 f3 ♕b6 16 fxe4 ♕xb5 and Black has earned equality.

13 a3

In the event of 13 ♔h1 Black has 13...b5 14 f3 ♕e8 15 a3 b4, or 13...h6!? 14 ♗e3 b5, with good play in either case. 13 a4 seriously compromises the queenside dark squares, e.g. 13...♕b6 14 ♔h1 ♘h5 15 g4 (Pyda-Socko, Krynica 1998) 15...h6! with an edge for Black. 15 ♖b1 improves, with a level game.

13...a4

Directed against 14 b4. Also possible is 13...h6 14 ♗e3 a4 (14...b5?! 15 b4) 15 ♕d2 ♔h7 with chances for both sides.

14 ♕d2

White has a wide range of continuations:

a) 14 ♘c1?! looks passive and therefore gives Black nothing to solve, e.g. 14...h6 15 ♗e3 ♕a5 (15...b5!? 16 ♕d2 is interesting) 16 ♖b1 ♖fc8 was Yermolinsky-Manion, Chicago 1995, given as unclear by Yermolinsky in *ECO*. Black was also doing okay after 14...♕e8 15 ♘1e2 b5 16 ♘g3 h6 17 ♗e3 ♕b8 18 ♘a2 in Dreev-Kazhgaleyev, Lucerne 1997.

b) 14 g4 is – for a change – unjustified here. Potapov-Neumann, Pardubice 2002, continued 14...♕b6 15 ♗e3 (15 ♔g2 h6 16 ♗e3 ♕a6 with advantage to Black) 15...♕a6 16 ♘g3 ♖fc8 with an edge for Black, while 14...h6!? 15 ♗e3, Roobol-Lane, Netherlands 2000 should also have favoured Black after 15...♘h7.

c) 14 ♔h1 prepares a kingside attack. Then 14...♕e8 15 ♕d2 (Bareev-Arduman, Heraklio 1997) 15...♘h5!? and 14...♕e7 15 ♕d2 ♖fc8 16 ♖ab1 b5, Ivanisevic-Tratar, Istanbul 2003 are unclear, while 14...b5!? 15 ♘g3 h6 16 ♗e3 (Roos-Kilgus, Ansfelden 2003) 16...♘h7 followed by ...♕h4 looks nice for Black.

However, the most popular choice is 14...♕b6 15 ♖b1 and:

c1) 15...♖fc8!? 16 f4 exf4 17 ♘xf4 ♘e8 and now instead of 18 ♘d3 with an advantage to White, Psakhis-Kuznetsov, St Petersburg 2002 saw 18 ♕f3?! f6!?, the forcing 19 ♘d3 ♘xd3

20 ♗xd3 fxg5 21 ♕f7+ ♔h8 22 ♕xd7 ♘f6 23 ♕b5 ♕d4 giving Black excellent counterplay due to the threat of ...♘h5 and the weak dark squares on the kingside.

c2) 15...♔h8 16 ♘g3 ♘g8 17 ♗e3 ♕a5 18 ♕d2 (Psakhis-Movsziszian, Balaguer 1998) 18...b5 and 16 g4 ♘g8 17 ♘g3 ♕a6 18 h4 ♕c4, Dreev-Fedorov, Maikop 1998 are both well balanced.

d) 14 f3 ♕a5 15 g4 h6 16 ♗d2, Motoc-Costantini, Plovdiv 2003 and now 16...♖fc8 with good play for Black.

14...♕b6 15 ♖ab1 ♖fc8

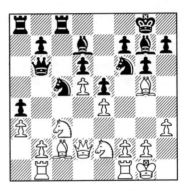

16 ♘g3

In reply to 16 ♔h1 Black plays 16...♗e8 to facilitate ...♘fd7. Then 17 ♗h6 ♘fd7 18 ♘g3 ♕d8 (18...♗xh6 19 ♕xh6 ♕d8 is also okay) 19 ♗xg7 ♔xg7 as in Mititelu-Planinec, Bath 1973 is given as equal in *ECO*, while 19 ♗g5 ♕b6 20 ♗h6?! ♕d8 21 ♗g5 ♗f6! 22 ♗e3 ♘b6 23 ♕e2 ♗g5! favoured Black in Yermolinsky-Kasimdzhanov, Wijk aan Zee 1999.

16...♕d8

16...♖c7 17 ♗e3 and the pin is unpleasant (Kramnik).

17 ♗h6 ♗xh6 18 ♕xh6 ♕f8 19 ♕e3 ♗e8 ½-½

Black has a good position with no weak points, and an attempt by White to generate activity with f2-f4 runs the risk of neglecting the dark squares after ...exf4. In fact this assessment refers to all positions after White's 16th move.

Summary

The Makogonov System should not cause Black any serious problems. Indeed Black has several interesting plans available that can lead to complex play with mutual chances. In the case of 6 ♗e3 Black is able to drum up good counterplay with ...c7-c5 (Game 32). Meanwhile ...e7-e5 (Game 33) also merits further study. After 6 ♗g5 both 6...♘bd7 (Game 34) and the variations involving ...c7-c5 followed by ...e7-e6 and ...exd5 (Game 36) are fine for Black. The most popular plan is still ...♘a6 followed by ...e7-e5, which is discussed in Games 39-45.

1 d4 ♘f6 2 c4 g6 3 ♘c3 ♗g7 4 e4 d6 5 h3 (D)
5...0-0 6 ♗g5
      6 ♘ge2 (*Game 31*)
      6 ♗e3
            6...c5 (*Game 32*)
            6...e5 (*Game 33*)
6...♘a6
      6...♘bd7 (*Game 34*)
      6...c5 7 d5
            7...b5 (*Game 35*)
            7...e6 (*Game 36*)
      6...h6 (*Game 37*)
      6...♕e8 (*Game 38*)
7 ♗d3
      7 g4 (*Game 39*)
      7 ♘ge2 c6 8 g4 (*Game 40*)
7...e5 (D)
      7...♕e8 (*Game 41*)
8 d5 c6
      8...♕e8 (*Game 42*)
9 ♘ge2 ♘c5 10 ♗c2 (D)
      10...♕b6 (*Game 43*)
      10...a5
            11 ♕d2 (*Game 44*)
            11 0-0 (*Game 45*)

5 h3

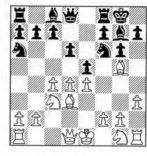

7...e5

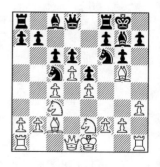

10...♗c2

CHAPTER FOUR

Averbakh System: 5 ♗e2 0-0 6 ♗g5 without ...c5

1 d4 ♘f6 2 c4 g6 3 ♘c3 ♗g7 4 e4 d6 5 ♗e2 0-0 6 ♗g5

Although the great grandmaster Yuri Averbakh's contribution to the development of ideas and analysis was undoubtedly the biggest, the variation named after him is not his invention. The first game was E.Andersen-Carls, Hamburg Olympiad 1930, but play transposed to the Modern Benoni. Unfortunately this idea remained unnoticed for over twenty years when, 1951, it appeared in two of Ivkov's games. After his duel with W. Niephaus (FRG-Yugoslavia Match), where Ivkov met with some problems playing with Black, he used this system very successfully with White against Udovcic in the Yugoslav championship.

The Averbakh System is directed against Black's counterplay involving ...e7-e5 and ...f7-f5. In most variations in this system Black must refrain from the otherwise natural push of the e-pawn (6...e5? 7 dxe5 dxe5 8 ♕xd8 ♖xd8 9 ♘d5) or decide to insert ...h7-h6, but this nudge of the h-pawn serves to weaken Black's kingside and, after ♗f4/e3, White can step up the pressure with ♕d2.

The Averbakh has been much more popular than other systems discussed in this book. As for those strong players whose relevant games are worth close study, the most signifi-

cant practitioners are Uhlmann, I.Farago, Kachiani Gersinska, Yakovich, Cs.Horvath and Petursson (it was also played by Polugaevsky), while Bareev and Yusupov also tend to include it in their armoury.

In this chapter we will discuss those plans for Black that are not connected with ...c7-c5 (see Chapter 5).

Game 46
Yusupov-Tseshkovsky
Oviedo Rapidplay 1993

1 d4 ♘f6 2 c4 g6 3 ♘c3 ♗g7 4 e4 d6 5 ♗e2 0-0 6 ♗g5

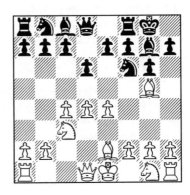

6...♘c6

This move is more typical of systems such

as the Sämisch or those lines with ♗g2 or ♗d3. The point is to exploit the fact that White's bishop is already committed and does not protect d4. However, as we will see, Black falls short of achieving his aim.

7 ♕d2

7 d5 is the knee-jerk reaction to the arrival of the knight on c6. After 7...♘e5 White has tried more than one way of dealing further with the enemy knight. The over-aggressive 8 f4 hits the knight again but is rather loosening, and after 8...♘ed7 9 ♘f3 c6 Black obtains counterplay by attacking White's exposed centre. Occasionally the e3-square might prove weak, e.g. 10 ♕c2?! ♘g4 with an edge for Black in Neyman-Teichgraeber, Germany 2001. Another move is 8 ♕d2, e.g. 8...c6 9 ♘f3 ♘xf3+ 10 ♗xf3 ♗d7!? 11 0-0 a6 12 h3 ♖c8 13 ♖fd1 cxd5 14 cxd5 b5 (Miralles-Piket, Cannes 1990) when 15 ♖ac1!? is a shade better for White. Finally there is the immediate 8 ♘f3, when 8...♘xf3+ 9 ♗xf3 h6 10 ♗e3 e6 11 0-0 (11 ♕d2!? ♔h7 12 h4 with initiative) 11...♖e8 (Korchnoi-Kasparov, Madrid 1988) 12 ♕d2 favours White according to Hazai, and 8...h6 9 ♗d2 ♘fd7 10 ♕c2 ♘xf3+ 11 ♗xf3 ♘e5 12 ♗e2 also failed to deny White an edge in Delaune-Karklins, Philadelphia 1992.

7...♘d7

7...e5 is not to be recommended here because after 8 dxe5 Black has to take with the knight in order to avoid 8...dxe5 9 ♕xd8 ♖xd8 10 ♘d5, which saw Black doomed in Lundin-Holst, Sweden 1999. Unfortunately for Black after 8...♘xe5 9 ♖d1 White threatens c4-c5. However, there is a playable alternative in 7...h6!? 8 ♗e3 (8 ♗xh6 ♗xh6 9 ♕xh6 ♘xd4 is harmless for Black) 8...♔h7 when ...e7-e5 is then a genuine possibility.

8 ♘f3 a6?! 9 0-0 f6

Black's position is rather passive.

10 ♗h6 e5 11 ♗xg7 ♔xg7 12 ♖ad1 ♖e8 13 ♕e3 ♘f8

13...exd4 14 ♘xd4 ♘xd4 15 ♕xd4 is hardly promising for Black but at least White

has no direct threats.

14 dxe5 fxe5 15 c5

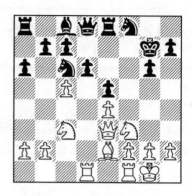

Only a brief appraisal of the diagram position is necessary to establish that White has a clear advantage, with more space, more active pieces and the superior pawn structure.

15...♗g4 16 cxd6 cxd6 17 ♖d2 ♘e6 18 ♖fd1 ♘ed4

Black is lacking one tempo in the desire to successfully place a knight on d4.

19 ♘xd4 exd4 20 ♕g3?!

20 ♕d3 is stronger, when 20...♗e6 21 ♘d5 ♖c8 sees Black struggling to hold on.

20...♗e6 21 ♘d5 ♗f7 22 ♗f3 ♖e5 23 h4 ♗xd5 24 exd5 ♘e7 25 ♗g4 ♕b6 26 ♗e6 ♖f8 27 b3 ♘f5

27...♘xd5 28 ♖xd4 ♖xe6 29 ♖xd5 secures a level game.

28 ♗xf5

28 ♕g4!? looks preferable, with the more pleasant game for White.

28...♖exf5 29 ♖xd4 ♖xf2 30 ♕xf2 ♖xf2 31 ♔xf2 h5 ½-½

Game 47
Eingorn-Chiburdanidze
USSR Championship, Tallinn 1980

1 d4 ♘f6 2 c4 g6 3 ♘c3 ♗g7 4 e4 d6 5 ♗e2 0-0 6 ♗g5 c6

Black wants to play ...a7-a6 and ...b7-b5 with the dual threats of chasing White's knight away from the defence of the e4-pawn with

...b5-b4 and the dismantling of White's centre with ...bxc4, ♗xc4 ...d6-d5 etc. 6...a6 tends to transpose.

7 f4

A very logical response to Black's rather slow plan. Moreover a thematic reaction to f2-f4 in related positions is for Black to challenge the centre and the dark squares with ...c5, but now this involves the loss of a tempo. White has also tried 7 ♕d2 a6 8 ♗h6 b5, when 9 ♗xg7 ♔xg7 10 a3 (Crouch-McShane, Edinburgh 1997) 10...bxc4!? 11 ♗xc4 d5 sees Black able to achieve his objective, the subsequent 12 exd5 cxd5 13 ♗e2 ♘c6 being unclear. In Moskalenko-Gunawan, Knjazevac 1988 White left his bishop on h6 with 9 a3, when 9...bxc4 10 h4 ♗xh6 11 ♕xh6 e5 12 dxe5 dxe5 13 h5 gave him a crushing attack. However, Black has an important improvement in 11...♕b6! 12 h5 ♕xb2 13 ♖c1 g5! with a good game.

7...a5

7...d5!? is worth a look, the point being that 8 e5 ♘e4!, as in Hermesmann-Gutman, Hamburg 1999, keeps Black well on level terms. Consequently White plays instead 8 ♗xf6 and now:

a) 8...exf6!? 9 exd5 cxd5 10 cxd5 (10 ♘xd5!? is the only try for advantage, although Black is not without counterplay, e.g. 10...♖e8 11 ♘f3 ♗e6 12 ♘e3 with an edge for White) 10...♕d6 11 ♕d2, Korchnoi-Miroshnichenko, Halkidiki 2002, and now 11...♖e8!? 12 ♘f3 ♗h6 results in excellent compensation.

b) 8...♗xf6 9 e5 ♗g7 10 ♘f3 (Rogers-Arakhamia Grant, Sydney 1991) 10...dxc4!? 11 ♗xc4 ♘d7 12 0-0 (12 e6 ♘b6 13 exf7+ ♔h8 14 ♗b3 ♗g4 with counterplay) 12...♘b6 13 ♗b3 a5 offers both sides sufficient play. White might consider 9 cxd5 cxd5, e.g. 10 ♘xd5 ♗g7 11 ♘f3 ♘c6 12 ♖c1 e6 13 ♘e3 ♘xd4 14 e5 ♘xf3+ 15 ♗xf3 with a small edge.

8 ♕d2 h6

8...e5 9 fxe5 dxe5 10 d5 (Sorin-Zapata, Americana 1997) 10...♘bd7!? is a shade better for White.

9 ♗h4 e5 10 fxe5 dxe5 11 d5

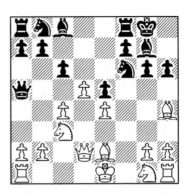

11...b5?!

11...cxd5!? 12 cxd5 ♘bd7 13 ♘f3 with the easier game for White.

12 cxb5?!

12 ♗xf6! doesn't look appropriate but is in fact the way to a big advantage after 12...♗xf6 13 cxb5 ♗h4+ (13...cxb5 14 ♘xb5) 14 g3 ♗g5 15 ♕d3 cxb5 16 h4 ♗f6 17 ♕xb5 etc.

12...g5 13 ♗f2?!

13 ♗g3!? cxb5 14 ♗d3 (14 b4!?) 14...b4 15 ♘d1 ♘h5 was played in Amura-Brustman, Azov 1990, and now 16 ♘e3!?, intending to meet 16...♘d7 with 17 ♘f5, favours White.

13...cxd5?

Black goes the wrong way – 13...cxb5! invites 14 ♗c5 but then after 14...b4 15 ♘b5 ♘a6 16 ♗xf8 ♗xf8 17 ♘f3 ♘xe4 Black has easily enough for the exchange.

14 exd5 ♖d8 15 ♗c4 a6

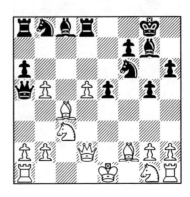

16 bxa6?!

Too accommodating. 16 ♗c5!? is preferable.

16...♗xa6 17 ♗b3 ♘c6 18 ♘ge2 ♘b4

Black is about to regain the pawn with an accompanying initiative.

19 0-0 ♘bxd5 20 ♕c2 ♘b4

20...♘xc3!? 21 bxc3 ♗d3 with a clear advantage for Black.

21 ♕g6 ♖d7 22 ♘e4 ♔h8 23 ♕f5 ♘xe4 24 ♕xe4 ♗d3 25 ♕f3 e4 26 ♕h3 f5 27 ♗e3? ♗xe2 28 ♖xf5 ♕a6 29 ♖xg5 ♖d3??

Missing 29...♖ad8! etc.

30 ♖xg7! ♔xg7 31 ♕g3+ ♕g6 32 ♕c7+??

White returns the favour by taking the losing check rather than 32 ♕e5+ ♔h7 (32...♕f6 33 ♗xh6+ ♔g6 34 ♕xe4+ ♔xh6 35 ♕xa8 with chances for both sides) 33 ♕e7+ ♔h8 34 ♕xb4 ♖ad8 with equality.

32...♔h8 33 ♗f4 ♖xb3 34 ♗e5+ ♔g8 35 ♖c1 ♘d5 36 ♕d7 ♖d3 0-1

Game 48
Portisch-Nunn
Linares 1988

---

1 d4 ♘f6 2 c4 g6 3 ♘c3 ♗g7 4 e4 d6 5 ♗e2 0-0 6 ♗g5 ♘bd7

By 'blocking' the d-file with the knight Black makes ...e7-e5 a realistic (sound) possibility, while ...c7-c5 might be another option.

7 ♕d2

The main line. Obviously White has tried other approaches:

a) 7 d5 ♘c5 8 ♕c2 c6 9 ♘f3 cxd5 10 cxd5 ♗d7 11 ♖c1 ♖c8 with a good game for Black, Uhlmann-Geller, Moscow 1967.

b) 7 ♕c1!? is an invention of GM Lev Alburt, who was first successful with it against Zapata in New York in 1980. The idea subsequently became more popular after his famous game with Kasparov at the Lucerne Olympiad in 1982, thus beginning a theoretical discussion. By using c1 on which to line up the queen and bishop – rather than the more logical looking d2 – White anticipates Black's adoption of the Benko-style plan involving ...b7-b5 and the opening of the queenside, the reasoning being that White's a1-rook will then be protected. Of course this is fine if Black obliges, but in other variations the queen is left artificially posted. Black can push the e-pawn but the most interesting test of Alburt's idea is 7...c5 8 d5 b5 (8...♕a5 9 ♗d2 a6 10 ♘f3 ♖e8 11 0-0 ♖b8 12 ♖e1 with a plus for White, Alburt-Zapata, New York MCC 1980) 9 cxb5 a6 10 a4 ♕a5 11 ♗d2 axb5 12 ♘xb5 (Kasparov gives 12 ♗xb5 ♗a6 13 ♘ge2 ♕b4! 14 f3 ♘e5 15 0-0 ♘c4 with an initiative for Black) 12...♕b6 (Alburt-Kasparov, Lucerne 1982) 13 f3!? (already assessed by Kasparov as favouring White) 13...♗a6 (13...e6 14 dxe6 fxe6 15 ♗e3 ♗a6 16 ♘h3 ♖fc8 17 0-0 with an edge for White) 14 ♘h3 ♖fc8 15 0-0 c4+ 16 ♗e3 ♕b7 17 ♘d4 ♘c5 18 ♖a3 with a slight advantage to White.

c) In the case of 7 f4 e5 8 dxe5 dxe5 9 ♘f3 h6 10 ♗h4, as in Agzamov-Yurtaev, USSR 1982, both sides can be content, although White's dark-squared bishop might be a cause for concern for Black. The most principled response is 7...c5, when 8 e5!? cxd4 9 ♕xd4 ♘e8!? 10 ♘f3 f6! provides Black with enough counterplay, e.g. 11 exf6 ♘exf6 12 ♕e3 ♕b6 ½-½, Agzamov-Mestel, Rakovica, Belgrade 1982.

This leaves 8 d5 with the following position:

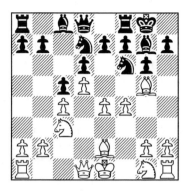

You won't be surprised to see Black's counterplay in the diagram position revolving around the thrust of the b-pawn – the question is when and how. In F.Portisch-Sinkovics, Hungary 1986 Black first inserted 8...h6 9 ♗h4 before pushing: 9...b5 10 cxb5 a6, and now 11 ♘f3!? axb5 12 e5 dxe5 13 fxe5 ♘h7 is unclear. 8...♕a5 9 ♕d2 a6 10 ♘f3 b5 (Forintos-Stein, Kapfenberg 1970) 11 ♕c2!? is also interesting.

Of course the meaty move is the immediate 8...b5!?, jumping straight into Benko waters. Note that here Black's approach appears entirely justified thanks to White's weakened dark squares caused by following up ♗g5 with the advance of the f-pawn. Meanwhile White must also pay attention to the defence of e4. Play has continued as follows – 9 cxb5 a6:

c1) 10 ♘f3 axb5 11 e5 (11 ♗xb5 ♘xe4 12 ♘xe4 ♕a5+ 13 ♘c3 ♗xc3+ 14 bxc3 ♕xb5 15 ♔f2 ♘f6 16 ♗xf6 exf6 with an edge for Black) 11...b4 12 ♘b5 (Rugman-Sakaev, USSR 1987) 12...dxe5! 13 fxe5 ♘e4 14 ♗f4 ♘b6 is great for Black.

c2) 10 bxa6 ♕a5 11 ♕d2 ♗xa6 12 ♘f3 (12 ♗xa6!? ♕xa6 with compensation) 12...♖fe8, Aguirre-Steinbaum, Villa Gesell 1971, and now 13 ♗xa6 ♕xa6 14 ♕e2 e6 15 ♕xa6 ♖xa6 with excellent compensation for the pawn. Black can also try 12...♖fb8!? here.

7...c6

An original plan. This time Black prepares to push with ...d6-d5, not concerned about the

reply e4-e5 because the knight can then jump into e4, attacking two pieces. In the meantime the text affords Black some flexibility for, depending on how White continues, all of 8...e5, 8...♕a5 and 8...a6 will be options.

Black has also played:

a) 7...c5 and now 8 ♘f3 cxd4 9 ♘xd4 ♘c5 10 f3 gives White the usual advantages associated with the Maróczy set-up, namely the more solid pawn structure and the greater presence in the centre. This tends to be enough for a modest but long-term edge, e.g. 10...♘e6 11 ♗e3 ♘xd4 12 ♗xd4 and now 12...♘e8 13 ♗xg7 ♔xg7 14 0-0 favoured White in Kramnik-Depner, Mainz 2001, while 12...♗e6 13 0-0 ♘d7 (Kallai-Schiffer, Wiesbaden 1992) 14 ♗xg7!? ♔xg7 15 f4 looks very good for White.

b) 7...a6 8 ♖d1!? c5 9 ♘f3 cxd4 10 ♘xd4 ♘c5 11 f3 ♘e6 12 ♗e3 ♘xd4 13 ♗xd4, Van Beek-Ribshtein, Apeldoorn 1999 is similar, again with advantage to White.

8 ♘f3

Continuing with development, White is willing to allow Black his planned advance in the centre. A couple of more aggressive moves have been tried.

a) 8 f4?! proved unsuccessful in Colon-Geller, Las Palmas 1980 after 8...e5 9 fxe5 dxe5 10 d5 ♘c5 11 ♗f3 ♕a5 12 ♖c1 cxd5 13 cxd5 b5 14 ♗e3 b4 15 ♗xc5 ♕xc5 and White's plan had seriously backfired. 9 dxe5!? dxe5 10 ♘f3 improves.

b) After 8 h4 Black can transpose to Browne-Fedorowicz, Game 50 with 8...e5 9 d5 ♘c5 10 f3 or decide on 8...c5 9 d5 b5!?, losing a tempo but judging that h2-h4 less than helps White, e.g. 10 cxb5 a6 (Nagl-Wahls, Vienna 1991) 11 ♘f3 ♕a5 with compensation. An alternative here is 9...h5.

8...d5 9 exd5

Taking this way is more flexible than 9 cxd5 cxd5, when White has to take again because 10 e5 ♘e4 is fine for Black, e.g. 11 ♕e3 ♘xg5 12 ♕xg5 ♘b8 (12...f6!?) 13 b4 (13 0-0!?) 13...a6 14 0-0 ♘c6 15 a3 h6 16 ♕e3

♗g4 with approximate equality in Seirawan-Boersma, Amsterdam 1983. Thus play continues 10 exd5 ♘b6 11 ♘e5 ♘bxd5 (11...♘fxd5!?) 12 ♗f3 ♗e6 with equality (*ECO*) in Gaprindashvili-Erenska-Radzewska, Bad Kissingen 1982, or 11 0-0 ♘bxd5 12 ♖fe1 ♘xc3 13 bxc3 ♘e4 14 ♕e3 ♘xg5 15 ♘xg5 e6 16 ♖ab1 b6 17 f4 ♗b7 with a level game in Moskalenko-Piket, Lvov 1988.

9...cxd5 10 0-0 ♘e4

Forcing, and preferable to the alternatives, which fail to deliver Black equality.

a) 10...a6 11 a4 dxc4 (11...♘e4 12 ♘xe4 dxe4 13 ♘e1 ♕e8 14 ♘c2 e5, Lukacs-Douven, Wijk aan Zee B 1988, and now 15 ♗h6!? favours White) 12 ♗xc4 ♘b6 (12...b6 13 ♖fe1 ♗b7, Karason-Nijboer, Reykjavik 1998, and now 14 d5!? secures White the lead) 13 ♗b3 ♕d6 14 a5 (Lukacs-Vukic, Tuzla 1981) 14...♘bd5 15 ♖fe1 ♗e6 16 ♘a4 with advantage to White (Gelfand).

b) 10...dxc4 11 ♗xc4 ♘b6 12 ♗b3 ♗f5 (12...♗d7 13 d5 ♘c8 14 ♖fe1 ♘d6 15 ♘e5, Farago-Martinovic, Dieren 1990, and 12...♘bd5 13 ♖fe1 ♗e6 14 ♗h6, Rashkovsky-Kupreichik, Vilnius 1980, with an edge for White in both cases) 13 ♖fe1 ♖c8 14 h3 (14 ♖ac1!?) 14...♘bd5 (Uhlmann-Guliev, Dresden 1994) 15 ♗xf6! ♘xf6 16 ♕e3 looks strong, but 14...a5!? limits White to a slight advantage.

11 ♘xe4 dxe4 12 ♘e1 f6

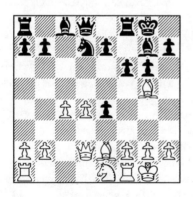

12...♘f6 13 ♘c2 ♕b6!? is an edge to White but 13...b6 14 ♖ad1 ♗b7 15 d5 was very poor

for Black in Uhlmann-Gross, Leipzig 1982.

13 ♗e3

White can also trade bishops: 13 ♗h6 ♗xh6 14 ♕xh6 e5 15 ♕d2 (15 ♘c2!? ♕e7 16 ♖ad1 f5 17 ♕e3 b6, Dokhoian-Guseinov, Klaipeda 1988, and now 18 f3!? secures White the more pleasant game) 15...f5 (15...exd4!? 16 ♕xd4 f5 17 ♖d1 ♕f6 18 f4 ♕xd4+ 19 ♖xd4 ♘c5 20 ♘c2 ♗e6 21 ♖fd1 ♘a4 with an equal ending) 16 d5 ♘f6 (16...f4!? with chances for both sides) 17 d6 (17 ♕c3 ♕e7 18 ♖d1 f4 is unclear) 17...f4 (17...♗e6!? 18 c5 b6 with counterplay) 18 c5 ♗e6, Gelfand-Glek, USSR 1985 is given as unclear in *ECO*.

13...e5 14 ♖d1

14 f3 exd4 15 ♗xd4 ♘c5 16 ♖d1 (Stohl-Gross, Stary Smokovec 1991) 16...♘e6! 17 ♘c2 ♘xd4 18 ♘xd4 f5 19 fxe4 fxe4 and Black's active bishop pair compensates for the weakness of the e4-pawn. However, after 15 ♕xd4 Black has problems.

14...exd4

Weaker is 14...♕e7 15 dxe5 ♘xe5 16 ♕d5+, Goehring-Rogozenko, Germany 1998, when the onus is on Black to demonstrate compensation for the pawn.

15 ♗xd4 ♕e7 16 ♘c2 f5 17 ♗xg7

After 17 f4!? ♗xd4+ 18 ♘xd4 ♘c5 19 ♕e3 ♘e6 20 ♘b5 b6 21 ♖d5 White's game is the more comfortable.

17...♕xg7 18 ♘d4 ♘e5 19 ♕a5 ♔h8 20 ♕d5 ♕f6 21 c5?!

The last chance of fighting for an advantage is with 21 f4!? exf3 22 ♗xf3 ♖d8 23 ♕c5.

21...♖d8 22 ♕b3 f4 23 ♖fe1 ♗g4 24 ♗xg4 ♘xg4 25 ♖xe4 ♕h4 26 ♕f3

Not 26 ♕xb7?? ♕xh2+ 27 ♔f1 f3! etc.

26...♕xh2+ 27 ♔f1 ♕h5 28 ♔g1 ♕h2+ 29 ♔f1 ♕h5 30 ♔g1 ½-½

Game 49
Petursson-Gallagher
San Bernardino 1992

1 d4 ♘f6 2 c4 g6 3 ♘c3 ♗g7 4 e4 d6 5 ♗e2 0-0 6 ♗g5 ♘a6

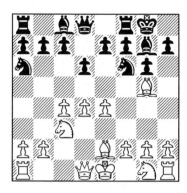

Yet another example of ...♘a6 (leaving the c8-bishop unobstructed) rather than ...♘bd7 (monitoring e5). Which is better? In many variations they tend to lead to the same positions, especially after 7...e5 8 d5. However, in a few lines there are some differences. First, after ...♘bd7 Black must contend with 7 f4!?, which was discussed in the notes to Portisch-Nunn, earlier, and secondly, 6...♘bd7 does not fit in well with 7...c5 as after 8 d5 Black does not have ...e7-e6 due to the weakness of the d6-pawn. Finally, in some variations, especially if White keeps the tension in the centre, it is important that the knight defends c7.

7 ♕d2 e5 8 d5

8 ♘f3 ♕e8 9 dxe5 (9 0-0?! exd4 10 ♕xd4 ♘xe4 11 ♕xe4 ♗xc3! – Hazai, while 9 d5 ♘h5 transposes to Game 60) 9...dxe5 10 ♖d1 ♘c5 (10...c6 11 ♕d6) 11 ♗xf6 ♗xf6 12 ♘d5 ♗d8 13 ♕e3 ♘e6! 14 ♘xe5 c6 15 ♘c3 ♗b6 16 ♕h6 ♗c7 (16...f5!?) 17 ♘g4 f5 18 exf5 ♘f4 19 fxg6 hxg6 20 ♘e3 ♖f7 21 ♕g5 ♗f5 22 g3? ♘h3 23 ♕h4 ♘xf2 24 ♔xf2 ♗b6 with a considerable advantage to Black in Uhlmann-J.Polgar, Aruba 1992.

8...♘c5 9 f3

9 b4?! leads to a dynamic queenless middlegame in which Black's chances are better: 9...♘cxe4 10 ♘xe4 ♘xe4 11 ♗xd8 ♘xd2 12 ♗xc7 ♘e4! 13 f3 ♘c3 and Black is believed to have a clear advantage here, although matters are rather complicated. 14 ♗xd6 ♖d8!? (Wyrwich-Hoppe, Ruhrgebiet 1999) 15 ♗e7! ♖d7

16 d6 (16 ♗c5 e4 17 ♖c1 b6 18 ♗e3 ♘xa2) 16...e4 17 ♘h3 a5 offers Black good chances, while 14...♖e8 15 ♔f1 e4 16 ♖e1 ♗f5 17 g4 ♗d7 produced a dynamic balance in Portisch-Kluger, Budapest 1957.

9...h6

9...♕d7 looks artificial, e.g. 10 g4 ♘e8 11 ♘h3 (11 h4 f5 12 h5 fxg4 13 fxg4 ♘f6 14 hxg6 hxg6 15 ♗xf6 ♖xf6 16 0-0-0 with an edge for White in Petraki-Voiska, Athens 1990) 11...f6 12 ♗e3 ♘a4 13 ♘xa4 ♕xa4 14 b3 (14 ♘f2!?) 14...♕d7 15 0-0-0 with a plus for White, Ulms-Hund, Altenkirchen 2003.

10 ♗e3

Obviously not 10 ♗xh6?! ♘fxe4 with a typical motif of both the King's Indian and Benoni. Black not only regains the pawn but also activates his pieces, especially the dark-squared bishop. After 11 fxe4 ♕h4+ 12 g3 ♕xh6 Black had an excellent game in Uksti-Kulaots, Polva 2000. Nor is 10 ♗h4 to be recommended, e.g. 10...a5 11 g4 ♗d7 12 ♗f2 (there is nothing left to stay for on the h4-d8 diagonal, from where the bishop must eventually leave) 12...♘h7 13 h3 f5 with counterplay in Kovacs-Sinkovics, Hungary 1995.

10...♘h5

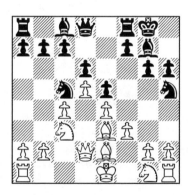

Or 10...♗d7 11 h4 h5 12 b4 (12 0-0-0!?) 12...♘a4 (Kogelov-Juferov, Correspondence 1986) 13 ♘xa4!? ♗xa4 14 ♗d3 with advantage to White.

11 0-0-0

11 g3!? ♔h7 12 0-0-0 ♕e7 (12...♕e8 13

♖e1 b6 14 ♗d1 ♗d7 15 ♘ge2 a6 16 g4 ♘f6 17 ♘g3 ♘g8 18 h4, Averbakh-Zaitsev, USSR 1970, and 12...♗d7 [Milov-Liberzon, Israel 1994] 13 ♗xc5! dxc5 14 f4 ♘f6 15 ♘f3 should be avoided by Black) 13 ♖e1 ♗d7 14 ♗d1 (14 ♗xc5!? dxc5 15 f4 ♘f6 16 ♘f3 with advantage to White) 14...c6 15 ♘ge2 ♘f6 16 ♗c2 (16 h4!?) 16...cxd5 17 exd5, Schulte-Bosboom, Bielsko Biala 1988, and now 17...b5! 18 cxb5 a6 with adequate gambit play.

11...♔h7

White has to solve the problem of how to develop his g1-knight.

12 ♗d3

An alternative plan involves a future ♘h3, e.g. 12 g4 ♘f4 13 h4 a5 14 ♘h3 a4 (14...♘xh3 15 ♖xh3 ♗d7 16 h5 g5 17 ♖hh1 ♕b8 18 b3 ♖d8 with equal chances in Tarjan-Grefe, USA Championship, Mentor 1977) 15 ♘xf4 (15 ♔c2 a3 16 b3 ♘a6, Kelecevic-Lputian, Sarajevo 1983, was unclear according to *ECO*) 15...exf4 16 ♗xf4 a3 17 b3 ♕f6 (17...♗d7 is less accommodating), Oral-Babula, Pardubice 1991, and now 18 ♗xh6!! is crushing.

12...♘xd3+ 13 ♕xd3 f5 14 ♘ge2 ♗d7

14...♘f4 is weak – 15 ♘xf4 exf4 16 ♗d4 (16 ♗xf4!?) 16...fxe4 17 ♘xe4 ♗f5 18 ♗xg7 ♔xg7 19 ♕d4+ ♔g8 20 ♖he1 with a big advantage, Loncar-Dueball, Germany 1997. However, 14...♕h4!? is worth a try in order to block the kingside. Indeed direct action works out fine for Black, e.g. 15 g3 fxe4! 16 ♘xe4 ♕h3 17 ♖hf1 ♘f6 18 ♘2c3 a5 19 ♘xf6+ ♖xf6 20 ♘e4 ♖f7 21 ♖f2 with a level game, or 15 ♘g3 f4 16 ♘xh5 ♖xh5 17 ♗f2 ♕g5 18 h4 ♕e7 and Black is doing fine. Consequently White should look to the other flank for an advantage, and 15 ♔b1 followed by c4-c5 should be enough to keep him slightly ahead.

15 exf5 gxf5 16 g4 e4 17 fxe4 fxg4 18 ♖df1?!

Missing 18 ♘g3! ♘xg3 19 hxg3 ♖f3 20 ♕d2 and Black is in trouble.

18...♗e5 19 ♕d2 ♖f3 20 ♘g3

Again White has stronger, this time in the shape of 20 ♖xf3 gxf3 21 ♘d4 etc.

20...♕h4 21 ♘ce2 ♖af8 22 ♖e1 ♘g7 23 ♗d4 ♕f6 24 ♗xe5 dxe5 25 ♔b1 h5 26 ♘c1 h4 27 ♘ge2 ♕g6 28 ♘c3 ♖f2 29 ♕d1 ♕g5 30 ♘d3 ♖g2 31 ♖e2 ♖xe2 32 ♕xe2 ♘h5 33 ♘c5 ♗c8 34 ♘b5 g3 35 hxg3?

35 ♘xc7 is called for.

35...♘xg3 36 ♕g2 ♕g4?!

Now it is Black's turn to come up with a series of poor moves. Better is 36...♕e3 37 ♖xh4+ ♔g8 etc.

37 ♘e6 ♖f2?

37...♖f4 wins, e.g. 38 ♘xf4 ♘xh1 39 ♕xh1 (39 ♕xg4 ♗xg4 40 ♘d3 h3) 39...exf4.

38 ♕xf2?

After 38 ♖xh4+ ♕xh4 39 ♕xf2 ♕xe4+ 40 ♔c1 ♗xe6 41 dxe6 ♘f5 the battle starts afresh.

38...♕xe4+ 39 ♕c2 ♕xc2+ 40 ♔xc2 ♘xh1 41 ♔d2 ♔g6 42 ♔e3 h3 43 ♔f3 ♔f5 44 ♘c5 ♔g5 45 ♘e4+ ♔h4 46 ♘xc7 ♗g4+ 47 ♔e3 h2 48 ♘e8 ♘g3 49 ♘f2 ♘f1+ 50 ♔d3 ♔g3 51 ♘f6 ♗f3 52 d6 ♔xf2 53 d7 h1♕ 54 d8♕ e4+ 55 ♔c3 e3 56 ♕f8 ♔g1 0-1

Game 50
Browne-Fedorowicz
USA 1984

---

1 d4 ♘f6 2 c4 g6 3 ♘c3 ♗g7 4 e4 d6 5 ♗e2 0-0 6 ♗g5 ♘bd7 7 ♕d2 e5 8 d5 ♘c5 9 f3 a5

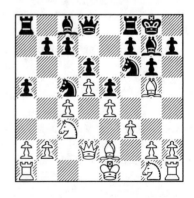

The key position, from which we can see that White plans to launch an offensive on the kingside while Black has already made arrangements on the other flank.

10 h4

Consistent in that it forms part of White's strategy, although 10 0-0-0 looks better (see below). With the text White judges that he might be able to get in h4-h5 without the preparatory g2-g4, thus saving a tempo.

a) In fact 10 g4 &d7 11 h4 c6 12 h5 cxd5 13 cxd5 a4 14 ⓓh3 ♕a5 15 ♖b1 b5 16 ⓓf2 b4 17 ⓓcd1 b3 18 a3 ♕xd2+ 19 ♔xd2 gave White a slight advantage in Kramnik-Ljubojevic, Monte Carlo 1999. Black can try the immediate 10...c6, e.g. 11 ⓓh3 cxd5!? 12 cxd5 &d7 13 ⓓf2 ♕b8 14 &b5 (14 h4!?) 14...♖c8 15 h4 ⓓe8 16 &e3 ⓓc7 17 &xd7 ⓓxd7 18 h5 b5 19 ⓓe2 ½-½, Kinsman-McShane, Edinburgh 1996. In Yakovich-Kindermann, Munich 1991 White captured on d5 with the knight, 11...a4 12 ⓓf2 &d7 13 h4 cxd5 14 ⓓxd5 ⓓe6 15 &xf6 &xf6 16 g5 &g7 17 ⓓg4 &c6 18 ⓓdf6+ &xf6 19 ⓓxf6+ ♔g7 resulting in an interesting struggle. Perhaps White can improve on this with 16 ⓓxf6+!? ♕xf6 17 ♕xd6 &c6 18 ⓓd3 ♖a5 19 g5 ♕g7 20 ♖d1, when Black does not have enough for the pawn.

b) 10 0-0-0!? shifts the king over to the queenside while simultaneously doubling on the d-file, this latter factor usually prompting Black to let the d6-pawn go in return for some activity on the queenside, e.g. 10...&d7 (10...a4 11 h4 a3 12 b3 &d7 13 h5, Ros Eskisabel-Bernal Moro, Spain 1990, and now 13...h6!? with a pull for White) 11 h4 (11 g4 c6 12 dxc6 &xc6 13 ♕xd6 ♕xd6 14 ♖xd6 ⓓe6 was Krueger-Summermatter, San Bernardino 1992, when 15 h4 was enough to secure White the advantage) 11...♕e8 12 g4 &a4 (after 12...c6 13 dxc6 &xc6 14 ♕xd6 ⓓe6 15 ⓓd5 &xd5, as in Krizsany-F.Portisch, Harkany 1998, 16 exd5 would have left Black with inadequate compensation) 13 ⓓxa4 ♕xa4 14 ♔b1 ♕b4 15 ⓓh3 with an edge for White,

Palatnik-Konig, Cattolica 1993.

10...c6

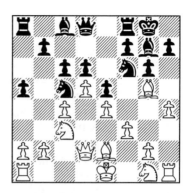

After 10...♕e8 Black fails to equalise, e.g. 11 ⓓb5 ♕d7 12 g4 h5 13 &xf6 &xf6 14 gxh5 ♕e7 (Ghinda-Georgiev, Baile Herculane 1982) 15 0-0-0 with the more pleasant game for White, or 11 g4 h5 12 0-0-0 hxg4 13 &xf6 &xf6 14 fxg4, when both 14...♕e7 15 g5 &g7 16 ⓓf3 f5 17 gxf6 ♖xf6 18 ♖dg1, Lerner-Georgiev, Moscow 1985, and 14...&g7 15 h5, Meins-Timagin, Groningen 1997, are great for White.

11 g4

11 h5 is obviously the consistent follow-up to White's play thus far, e.g. 11...cxd5 12 cxd5 (12 ⓓxd5!?) 12...&d7 13 ⓓh3 a4 14 ⓓf2 ♕a5 15 hxg6 fxg6 16 ⓓd3 ♖fc8. This is evaluated as unclear in *ECO* but it seems White has chances of obtaining an advantage, e.g. 17 ⓓxc5 ♖xc5 18 &xf6 &xf6 19 ♕h6 &e8 20 ♕xh7+ ♔f8 (Whitehead-Tarjan, USA 1983) 21 ♖b1 and Black has problems. With this in mind 16...ⓓh5 should be an improvement for Black, hoping to put the f8-rook to good use. Then 17 ⓓxc5 ♕xc5 is level.

11...cxd5

11...a4 is possible. Retaining the tension in the centre sometimes has its advantages as the e2-bishop stays closed in, but in this case Black's counterplay revolves around efforts on the queenside with ...♕a5, &d7 and ...b7-b5, so sooner or later Black will be forced to take on d5 anyway. Therefore play is likely to continue 12 h5 ♛a5 13 ♘h3 cxd5 14 cxd5 etc. Note that Black cannot play 13...b5? in view of 14 cxb5 cxd5 15 ♗xf6 ♗xf6 16 ♘xd5 ♗h4+ 17 ♔d1 with a decisive lead – Fedorowicz.

12 cxd5 a4

12...♗d7 13 ♘h3 (or 13 ♖c1 ♛e8 14 ♘h3 b5 15 ♘f2 b4 16 ♘cd1 with a slight advantage to White, Kabatianski-Neverovsky, Podolsk 1990) 13...b5 14 ♘xb5 (14 ♘f2!? with a plus for White) 14...♘fxe4 15 fxe4 f6 16 ♗e3 ♘xe4 17 ♛c2 f5, Diaz-Perez, Cuba 1997 is given as unclear in *ECO*.

13 ♘h3 ♗d7 14 ♘f2 ♛a5 15 h5

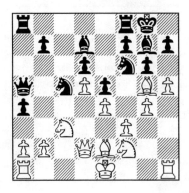

Less accurate is 15 ♘cd1 ♛xd2+! 16 ♗xd2, Wilder-Gallagher, Saint John 1988, allowing 16...h5! with chances for both sides.

15...b5

Black has also tried a couple of other moves here.

a) 15...a3 16 b3 ♖fc8 17 ♘cd1 (Seirawan-Ivanovic, Niksic 1983) 17...♛xd2+ 18 ♔xd2 h6 19 ♗e3 with advantage to White.

b) With 15...♖fc8 Black deprives himself of the defensive resource (after h5xg6 ...f7xg6) ...♖f7 to protect h7, but after 15...♖ac8 White has 16 ♘b5 ♛b6 17 ♘a3 with an advantage. Thus (after 15...♖fc8) play can develop as follows: 16 hxg6 fxg6 17 ♗xf6 ♗xf6 18 ♛h6 ♗e8 19 ♛xh7+ ♔f8 20 ♖b1 b5. Then 21 ♛h6+ ♗g7 22 ♛d2 (Alburt-Spraggett, Taxco 1985) 22...b4 23 ♘cd1 b3 24 a3 ♛xd2+ 25 ♔xd2 ♗f6 gives Black some compensation for the pawn, but White has an interesting

attempt at advantage in 21 g5!?, when 21...♗g7 walks into trouble, e.g. 22 ♘g4 b4 23 ♘h6 ♗f7 24 0-0! ♛b6 (24...bxc3 25 ♘xf7 c2 26 ♖bc1 etc.) 25 ♔g2 with the idea of pushing the f-pawn with a strong attack. Instead the circumspect 21...♖c7! 22 ♛h4 ♗g7 23 0-0 b4 24 ♘cd1 b3 25 a3 leads to an unclear situation, e.g. 25...♛d2 26 ♘c3 ♖f7 27 ♔g2 ♗d7 28 ♖fd1 ♛e3.

Returning to 15...♖fc8, 16 ♖b1 ♗e8 was seen in Bykhovsky-Ye Jiangchuan, Belgrade 1988, and now White has 17 hxg6!? fxg6 18 f4!? b5 19 fxe5 dxe5 20 ♗xf6 ♗xf6 21 ♛h6 with initiative, e.g. 21...♖a7 22 g5 b4 23 gxf6 bxc3 24 0-0 cxb2 25 ♗g4 etc.

16 ♘cd1

Solid – which cannot be said of the alternatives:

a) 16 ♘d3? b4 17 ♘d1 ♘fxe4 18 fxe4 ♘xe4 and White was on his way to an early demise in Facchini-Gutierrez, Bratislava 1993.

b) 16 ♗h6?! was a dubious attempt to trouble Black's king in Bialas-Bero, Correspondence 1991. With 16...♗xh6! 17 ♛xh6 a3 Black could have generated strong counterplay and, in doing so, guarantee the better chances, e.g. 18 g5 ♘xh5 and there is no clear way for White to continue his attack, whereas the situation on the queenside is tragic. You might have noticed here that 18...axb2?? loses in view of 19 gxf6 bxa1♛+ 20 ♘fd1 ♛1xc3+ 21 ♘xc3 ♛xc3+ 22 ♔f1 etc.

c) 16 ♔f1 ♖a7 (16...♖fc8!? and 16...b4!? are unclear) 17 ♔g2 (Petursson-Belotti, Novi Sad 1990) 17...b4 18 ♘cd1 ♗b5 19 ♗xb5 ♛xb5 with chances for both sides.

16...♛xd2+

The ending that results from this exchange is a bit better for White but Black has no convenient way to avoid it. 16...♛b6 (Whitehead-Benjamin, Pasadena 1983) 17 ♗e3!? ♖fc8 18 ♘d3 ♛c7 19 ♘1f2 ♘xd3+ 20 ♗xd3 is awful for Black, while 16...b4 17 ♘e3 (White owns the c4-square) and 16...♖fc8 17 ♛xa5 ♖xa5 18 h6 ♗h8 19 ♗d2 ♖a7 20 ♘d3 ♘xd3+ 21 ♗xd3, Mirumian-Balogh, Zagan 1997, both fail to deny White a definite advantage.

The picture is also pretty grim for Black after 16...♕a7, when 17 ♖c1 ♖ac8 18 ♕b4 followed by ♘c3 is very unpleasant for Black due to the problems with his queenside pawns. And 17 ♗h6! is even more effective because, in comparison with 16 ♗h6, White can count on a few tempi more! Now 17...♗xh6 is too late, e.g. 18 ♕xh6 ♕a5+ 19 ♔f1! ♕d8 20 ♔g2 b4 21 ♘e3 ♖b8 22 ♖h2! and White is ready with ♖ah1, ♘f1-g3, hxg6 and g4-g5, a plan against which Black has nothing useful. 17...♗xg4!? 18 ♗xg7 ♔xg7 was Babu-Thipsay, Indian Championship 1987, and now 19 ♘xg4! ♘xg4 20 ♕g5!, given by Thipsay & Tilak, is strong.

17 ♗xd2 ♖fc8 18 ♘d3 ♘xd3+ 19 ♗xd3 a3 20 ♖b1 axb2 21 ♖xb2 ♘e8 22 ♔e2

22 ♘c3 is strong.

22...f5?

Opening the g-file is only grist to White's mill. After the superior 22...♖a3 (directed against ♘c3) 23 ♗b4 ♖a4 24 a3 ♗f6 25 ♖c2 ♖xc2+ 26 ♗xc2 ♖a8 27 ♗d3 ♗e7 28 ♘c3 ♘c7 29 ♖c1 ♖a7 30 ♖b1 a draw was agreed in Wagner-Britton, London 1994.

23 gxf5 gxf5 24 ♖g1 ♔f7 25 ♘c3 ♘f6 26 ♗xb5 ♖cb8 27 h6 ♗f8 28 ♖gb1 fxe4 29 fxe4 ♗xb5+ 30 ♖xb5 ♖xb5 31 ♖xb5 ♔g6 32 ♖b6 ♖a3 33 ♖c6?!

A loss of a tempo. White should play 33 ♔d3.

33...♗xh6 34 ♖xd6 ♔f7 35 ♖c6

35 ♖e6 meets with 35... ♗f4 and Black has counterplay, and 35 ♗xh6 ♖xc3 36 ♖e6 ♖h3 37 ♗d2 ♘xe4 is unclear.

35...♗xd2 36 ♔xd2 h5 37 ♖c7+ ♔f8 38 ♔e3?! h4 39 ♔f3 h3 40 d6?

Missing 40 ♖c8+ ♔e7 41 ♖c7+ ♔e8 42 ♖c6 ♘h5 43 ♔f2 ♘f4 with an edge for Black.

40...♔e8 41 ♖e7+

41 d7+ ♔d8 42 ♖c6 ♘h5 etc.

41...♔f8??

So near and yet so far! 41...♔d8 42 ♖c7 ♘e8 is decisive.

42 ♖c7 ½-½

1 d4 ♘f6 2 c4 g6 3 ♘c3 ♗g7 4 e4 d6 5 ♗e2 0-0 6 ♗g5 h6

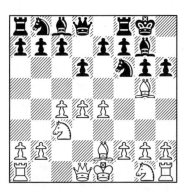

Driving away the dangerous bishop is obviously desirable but of course has its downside, most notably the fact that after a retreat on the c1-h6 diagonal White will double his influence there with ♕d2, attacking the h6-pawn and causing a certain amount of potential inconvenience for Black in the process. Additionally, the pawn cover in front of Black's king has also been irrevocably – albeit only slightly – damaged.

7 ♗e3 ♘bd7

Alternatives other than 7...c5?! and 7...e5, which are dealt with in the following main games, are:

a) 7...♘a6 8 ♕d2 ♔h7 and now 9 h4!? is rather blunt but quite interesting. A feasible continuation is 9...c5 10 d5 ♘g4 11 ♗xg4 ♗xg4 12 f3 ♗d7 13 h5 g5 14 ♘ge2 ♘c7 (Moskalenko-Volke, Groningen 1990) when 15 ♕d3!? favours White, e.g. 15...♖b8 16 f4 g4 (16...gxf4 17 ♗xf4 ♔h8 18 ♕e3 ♔h7 19 e5) 17 0-0 b5 18 e5+ ♔g8 19 b3 bxc4 20 bxc4. After the more conservative, unambitious 9 h3 Black should seek to exploit the disharmony of White's forces with 9...e5 10 d5 ♘c5!?, e.g. 11 f3 as in Sanjuan Morigosa-Mozo Diaz,

Aviles 2001, when Black could have obtained excellent play with 11...♘h5, concentrating on the weakened dark squares on the kingside. 11 ♕c2 is better, with chances for both sides.

b) 7...♘c6 8 d5 ♘e5 9 f4 ♘ed7 10 ♘f3 (10 ♘h3 ♖e8 11 0-0 ♘f8 12 ♘f2 with a slight advantage to White in Dydyshko-Chiburdanidze, Ivano Frankovsk 1982) 10...c6 (10...c5 11 ♕d2 ♘g4 12 ♗g1 a6 13 h3 ♘gf6, Kartsev-Baranov, Russia 2000, and now 14 ♗h2! is an edge for White) 11 0-0 a6 12 ♘d4 (12 ♕e1!?) 12...c5 13 ♘c2 with advantage to White in Jasnikowski-Borkowski, Lublin 1988.

Returning to the position after 7...♘bd7 it is not difficult to guess what White's most obvious move is.

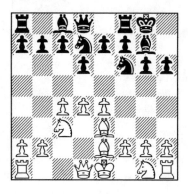

8 ♕d2

Consistent. White has also tried:

a) 8 f3 ♔h7!? (8...e5 9 d5 ♘h5 10 ♕d2 ♔h7 11 0-0-0 ♘c5 12 g4 ♘f4 13 ♗f1, Larrea-Gutierrez, Medellin 1996, and now 13...a5 14 h4 a4 15 ♔b1 earns White a plus) 9 ♕d2 c5 10 dxc5 ♘xc5 11 e5 ♘fd7 12 exd6 exd6 13 ♘h3 ♘b6 14 ♘f4 ♘ca4 15 ♘xa4 ♘xa4 16 ♗d4 ♗xd4 17 ♕xd4 ♕a5+ 18 ♔f2 ♕e5 with equality, Korchnoi-Schebler, Netherlands 2001.

b) 8 h3 c5 (8...e5!?) 9 d5 b5 (9...♕a5 10 ♕d2 a6 11 a4 ♔h7 12 ♘f3 b5 13 cxb5 axb5 14 ♗xb5 ♘xe4! 15 ♘xe4 ♕xb5 16 axb5 ♖xa1+ 17 ♔e2 ♖xh1 with an excellent game for Black (Lanka), Boudiba-Garcia Paolicchi, Manila 1992, although more typical of this

kind of position is the prophylactic 12 ♖a3!, which looks stronger) 10 cxb5 ♕a5 (10...a6 11 bxa6 ♕a5 12 ♕d2 ♘h7 13 ♖b1, Polak-Nevednichy, Budapest 2000, and here 13...♗xa6 14 ♗xa6 ♕xa6 15 ♘ge2 secures White a plus) 11 ♕d2 (11 ♗d2!?) 11...♔h7 12 ♖c1 (12 g4!? followed by g4-g5) 12...a6 13 b6 (13 bxa6!? is of course possible, when Black has sufficient compensation) 13...♘xb6 14 ♕c2 (14 ♘f3 ♘a4 15 ♗d3 ♘xc3 16 bxc3 ♖b8 ½-½, Luft-Roos, Germany 2000) 14...e6 15 ♗d2 ♖b8 16 b3 c4 with a position considered to favour Black but, after the simple 17 ♘f3, favours White. Note that 16...exd5?? 17 ♘b1, the disastrous course of Yusupov-Shirov, Moscow 1992, is a blunder to remember.

8...c5 9 ♖d1

After the effective 9 d5 the d7-knight hinders the generation of counterplay with ...e7-e6.

9...cxd4 10 ♗xd4 a6 11 ♘f3 b6 12 ♗e3

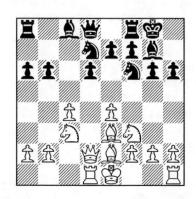

White has two heavy pieces on the d-file and he wants to engineer a timely push of the e-pawn. After 12 e5 dxe5 13 ♘xe5 ♘xe5 14 ♗xe5 ♕xd2+ 15 ♖xd2 ♗e6 and 12 0-0 ♗b7 13 ♕c2 ♖c8 14 e5 dxe5 15 ♘xe5 e6 White can claim only a tiny advantage.

12...♗b7

Black has two more promising continuations in 12...♔h7 13 e5 dxe5 14 ♘xe5 ♕c7, when he is fine, and 12...♘g4:

a) After the sharpest 13 ♗f4 Black can settle for a slight disadvantage in the case of 13...♔h7 14 0-0 ♗b7 15 h3 ♘ge5 16 ♘xe5 ♘xe5 17 ♗e3 ♖c8 18 b3 b5 19 f4 or jump into the complexities of 13...♘c5 14 e5 ♗b7 etc.

b) 13 ♗d4 and now 13...♘gf6!?, inducing e4-e5 (see the notes to White's 12th move, above), or 13...e5 14 ♗e3 ♗b7 15 0-0 ♘df6 16 ♘e1 ♘xe3 17 ♕xe3 with chances for both sides (Black has the bishop pair in return for the weakness on d5).

13 ♗xh6 ♘c5

After both 13...♘xe4 14 ♘xe4 ♗xe4 15 h4 ♘f6 16 h5 and 13...♗xe4 14 h4 ♖c8 (14...♘c5 15 h5 gxh5 16 g4) 15 h5 White has strong threats on the kingside.

14 ♗xg7 ♔xg7 15 ♘g5! ♘cxe4 16 ♘cxe4 ♗xe4 17 ♘xe4 ♘xe4 18 ♕d4+ ♘f6 19 g4 e5

Black sacrifices a pawn in the hope of drumming up an initiative in the ending. After 19...♔g8 20 h4 ♕d7 21 h5 White has a clear advantage.

20 ♕xd6 ♕xd6 21 ♖xd6 b5 22 h3 ♖fd8

22...♖fc8!? 23 b3 ♘e4 looks preferable.

23 ♖xd8 ♖xd8 24 cxb5 axb5 25 ♗xb5 ♘d5 26 a4 ♖b8 27 ♔d2 ♘c7 28 ♔c3 ♘xb5+ 29 axb5 ♖xb5 30 b4 f5 31 ♖g1

31 ♔c4 ♖b8 32 gxf5 gxf5 33 b5 is the simplest route to the full point.

31...♔f6 32 ♔c4 ♖b8 33 b5 e4 34 gxf5 gxf5 35 f4?!

Again missing the easiest continuation – this time 35 ♖b1 ♔e5 36 b6 wins very easily.

35...♖c8+?!

Black must try 35...exf3, when some accuracy is required of White in order to earn the win: 36 ♖f1 ♔e5 37 ♖xf3 ♔e4 38 ♖f1 f4 39 ♔c5 f3 40 b6 ♔e3 41 ♔c6 ♖c8+ 42 ♔d6 ♖d8+ 43 ♔c7 ♖d2 44 ♖b1 ♖c2+ 45 ♔d7 ♖d2+ 46 ♔e7 f2 47 b7 f1♕ 48 ♖xf1 ♖b2 49 h4 ♖xb7+ 50 ♔f6 etc.

36 ♔d5 ♖c2 37 b6 ♖d2+ 38 ♔c6 ♖c2+ 39 ♔d7 ♖d2+ 40 ♔c7 ♖c2+ 41 ♔b8 e3 42 h4 ♖c4 43 b7 ♖xf4 44 h5 e2 45 ♔c7 ♖c4+ 46 ♔d6 ♖b4 47 ♔c6 ♖b3 48 h6

♖c3+ 49 ♔b6 ♖b3+ 50 ♔c7 ♖c3+ 51 ♔d8 ♖d3+ 52 ♔e8 ♖b3 53 h7 e1♕+ 54 ♖xe1 ♔g7 55 ♖e7+ ♔h8 56 ♔d8 f4 57 ♔c8 f3 58 b8♕ 1-0

Game 52
Keene-Sigurjonsson
Hastings 1975/76

---

1 d4 ♘f6 2 c4 g6 3 ♘c3 ♗g7 4 e4 d6 5 ♗e2 0-0 6 ♗g5 h6 7 ♗e3 c5?!

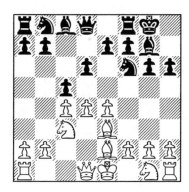

In reply to the push of the c-pawn d4-d5 is a standard response, but the insertion of 6...h6 and 7 ♗e3 gives White two logical and strong continuations in 8 dxc5 and 8 e5!, which is dealt with in the next main game, Onischuk-Forster.

8 dxc5 ♕a5

8...dxc5 and now 9 e5 ♕xd1+ (9...♘fd7!?) 10 ♖xd1 ♘g4 11 ♗xc5 ♘xe5 12 ♘d5 ♘bc6 13 f4 ♘g4 14 h3 ♘f6 15 ♗f3 ♗f5 16 ♘e2, Kachiani Gersinska-Peng, Azov 1990, and 9 ♕xd8 ♖xd8 10 ♗xc5 ♘c6 11 ♘f3 b6 12 ♗a3 a5 (Yakovich-Blees, Ostend 1993) 13 e5! ♘g4 14 ♘d5 are good for White.

9 ♗d2

9 ♕d2 dxc5 10 ♗xh6 leads to sharp play with chances of both sides, e.g. 10...♖d8 11 ♕e3 ♗xh6 12 ♕xh6 ♘xe4 13 ♖c1 ♘c6 14 ♘f3 ♘d4 15 h4, Seirawan-Timman, Tilburg 1990, which *ECO* gives as unclear.

9...♕xc5

Better than 9...dxc5 10 e5, and now:

a) 10...♘e8 11 ♘f3 (11 f4!? followed by ♘f3 looks okay) 11...♘c6 12 0-0 ♗g4 13 ♕c1 ♗xf3 (13...h5) 14 ♗xf3 ♘xe5 15 ♗xb7 ♖b8 16 ♗e4! ♘xc4 17 ♗xh6 ♗xh6 18 ♕xh6 e6 (18...♖xb2 19 ♘d5) 19 ♖ad1 and White was already on her way to victory in Levitina-Matveeva, Manila 1992, when there followed 19...♘xb2 20 ♗xg6! fxg6 21 ♖d7 ♖f7 22 ♕xg6+ ♖g7 23 ♕xe6+ ♔h8 24 ♕e5! ♕b4 25 ♘d5 ♕b5 26 ♕h5+ ♔g8 27 ♘e7+ ♔f8 28 ♕h8+ ♔f7 29 ♘c6+ ♔e6 30 ♘xb8 1-0 .

b) 10...♘h7 11 f4 ♘c6 12 ♘f3 and now both 12...f6 13 ♘h4! and 12...♕d8 13 0-0 ♘d4 (Rashkovsky-Temirbaev, Kujbyshev 1986) 14 ♘xd4!? ♕xd4+ 15 ♔h1 spell trouble for Black, leaving 12....♗f5. Then 13 ♘h4!? was an edge for White in De Winter-Hernandez, Mexico 1999, while 13 ♘d5!? is interesting, but the simple 13 0-0 is equally playable, e.g. 13...♖ad8 14 ♘d5 (14 ♕e1 ♖d7 15 ♕f2 ♕d8 16 ♗e3 ♘d4 17 ♖fd1 ♘xe2+ 18 ♕xe2 b6 19 ♖xd7 ♕xd7 20 ♖d1 ♕b7, Beliavsky-Yurtaev, Elista 1998, and now 21 h3!? with the more pleasant game for White according to Beliavsky) 14...♕a6 15 a3! b6 16 b4 ♕b7 17 b5 ♘b8 (Volzhin-Kovalev, Gistrup 1996) 18 ♕e1! e6 19 ♘e3 with a massive advantage for White. Nor does 17...♘d4 improve here in view of 18 ♘xd4 cxd4 19 ♗b4 etc. Black should play 15...e6 16 ♕e1 ♕a4 17 ♘e3 ♗d3 18 ♗xd3 ♖xd3 19 ♗c3 with a slight advantage to White.

10 ♘f3

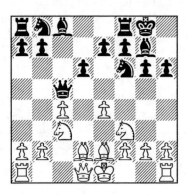

10...♗g4

The most frequently played move, although Black has two decent alternatives.

a) 10...♘bd7!? 11 0-0 a6 (11...♘e5!?) 12 ♖c1 ♕c7 (Kinsman-Van den Doel, Wrexham 1997) 13 ♘d5 with advantage to White.

b) 10...♘c6 looks fine for Black. 11 0-0!? ♘d4 12 ♘xd4 ♕xd4 13 ♕c2 ♕e5 14 ♔h1 (Tarjan-Vukic, Novi Sad 1975) 14...♗d7 is level. After 11 h3 ♘d4 (11...♘e5!?) 12 ♘xd4 ♕xd4 13 ♕c2 ♗e6 (13...♗d7!?) 14 ♗e3 ♕e5 15 f4 ♕a5 16 0-0 ♖fc8 the situation was even in Horvath-Kotronias, Gausdal 1994, and 14 0-0 ♕c5 15 ♗e3 ♕a5 was seen in Uhlmann-Gligoric, Amsterdam 1971, when 16 ♘d5!? might be very slightly favourable for White.

11 0-0

11 ♖c1 ♘c6 12 ♗e3 ♕b4 13 ♕d2 ♗xf3 14 gxf3 ♔h7 15 ♘d5 ♕xd2+ 16 ♔xd2 ♘d7 failed to achieve more than a level game for White in Sanguinetti-Liberzon, Biel 1976, while 11 ♗e3 has also been played with a view to emerging from the opening phase with something tangible, e.g. 11...♕a5 (11...♕h5 12 h3 ♘c6 13 0-0 ♗xf3 14 ♗xf3 ♕a5 15 ♕d2 ♔h7 16 ♖ac1 with a plus for White in Bagirov-Sasikiran, Biel 1999) 12 ♘d2 (12 0-0!?) 12...♗xe2 13 ♕xe2 ♘fd7 (13...♖c8 is worth a try, and 13...♘c6 14 0-0 ♕h5! should be equal) 14 ♖c1 (14 0-0 ♗xc3 15 bxc3 ♔h7 is given as unclear in *NCO*) 14...♖c8 15 0-0 ♘c6 16 ♖fd1 h5?! 17 a3 (17 f4!?, when 17...♕a6 18 ♘f3 is excellent for White) 17...♕a6 and the position is evaluated as unclear in *ECO*. We think that this assessment is definitely too optimistic. Black has nothing to show for his cramped position and weakened kingside, e.g. 18 ♘f3 ♘b6 (18...♘de5 19 ♘xe5 dxe5 20 ♘b5) 19 ♗xb6 and now:

a) After Gulko's 19...♕xb6 20 b4 ♗xc3 21 ♖xc3 a5 White has a clear advantage after both 22 c5 dxc5 23 bxc5 and 22 b5 ♘e5 (22...♖d8 23 e5) 23 ♘xe5 dxe5 24 ♖d7.

b) 19...axb6 20 ♘d5! e6 21 ♘c3 (21 ♘e3! looks very good) 21...♘a7 22 ♖xd6 ♖xc4 23 ♕e3 was Gulko-Ivanchuk, Biel 1993, when

Black should have played 23...♗xc3! 24 ♖xc3 ♖xc3 25 bxc3 ♕xa3 26 ♖xb6 ♕a1+ 27 ♕e1 ♕xe1+ 28 ♘xe1 ♘c6 29 ♖xb7 ♖a3 with a probable draw.

11...♘c6

Or 11...♗xf3 (11...♘bd7 12 ♗e3 ♕a5, Uhlmann-Boudy, Cienfuegos 1973, and now 13 h3!? ♗xf3 14 ♗xf3 with advantage to White) 12 ♗xf3 ♘c6 (12...♕xc4? 13 e5) and now:

a) 13 ♗e2 ♕a5 14 ♔h1 (14 ♘d5!? ♕d8 15 ♘xf6+ exf6 16 ♗c3 looks strong) 14...♖ac8 15 ♖b1 (Petursson-Markzon, Linares 1994) with a pull for White – Gulko.

b) 13 b3 ♘d4 (13...♘h7 14 ♖c1 with advantage to White) 14 ♖c1 ♘xf3+ 15 ♕xf3 ♖fe8 16 ♕e2 (16 ♘d5!? is good for White) 16...♔h7 (Petursson-Fedorowicz, New York 1992) 17 ♘d5 with an edge for White.

12 ♗e3 ♕a5 13 ♕d2

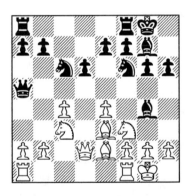

13 ♘d2 ♗xe2 14 ♕xe2 ♖fc8 15 ♖fc1 (Tukmakov-Dam, Lugano 1989) 15...♕h5! and Black does not have any problems.

13...♖fc8

13...♔h7!? is obvious but interesting, e.g. 14 ♖ac1 ♖ac8 15 b3 a6 16 h3 ♗xf3 17 ♗xf3 b5, or 14 h3 ♗xf3 15 ♗xf3 ♖fc8 16 ♗e2 ♘e5 17 b3 b5 as in Gruenberg-Vogt, Leipzig 1973, with counterplay in both cases.

14 b3

After 14 ♗xh6 Black easily regains the pawn and obtains an excellent position, e.g. 14...♗xf3 15 ♗xf3 ♘e5 16 ♗e2 ♘xc4 17

♗xc4 ♖xc4 18 ♖ae1 ♗xh6 19 ♕xh6 ♖ac8 with chances for both sides. White should definitely prefer this to 15 gxf3 ♕h5 16 ♗f4 ♘e5 with compensation, or 15...♗xh6 16 ♕xh6 ♘d4 17 ♖fc1 ♕e5 with an initiative for Black.

14...♗xf3

14...♘h7 15 ♖ac1 a6 16 h3 ♗xf3 17 ♗xf3 b5 18 e5 dxe5 19 ♘d5 ♕xd2 20 ♘xf6+ ♗xf6 21 ♗xd2 b4 ½-½, Rodriguez Garcia-Moreno Carnero, Navalmoral de la Mata 2000.

15 ♗xf3 ♘g4

ECO gives this position as equal but matters are not so simple. For example 15...♘h7! deserves attention, e.g. 16 ♖ac1 (16 ♖fc1 ♘g5 17 ♗xg5 ♕xg5 18 ♕xg5 hxg5 19 ♖ab1 ♘d4 with advantage to Black) 16...♘g5! 17 ♗g4 (17 ♗xg5 ♗xc3 18 ♖xc3 ♕xg5 19 ♕xg5 hxg5 with a level game, or 17...hxg5 18 ♖fd1 ♗e5 with chances for both sides) 17...♖f8 (intending ...f7-f5) 18 f3 (18 ♗xg5 ♕xg5 19 ♕xg5 hxg5 with equality) 18...f5 19 exf5 gxf5.

16 ♗xg4 ♗xc3 17 ♕c2?!

17 ♕d5! is awkward for Black, as was demonstrated in Garcia Vicente-Kouvatsou, Istanbul 2000: 17...♗xa1 (17...♖c7 18 ♕xa5 ♘xa5 19 ♖ad1) 18 ♗xc8 ♖xc8 19 ♕xa5 ♘xa5 20 ♖xa1 ♘c6 (20...a6 21 ♗xh6 b5 22 cxb5 axb5 hardly helps the defender) 21 ♗xh6 and Black was in dire straits.

17...♗xa1 18 ♗xc8 ♖xc8 19 ♖xa1 ♘e5 20 ♕e2 h5 21 h3

21 ♖d1!? a6 22 ♕b2 with a slight edge.

21...a6 22 ♖d1 ♕b4 23 ♗d4 ♘c6 24 ♗a1 b5 25 ♕b2 f6 26 a3 ♕a5 27 cxb5 axb5 28 ♕e2 ♕xa3 29 ♕xb5 ♕c5 30 ♕xc5 ½-½

Game 53
Onischuk-Forster
World U16 Championship, Mamaia 1991

---

1 d4 ♘f6 2 c4 g6 3 ♘c3 ♗g7 4 e4 d6 5 ♗e2 0-0 6 ♗g5 h6 7 ♗e3 c5 8 e5

White steers the game to an ending in which he hopes to secure and improve an early advantage.

8...dxe5

Trying to avoid the exchange of queens is futile and leads to a poor game for Black.

a) 8...♘h7?! 9 exd6 cxd4 10 dxe7 ♕xe7 11 ♗xd4 ♗xd4 12 ♕xd4 ♘c6 13 ♕d2 and Black has no compensation for the pawn, Zakharevich-Nikolaev, St Petersburg 1998.

b) 8...♘fd7 9 exd6 exd6 10 ♘f3 ♘c6 11 0-0 b6 (11...f5!?) 12 ♕d2 ♔h7 13 ♖ad1 with a plus for White in Alburt-Lukin, Tbilisi 1974.

c) 8...♘e8 9 dxc5 ♕a5 10 exd6 exd6 (Kallai-Ryskin, Kobanya 1992) 11 ♕d2!? ♔h7 12 ♘b5 ♕xd2+ 13 ♔xd2 is poor for Black.

9 dxe5 ♕xd1+

Weaker is 9...♘fd7 10 f4, e.g. 10...♘c6 11 ♘f3 f6 12 ♘h4 fxe5 13 ♘xg6 and Black's position was a mess in Palatnik-Paschall, New York 1995.

10 ♖xd1 ♘g4

Again 10...♘fd7?! helps only White, Seirawan-Gudmundsson, Reykjavik 1990 continuing 11 f4 ♘a6 12 ♗f3 ♖e8 13 ♘ge2 ♘f8 14 ♔f2 f6 15 exf6 ♗xf6 16 ♖d2 ♔g7 17 ♘e4 ♘e6 18 ♘xf6 exf6 19 ♖hd1 and White was too far in front.

11 ♗xc5

The critical position for this variation. White wins a pawn but the advantage is not absolutely beyond doubt, as the win of material takes time and Black is able to generate counterplay. Since the 1970s the ending has been analysed and tested in the practice and,

although statistics are not bad for Black, in our opinion White does indeed stand better.

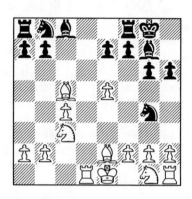

11...♘xe5

Black has also played 11...♘a6 12 ♗xe7 ♖e8 13 ♘d5 ♘xe5 14 ♗a3 (14 ♘f6+ ♗xf6 15 ♗xf6 ♘xc4 16 ♘f3 ♗g4 17 ♔f1 with the more pleasant game for White in Nendick-Dilleigh, Bristol 1991) 14...♗e6 15 ♔f1. Then 15...♔h7 (Milov-Fleish, Israel 1992) 16 f4!? ♘g4 17 h3 ♘f6 18 ♘xf6+ ♗xf6 19 g4 sees Black fail to get enough compensation for the pawn, while 15...♖ad8 16 f4 (Petursson-Kotronias, Gausdal 1995) 16...♘g4 17 ♗xg4 ♗xg4 18 ♘f3 favours White according to Petursson.

12 ♘d5

Stronger than 12 ♗xe7 ♖e8 13 ♘d5 ♗e6!, e.g. 14 ♗a3 (14 ♘c7 ♖xe7 15 ♘xa8 ♘ec6 with compensation) 14...♗xd5 15 cxd5 ♘c4 16 ♔f1 ♘xa3 17 bxa3 ♘d7 18 h4 ♖ac8 as in Polak-Mochalov, Litomysl 1994, with enough for Black according to Polak in *ECO*.

12...♘bc6

Or 12...♘a6 13 ♗a3 (13 ♗xe7!? ♖e8 14 b3 ♗f5 15 ♔f1 ♘c6 16 ♗f6 with advantage to White) 13...♘c6 14 ♘f3, when 14...♗e6 15 0-0 ♖fd8 16 ♖fe1 favoured White in Kallai-Pinchuk, Kobanya 1991, but 14...♖e8!? 15 0-0 e6 16 ♘c3 ♗xc3 17 bxc3 e5!? seems to improve, when Black, with ...♗g4 coming, has ample activity.

13 f4

Not White's only good continuation.

a) 13 ♘f3 ♗e6 14 b3 ♖fd8 15 0-0 ♖d7 16 ♘f4 ♗f5 17 ♘xe5 ♗xe5 18 ♖xd7 ♗xd7 19 ♖d1 ♖d8 20 ♘d5 ♔f8 with slightly better chances for White, Petursson-Piket, Wijk aan Zee 1990.

b) 13 b3!? and now 13...♗f5 (Seifert-Feige, Winterberg 2002) 14 ♗xe7 ♖fe8 15 ♗f6 ♖ac8 16 ♗xg7 ♔xg7 17 ♘e3 is awful for Black and best replaced with 13...♗e6, e.g. 14 ♘c7 (14 f4!? offers White chances of an advantage) 14...♖ad8 15 ♘xe6 fxe6 16 ♘f3 b6 17 ♗e3 ♘xf3+ (17...♘b4 18 0-0 with an edge for White in Alburt-Tukmakov, Odessa 1974) 18 ♗xf3 ♗c3+ 19 ♔e2 ♘d4+ 20 ♗xd4 ♖xd4 and White did not even try to realise his better pawn structure in Khalifman-Yurtaev, Riga 1988, the players agreeing a draw.

13...♘g4

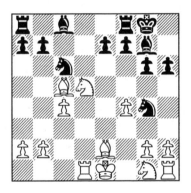

14 h3

Or 14 ♗f3 ♗f5 15 ♘e2 (15 h3!? ♘f6 16 g4 ♗c2 17 ♖d2 with a pull for White) 15...♖fd8 (not 15...♗xb2? 16 h3 ♘f6 17 ♖d2 etc.) 16 h3 ♘f6 17 ♘g3 (17 g4!? ♗c2 18 ♘xe7+ ♘xe7 19 ♖xd8+ ♖xd8 20 ♗xe7 with a plus for White, while 17 ♘xe7+ ♘xe7 18 ♖xd8+ ♖xd8 19 ♗xe7 ♖e8 20 ♗xf6 ♗xf6 21 b3 ♗b1 22 ♔d2 ♗xa2 23 ♘c1 ♗b1 24 ♘d3 ♗xd3 25 ♔xd3 b6 is only a shade worse for Black) 17...♗c2 18 ♖d2 (18 ♘xe7+!? ♘xe7 19 ♖xd8+ ♖xd8 20 ♗xe7) 18...♗b1 19 b3 ♘xd5 20 cxd5 ♗c3 (Bareev-Yurtaev, Moscow 1990) with equality according to *ECO*.

14...♘f6 15 ♗f3 ♗f5

Both 15...♘d7? 16 ♗xe7 ♖e8 17 ♘e2 and 15...♘xd5 16 cxd5 ♘b8 17 ♘e2 ♖e8 18 ♗a3 ♘d7 19 ♘d4 a6 20 ♔f2, Normantas-Strand, Correspondence 1986/91, are much worse.

16 ♘e2

More effective than 16 g4 ♗c2 17 ♖d2 ♘e4 18 ♗xe4 (18 ♗xe7!? ♘xd2 19 ♔xd2 ♗b1 20 ♗xf8 ♔xf8 21 ♘c3 ♗xc3+ 22 ♔xc3 with advantage to White) 18...♗xe4 (Black has obtained the two bishop pair) 19 ♖hh2 ♖fd8 (19...♖fc8!? with equality) 20 ♖he2 ♗b1 (Bai Min-Chen De, China 1987) 21 ♗xe7 with chances for both sides.

16...♗c2?!

16...♖fd8 transposes to 14 ♗f3, above.

17 ♖c1

17 ♖d2 ♘e4 18 ♗xe7 ♘xd2 19 ♔xd2 ♗f5 20 g4? ½-½, Engel-Milvydas, Correspondence 1988/93. Instead the big improvement 20 ♗xf8 ♔xf8 21 b3 puts the onus on Black to justify the pawn sacrifice.

17...♗d3 18 ♔f2 ♘e4+ 19 ♗xe4 ♗xe4 20 ♘g3 ♗d3 21 b3 ♖fd8 22 ♘xe7+ ♘xe7 23 ♗xe7 ♖e8?!

23...♖d7 is better.

24 ♗c5 ♖ac8 25 ♗e3 h5 26 ♖hd1 ♖cd8 27 ♖d2 h4 28 ♘e2 ♗e4 29 ♖xd8 ♖xd8 30 ♘g1 ♗b2 31 ♖e1 ♗c3 32 ♖f1 a5 33 ♘f3 ♗f6 34 ♖e1 ♗c3 35 ♗d2 ♗xf3 36 ♗xc3 ♗c6 37 ♖e2 a4 38 b4 b5 39 cxb5 ♗xb5 40 ♖e5 ♗d3 41 ♖c5 f5 42 ♗e5 ♗d7?!

42...♖d2+!? is less accommodating.

43 b5 ♗xb5 44 ♖xb5 ♖d2+ 45 ♔g1 ♖xa2 46 ♖b7 a3 47 ♖a7 ♖c2 48 ♖xa3 ♔h7 49 ♖a8 ♖c1+ 50 ♔h2 ♔h6 51 ♖h8 mate

Game 54
Yakovich-Zakharevich
Petrov Memorial, St Petersburg 1998

1 d4 ♘f6 2 c4 g6 3 ♘c3 ♗g7 4 e4 d6 5 ♗e2 0-0 6 ♗g5 h6 7 ♗e3 e5 8 d5

Having forced the bishop back to e3 and achieved ...e7-e5 Black has had to pay the price of giving White the tempo-gaining ♕d2 sooner or later. In the meantime a standard King's Indian central pawn configuration has been created, and with the bishop no longer on g5 Black can entertain the often thematic ...c7-c6 followed by the trade on d5 without having to weigh up the implications of White recapturing with the knight.

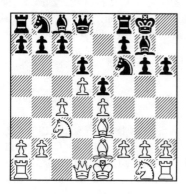

White (depending on Black's reaction) has two different plans. One involves generating a kingside attack by launching the 'g' and h-pawns while the other is a case of stabilising the situation on the kingside in order to step up the pace on the queenside. However, in most instances Black is the one looking for activity on the queenside.

Note that 8 dxe5 cannot be recommended as after 8...dxe5 White gains nothing from either keeping the tension in the centre with 9 ♘f3 ♘bd7 10 ♘d2 ♖e8 11 0-0 ♘f8 12 ♘b3 c6 13 ♕xd8 ♖xd8 14 f3 ♘e6 15 ♖fd1 ♖e8 16 ♗d2 h5 with a level game, Damljanovic-Kljako, Trnava 1982, or heading for the ending with 9 ♕xd8 ♖xd8 10 ♘d5. Then Black has two options. 10...♘a6 11 0-0-0 (Agzamov-Kupreichik, Yerevan 1982) 11...♗e6!? looks fine for Black because 12 ♘xf6+ ♗xf6 13 ♗xh6 can be met with 13...♘c5 14 f3 g5 15 h4 gxh4 16 ♗e3 ♗e7. There is also 10...♘xd5 11 cxd5 c6 12 ♗c4 cxd5 13 ♗xd5 ♘c6 14 ♗xc6 bxc6 when the bishop pair, superior development and the initiative on the queen-side more than compensate for Black's worse

pawn structure. For example 15 ♖c1 ♗e6 16 b3 a5 17 ♖xc6 a4 was equal in Garcia-Barbera Estelles, Spain 1992, and 15 ♘f3 ♗e6 16 ♘d2 a5 17 ♔e2 ♖db8 18 b3 a4 19 ♖hc1 axb3 20 axb3 ♖xa1 21 ♖xa1 ♗xb3 22 ♘xb3 ♖xb3 23 ♖c1 was agreed drawn in Dokhoian-Seredenko, Aktjubinsk 1985.

8...♘a6

For 8...c6 see Campbell-Roach, Game 56.

9 ♕d2

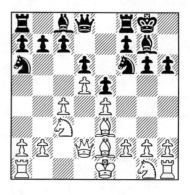

For 9 h4 see the next main game.

9...♘c5

Note that this position could have arisen after 8...♘bd7 9 ♕d2 ♘c5. Other continuations also fail to give Black equality.

a) 9...h5 10 f3 ♘h7 (10...♘c5 11 b4 ♘a6 12 a3 ♘h7 13 ♖c1 f5 14 exf5 gxf5 15 f4 was the unfortunate course of Gamota-Mirzoeva, Moscow 1997, which shouldn't be repeated by Black) 11 0-0-0 ♕e8 (11...♗f6 12 g3 ♘c5 13 h4 and the storm clouds already hovered over Black in Berg-Holst, Denmark 1991) 12 h4 f5 13 ♘h3 f4 14 ♗f2 with a big advantage to White in Ryskin-Mrva, Bratislava 1993.

b) 9...♔h7 10 f3 ♘c5 (10...♗d7 11 g4 ♘c5 12 h4 ♘e8 13 h5 g5 14 ♘h3 with advantage to White, Santolini-Ceschia, Barcelona PG 1981) 11 ♗d1 a5 12 ♗c2 ♗d7 13 ♘ge2 ♕e8 14 g4 and White was better in Polak-Kupruks, Stockerau 1992.

10 f3 a5

10...♘h5 11 0-0-0 (11 ♗d1 ♘f4!, or 11 ♗xh6? ♕h4+ etc.) 11...♔h7 12 g3 helps

White. For example 12...♕e7 13 ♖e1 a5 (Ubilava-Yermolinsky, Telavi 1982) 14 ♗xc5! is a characteristic of this kind of position, affording White an advantage in the centre after 14...dxc5 15 f4! ♘f6 16 ♘f3. This theme also crops up after 12...♕e8 13 ♖e1 ♗d7 (Stuart-Gollogly, New Zealand 1984) 14 ♗xc5! (14 ♗d1 with advantage to White in Gaprindashvili-Levitina, Lvov 1983) 14...dxc5 15 f4 ♘f6 16 ♘f3 and 12...a6 13 ♗xc5 dxc5 14 f4 ♘f6 15 ♘f3, which was very poor for Black in Lukin-Ignatiev, St Petersburg 2000. Finally 12...a5 (Ubilava-Tseitlin, Telavi 1982) 13 f4 with an initiative for White.

11 0-0-0

11 g4!? h5 12 h3 ♘h7 13 h4 hxg4 14 fxg4 ♘f6 15 ♗g5 ♘cxe4 16 ♘xe4 ♘xe4 17 ♗xd8 ♘xd2 18 ♗xc7 ♘e4 19 ♗f3 was bad news for Black in Serper-Novik, St Petersburg 1993. White can also play 11 h4, e.g. 11...h5 12 ♘h3 ♘h7 (12...♗xh3 13 ♖xh3 with a slight advantage to White in Seirawan-Balashov, Toluca 1982) 13 ♘f2 f5 14 exf5 gxf5 15 g4 e4 16 gxh5 f4 17 ♗xc5 dxc5 18 ♘cxe4 ♗d4, Seirawan-Kinley, London 1981 is given as unclear in *ECO*, but in our opinion Black does not have sufficient compensation for the pawns. 11...♔h7 12 g4 h5 13 0-0-0 ♖h8 (Benjamin-Kr.Georgiev, Saint John Open II 1988) and now 14 g5 ♘g8 15 ♘h3 with advantage to White. In S.Ivanov-Zakharevich, Kazan 1995 Black didn't have a pawn's worth of compensation after 11...♘h5 12 ♗xh6 ♘g3 13 ♖h2.

11...♔h7 12 g4 ♖h8

Or 12...♗d7 (Popov-Bobotsov, Varna 1968) 13 h4 and White is in control.

13 h4 h5 14 ♗g5 hxg4 15 h5 ♔g8

15...g3!? is interesting.

16 fxg4 ♗d7 17 ♗f3 ♕c8?

This is an obvious blunder but there is no clear way for Black to emerge from the pressure intact.

18 h6 ♘xg4 19 hxg7 ♖xh1 20 ♗xh1 f6 21 ♗e3 ♘xe3 22 ♕xe3 ♔xg7 23 ♗g2 ♕h8 24 ♗h3 ♗xh3 25 ♘xh3 ♕h4 26 ♘f2 ♖h8 27 ♘b5 ♕h6 28 ♕xh6+ ♖xh6 29 ♘xc7 ♔f7 30 ♔d2 f5 31 ♘b5 ♔e7 32 ♘c3 ♔f6 33 ♔e3 ♖h4 34 ♖h1 ♖xh1 35 ♘xh1 b6 36 ♘f2 ♔g5 37 ♘b5 ♘b7 38 ♔f3 1-0

1 d4 ♘f6 2 c4 g6 3 ♘c3 ♗g7 4 e4 d6 5 ♗e2 0-0 6 ♗g5 h6

N.B. The actual move order was 6...♘a6 7 h4 e5 8 d5 h6 9 ♗e3.

7 ♗e3 e5 8 d5 ♘a6 9 h4

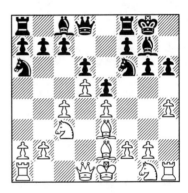

Not too subtle, perhaps, but this simplistic show of aggression should by no means be underestimated. With the centre closed and stable White can turn to the kingside, concentrating on opening the h-file and trading dark-squared bishops in order to eliminate a key defender. However – perhaps not surprisingly given that Black has thus far played only decent King's Indian moves – Black has sufficient resources with which to counteract White's offensive. In fact Black's treatment of the situation in this game suggests that this move order is inaccurate, so 9 ♕d2 looks preferable..

9...♘c5

9...c6 10 g4 ♕a5 11 f3 h5 12 g5 ♘e8 13 ♘h3 ♗d7 14 ♕d2 ♘c5 15 ♖b1 with an edge for White in Babu-Gallagher, Kuala Lumpur 1992, while the immediate 9...h5 10 f3 c6 11

♘h3 cxd5 12 cxd5 ♗d7 13 ♘f2 also favoured White in Alburt-Hort, La Valetta 1980.

10 ♕c2

White finds himself posting the queen on c2 rather than the usual d2-square because now after 10 f3 would have ...♘h5. Unfortunately the c2-square is not ideal. Apart from not enabling White to exert pressure on Black's kingside (as is the case after ♕d2), the queen might also require attention should Black begin proceedings on the c-file.

10...c6

The logical response. In Fayard-Pour Rahnama, France 1994 Black tried 10...♘g4 but was punished after 11 ♗xg4 ♗xg4 12 f3 ♗d7 13 g4 a5 14 ♘ge2 f5 15 gxf5 gxf5 16 0-0-0 f4 17 ♗f2 with a big lead for White. 10...h5 11 f3 is playable but not as accurate as the text, e.g. 11...a5!? 12 ♘h3 ♘h7 13 ♘f2, Dzuban-Majorovas, Moscow 1983, or 11...c6 12 b4 ♘a6 13 a3 cxd5 14 cxd5 ♗d7 15 ♘h3, Polugaevsky-Donner, Amsterdam 1970, with a plus for White in both cases.

11 h5

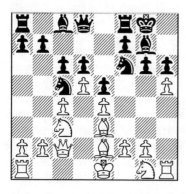

White continues the march of the h-pawn, which is particularly important now that Black is seeking to generate activity elsewhere. Indeed the advance serves to keep Black on his toes and tests out the waters in terms of how Black responds to the challenge to the defensive wall.

11...cxd5

Black is not phased by the intruder, calmly

getting on with his own aggressive strategy. Instead after 11...g5 12 f3 a5 13 g4 the kingside takes on a different shape, when play continues as follows: 13...♗d7 14 ♘h3 a4 (14...cxd5 15 cxd5 ♘e8 16 ♗b5 ♗c8 17 0-0 ♘c7 with equality in Gervasio-V.Gurevich, Le Touquet 1996) 15 ♕d2 (15 ♘f2 cxd5 16 cxd5 ♕a5 and Black prepares to push the b-pawn, Bareev assessing the situation as level, Stettler-Habermehl, Correspondence 1999) 15...cxd5 16 cxd5 and White has had some kind of success but without achieving too much. Then 16...♕a5 17 ♘b1 ♕xd2+ 18 ♘xd2 b5 is equal according to Bareev, 19 ♖c1 ♖fc8 20 ♔f2 ♗f8 21 ♔g2 ♘e8 22 ♘f2 ♗e7 23 ♖hd1 ♖c7 24 ♖c2 agreed drawn in De Boni-Berdichesky, Correspondence 1994. Much less clear is 17...♘fxe4 18 fxe4 ♘xe4 19 ♕xa5 ♖xa5 with compensation, as in Bareev-Kasparov, Linares 1992, but if somebody wants to play this position, he must be Kasparov!

12 cxd5 ♕a5!

Others:

a) 12...♗d7?! 13 b4! ♘a6 14 a3 leaves the a6-knight out of play. Now Black has tried 14...♖c8 (14...g5 15 f3 gives White, who plans to push the g-pawn, a commanding advantage across the board, 14...♘xh5? 15 ♗xh5 gxh5 16 ♖xh5 ♖c8 17 ♗xh6 ♗xh6 18 ♖xh6 ♔g7 19 ♕d2 [19...♖xc3?? 20 ♖h1] is excellent for White and 14...gxh5 [unclear according to S.Ivanov in *ECO*] 15 ♕d2 ♔h7 16 f3 – intending g2-g4 or ♗xa6 (♗d3), ♘e2-g3 and so on – also looks very poor for Black) 15 ♕d2 gxh5 (15...♖xc3 16 ♕xc3 ♘xe4 17 ♕c4 and 15...g5 16 f3 are awful) 16 ♗xh6! ♘h7 17 ♖xh5 ♕f6 18 g4 ♕g6 19 ♗xg7 ♔xg7 20 f3 with a big advantage in Lugovoi-Degraeve, Paris 1996.

b) In the event of 12...g5 13 b4?! Black can get away with 13...♘cxe4 14 ♘xe4 ♘xd5 15 ♕d2 ♗e6 16 g4 a5 17 b5 (Bönsch-Bielicki, Germany 1993) 17...♘xe3 18 fxe3 ♕b6 with compensation. Therefore White should play 13 f3, e.g. 13...a5!? (13...♗d7 14 g4 ♖c8 15 ♕d2 ♕a5 16 ♖b1 with a slight advantage to

White in Shereshevsky-Gufeld, Tbilisi 1974) and now instead of 14 ♗b5 as in Bellmann-Gwozdz, E-mail 2000, when 14...♘e8!? followed by ...♘c7 would have left Black doing fine, White has 14 ♘b5, with an edge, or 14 g4 with the following position:

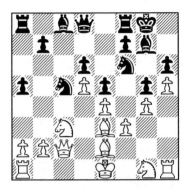

This situation is similar to the game De Boni-Berdichesky, mentioned in the note to Black's 11th move, the only difference being the trade on d5. Despite the fact that White has achieved nothing special in the games played thus far, this factor is rather advantageous for White because the b5-square is available.

b1) 14...♗d7 15 ♗b5 (15 ♗xc5 dxc5 16 ♗b5 ♕b6 17 a4 c4, Magerramov-Chiburdanidze, Baku 1980 is given as unclear in *ECO*) 15...♖c8 was seen in Hutschenreiter-Koppe, Correspondence 1987, and now 16 ♖c1!? looks a shade better for White.

b2) 14...a4!? 15 ♗b5 (15 ♘b5!?) 15...♗d7 16 ♘ge2 affords White an effective development for his knight on e2, from where it can head for f5. The subsequent 16...♕a5 17 ♗xc5 dxc5 18 ♗xd7 ♘xd7 was unclear in Dziggel-Hesse, Correspondence 1995.

13 ♗d2

Alternatives fall short and even look favourable for Black. For example 13 ♖b1? walks into 13...♘cxe4 14 b4 ♕c7, while 13 ♕d2? ♘b3 14 axb3 ♕xa1+ was winning for Black in Seifert-Balcerak, Oberhof 1999.

After 13 ♔f1 ♗d7! 14 hxg6 fxg6 15 ♖c1

b5 is nice for Black, so preference has been for 15 ♗xh6, and now:

a) 15...♗xh6 16 ♖xh6 ♔g7 17 ♖h4 (17 ♖h1 b5 18 ♗f3 b4 19 ♘ce2 ♗b5 is great for Black) 17...b5 18 b4 (18 ♕c1 ♖h8 19 ♖xh8 ♖xh8 20 f3 ♖f8 looked very gloomy for White in Gyurkovics-Khamatgaleev, Gyongyos 1999) 18...♕xb4 19 ♖b1 ♕a5 20 ♗xb5, Raetsky-Golubev, Lucerne 1994, and now 20...g5! puts White in trouble.

b) 15...b5 leads to more complicated positions, e.g. 16 ♕c1 (16 a3 b4, or 16 ♗g5 b4 17 ♗xf6 ♖xf6 18 ♘d1 ♖f4 with serious problems for White) 16...b4 17 ♗xg7 ♔xg7 and Black had the upper hand in M.Hansen-Geenen, Correspondence 1998.

13...♗d7!

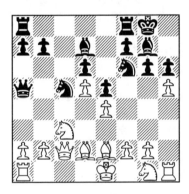

It is imperative that Black maintains his presence on the queenside, although his harmonious forces should afford him good play on both flanks in view of the dark squares on the kingside, the uncertain position of White's king and, unexpectedly, the open h-file. After 13...g5 14 a3 White has a definite advantage, while 13...♘xh5 should have been punished in Kachiani Gersinska-Volke, Germany 1997 by the clever 14 a3! etc. Raetsky-Hitzgerova, Baden 1998 went 13...a6 14 a3 ♕d8? (14...♕c7 is a lesser evil) 15 b4 ♘cd7 16 hxg6 fxg6 17 ♗xh6 ♗xh6 18 ♖xh6 ♔g7 19 ♕d2 and White was in the driving seat.

14 hxg6

An alternative is 14 ♖b1, e.g. 14...♕b4 15

a3 ♕b6 16 hxg6 fxg6 17 ♗e3 (not 17 b4? ♘cxe4 18 ♘xe4 ♖ac8! etc.) 17...♕c7 18 ♖c1 ♖ac8 19 ♕d1 ♕d8 20 f3 (20 ♗f3 has the advantage of not compromising the dark squares – 20...a5 21 b4 axb4 22 axb4 ♘a6 and White's chances are a little better) 20...♘h5 21 b4 ♘f4!! 22 ♔f2 (22 bxc5?! ♘xg2+ 23 ♔f2 ♘xe3 24 ♔xe3 ♖xc5 and now the best continuation is given by Hazai – 22 ♗xf4 exf4 23 bxc5 ♖xc5 24 ♕d2 ♕a5 25 ♘d1 ♕xa3 with compensation for the sacrificed piece) 22...♗a4! 23 ♘xa4 ♘xe4+! 24 fxe4 ♖xc1 25 ♗xc1 ♘d3+ 26 ♔g3 ♘f2 27 ♕e1 ♘xh1+ 28 ♔h2 ♘f2 29 ♘f3 was Buhmann-Vouldis, Fuerth 2002. Then Hazai gives 29...♘xe4 30 ♗d3 ♘f6 31 ♘c3 ♕e8 with compensation.

Overall we suggest 14...♕b6!?, when 15 b4? ♘cxe4 16 ♘xe4 ♘xe4 17 ♗e3 ♕d8 18 hxg6 f5 is an edge for Black, and 15 hxg6 fxg6 will transpose to the main line.

14...fxg6 15 f3

White has two other logical continuations. 15 ♖b1 ♕b6 16 ♗e3 a5 17 ♘h3 ♖ac8 18 ♕d2 a4, Hauchard-Hebden, Cappelle la Grande 1998 is given as unclear in *ECO*. Then there is 15 a3:

a) 15...♕b6 16 b4 ♘a4 (16...♘cxe4!? 17 ♘xe4 ♕d4 18 ♘c3 ♘g4 19 0-0-0 ♗f5 and Black gets enough play for his investment) 17 ♘xa4 ♗xa4! 18 ♕xa4 ♘g4 19 0-0-0!? (19 ♘h3 ♘xf2 20 ♘xf2 ♕xf2+ 21 ♔d1 ♕xg2 22 ♖e1 ♕xe4 23 ♕c2 is unclear) 19...♘xf2 20 ♘f3 ♘xe4 21 ♔b1!? ♖xd2+!? (much better than 21...♘g3 22 ♗xh6 ♘xe2 23 ♕c2 ♘f4 24 ♗xf4 ♖xf4 25 ♕xg6 etc.) 22 ♘xd2 ♖f2 23 ♖he1 ♕d4 24 ♕c2 e4 25 ♔a2 and White's chances are preferable.

b) 15...♕c7!? was Coathup-Lane, Port Erin 2003. Then 16 ♗f3 ♔h7 17 b4 ♘a4 is unclear, while 16...a5!? is interesting, with the idea of continuing 17 ♗xh6 ♗xh6 18 ♖xh6 ♔g7 19 ♖h1 ♖h8 with more than enough compensation for the pawn.

15...♖ac8!

Black cannot afford to waste time defending the h6-pawn. For example after 15...♘h5

or 15...g5 White unleashes a trick on the other flank with 16 b4! ♕xb4 17 ♘b5 ♕a4 18 ♕xa4 ♘xa4 19 ♘xd6 ♘c5 20 ♗e3 b6 21 ♖b1 ♘f4 22 ♗f1 and the ending is quite unpleasant for Black, Yakovich-Bekker Jensen, Gothenburg 2000. However, 15...♕b6!? is worth a try as long as Black is aware of 16 b4 ♕xb4? 17 ♘b5 etc. Instead after 16 b4 there is 16...♘a4! 17 ♘xa4 ♗xa4 18 ♕xa4 ♘xe4! 19 fxe4 ♕f2+ 20 ♔d1 ♕xg2 and White would rather start again. Consequently White has to play 16 ♕c1 ♘h5 17 ♗xh6 ♘f4 18 ♗xf4 exf4 when Black has compensation for the pawn.

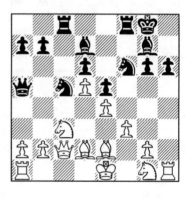

16 ♖b1

a) This time after 16 b4 ♕xb4 17 ♘b5 Black has a pleasant choice between the positional queen sacrifice 17...♕xb5! 18 ♗xb5 ♗xb5 19 ♕b1 ♗d3! 20 ♕b4 (20 ♕d1 ♘fxe4) 20...♗a6 21 ♔d1 ♘d3 with a great game or the simple 17...♘cxe4 18 ♕xe4 ♕xe4 19 fxe4 ♘xe4 20 ♗xh6 ♘g3 21 ♘xd6 ♘xh1 22 ♘xc8 ♗xh6 with a clear advantage in the ending.

b) 16 ♗xh6 ♗xh6 17 ♖xh6 ♔g7 is Black's main idea, after which he can exploit the factors mentioned in the note to Black's 13th move, e.g. 18 ♖h1 (18 ♕d2? ♘g8 19 ♖h1 ♘b3 and 18 ♕c1 ♘a4 19 ♖h1 ♘xb2 20 ♕xb2 ♖xc3 21 ♕d2 ♘h5 are quite poor for White) 18...♘h5! 19 ♗f1 ♘g3 20 ♖h4 (20 ♖h2? ♘cxe4!) 20...♕d8 21 ♖h2 ♕g5 etc.

c) 16 g4!? is cunning, when 16...g5 17 ♘h3 followed by ♘f2 favours White. Instead there can follow 16...h5 17 g5 ♘h7 18 b4 ♕xb4 19 ♘b5 ♕xb5 20 ♗xb5 ♗xb5 21 ♕b1 and White has a much better position than is the case with 16 b4, above, as the h7-knight is temporarily out of play. However, after 21...♗d3 22 ♕d1 ♘xe4! Black still has the advantage, with two pieces, two pawns and a strong initiative for the queen.

16...♕d8!

Not 16...♕c7 17 g4 h5 (17...♕d8 18 ♗e3 b5 19 ♕d2 b4 20 ♘d1) 18 g5 ♘h7 19 ♗e3 ♕d8 20 ♕d2, when White rearranges his pieces in time.

17 ♗xh6

If White does not take this pawn he might well find himself playing a similar position but with equal material. For example after 17 ♕d1 ♘h5, homing in on f4, or 17 g4 h5 Black has a strong initiative without any investment. The only decent alternative is 17 ♕c1, although 17...g5 (17...♘h5! 18 ♗xh6 ♘f4 19 ♗xf4 exf4 with good play for Black) 18 ♕d1 (18 ♗e3!?) 18...♕e8 19 ♗e3 ♘h5 gave Black a healthy initiative in Felzmann-Utesch, E-mail 2002.

17...♗xh6 18 ♖xh6 ♔g7 19 ♖h1 ♘h5

19...♖h8 20 ♖xh8 ♕xh8 deserves attention, e.g. 21 ♗f1 b5 22 a3 a5 23 ♕e2 b4 24 axb4 axb4 25 ♘d1 ♖f8 with a strong initiative.

20 ♕d2 ♖h8 21 ♗f1 ♕b6 22 ♘ge2

22 ♕g5!? might be better.

22...♘f4 23 ♖xh8 ♘cd3+

23...♘fd3+!? 24 ♔d1 ♖xh8 is unclear.

24 ♔d1 ♖xh8 25 ♘xf4 ♘xf4

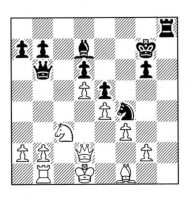

26 ♔c2

Smirin gives 26 g3 ♕g1 27 gxf4 ♕xf1+ 28 ♔c2 ♕xf3 29 fxe5 dxe5 as unclear.

26...♖h2 27 ♖c1 ♘h3 28 ♘a4 ♕d4 29 ♕xd4 exd4 30 ♔b3 ♗xg2 31 ♗xg2 b5!

Thanks to this excellent move Black is rewarded with a clearly better ending.

32 ♘b6

White should probably try 32 ♗f1!? bxa4+ 33 ♔xa4 ♖xb2, although Black still has a better ending.

32...axb6 33 ♗f1 d3

33...♖f2!? 34 ♗xb5 ♖xf3+ 35 ♔c4 d3 (Smirin) puts White in serious trouble.

34 ♔c3

After 34 ♖d1 ♖f2 35 ♗xd3 ♖xf3 White has the trick 36 ♖f1 ♖xd3+ 37 ♔c2 g5 (37...♖e3 38 ♖xf4 g5 39 ♖g4 ♔g6 40 ♔d2 ♖h3 41 ♖g2, or 37...♖d4 38 ♖xf4 g5 39 ♖g4 ♔g6 40 ♔c3 ♖a4 41 b3 ♖xa2 42 ♔b4) 38 ♖xf4 ♖xd5 39 ♖f2 ♖e5 40 ♔d3 ♔g6 41 ♔d4 g4 42 ♖d2 ♔g5 43 ♔e3 with drawing chances in all variations.

34...♖h1?

34...♖f2! is strong.

35 ♖d1 ♔f6 36 ♔d4 b4 37 ♖b1

37 a3!? might improve.

37...♘e2+! 38 ♔e3 g5?

38...♔e5!? 39 a3 b3 40 ♖d1 ♘g3 41 f4+ ♔f6 42 ♔f2 ♘xe4+ 43 ♔g2 d2 is strong (Hazai).

39 ♔f2?

39 a3 b3 (Hazai).

39...♘f4?

39...♔e5!? deserved serious attention, e.g. 40 ♔g2 ♖g1+ 41 ♔f2 g4.

40 ♔e3 ♘e2 41 ♖d1 ♘f4?

Much stronger is 41...♘g3! 42 ♔f2 ♘xf1 43 ♖xf1 ♖xf1+ 44 ♔xf1 ♔e5 45 ♔e1 ♔f4 and Black is approaching the finishing line:

a) 46 ♔f2 b5 47 ♔e1 (or 47 b3 g4 48 fxg4 ♔xe4 49 g5 ♔f5 50 ♔e3 ♔xg5 51 ♔xd3 ♔f5 52 ♔d4 ♔f4) 47...♔xf3 48 e5 g4 49 e6 g3 50 e7 g2 51 e8♕ g1♕+ 52 ♔d2 ♕g5+ 53 ♔xd3 (53 ♔d1 ♕e3) 53...♕xd5+ 54 ♔c2 b3+ 55 axb3 ♕e4+ etc.

b) 46 ♔d2 ♗xf3 47 e5 dxe5 48 d6 e4 49 d7 e3+ 50 ♔xd3 e2 51 d8♕ e1♕ 52 ♕d5+ (52 ♕xg5?? ♕e2+ 53 ♔d4 ♕e4 mate) 52...♔g4 and Black should win the queen ending.

42 ♖b1 d2! 43 ♔xd2 ♖h2+ 44 ♔e3 ♔e5 45 ♗a6?!

After both 45 ♖c1 and 45 a3 White has good chances to equalise.

45...♘g2+ 46 ♔d3 ♘f4+

46...♔f4 47 ♖g1 ♘e3 (47...♔xf3 48 ♖f1+ ♔g3 49 ♖f6 with counterplay) 48 ♖xg5! ♔xg5 49 ♔xe3 ♖xb2 50 ♗c4 ♖c2 51 f4+ ♔f6 52 ♗b3 with equality (Smirin).

47 ♔e3 ♖h3 48 ♖f1?

The only move is 48 ♖g1.

48...g4 49 ♗e2??

Disaster – after 49 ♗c8 ♖h2 50 fxg4 ♖e2+ 51 ♔f3 ♖xb2 a draw beckons.

49...♘g2+ 50 ♔d2 g3 51 ♖g1 ♖h2 52 ♗a6 ♔f4 53 e5 ♔xe5 0-1

Game 56
Campbell-Roach
Correspondence 1978

---

1 d4 ♘f6 2 c4 g6 3 ♘c3 ♗g7 4 e4 d6 5 ♗e2 0-0 6 ♗g5 h6 7 ♗e3 e5 8 d5 c6

Rather than commit his queen's knight Black gets to work on chipping away at the centre and opening the c-file. The text also introduces the possibility of using the c6-pawn to push with ...b7-b5, but in the main such a plan does not quite work.

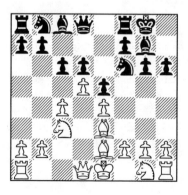

9 ♕d2

The by now familiar, tempo-gaining development of the queen looks best of White's available options.

a) Less ambitious is 9 dxc6 (which Black could well be tempting White into by selecting the early ...c7-c6), when Black has good play after both 9...bxc6 10 ♕d2 ♔h7 11 ♖d1 (11 h3!? looks good for White) 11...♕a5 12 f3 ♖d8, which was unclear in McSweeny-Stables, London 1993, and 9...♘xc6!? 10 ♕d2 (10 ♘f3 ♘g4; 10 h3 ♘d4) 10...♘d4 11 ♗xd4 exd4 12 ♕xd4 ♖e8 13 ♕e3 ♕a5 14 0-0-0 (14 f3?! d5 15 e5 dxc4) 14...b5 (14...♘g4 15 ♗xg4 ♗xg4) 15 cxb5 ♘xe4 16 ♘xe4 ♗b7 17 f3 d5 with an excellent position for Black, Nizard-Emmenecker, France 2001.

b) 9 h4 is interesting.

b1) 9...b5 10 cxb5 cxb5 (10...cxd5 11 exd5 a6 12 b6 with a plus for White in Salvermoser-Schneider, Germany 1994, or 12 g4!? with initiative) 11 a3 h5 (11...a6 12 g4 with an edge for White, Bertuli-Cordier, Correspondence 1990) 12 ♘h3 ♗g4 13 ♘g5 (13 ♗xg4!? ♘xg4 14 ♗g5 with the more pleasant game for White, while 13 f3 ♗xh3 14 ♖xh3 a6 15 ♘a2 is also enough for a slight edge) 13...♗xe2 14 ♕xe2 a6 15 f3 ♘bd7, as in Meduna-Barczay, Trnava 1982, is given as unclear in *ECO*.

b2) 9...cxd5 10 cxd5 h5 (10...♕a5 11 ♕d2 h5 12 f3 a6 13 b4 ♕d8 14 ♘h3, Alburt-Mortensen, Lucerne 1982 and 10...♘bd7 11 g4 ♘c5 12 f3 h5 13 b4 ♘cd7 14 ♘h3 a5 15 a3, Alburt-Velasquez Ojeda, Santiago 1981 both favour White) 11 f3 ♘bd7 12 ♕d2 a6 13 ♘h3 ♘h7 (13...b5 14 ♘f2 ♘b6 15 b3 ♗d7 16 ♖c1 and White stood better in Agzamov-Paehtz, Potsdam 1985) 14 ♘f2 b5 (14...f5!? 15 exf5 gxf5 16 ♗h6 with a plus for White) 15 ♘d3 f5 16 ♘b4 ♕e8 17 ♘c6, Lputian-Uhlmann, Sarajevo 1983, is slightly better for White.

9...cxd5

9...h5 10 h3!? cxd5 11 cxd5 ♘bd7 12 ♘f3 ♘c5 13 ♕c2 ♕c7 14 ♖c1 ♗d7 15 b4 (15 ♕b1!?) 15...♘a4 16 ♕b3 ♘xc3 17 ♖xc3 ♕d8

18 ♘g5 a5 19 b5 a4 20 ♕b4 ♘e8 was agreed drawn in Kallai-Groszpeter, Hungary 1992 but, in our opinion, White has a clear advantage. Note that 10...b5?! 11 cxb5 cxd5 12 exd5 is not enough for the pawn, Gaprindashvili-Ioseliani, Georgia 1990, and 10...a6 should have been punished in Mohr-Uhlmann, Debrecen 1989 by 11 dxc6 ♘xc6 12 ♘f3 ♗e6 13 0-0 etc.

10 cxd5 ♔h7 11 h4

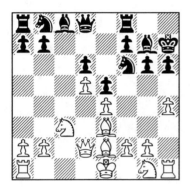

11...♘g4

11...h5 12 ♘f3 (12 f3 a6 13 ♘h3, Meins-Lauzeningks, Germany 2001 and 12 ♘h3!? both seem to favour White) 12...♗d7 13 ♘g5+ ♔g8 14 f3 ♘a6 15 0-0 was excellent for White in Milov-Damaso, Mulhouse 1997.

12 ♗xg4 ♗xg4 13 h5 g5 14 ♖c1

Black's bishop must relocate soon so there is no need to drive it away, e.g. 14 f3 ♗d7 15 g4?! (15 ♘ge2!?) 15...♕f6 16 ♔e2 (16 ♘ce2 ♖c8 17 ♘g3 a5 18 ♘f5 is unclear) 16...♖c8 with a good game for Black, Alburt-Gligoric, Odessa 1975.

14...♘a6

As ...♘d7 denies the bishop a retreat square Black must use a6.

15 ♘b5!

Inflicting upon Black long-term problems due to his vulnerable queenside.

15...♕e7 16 ♘e2 ♗d7 17 a4 ♖ac8

17...♘c5!? 18 ♗xc5 dxc5 19 d6 with advantage to White.

18 ♖xc8 ♖xc8 19 ♗xa7!

Black does not have compensation for the sacrificed pawn. Less accurate but still leaving White with an advantage is 19 ♘xa7?!, when Uhlmann-Gligoric, Vrbas 1977 continued 19...♖c4 20 ♘c3 ♗xa4 21 ♘c8! ♖xc8 22 ♘xa4.

19...♖c4 20 ♘ec3 ♗xb5

20...♘c5!? might put up more of a fight.

21 axb5 ♘c5 22 ♗xc5 ♖xc5 23 0-0 ♖c8 24 ♖a1 ♕d8 25 ♖a7 ♕b6 26 ♕e3 ♕c7 27 b6 ♕d7 28 ♕e2 ♖c5 29 ♕a6 ♕g4 30 ♖xb7 ♕f4 31 ♖c7 ♕c1+ 32 ♕f1 ♕xb2 33 ♖xc5 dxc5 34 ♕b1 ♕xb1+ 35 ♘xb1 ♗f8 36 ♘a3 1-0

Game 57
Onischuk-Wegener
Berlin 1993

---

1 d4 ♘f6 2 c4 g6 3 ♘c3 ♗g7 4 e4 d6 5 ♗e2 0-0 6 ♗g5 ♘a6

The popular, modern approach.

7 h4

The direct approach, and one that – not surprisingly – attracts those adventurous players not satisfied with the standard strategy beginning 7 ♕d2 (see Games 60-64). For 7 ♕c2 see Bönsch-Gallagher, next, while 7 f4 is the subject of Sorin-Foisor, Game 59.

7...c5

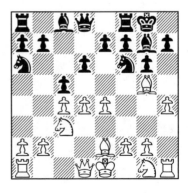

Following the recommended recipe of answering aggression on the flank with aggression in the centre. Of course the text both hits d4 (and hence the dark squares) and fits in with future play on the queenside, thus increasing the pressure on both sides. Consequently Black's approach, while logical, is also a little risky in view of the complications that can follow. Additionally, counterplay sometimes comes at the price of a pawn, and it is not clear that White can be denied an advantage. Therefore, although 7...c5 might appeal to aggressive players – provided that improvements are found – we recommend 7...e5 or 7...h6 8 ♗e3 e5. After 7...e5 8 d5 c6 9 h5 cxd5 10 cxd5 ♘c5 11 b4 ♘cd7 12 h6 ♗h8 13 ♘f3 ♕b6 14 a3 ♘g4 15 0-0, Onischuk-Dydyshko, Erfurt 1993, 9...♕b6 (Obodchuk-Bronznik, Bratislava 1992) 10 ♖b1!? and 9...♕a5 (A.Petrosian-Xie Jun, Shenzhen 1992) 10 ♗xf6!? ♗xf6 11 a3 White manages to stay ahead, but 9...h6 looks okay for Black, e.g. 10 ♗e3 g5 11 g4 (11 ♕d2!?) 11...♗d7 12 f3 ♕b8 (12...c5!? is unclear) 13 ♘h3 ♖c8 with equal chances in Horvath-Seres, Budapest 1996.

8 d5

Now Black must decide whether to continue with the plan in the centre or to take time out to address the threatened h4-h5 etc.

8...♘c7

Supporting both the desired ...b7-b5 and the thematic ...e7-e6, after which the subsequent dxe6 can be met with ...♘xe6, attacking the g5-bishop and monitoring the d4-square. Neither move with the h-pawn is good for Black: 8...h6 9 ♗e3 e5 10 dxe6 ♗xe6 11 ♕d2 h5 12 ♗h6 was an edge for White in Alterman-Xie Jianjun, Beijing 1997, and 8...h5 9 ♕d2 ♖e8 10 f3 ♕a5 11 ♘h3 ♗d7 12 ♘f2 left White with an initiative in Baer-Timpel, Germany 2000.

Instead Black has 8...e6, when it is White's turn to make a decision:

a) 9 dxe6 is aimed at proving the now inappropriate posting of the knight on a6. 9...♗xe6 10 ♕d2 ♘b4 11 h5 ♕a5 12 ♘h3 (12 ♖d1 secures White the advantage without risk) 12...♕a6 (Yakovich-Voitsekhovsky, Nizhnij Novgorod 1998) 13 ♘f4!? ♗xc4 (13...♖ae8 14

hxg6 fxg6 15 ♘xe6 ♖xe6 16 f3 ♘h5 17 ♖h3 ♗e5 18 ♘d5 with an edge) 14 ♗xf6 ♗xf6 15 ♘fd5 with advantage to White. Hazai points out that Black is in big trouble after 12...♗xh3 13 ♖xh3 ♖ae8 14 hxg6 fxg6 15 f3 etc.

c2) Also very good is 9 ♕d2, e.g. 9...exd5 10 exd5 (10 cxd5 leads to an unusual and interesting Modern Benoni set-up, e.g. 10...♕b6 11 h5 ♖e8 12 hxg6 fxg6 13 f3 with advantage to White, Pietrasanta-Sorin, France 1998) 10...♕e8!? (10...♖e8 11 h5 ♗f5 12 ♔f1 gxh5 13 ♘h3 ♕d7 14 ♘f4 with a slight advantage to White, S.Ivanov-Likavsky, Cappelle la Grande 2000) 11 ♔f1 (11 h5!?) 11...♘e4 12 ♘xe4 ♕xe4 13 ♖d1 ♗f5 with chances for both sides, Lerner-Golod, Tel Aviv 2002.

9 ♕d2

White can consider simply marching forward: 9 h5 a6 (9...h6 10 ♗e3 g5 11 f4 gxf4 12 ♗xf4 with a plus for White) 10 hxg6 fxg6 (10...hxg6 11 ♕d2 and Black's king was in for a rough ride in Stassen-Vollmar, Wallertheim 1992) 11 a4 (11 f4 b5! earned Black counterplay in Shainswit-Hearst, New York 1956, while 11 ♘f3!? is an edge for White) 11...♖b8 (Vonk-Abels, Correspondence 1991) 12 a5 with advantage to White.

9...e6

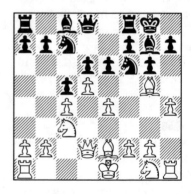

In Salus-Daly, Clichy 1997 Black didn't bother with the e-pawn and instead spent the tempo on preparing the launch of the b-pawn – after 9...a6 10 h5 b5 11 ♗h6 best seems 11...b4!?, when 12 ♗xg7 ♔xg7 13 ♘a4 ♘xe4

14 ♕e3 ♘f6 15 hxg6 fxg6 16 g4 gives White an initiative for the modest investment.

10 h5

White has two alternatives.

a) 10 e5 dxe5 11 d6 ♘ce8 12 ♖d1 (12 0-0-0 ♕d7 13 h5 b5! 14 cxb5 ♗b7 15 hxg6 fxg6 was unclear in Antreasyan-Andersen, Copenhagen 1994) 12...♕d7 13 h5 b5 (13...e4!? is unclear) 14 cxb5 ♗b7 (Zakharevich-Dolmatov, Kazan 1995) and now 15 hxg6 fxg6 16 ♘f3 is given by Zakharevich in *ECO* as unclear, but perhaps 15 ♘f3 is stronger.

b) 10 dxe6 is believed to be incorrect due to 10...♘xe6 with an advantage for Black. Nevertheless, this is rather difficult to prove, e.g. 11 0-0-0!? ♖e8 (11...♕a5 12 ♗h6 ♗xh6 13 ♕xh6 ♘d4 14 ♕f4 ♘xe2+ 15 ♘gxe2, 11...♘d4 12 h5 ♗e6 13 ♘f3 ♘xe2+ 14 ♕xe2 h6 15 ♗f4 ♘xh5 16 ♗xd6 and 11...♘xg5 12 hxg5 ♘g4 13 ♘h3 ♕a5 14 f3 ♘e5 15 ♘f4 ♗e6 16 ♕e1 are all dismal for Black) 12 ♗d3 (12 ♗h6 ♘d4 13 h5 ♗xh6 14 ♕xh6 ♗e6 15 hxg6 fxg6 16 ♗d3 with a considerable advantage for White) 12...♖b8 13 f3 a6 14 ♘ge2 ♗d7 15 ♗c2 ♗c6 16 ♔b1 and White is well in control.

10...exd5 11 exd5 b5

Not Black's only option.

a) 11...♖e8 12 hxg6 hxg6 13 0-0-0 b5 14 cxb5 a6 15 ♗h6 ♗h8 16 bxa6 ♗xa6 17 ♗g5 ♗g7 18 ♗xa6 ♖xa6 19 ♕f4 with a big advantage for White in Berdichesky-Pyrich, E-mail 1997.

b) 11...♕d7 12 ♗h6 ♖e8 13 ♗xg7 ♔xg7 14 ♘f3 b5 15 cxb5 ♗b7 16 0-0-0 ♕e7 (16...♘cxd5 17 hxg6 ♘xc3 18 ♕xc3 fxg6 was played in Yakovich-Dolmatov, Elista 1996, but 19 ♖xh7+! is final) 17 hxg6 fxg6 18 ♘g5! looked very good in Alterman-Kindermann, Bad Homburg 1997.

c) 11...a6!? 12 ♕f4 ♘ce8 13 hxg6 (13 ♗d3?!, as in Kekki-Yrjola, Finland 1994, walks into 13...♘xh5! and White lacks sufficient compensation) 13...fxg6 14 ♕h4 ♕b6 15 0-0-0 ♕a5 followed by ...b5 with counterplay.

12 cxb5 ♗b7

12...a6 13 hxg6 fxg6 14 bxa6 ♖e8 15 ♔f1

♗xa6 16 ♗xa6 ♖xa6 17 ♘ge2 left Black with too little for the pawn in Levin-Mellem, Hamburg 1999.

13 ♗f3

13 0-0-0! appears to be strong, although White continues to prefer alternatives.

13...♕d7 14 ♘ge2 ♘xb5 15 ♕f4 ♘xc3 16 ♘xc3 ♖fe8+ 17 ♔f1 ♕f5

17...♘xh5!? 18 ♗xh5 gxh5 is unclear.

18 ♕xf5 gxf5 19 h6 ♗h8 20 ♖h4

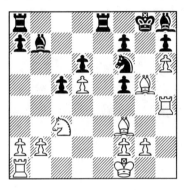

Having had some fun on the kingside White now switches his sights to the other flank, the point being to swing the rook over to a4 to draw attention to the a7-pawn.

20...♖ab8

Others:

a) 20...♗a6+ 21 ♔g1 ♘d7 22 ♖a4 ♗d3 is okay for Black.

b) 20...♘d7!? 21 ♗e2 (21 ♖f4 ♗a6+ 22 ♔g1 ♗d4 with an excellent position) 21...♘b6 22 ♖d1 ♗xc3 23 bxc3 ♗xd5 24 g4 and White has considerable activity for the pawn.

21 ♖a4 ♘e4 22 ♘xe4?!

The superior 22 ♗xe4 fxe4 23 ♗f4 favours White, but Black now latches on to the wrong plan and even contrives to create good losing chances.

22...fxe4 23 ♗xe4 ♗xb2

23...a5! is equal.

24 ♖b1 c4??

24...a5!? 25 ♗d2 with a slight edge.

25 ♖xb2 ♖xe4 26 ♗d2

26 ♖b1! is more to the point.

26...c3 27 Ïxb7 Ïxb7 28 Ïxe4 f5 29 Ïe6 cxd2 30 êe2 Ïb4 31 Ïe7 Ïd4 32 êd1 a5 33 Ïg7+ êh8?! 34 Ïf7 êg8 35 Ïxf5 a4 36 f3 a3 37 g4 Ïd3 38 g5 Ïd4 39 f4 Ïd3 40 Ïf6 Ïxd5 41 f5 Ïd3 42 g6 hxg6 43 fxg6 Ïh3 44 g7 1-0

Game 58
Bönsch-Gallagher
Bundesliga Germany 2002/3

---

1 d4 Ìf6 2 c4 g6 3 Ìc3 êg7 4 e4 d6 5 êe2 0-0 6 êg5 Ìa6 7 Ëc2

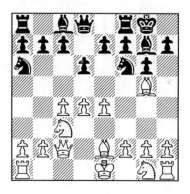

Uhlmann's idea. The queen turns down the natural home on d2 in order to grant any action on the d-file to the rook. For example after ...e7-e5 White has dxe5 followed by Ïd1.

7...h6

Of course this is not the only reply to the 'quiet' Ëc2.

a) 7...c5 8 d5 (8 dxc5 Ìxc5 9 Ìf3 a5 10 0-0 êd7 was unclear in Uhlmann-Klebaner, Naumburg 2002) 8...h6 9 êe3 e6 10 dxe6 êxe6 11 Ïd1 (11 Ëd2!?) 11...Ëa5 (11...Ìg4!? should be okay for Black) 12 a3 Ïfe8 (12...Ïad8 13 h3 with advantage to White) 13 Ìf3 (13 Ïxd6!?) 13...Ïad8 (13...Ìg4 14 êd2 with a plus for White) 14 0-0 êg4 15 Ïd2 with an excellent game for White in Bischoff-Machelett, Germany 1999.

b) 7...c6 8 Ìf3 (8 Ïd1!? Ìc7 9 Ìf3 was Bönsch-Kempinski, Germany 2000, when 9...d5!? leaves White only a shade better) 8...h6

9 êd2 Ëe8 10 Ïd1 e5 11 dxe5 dxe5 12 0-0 Ìh5 (heading for f4; 12...êg4 13 êe3 with a pull for White) 13 Ëc1 êh7 14 Ìe1 Ìf4 15 êxf4 exf4 16 Ëxf4 f5 17 Ëe3 with the more pleasant game for White in Uhlmann-Brendel, Germany 1995.

c) 7...e5 8 dxe5 dxe5 9 Ïd1 Ëe8 10 Ìd5 Ëe6 (10...Ìxd5 11 cxd5 f5 12 êxa6 bxa6 13 Ìe2 h6 14 êd2 Ïb8 15 b3 f4 16 f3 and Black was struggling in Uhlmann-Heissler, Germany 1995) 11 êxf6 êxf6 12 êg4 Ëc6 13 êxc8 Ïaxc8 14 b4 Ëe6 15 Ìf3 with a slight edge to White, Uhlmann-Reschke, Germany 1995.

d) 7...Ëe8 8 Ìf3 e5 9 dxe5 dxe5 10 c5 Ìb4 11 Ëb3 a5 12 0-0 favoured White in Uhlmann-Podzielny, Germany 1995.

8 êf4

A good continuation is 8 êe3 e5 9 dxe5 dxe5 10 Ïd1 Ëe8 (10...Ìd7 11 c5 c6 12 êxa6 bxa6 13 Ìge2 with a plus for White. Uhlmann-Voekler, Germany 1996) 11 Ìf3 Ìg4 12 êc1 f5 13 0-0 Ìb4 14 Ëb3 Ìc6 as in Uhlmann-Gallagher, Dresden 1998, when 15 c5+ êh7 16 êb5 secures White an edge.

8...c5

8...Ìb4!? looks bizarre but in fact offers Black healthy counterplay, e.g. 9 Ëd1 (9 Ëb3 c5, or 9 Ëd2 e5 10 dxe5 dxe5 when 11 êxe5 runs into 11...Ëxd2+ 12 êxd2 Ìxe4+) 9...e5!? 10 dxe5 dxe5 11 êxe5 Ëe7 12 êxf6 (12 Ìf3 Ïd8, intending ...Ìxe4) 12...Ëxf6 13 Ìf3 êg4 with compensation.

9 d5 e5 10 dxe6 êxe6

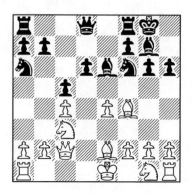

11 ♖d1

11 0-0-0?! (Bagirov-Smirin, Batumi 1999) also brings the rook to the d-file, but White shouldn't send his king to the queenside as 11...♘b4! 12 ♕b1 ♕a5 is excellent for Black and 12 ♕d2 ♘xa2+ 13 ♘xa2 ♘xe4 is even more serious.

11...♘b4 12 ♕b1

12 ♕d2 ♖e8 13 ♗xh6 ♗xh6 14 ♕xh6 ♘c2+ 15 ♔f1 ♘d4 with play (Hazai).

12...♖e8?!

The right place for this rook is d8! Hazai recommends 12...♕a5! 13 ♘f3 (13 ♗xd6 ♖fd8! 14 ♘f3 ♘e8 with counterplay) 13...♗g4 14 0-0 (14 ♗xd6 ♘xa2!) 14...♘e5 with an assessment of unclear.

13 ♗xd6?!

More reasonable was to finish the development. A threat is stronger than its execution! 13 ♘f3! lead to a very unpleasant position for Black where in most variations White has a small but long-term advantage without any counterplay. 13...♘xe4 (13...♗g4 14 0-0 ♘c6 15 ♗xd6 ♘d4 16 ♘xd4 cxd4 17 ♖xd4 ♘xe4 18 ♖xe4 ♗xe2 19 ♖xe8+ ♕xe8 20 ♘xe2 ♕xe2 21 b3 ♗d4 22 ♗g3 with advantage to White – Meyer) 14 ♘xe4 ♗f5 15 ♘fd2 d5 16 cxd5 ♘xd5 17 ♗g3 ♕e7 18 ♗d6!? ♕e6 19 0-0 ♗xe4 20 ♘xe4 ♕xe4 21 ♕xe4 ♖xe4 22 ♗f3 ♘f6 with a slight advantage to White (Meyer).

13...♕a5 14 a3?!

14 ♘f3 ♘xe4! 15 ♘xe4 (15 ♕xe4 ♘xa2 16 0-0 ♗xc3 17 bxc3 ♘xc3 18 ♕c2 ♖ad8 19 ♗e5 ♘xd1 20 ♗xd1 with chances for both sides) 15...♗f5 (15...♘d3+ 16 ♔f1 ♘xb2 17 ♖e1 ♗f5 18 ♘fd2 ♖ad8 19 ♗f4 is also unclear) 16 ♘fd2 ♖xe4 17 ♘xe4 ♘c2+ 18 ♔f1 ♗xe4 19 ♗d3 ♗xd3+ 20 ♖xd3 ♖e8 21 ♖d1 ♘d4 with compensation (Meyer).

14...♘c6 15 ♘f3

15 ♖d2 makes sense, unpinning the c3-knight.

15...♘xe4!

This sacrifice has been hanging in the air for some time.

16 ♕xe4 ♗h3 17 ♕d3 ♗xg2 18 ♖g1 ♗xf3 19 ♕xf3 ♘d4 20 ♖xd4 cxd4 21 ♗b4 ♕c7 22 ♘e4??

A terrible blunder. After the forced 22 ♘d1 ♕xc4 23 ♔f1 ♕c2 Black is still better but at least White is in the game and can hope to mount some kind of resistance.

22...♕c6 23 ♔f1 ♖xe4 24 ♕d3 ♕e6 25 ♖g3 ♖e8 26 ♗f3 f5 27 ♗d2 ♔h7 28 c5 h5 29 b4 h4 30 ♖h3 ♗f6 31 ♗d1 ♕d5 32 ♗f3 ♕a2 33 ♔g2 ♖g4+ 34 ♗xg4 fxg4 0-1

> ### Game 59
> ## Sorin-Foisor
> *Olot 1992*

---

1 d4 ♘f6 2 c4 g6 3 ♘c3 ♗g7 4 e4 d6 5 ♗e2 0-0 6 ♗g5 ♘a6 7 f4

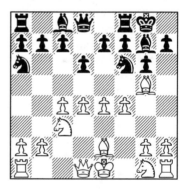

Another hyper-aggressive reaction to Black's...♘a6, White staking a further claim to the centre. Of course the position now closely resembles the Four Pawns Variation, but the question is whom do ♗g5 and ♘a6 most benefit? A brief appraisal of the diagram position suggests that the bishop looks more useful than the knight, occupying an active post compared with the effectively intermediate location on a6. On the other hand the bishop might prove vulnerable in some circumstances, while White could also find himself under pressure on the dark squares.

7...c6

7...c5?! does not fit in well with ...♘a6 after 8 d5, e.g. 8...♕a5 9 ♕d2 e6 10 dxe6 ♗xe6 11 ♘f3 ♗g4 12 0-0 and Black was already in serious difficulties in Tukmakov-Barbero, Wijk aan Zee 1991.

7...♕e8 is a very logical move which Black plans to follow up with ...e7-e5. After subsequent exchanges in the centre the c5-square can be prepared for the knight. Meanwhile White can suffer on the dark squares in some variations, and Black can also look to ...f7-f5 to help the cause. Here are some sample lines:

a) 8 ♕d2 h6 (8...e5 9 fxe5 dxe5 10 d5 ♘c5 11 ♗f3!? a5 12 ♘ge2 ♘fd7 13 ♘b5 was very poor for Black in Alterman-Polgar, Haifa 1998) 9 ♗h4 e5 10 fxe5 dxe5 11 d5 ♘d7 12 g4 f5 13 gxf5 gxf5 14 0-0-0 was unclear in Mohr-Panzer, Germany 1991.

b) 8 e5!? spoils Black's plans. After 8...♘d7 White is unable to maintain the formidable looking centre because ...c7-c5 is coming, but Black's pieces occupy awkward positions and this important factor contributes to White's ultimate advantage, e.g. 9 ♘f3 c5 10 0-0 (10 ♘d5!? looks good) 10...♘b6 (10...cxd4 11 ♘d5 f6 12 exf6 ♘xf6 13 ♗xf6 ♗xf6 14 ♘xf6+ ♖xf6 15 ♘xd4 with a pull for White, Yakovich-Trygstad, Bergen 2000) 11 d5 (11 ♘d5!?) 11...f6 12 ♗h4 fxe5 13 fxe5 dxe5 14 ♗g3 e4 15 ♘xe4 ♗xb2, Grabuzova-Umanskaya, Moscow 1992, and 16 ♖b1 gives White easily enough play.

c) 8 ♘f3

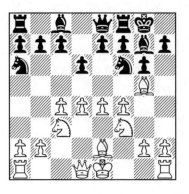

Now 8...e5 9 fxe5 dxe5 10 dxe5!? ♘g4 11 ♘d5 ♘xe5 12 ♗f6!? c6 13 ♘e7+ ♔h8 14 ♕d6, Hoang Thanh Trang-Szuk, Hungary 1998 is well worth remembering (and, for Black, avoiding). Instead Black can preface the push of the e-pawn with 8...h6!?, when 9 ♗h4 e5 10 dxe5!? dxe5 11 ♘xe5 ♘c5 12 ♘d5!? ♘xd5 13 exd5 is a plus for White. A different structure results from 10 fxe5 dxe5 11 d5 ♘g4 12 ♕d2 f5, e.g. 13 h3 ♘f6 14 exf5 (14 0-0, Yakovich-Van den Doel, Leeuwarden 1997, and now 14...♘xe4!? 15 ♘xe4 fxe4 16 ♘h2 is complicated) 14...e4 15 ♘d4 gxf5!? (15...e3 16 ♕c2 g5 17 ♗g3 ♘b4 18 ♕b3 ♘e4 19 ♘xe4 ♕xe4, Sorin-Zarnicki, Buenos Aires 2000, when 20 0-0! would have kept White slightly ahead according to Hazai) 16 ♖f1 (16 0-0-0!?) 16...e3 17 ♕c1 ♘xd5 18 ♘xd5 ♗xd4 19 ♗e7 c6 20 ♗xf8 ♕xf8 with compensation (Hazai).

8 ♘f3 ♘c7

Suddenly the knight looks useful, the threat being to jump across to e6 with a double attack on the bishop and the f4-pawn. Additionally the knight supports ...b7-b5 or ...d6-d5. However, two other continuations are also worth investigating.

a) 8...♗g4!? 9 0-0 ♘c7 10 e5 (Bagirov-Sale, Abu Dhabi 2002) 10...♘h5! with chances for both sides.

b) 8...b5!? (Korchnoi's idea) 9 cxb5 cxb5 10 ♗xb5 ♖b8 11 ♕e2 ♘c7 12 ♗c4 d5 13 exd5 (13 ♗xf6!? exf6! 14 ♘xd5 ♘xd5 15 ♗xd5 f5 16 ♘e5 fxe4 17 ♘c6 ♕d6 is unclear) 13...♘cxd5 14 ♗xf6 ♘xf6 15 0-0 ♘h5 16 ♖ad1 ♘xf4 (16...♗g4 17 g3 e6 with compensation according to Gulko in *ECO*) 17 ♕e4 ♘h5! 18 ♘e5 ♘f6 19 ♕e2 ♗b7, Gulko-Barsov, Montreal 1992 (with an assessment of unclear from Gulko in *ECO*).

9 ♗h4

Let's see other continuations:

a) 9 d5 ♘h5 10 ♕d2 f6 11 ♗h4 ♗h6 12 g3 e5 was the course of Chjumachenko-Nadyrhanov, Novorossijsk 1997, when 13 dxc6!? bxc6 14 c5 exf4 15 cxd6 ♘e8 is unclear according to *ECO*. However, after 16 ♖d1 (preparing d6-d7 and ♘e5) Black appears to have serious problems. Black should prefer 9...♘a6!? 10 ♘d2 ♕b6 11 ♖b1 ♖e8 12 a3 ♖b8 with counterplay in Degerhammar-Scheuermann, E-mail 2001, or 9...cxd5 10 cxd5 ♘a6!? 11 ♘d2 ♘e8 12 ♖b1 (12 ♖c1!?) 12...f5 13 0-0 ♘c5 14 exf5 &xf5 with a good game, Sturua-Kempinski, Leon 2001.

b) 9 ♕d2 and now:

b1) 9...&g4 10 h3 &xf3 11 &xf3 ♘e6 (11...♘d7 12 f5 with a healthy initiative for White in Lalic-McShane, Millfield 2000) 12 &h4 ♘d7 13 ♘e2! c5 14 dxc5 dxc5 15 0-0-0! ♘d4 16 e5 and White could be confident of earning the full point in Yakovich-Xie Jun, Moscow 1992.

b2) 9...♘e6!? 10 0-0-0 (10 &h4!?) 10...♘xg5 11 fxg5 ♘d7 12 h4 and now both 12...c5, Singleton-Finnie, Correspondence 1992, and 12 ♖hf1 are unclear.

b3) 9...♕e8 10 0-0 b5 11 e5 (11 cxb5!? cxb5 12 ♖ac1 with a slight advantage to White) 11...b4 12 exf6 (12 ♘d1!?) 12...exf6 13 &h4 bxc3 14 bxc3! is equal according to *NCO*, but in our opinion White has slightly the better chances, e.g. 14...&f5 (14...f5 15 ♖fe1, or 14...&e6 15 ♖ab1 with the more pleasant game for White in either case) 15 &d3 &xd3 16 ♕xd3 with advantage to White. Note that 14 ♕xc3? ♕xe2 15 ♖fe1 ♘b5! 16 ♖xe2 ♘xc3 17 bxc3 (Yakovich-Atalik, Beijing 1997) favours Black after 17...&e6 18 ♘d2 ♖ab8.

b4) 9...d5 10 &xf6 exf6 (10...&xf6 11 cxd5 cxd5 12 e5 &g7 13 h4 h5 14 &d3 &h6 15 0-0 ♘e6 16 g3 with a slight advantage to White, Moskalenko-Zlochevsky, Alushta 1993) 11 exd5 (11 cxd5!? cxd5 12 e5 &g4 13 0-0 fxe5 14 dxe5 f6 was Bursztyn-Bolbochan, Netanya 1993, when 15 ♖ad1 would have secured White an edge) 11...cxd5 12 c5 &f5!? 13 0-0 &e4 (13...♖e8 14 ♖ad1 ♕d7 15 b4 ½-½, Bekker Jensen-Zesch, Gelsenkirchen 2001) 14 b4 ♘e6 15 ♖ad1 f5 16 ♘e5 (Meins-Kempinski, Groningen 1996) 16...f6!? with chances for both sides.

b5) 9...b5

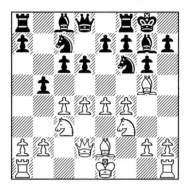

Another attempted justification of Black's set-up, and this one looks sound. For example after 10 e5 b4 11 exf6 bxc3 12 bxc3 exf6 13 &h4 ♕d7 Black was fine in Wang Lei-Kovalevskaya, Shanghai 2001, and nor did 10 cxb5 cxb5 11 e5 b4 12 exf6 bxc3 13 bxc3 improve White's lot in Meins-Reschke, Germany 1998.

This leaves 10 &xf6, avoiding the loss of a tempo caused by an attack on the bishop (after ...e7xf6, above) by simply removing the problem piece. Then 10...exf6 11 cxb5 cxb5 12 0-0 b4 (Mirkovic-Brenjo, Kladovo 1994) 13 ♘d1!? f5 leaves much play, while 10...&xf6 11 e5 &g7 12 cxb5 cxb5 is more sober, with Black holding his ground after either 13 ♘xb5 ♘xb5 14 &xb5 ♕b6 with play, or 13 0-0 b4 14 ♘e4 &b7 15 &d3 dxe5 16 dxe5 ♘e6 17 ♖ad1 ♕b6+ 18 ♔h1 ½-½, Korotylev-Lomineishvili, UKR 1999 (Black has an edge).

9...d5

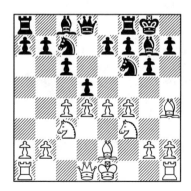

9...♘e6 is again dubious: 10 ♕d2 ♘h5 11 g3 ♗h6 (11...♘f6 12 e5 with advantage to White) 12 ♘g5 ♘eg7 13 0-0-0 f6 14 ♔b1 ♕c7 15 d5 was crushing in Yakovich-Glavina Rossi, Oviedo 1991. But Black can try 9...b5 10 e5 ♘g4! thanks to weakness of the e3-square (Black wins a tempo), e.g. 11 ♕d2 dxe5!? 12 ♘xe5 (12 dxe5 ♘e6 13 h3 ♕xd2+ 14 ♔xd2 b4 15 ♘e4 ♖d8+ 16 ♔e1 ♘e3 17 ♗xe7 ♘c2+ 18 ♔f2 ♖d7 19 ♖ac1 ♖xe7 with equality; 12 fxe5 f6 gives Black counterplay) 12...♘xe5 13 dxe5 ♕xd2+ 14 ♔xd2 b4 15 ♘e4 f6 16 exf6 exf6 and the game looks level. Indeed Salceanu-Jorgensen, E-mail 2000 continued 17 ♖ad1 ♘e6 18 ♖hf1 ♘d4 19 ♗d3 ♗g4 20 ♖de1 b3 21 h3 ♗f5 22 ♗f2 ♖fd8 23 axb3 ♘xb3+ 24 ♔c2 ♖ab8 25 ♘c5 ½-½.

10 cxd5

Alternatives achieve nothing.

a) 10 ♗xf6 exf6! 11 cxd5 (11 0-0 dxe4 12 ♘xe4 ♗g4 followed by ...f6-f5 with advantage to Black, or 11 exd5 cxd5 12 c5 ♗g4 with chances for both sides) 11...cxd5 12 e5 ♗h6 and Black is holding his ground well.

b) 10 e5 ♘e4 (10...♘h5 11 g3 dxc4 12 ♗xc4 with a plus for White) 11 ♘xe4 (11 0-0 f6 12 ♘xe4 dxe4 13 ♘e1 ♘e6 14 ♘c2 g5 15 fxg5 fxe5 16 ♖xf8+ was seen in Illescas-Comas, Spain 2002, and now 16...♗xf8!? is unclear) 11...dxe4 12 ♘g5 f6! 13 ♘xe4 ♘e6 14 d5 (14 exf6!? exf6 15 0-0 ♘xd4 with a level game) 14...cxd5 (14...♘xf4!? 15 0-0 fxe5 secures an edge for Black) 15 exf6 (15 cxd5 ♘xf4 16 0-0 fxe5!? 17 d6 ♗f6! is given by Golubev as unclear) 15...exf6 16 cxd5 (16 ♕xd5 ♕xd5 with an edge for Black) 16...♘xf4 17 0-0 g5 (17...♘xe2+ 18 ♕xe2 ♕xd5 19 ♘xf6+ ½-½, Cs.Horvath-Poldauf, Austria 1999) 18 ♗c4 (18 ♖xf4 gxf4 19 d6 ♔h8 with compensation – Golubev in *ECO*) 18...♕c7 with much to play for in Wang Lei-Ye Jiang-chuan, Shanghai 2000.

10...cxd5 11 e5 ♘e4! 12 ♕b3 ♗h6 13 g3

13 ♗g5!? ♗g7 (13...♗xg5 14 ♘xg5 ♘xc3 15 ♕xc3 f6 16 ♖c1 fxg5 17 ♕xc7 gxf4 18 ♖c3 ♗f5 is a decent alternative) 14 ♖c1 ♘xc3

15 ♖xc3 ♘e6 with chances for both sides.

13...b6

13...♗h3!? is also possible.

14 0-0 ♗b7 15 ♖ad1 ♘e6 16 ♘e1 ♘xc3 17 ♕xc3 f6 18 ♘g2 ♕d7 19 ♗g4 ♗a6 20 ♖fe1 f5 21 ♗f3 g5 22 fxg5 ♗xg5 23 ♗xg5 ♘xg5 24 e6

24 ♘f4!? is another option.

24...♕d6

More accurate is 24...♘h3+ 25 ♔h1 ♘f2+ 26 ♔g1 ♘h3+ with a perpetual check.

25 ♖e5?

Missing 25 ♘f4! ♘e4 26 ♕b3 with an edge for White.

25...♘h3+ 26 ♔h1 ♘f2+ 27 ♔g1 ♘xd1 28 ♗xd1 ♖ac8 29 ♕d2 ♕c7 30 ♕g5+ ♔h8 31 ♘f4? ♕c1 32 ♖e1 ♖f6 33 h4 ♕xb2 34 ♘xd5 ♕xd4+ 35 ♘e3 ♖g8 36 ♕h5 ♖xg3+ 37 ♔h2 ♕f4 38 ♘g2 ♖xg2+ 39 ♔xg2 ♖g6+ 40 ♔h1 ♗b7+ 0-1

Game 60
Kachiani Gersinska-Kovalev
Helsinki 1996

1 d4 ♘f6 2 c4 g6 3 ♘c3 ♗g7 4 e4 d6 5 ♗e2 0-0 6 ♗g5 ♘a6 7 ♕d2

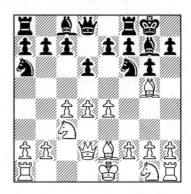

The most logical and flexible move, developing the queen actively by teaming up with the bishop.

7...e5

Black, too, responds in standard fashion, staking a claim in the centre. Of course there are other moves available but, unless Black is intent on doing without ...e7-e5, he might as well play it now.

a) 7...♕e8!? tends to transpose to lines covered below after 8 h4 e5 9 d5 or 8 f3 e5 etc.

b) 7...c5?! 8 d5 e6 9 ♘f3 (9 dxe6!? ♗xe6, Solmajer-Breznik, Slovenia 1993 and 10 ♘f3 favours White) 9...exd5 10 exd5 ♖e8 (10...♗g4 11 ♕f4 with advantage to White) 11 0-0 ♕b6 12 ♗d3 (12 ♖ae1 is also good enough for a plus) 12...♗d7 (12...♗g4 13 ♕f4) 13 h3 ♘b4 14 ♗b1 h5 15 a3 ♘a6 16 ♗d3 and Black was struggling in Bareev-I.Sokolov, Biel 1993.

c) 7...c6 8 f3!? ♘c7 9 0-0-0 (9 ♖d1!?) 9...b5!? (9...♘e6 10 ♗e3 ♕a5 11 ♔b1 is better for White) 10 cxb5 cxb5 11 ♗xb5 (11 ♘xb5 ♘xb5 12 ♗xb5 ♕b6 with compensation) 11...♘xb5 12 ♘xb5 ♗e6 with enough activity for the pawn. Black can also try 8...♖b8!?, e.g. 9 g4 ♕a5 10 h4 (Sakaev-Motylev, Moscow 1998) 10...c5!? 11 ♘d5 ♕xd2+ 12 ♔xd2 ♘xd5 13 cxd5 f6 with an interesting position.

8 d5 ♕e8

Black wants to unpin immediately.

9 h4

This thrust is certainly a key theme in this system! 9 ♗d1 is covered in the next main game, while others are discussed below.

a) 9 0-0-0 ♘c5 (9...♗d7 10 f3 ♘h5 11 g3 f5 12 ♗e3 ♘c5 13 exf5 gxf5 was unclear in Hernando Rodrigo-Barrero Garcia, Barcelona 2000) 10 f3 ♘h5 11 b4 ♘a6 12 a3 ♘f4 13 ♗f1 (13 g3 ♘xe2+ 14 ♘gxe2 f5 with chances for both sides according to Golubev in *ECO*) 13...f6 14 ♗h4 ♗h6 15 ♔b2 f5 16 ♕c2 fxe4 17 ♘xe4 ♗f5 18 ♗f2 ♘b8 and both sides could be reasonably content in Raetsky-Golubev, Biel 1994.

b) 9 ♘f3 ♘h5!? 10 g3 (10 0-0-0 ♘f4 11 ♗xf4 exf4 12 ♖de1 ♘c5 13 ♗d1 a6 14 ♗c2 b5 15 ♕xf4 b4! was fine for Black in Dao Thien Hai-Paragua, Manila 2001, while Black generated good play after 10 0-0 f5 11 ♘e1 f4 12 f3 h6 13 ♗h4 g5 14 ♗f2 ♕g6 15 ♘d3 g4 in Pisulinski-Toczek, Lubniewice 2002) 10...f5 11 exf5 (11 ♘h4 f4 12 g4 ♘f6 13 f3 h5 14

gxh5 ♘h7 15 ♘xg6 ♘xg5, Tisdall-Watson, Oslo 1991, and now 16 h4!? ♘h7 17 ♘xf8 ♘xf8 18 0-0-0 ♕xh5 19 ♖dg1 keeps the fire burning) 11...gxf5 12 ♗h6 f4 13 ♗xg7 ♘xg7 with equality, Gulko-Djurhuus, Manila 1992.

c) 9 ♗d3

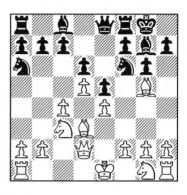

c1) 9...♘h5 10 ♘ge2 f5 11 f3 (11 exf5 ♗xf5 12 ♗xf5 gxf5 failed to trouble Black in Baragar-Yoos, Winnipeg 1997) 11...♘c5 (11...f4 12 ♗h4 g5 13 ♗f2 g4 14 0-0-0 ♔h8 15 ♔b1 ♗f6 16 ♘c1 gxf3 17 gxf3 ♕e7 18 ♘b5 c5 19 dxc6 bxc6 20 ♘c3 ♘g7!, as in Dao Thien Hai-David, Wijk aan Zee 1997, is unclear according to Hazai) 12 ♗c2 a5 13 exf5 gxf5 14 0-0 (14 0-0-0 ♗d7 15 h3 f4 16 ♗h4 a4 17 ♗f2 b6 with chances for both sides, Bekker Jensen-Hunt, Witley 1999) 14...♗d7 (14...f4!?) 15 ♖ae1 f4 16 g4 fxg3 17 hxg3 ♘f6 with a balanced middlegame, Horvath-Kindermann, Austria 1997.

c2) 9...♘d7 also releases the f-pawn. In Hoang Thanh Trang-Coleman, Amsterdam 1996 Black should have met 10 ♘ge2 with the immediate 10...f5!? 11 exf5 gxf5 with healthy counterplay. After 10 ♖d1 ♘dc5 11 ♗b1 f6 12 ♗e3 f5 13 f3 ♗d7 the tension builds, while 10...f5 was the more direct course taken in Najer-Umanskaya, Moscow 1996, which went 11 ♘ge2 f4 12 f3 ♗f6 (12...h6 13 ♗h4 ♘dc5 14 ♗b1 ♗d7 with chances for both sides) 13 ♗xf6 ♗xf6, and now in *ECO* Umanskaya gives 14 a3 c5! 15 dxc6 bxc6 16 b4 ♘c7 with chances for both sides.

Let's return to 9 h4, with the following position:

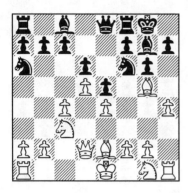

9...♘c5!?

Black has also tried 9...♘h5 10 ♗xh5 (10 ♘h3 f6 11 ♗h6 ♗xh6 12 ♕xh6 ♗xh3 13 ♗xh5 with a level game in Sorin-Nadyrhanov, Moscow 1994) 10...gxh5 11 ♘ge2 f5 12 exf5 ♗xf5 13 ♘g3 ♕g6 14 ♘xf5 ♕xf5 15 0-0 ♘c5 16 f3 and White stood slightly better in Fitzpatrick-Guizar, Correspondence 1999.

10 ♕c2

10 f3?! unnecessarily weakens the dark squares – 10...♘h5 11 g4 (11 b4 ♘a6 12 a3 f5 and Black is doing fine) 11...♘g3 12 ♖h3 ♘xe2 13 ♘gxe2 (13 ♕xe2 f5 with the usual activity for Black in Borbjerggaard-Sosnicki, Koszalin 1997) 13...f5 and Black has no complaints, Petran-Tratar, Austria 1996.

10...a5

10...h6 11 ♗e3 ♘g4 12 ♗xg4 ♗xg4 (Tjiam-Piket, Holland 1996) is a trade that deserves further tests.

11 h5

White presses on rather than take time out to castle, which resulted in a complex position in Nielsen-Lambert, Correspondence 1998 after 11 0-0-0 ♗d7 12 ♘h3 ♘a4!? 13 ♖d3 (13 ♘b5!?) 13...♘xc3 14 ♖xc3.

11...♘xh5 12 ♗xh5 gxh5 13 ♗e3 ♘a6 14 ♘ge2 f5 15 f3 ♕g6 16 ♖h2 c6

Black should not open up the position. The flexible 16...♗d7!? is preferable, with dynamic equality.

17 ♕d2 fxe4 18 ♘xe4 cxd5 19 cxd5 ♗d7 20 ♘2g3 ♖ac8 21 a3 ♖c4?!

21...♘c5!? looks better.

22 b3 ♖xe4?! 23 ♘xe4 ♗f5 24 ♖h4 ♗xe4 25 ♖xe4 ♘c7 26 ♖c1 ♕f7 27 ♖d1 ♘e8 28 ♗g5 ♕g6 29 ♖c1 ♗f6 30 ♗e3 ♗d8 31 ♖ec4 ♘f6 32 ♖c8?! e4 33 ♗h6?! exf3 34 ♕g5??

A serious mistake. Instead the cold-blooded 34 gxf3 ♕g1+ 35 ♔e2 ♖e8+ 36 ♔d3 ♕g6+ 37 ♔c4 is brutal.

34...f2+?

One mistake often seems to prompt another in reply. This time there is the simpler 34...fxg2 (or, with different move order, 34...♕xg5 35 ♗xg5 fxg2) 35 ♔e2 ♕xg5 36 ♗xg5 ♗b6 37 ♖xf8+ ♗xf8 38 ♗xf6 g1♕ 39 ♖xg1 ♗xg1 with which Black steers the game to a winning ending!

35 ♔e2 ♕xg5?

Luck goes in cycles, and here it smiles on White, who would only be able to claim a modest plus after 35...♖e8+ 36 ♔f1 ♔f7 37 ♕xg6+ ♔xg6 38 ♗f4 ♘e4 39 ♖1c2.

36 ♗xg5 ♘e4 37 ♖xd8 ♘g3+ 38 ♔d3 f1♕+ 39 ♖xf1 ♘xf1 40 ♖xf8+ ♔xf8 41 ♗f4 h4 42 ♗xd6+ ♔e8 43 a4 ♔d7 44 ♗f4 ♘g3 45 ♔c4 ♘e4 46 ♔d4 ♘f2 47 ♗e3 h3 48 gxh3 ♘xh3 49 ♔c5 h6

49...h5 50 ♔b5 ♔d6 51 ♔xa5 ♔xd5 52 ♔b6 is decisive.

50 ♗xh6 ♘f2 51 ♔b6 ♘e4 52 ♔xa5 ♘f6 53 ♔b6 ♔c8 54 d6 ♘d7+ 55 ♔b5 ♔b8 56 ♗g7 ♔c8 57 b4 ♔b8 58 a5 ♔c8 59 ♔c4 ♘b8 60 b5 ♔d7 61 ♔d5 ♔e8 62 ♗d4 ♔d7 1-0

Game 61
Leitao-Gormally
Mermaid Beach 1998

---

1 d4 ♘f6 2 c4 g6 3 ♘c3 ♗g7 4 e4 d6 5 ♗e2 0-0 6 ♗g5 ♘a6 7 ♕d2 e5 8 d5 ♕e8 9 ♗d1

At first glance a little strange, dropping the bishop back to d1 is in fact quite logical – and very popular in modern practice. White wants to defend the e4-pawn with ♗c2, while the mini-manoeuvre also frees e2 for the king's knight. Note the connection with positions in the 5 ♗d3 system (with Black's queen on e8 instead of d8).

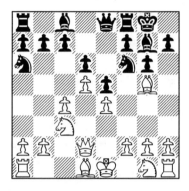

9...♘h5

Black's justification for this radical response is the 'gain' of a tempo and the fact that the queen will offer protection on the h5-e8 diagonal after the planned ...f7-f5 etc. However, this strategy is not without some positional risk and, consequently, is probably not the best of Black's options, which we can take a look at below.

a) 9...c6 10 ♘ge2 cxd5 11 ♗xf6 ♗xf6 12 ♘xd5 ♗h4 13 0-0 ♗e6 14 ♘ec3 ♕d8 15 g3 ♗g5 16 f4 exf4 17 gxf4 with advantage to White, Mascarenhas-Barkwell, E-mail 1997.

b) 9...♘c5 10 ♗c2 a5 11 ♘ge2 ♗d7 (11...♘h5?! 12 ♘b5 ♕d7 13 0-0-0 b6 14 f3 a4 was tried in Seirawan-Piket, Wijk aan Zee 1991, when Piket suggests 15 ♗e3! followed by ♘ec3 with a very big lead) 12 f3 b5 (12...♔h8 13 0-0 ♘g8 14 ♖ae1 f6 15 ♗e3 f5 16 exf5 gxf5, Tisdall-Manninen, Gausdal 1991, and now 17 ♗xc5!? dxc5 18 ♘c1 b6 19 ♘d3 looks strong; 12...h5 13 ♗e3 ♘h7 14 0-0-0 [Petursson-Djurhuus, Gausdal 1995] 14...a4!? 15 ♔b1 a3 16 b3 with a plus) 13 cxb5 ♗xb5 14 ♘xb5 ♕xb5 (Valeriani-Stilling, Correspondence 1991) and now 15 ♖b1 followed by 0-0, gives White an edge according to Piket.

c) 9...♗d7 is probably best. Then 10 h3 ♘c5 11 ♗c2 a5 12 g4 b5 13 cxb5 ♗xb5 14 ♘ge2 ♖b8 was good for Black in Cranbourne-Buraschi, Correspondence 1999, so White should play 12 ♘ge2!? with chances for both sides. Instead 10 ♘ge2 ♘h5 11 ♘g3 ♘f4 12 0-0 ♘c5 13 ♗c2 a5, when Yusupov gives the following: 14 a4 ♕b8 15 ♖ab1 (Black is fine after either 15 ♗xf4 exf4 16 ♕xf4 ♕a7 or 16...c6) 15...♕a7 16 ♘ge2 ♘xe2+ 17 ♕xe2 ♕b8 with equality, Yusupov-Nikolaidis, Yerevan 1996.

10 ♗xh5!

This principled capture appears effective but it is not White's only promising continuation.

a) 10 ♘ge2 f5 11 exf5 gxf5 12 ♘g3 ♘f6 13 ♗c2 ♕g6 14 f3 ♗d7 15 0-0 ♖ae8 with mutual chances, Leitao-Marques, Sao Paulo 1997.

b) 10 ♗a4!? ♗d7 11 ♗xd7 ♕xd7 12 ♘ge2 f5 13 f3 ♘c5 (13...♘f6 14 ♘c1 ♘c5 15 ♘d3 ♘xd3+ 16 ♕xd3 fxe4 17 ♘xe4 ♘xe4 was agreed drawn in Sapis-Umansky, Legnica 1996, although White has the advantage here) 14 b4 ♘a4 15 0-0 a5 16 a3 ♘f6 17 ♖ab1 ♘xc3 18 ♘xc3 with an edge for White, Heinig-Schenk, Bad Woerishofen 2001.

c) 10 f3 f5 11 ♘ge2 ♗d7 (11...fxe4 12 ♘xe4 ♘f4 13 0-0, Ivanov-Sokolin, Russia 1992, and now 13...♕f7 14 ♗c2 h6 15 ♗h4 g5 16 ♗g3 favours White; 11...♘c5 12 b4 fxe4 13 bxc5 exf3 14 gxf3 ♖xf3 would have led to trouble for Black in Krizsany-Czebe, Budapest 1993 had White found 15 ♘e4!, clamping down on Black's King's Indian bishop, so Black should play 12...♘a6 13 ♗a4 ♕f7 14 a3 with advantage to White) 12 a3 f4 13 ♗h4 ♗f6 14 ♗f2 ♕e7 15 ♗c2 (15 ♗a4!?) 15...♗h4 16 g3 ♗g5 17 g4 ♘g3 (Yakovich-Nadyrhanov, Smolensk 1997) 18 ♖g1 ♘xe2 (18...♗xg4 19 h4!) 19 ♕xe2 ♗h4 with a balanced game according to Nadyrhanov in *ECO*.

Returning to the position after 10 ♗xh5, below, the recapture is not forced.

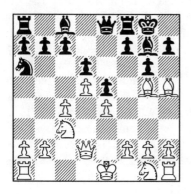

10...gxh5

Rather than the automatic recapture Black can hope for more with 10...f6, e.g. 11 ♗h6 ♗xh6 12 ♕xh6 gxh5 13 ♘ge2 ♕g6 14 ♕d2 f5 15 f3 b6 16 exf5 ♗xf5, which is given as equal in *ECO*. However after 17 ♘g3 ♗d7, as in Petursson-Grivas, Katerini 1993, White should play 18 0-0-0 with an edge.

11 ♘f3!?

11 ♘ge2 f5!? 12 exf5 ♗xf5 13 ♘g3 e4 14 0-0 ♕g6 15 ♗e3 ♖ae8 (Petursson-Glek, Belgrade 1988) 16 ♘xf5 ♖xf5 17 ♔h1 with f2-f3 to follow, and White should be better here.

11...f5 12 exf5 ♗xf5 13 ♘h4 ♘c5 14 ♘xf5 ♖xf5 15 0-0 ♕g6 16 ♗e3 ♖af8 17 ♖ad1

Stronger is 17 ♗xc5 dxc5 18 ♘e4, e.g. 18...♖f4 19 ♘xc5 ♖xc4 20 ♘e6 ♖f7 21 ♕e3 with an edge (Leitao), or 18...b6 19 ♕e2 etc.

17...h4 18 ♗xc5 dxc5

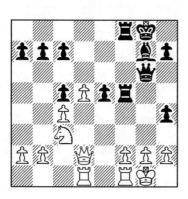

19 d6?!

Tempting, but more promising winning prospects are offered by 19 ♘e4 or 19 ♕e2, although after 19...h3 20 g3 White's potential problems on the light squares present him with technical difficulties as far as converting the advantage is concerned.

19...cxd6 20 ♕d5+ ♔h8 21 ♖xd6 ♕xd6?

Missing 21...e4! 22 ♘xe4 ♗xb2 23 ♕xg6 hxg6 with equality.

22 ♖xd6 ♖f4 23 ♖d7?!

Preferable is 23 b3 e4 24 ♘d5 with a plus.

23...b6

After 23...♖xc4 24 ♖xb7 e4 25 ♖xa7 ♗xc3 26 bxc3 ♖xc3 Black should draw the ending.

24 b3 e4 25 g3 hxg3 26 hxg3 ♖g4 27 ♘e2 a5 28 ♖fd1 1-0

Obviously White has a clear advantage – his active pieces combined with the weakness of Black's pawn structure will sooner or later result in the win of a pawn. However, Black could still have put up a bit more resistance.

Game 62
I.Farago-Rotstein
Maribor 1994

---

1 d4 ♘f6 2 c4 g6 3 ♘c3 ♗g7 4 e4 d6 5 ♗e2 0-0 6 ♗g5 ♘a6 7 ♕d2 e5 8 d5 c6

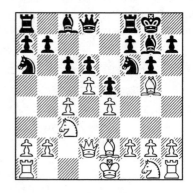

More active than 8...♕e8, Black wastes no time seeking counterplay on the queenside. However, opening the c-file is not always advantageous for Black...

9 ♗f3

This move has been popularised by GM Ivan Farago. On f3 the bishop protects the e4-pawn and frees the e2-square for the knight, while the main idea behind the text is to eventually target Black's backward d6-pawn. However, this is the second move with the same piece, and to a post that is far from perfect! With this in mind White should look elsewhere for more threatening continuations. 9 h4 and 9 f3 are dealt with in the next two main games, while here are the other alternatives:

a) 9 ♗d1?! does not work out well for White in this particular scenario, allowing Black immediate counterplay, e.g. 9...cxd5 10 cxd5 (the key factor here is the unprotected b5-square) 10...b5!? 11 a3 (11 ♘xb5 ♕b6 is okay for Black) 11...♘c5 12 f3 a5 13 ♘xb5 a4! 14 ♘c3 ♗a6 (14...♕a5 with compensation – Petursson in *ECO*) 15 ♗c2 ♕b8 16 ♘ge2 ♕xb2 17 0-0 ♘b3 18 ♗xb3 ♕xd2 19 ♗xd2 axb3 and Black had an excellent position in Leitao-Sorin, Sao Paulo 1991.

b) After 9 ♘f3 ♘c5 White's pieces look poorly placed, and there is no convenient way to defend the e4-pawn. Bareev-Kuzmin, USSR Championship 1990 went 10 ♗xf6 ♕xf6 11 b4 ♘a6 12 a3 c5 13 ♖b1 ♕e7 14 0-0 f5 15 ♘e1, when Bareev gives 15...fxe4 16 ♘xe4 ♗f5 17 ♗f3 b6 18 ♘d3 ♖ac8 19 bxc5 ♗xe4 20 ♗xe4 ♘xc5 as equal.

c) 9 ♗d3

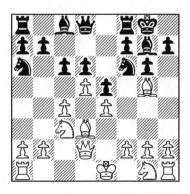

Another move of the light-squared bishop.

The diagram position is not unlike those encountered in the 5 ♗d3 variation, except that here White has lost a move. Nonetheless it is a little more accurate to prefer d3 over d1 here. 9...♘c5 10 ♗c2 and now:

c1) 10...a5 11 ♘ge2 cxd5 12 exd5!? ♗d7 13 0-0 ♕c7 14 b3 ♖fe8 was unclear in Bettalli-Pantaleoni, Correspondence 1992.

c2) 10...♕b6 11 ♖b1 ♕b4 (11...a5 12 ♘ge2 with an edge for White) 12 ♘ge2 h6 (12...a5 13 a3 ♕xc4 14 ♗xf6 ♗xf6 15 b4 axb4 16 axb4 cxd5 17 bxc5 and Black was on the ropes in Petursson-Nunn, Reykjavik 1990) 13 a3 ♕xc4 14 ♗xf6 ♗xf6 15 b4 ♗g5 16 ♕d1 cxd5 17 bxc5 d4 18 ♘d5 ♕xc5 19 0-0 ♗e6 and now an assessment of unclear is given in *ECO*, but White is doing well, e.g. 20 ♗b3 (20 ♗d3!? is also interesting, 20...♗xd5 21 exd5 f5 22 ♕a4 ♕c7 23 ♕b3 ♕g7 24 ♕xb7 ♕xb7 25 ♖xb7 being excellent for White) 20...♖ac8 21 ♔h1 ♕xa3 22 f4 ♗h4 23 f5 gxf5 24 exf5 ♗xd5 25 ♗xd5 ♖c5 26 ♖b3 ♕a5 (Silman-Root, California 1990) 27 ♗xb7 with a slight advantage to White.

c3) 10...cxd5!? 11 cxd5 (11 exd5 a5 12 ♘ge2 leads back to 10...a5, but 11...♕b6!? is quite possible) 11...a5 12 ♘ge2 ♗d7 (12...b5!? 13 ♘xb5 h6 14 ♗xf6 ♗xf6 15 h4 h5 was unclear in Lyukmanov-Beroun, Correspondence 1990, and after 14 ♗xh6 ♘cxe4! 15 ♗xe4 ♘xe4 16 ♕e3 ♗xh6 17 ♕xe4 ♗f5 the bishop pair gives Black good compensation for the pawn) 13 f3 b5 14 0-0 b4 15 ♘d1 ♗b5 (15...♕b6 16 ♗e3 ♗b5 17 ♘f2 ♕a6 18 ♖fe1 ½-½, Silman-Rey, San Francisco 1999) 16 ♖e1 ♕b6 with an interesting struggle in Gislason-Kilgour, Correspondence 1990/94.

9...cxd5

a) 9...♕e8 10 dxc6 ♕xc6 11 ♖c1 ♗e6 12 b3 (12 ♘ge2!? with advantage to White) 12...♘c5 13 ♘ge2 h6! 14 ♗xf6 ♗xf6 15 ♖d1 ♗g5 16 ♕c2 h5 was equal in Horvath-Dydyshko, Harkany 1991.

b) 9...♕a5 10 ♘ge2 cxd5 (10...♘c5 11 0-0 cxd5 12 ♘xd5 ♕xd2 13 ♘xf6+ ♗xf6 14 ♗xd2 with a pull for White [I.Farago in *ECO*] in Farago-Wells, Hungary 1995, when White had achieved his aim of reaching an ending with the backward pawn) 11 cxd5! and Black must justify sending the queen to a5. After 11...♘c5 12 ♖b1 Black loses time thanks to his awkward pieces, e.g. 12...♕b4 13 0-0 ♗d7 14 a3 ♕b3 15 ♘c1 ♕b6 16 b4 with advantage to White. This leaves 11...b5 12 a3 ♖b8 13 0-0 b4 14 ♘a2 ♕b6 15 ♘xb4 ♘xb4 16 ♗e3 ♕b7 17 axb4 ♕xb4 18 ♘c3 ♕xb2 19 ♕xb2 ♖xb2 20 ♖xa7 with advantage to White. We can also consider 11 ♘xd5 ♕xd2+ 12 ♗xd2 ♘xd5 13 cxd5 f5 14 0-0 ♗d7 15 b4 ♗b5 16 ♖fe1 ♖ac8 17 ♘c3 ♗d3 18 a3 ♖c7, which was seen in Hort-Xie Jun, London 1996, when the c-file played a part: 19 ♖ac1 ♖fc8 20 ♗e2 ♗xe2 21 ♘xe2 ♖c2 22 ♘g3 ♖8c7 23 b5 ♖xc1 24 ♖xc1 ♖xc1+ 25 ♗xc1 ♘c7 and a draw was agreed.

10 ♘xd5

10 cxd5 is harmless: 10...♗d7 11 ♖b1 ♕e8 12 ♘gc2 h5 13 0-0 ♘h7 14 ♗h6 ♗xh6 15 ♕xh6 ♕e7 16 g3 ♕g5 with equality, Beliavsky, Bönsch-Maiwald, Dresden 2000.

10...♘c5

10...♗e6 11 ♘e2 ♖c8 12 ♘xf6+ (12 b3 ♗xd5 13 ♗xf6 ♗xf6 14 ♕xd5 ♖c5 15 ♕d2 b5 with counterplay in Rezsek-Grabics, Hungary 1995) 12...♗xf6 13 ♗xf6 ♕xf6 14 b3 ♕e7 15 0-0 ♘b8 16 ♖fd1 ♖fd8 17 ♖ac1 ♘c6 with chances for both sides, Farago-Paehtz, Budapest 1991 (this is similar to the main line, below).

11 ♗xf6 ♗xf6 12 ♘xf6+ ♕xf6 13 ♘e2

The diagram position is what White was looking for when he embarked on this line – Black's d6-pawn is backward and the d5-square is a potential problem. But the price is vulnerability on the dark squares and a passive bishop, which now looks fairly lacking on f3. Moreover, as for the d5-square, this feature is less worrying for Black than it might first seem, for as soon White sends the knight there Black will be ready to remove it with ...Bxd5, leaving Black with the superior minor piece. Meanwhile the d6-pawn is easy to defend. Consequently the game is well balanced.

13...♗e6

Wasting no time in monitoring d5. Others:

a) 13...♘e6 14 ♖c1 ♖d8 15 0-0 ♘g5 16 ♘c3 with the better prospects for White, Farago-Deak, Hungary 1993.

b) 13...♕h4 14 g3 ♕e7 15 0-0 ♗h3 16 ♖fd1 ♖ad8 17 ♘c3 f6 18 ♕e3 a6 19 ♖d2 ♘e6 20 ♗g2 ♗xg2 21 ♔xg2 and Black has made the mistake of trading bishops in Beliavsky, Farago-Groszpeter, Zalakaros 1994, being suitably punished with a disadvantage following the subsequent 21...f5 22 exf5 gxf5 23 f4 ♕c7 24 b3 ♕c5 25 ♖e1 ♕xe3 26 ♖xe3 e4 27 ♘d5 etc.

c) 13...b6 14 0-0 (14 b3 ♗b7 15 ♘c3 ♘e6 16 0-0 ♘d4 17 ♗e2 ♕h4 ½-½, Farago-Groszpeter, Budapest 1993) 14...♗b7 15 ♕e3 (Farago-Seres, Hungary 1994) 15...♖ad8 16 ♖fd1 ♕h4 17 g3 (17 ♘c3 f5) 17...♕e7 and Black has counterplay in the form of ...f7-f5. Another Farago game, Farago-Szuk, Hungary 1995, went instead 15 ♘c3, when Black should have continued 15...♖ad8!? 16 ♖ad1 ♘e6 with chances for both sides.

14 ♖c1 ♕h4!? 15 g3 ♕e7 16 0-0 a5 17 b3 a4

Black has succeeded in generating a level of counterplay to afford him a level game.

18 ♖b1 f5 19 exf5 ♗xf5 20 ♖bd1 axb3 21 axb3 ♗e6 22 ♗d5 ♘xb3 23 ♗xe6+ ♕xe6 24 ♖xd6 ♕xc4 25 ♕xe5 ♖ae8 26 ♕c3 b5 27 ♖d7 ♖f7 28 ♖xf7 ♔xf7 29 ♕xc4+ bxc4 30 ♘c3 ♖d8 31 ♖e1 ♖d3 32

♖e3 ♖xe3 33 fxe3 ♔e6 34 ♔f2 ♔e5 35 ♔e2 ♘c5 36 ♔f3 h5 37 h4 ♘e6 38 g4 ♘c5 39 gxh5 gxh5 40 ♔e2

40 ♘e2 ♘e4 41 ♘f4 ♘f6 42 ♘e2 is equal.

40...♘e6 41 ♔f3 ♘g7 42 ♘e2 ♘e8 43 ♘g3 ♘f6 44 ♔e2 ♔d5 45 ♔d2 ♔c5 46 ♔c2 ½-½

Game 63
Yakovich-Beckhuis
Berlin 1996

---

1 d4 ♘f6 2 c4 g6 3 ♘c3 ♗g7 4 e4 d6 5 ♗e2 0-0 6 ♗g5 ♘a6 7 ♕d2 e5 8 d5 c6 9 h4

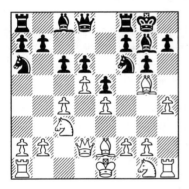

(N.B. 9 f3 cxd5 10 cxd5 ♗d7 11 h4 was the game's actual move order)

Here we go again! Expect to see White's g-pawn play a part in this flank offensive sooner or later.

9...cxd5 10 cxd5 ♗d7

Of course this is not the only way to get Black's queenside counterplay rolling:

a) 10...♕a5 11 f3 (11 a3!?) 11...♘h5 (11...♗d7 – 10...♗d7) 12 g4 ♘g3 13 ♖h3 ♘xe2 14 ♘gxe2 is Serper-Ye Jiangchuan, Jakarta 1994, when 14...♘c5!? maintains the balance.

b) 10...♕e8 11 f3 ♗d7 12 g4 (12 ♘h3 ♘c5 13 g4 h5 14 ♘f2, Ivanchuk-Topalov, Yerevan 1996, with a slight advantage to White according to *NCO*; 12 h5!? ♘xh5 13 ♗xa6 bxa6 14 g4 ♘f4 15 ♕h2 h5 16 ♗xf4 exf4 17 gxh5 is

another possibility, and one which looks quite dangerous) 12...h5 13 ♗xf6!? ♗xf6 14 gxh5 ♔g7, Gaprindashvili-Makropoulou, Kuala Lumpur 1990. The evaluation of this position in *NCO* is that there is compensation, but after 15 ♗xa6!? bxa6 16 hxg6 fxg6 17 ♕g2 the bishop pair is not enough for the pawn.

c) 10...♘c5!? 11 f3 (11 h5 ♘cxe4 12 ♘xe4 ♘xe4 13 ♗xd8 ♘xd2 14 ♗e7 ♖e8 15 ♗xd6 ♘e4 16 ♗a3 ♗d7 with a level game, De Haro-Giaccio, Montevideo 2000) 11...♕b6!? 12 g4 h5 (12...♗d7 13 h5 a5 14 ♖c1 a4, Mikenas-Mickiewicz, Bydgoszcz 2001, and now 15 ♗e3 leaves both sides with something to aim at) 13 ♗xf6 ♗xf6 14 gxh5 gxh5 15 ♘h3 (Berkley-Garnett, Correspondence 2000) 15...♗xh3!? 16 ♖xh3 ♔h7 with equal chances.

11 f3

11 ♗xa6!? might not be to everyone's taste, but perhaps parting with the bishop is the best option. Ironically, presenting Black with the b-file looks like the best chance for White to undermine Black's counterplay on the queenside because much of this lies in the pieces' harmony and dynamism. Additionally, White can also bring his knight to e2. After 11...bxa6 White has tried a couple of moves.

a) 12 f3 and now 12...♕b6 13 ♘ge2 ♖ab8 14 ♖b1 a5 gives Black something but probably not enough, e.g. 15 g4 h5 16 ♗xf6 ♗xf6 17 gxh5 with an advantage to White. Glek's assessment of unclear after 12...♕a5 13 g4 h5 might need another look, as 14 ♗xf6 ♗xf6 15 gxh5 leaves Black with serious problems, e.g. 15...♕d8 16 hxg6 ♗xh4+ 17 ♔d1 etc. Meanwhile 12...h5!? 13 ♘ge2 ♕a5 14 ♖c1 ♘h7 15 ♗e3 is an edge for White.

b) 12 h5 ♕a5 13 ♘ge2 (White should prefer 13 hxg6!? fxg6 14 f3, as is the case on the next two moves) 13...♖ab8 14 f3 ♕b6 15 ♗e3?! (it makes no sense to give up the pawn – after 15 hxg6!? fxg6 16 b3 a5 Black is not deprived of counterplay but White's chances are better) 15...♕xb2 16 ♕xb2 ♖xb2 with a complicated, balanced game in Moskalenko-Glek, Odessa 1989.

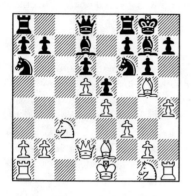

Back to the position after 11 f3.

11...♛b6

11...♛a5!? and now 12 ♘h3 ♖ab8 13 ♘b5 ♘b4 14 ♘a3 ♖fc8 was unclear in Hoang Thanh Trang-Pinter, Budapest 1998. 12 g4 h5 13 ♗xf6 ♗xf6 14 gxh5 ♔g7 15 hxg6 fxg6 quickly saw the kingside undergo alterations in Gaprindashvili-Ioseliani, Tbilisi 1991, Black's return for the pawn being enough according to *NCO*. Meanwhile 12 ♘d1 ♘b4 13 ♘e3 ½-½, Herraiz Hidalgo-Arizmendi Martinez, Ayamonte 2002 was not quite so exciting.

12 g4 h5 13 ♗e3

13 ♗xf6 ♗xf6 14 gxh5 ♔g7 is fine.

13...♘c5 14 g5 ♘e8 15 ♘h3 a5 16 ♖c1

White achieved no more than approximate equality with 16 ♘f2 ♘c7 17 0-0 in De Santis-Horvath, Budapest 1999.

16...♘c7 17 ♘f2 ♘7a6 18 ♔f1 ♖fc8 19 ♔g2 ♗f8 20 ♖hd1 a4 21 ♖b1 ♖ab8 22 ♖dc1 ♛b4 23 ♘b5 ♗e7 24 ♘d1

24 f4!? is also possible.

24...♗xb5

It is certainly not necessary to make this exchange, and Black would do better to maintain a wait-and-see policy, e.g. 24...♖a8!? with a level game.

25 ♛xb4 ♘xb4 26 ♗xb5 ♘cd3

26...♘xa2 27 ♖c4 is futile.

27 ♖xc8+ ♖xc8 28 a3 ♘c2 29 ♗xd3 ♘e1+ 30 ♔f2 ♘xd3+ 31 ♔e2 ♘f4+ 32 ♗xf4 exf4 33 ♘c3 f6 34 ♖g1 fxg5 35 hxg5 b5 36 ♔d3 ♖c5 37 ♘e2 ♗f8 38

♘xf4 ♗g7 39 ♘e6 ♗xb2 40 ♘xc5 dxc5 41 ♖b1 c4+ 42 ♔c2 c3 43 d6 ♔f7 44 e5 ♔e6 45 f4 h4 46 ♖d1 ♗xa3 47 d7 1-0

Game 64
Kachiani Gersinska-Wang Pin
Subotica Interzonal (Women) 1991

1 d4 ♘f6 2 c4 g6 3 ♘c3 ♗g7 4 e4 d6 5 ♗e2 0-0 6 ♗g5 ♘a6 7 ♛d2 e5

In order to better accommodate variations we have altered the actual move order, which was 7... c6 8 f3 e5 9 d5.

8 d5 c6 9 f3

Before stepping up the pressure on the kingside White reinforces the centre. Of course play can sometimes run along the lines of the previous game, but there are other interesting avenues. In this game, for example, White uses the g-pawn only to address Black's desired ...f7-f5 advance.

9...cxd5

Or 9...♛a5 10 g4 (after 10 dxc6 bxc6 11 ♛xd6 ♘b4! Black has more than enough compensation for the pawn) 10...h5 and now:

a) 11 h3 cxd5 (11...♘c5!? 12 0-0-0 cxd5 13 ♗xf6 ♗xf6 14 ♘xd5 ♛xd2+ 15 ♔xd2 ♗g5+ 16 ♔c3 h4 with approximate equality, while 11...♗d7 12 0-0-0 cxd5 13 ♘xd5 ♛xd2+ 14 ♖xd2 ♘xd5 15 ♖xd5 ♗e6 16 ♖xd6 ♖fc8 17 ♔b1 gave White the more pleasant game in Wang Yaoyao-Smirin, Beijing 1996) 12 ♘xd5 ♛xd2+ 13 ♔xd2 ♘xd5 14 cxd5 f6 15 ♗e3 f5 was played in Yusupov-Smirin, Yerevan 1996. Smirin considers this position to be unclear but we think that it is better for White

b) 11 h4!? looks effective. Then 11...♘c5 12 ♖b1 ♛c7 13 b4 ♘a6 14 a3 is nice for White, while 11...hxg4 12 ♗xf6 ♗xf6 13 fxg4 ♘c5 14 g5 ♗e7 15 0-0-0 followed by pressing on with the h4-h5 gives White a menacing initiative.

10 cxd5

10 ♘xd5!? also looks favourable for White but the game is more simplified, e.g. 10...♘c5 11 ♗d3 ♗e6 (11...♘e6 was Jordan-Wegener, Schoeneck 1996, when 12 ♗h4 ♘c7 13 ♘e2

♘cxd5 14 cxd5 would have secured White a plus) 12 ♘e2 ♗xd5 13 cxd5 ♘xd3+ 14 ♕xd3 ♕b6 15 ♕d2 ♘d7 16 ♗e3 ♕a6 17 0-0 f5 18 ♘c3 f4 19 ♗f2 ♖ac8 20 ♖ac1 with an edge for White in Szeberenyi-Berta, Budapest 1995.

10...♗d7

Or 10...♕a5 11 g4 ♗d7 12 ♘h3 and now:

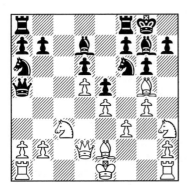

a) 12...♖ab8 13 ♘f2 b5 14 ♘cd1 ♕xd2+ 15 ♗xd2 ♘c5 16 b3 with a pull for White, Kaidanov-Gallagher, Chicago 1999.

b) 12...♖ac8 13 ♘f2 ♘c5 14 ♖b1 ♕c7 15 0-0 ♘a4 16 ♘b5 ♕b8 17 ♕a5 with advantage to White, Dao Thien Hai-Oral, Szeged 1994.

c) 12...♘c5 13 ♖b1 ♕b4 (13...♘a4 14 ♘b5! ♕d8 15 ♘f2 ♕e7 16 b3 ♘c5 17 ♘c3 ♖fc8 18 0-0 with advantage to White, Lugovoi-Saulin, Kstovo 1994) 14 ♘f2 (14 ♘b5!? looks good) 14...a5 15 ♗e3 ♕b6 (Petursson-Lane, Cappelle la Grande 1993) 16 ♘d3!? with a plus for White.

d) 12...♖fc8 13 ♘f2 (13 0-0 ♘c5 14 ♘f2 a6 15 ♖ab1 ♕d8 16 ♗e3 with a slight advantage to White, Seirawan-Xie Jun, Ji Nan 2003) 13...♘c5 14 ♖b1 ♕b4 (14...♘a4 walks into 15 ♘b5!, while 14...♕b6 15 h4 ♘a4 16 ♘fd1 ♘xc3 17 ♘xc3 h5 18 ♗e3 ♕d8 19 g5 ♘h7 20 ♘b5 ♗xb5 21 ♗xb5 was good for White in Dao Thien Hai-Stocek, Budapest 1996, as was 14...♕d8 15 h4 ♖c7 16 h5 ♖ac8) 15 ♘b5 (15 h4!? with advantage to White) 15...♕xd2+ 16 ♔xd2 ♘e8 17 ♖hc1 a6 18 ♘c3, as in Petursson-Kotronias, Reykjavik 1992, favours White according to Petursson in *ECO*.

11 g4

Not the only decent move.

a) 11 ♗b5 ♗xb5 12 ♘xb5 ♕b6 13 ♘c3 ♘c5 and here 14 ♖d1 a5 15 ♘ge2 (Valdes-Cabreja, Cuba 1995) 15...a4 is fine for Black (Dolmatov), while 14 b3 ♘h5, Petursson-Dolmatov, Lucerne 1993 and 14 ♘ge2!? ♖ac8 15 ♖b1 a5 16 ♗e3 ♕a6, Goriatchkin-Leskinen, Orsk 2000, were unclear. This leaves 14 ♖b1 ♘h5 (14...a5!?) 15 ♗e3 ♘f4 16 g3 ♘fd3+ 17 ♔f1 ♕b4! 18 ♔g2 ♖ac8 (18...a5!?) 19 ♘h3 with chances for both sides (*ECO*), Yusupov-Gelfand, Dortmund 1997.

b) In the event of 11 ♗xa6 bxa6 the evaluation of the game depends upon which factor has the most significance – Black's bishop pair or the structural damage. Obviously the situation is complex, but White seems to be better, e.g. 12 ♘ge2 ♕b6 13 ♗e3 ♕b7 14 0-0 and now Dolmatov analyses the following: 14...♘h5!? 15 g4 ♘f6 with chances for both sides (15...♘f4 16 ♘xf4 exf4 17 ♗xf4 with a slight advantage to White).

With 11 g4 (see diagram below) White's strategy of containment serves to frustrate Black, who needs to generate some kind of activity in order to avoid drifting into passivity.

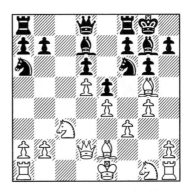

11...♕b6

Stepping out of the pin and giving the queen a clear view of the enemy. Black has also tried 11...h6 12 ♗e3 (12 ♗xh6? ♘xe4 13 ♘xe4 ♕h4+) 12...h5 (12...♘c5 13 h4 h5 14 g5 ♘e8, Lew-Rogalewicz, Correspondence 1990,

15 b4!? ②a4 16 ②xa4 ♗xa4 17 ♖c1 with an edge for White) 13 g5 ②h7 14 h4 (14 ②b5 ♕e7 15 h4 f6 16 ♖h2 fxg5, Hedman-Gonzalez, Budapest 1995, and here 17 hxg5 ♖f4! 18 ♗xf4 exf4 19 ②h3 ♗xh3 20 ♖xh3 ②xg5 with an initiative – Cu.Hansen). 14...f6 15 ②h3 (15 gxf6!? with a plus for White, e.g. 15...♗xf6 16 ♗xa6 bxa6 17 ♕f2, or 15...♖xf6 16 ②b5) 15...♗xh3 16 ♖xh3 fxg5 17 hxg5 (Valdes-Pupo, Pinar del Rio 1997) 17...♖f4!? 18 ♗xf4 exf4 19 ♕xf4 ♗e5 20 ♕d2 ②xg5 21 ♖h1 ♕f6 with compensation (Cu.Hansen).

c) 13 h3

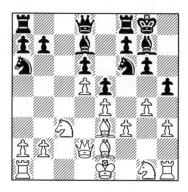

Now 13...♕b8 14 ♗b5 ♕e8 15 ♗xd7 ♕xd7 (Wagner-Xie Jun, Cannes 1997) 16 ②ge2!? favours White, while 13...♕a5 14 a3 ♖fc8 15 ♖b1 ♕d8 16 b4 ②c7 17 ♗d3 ②h7 18 gxh5 ♕h4+ 19 ♕f2 ♕xh5 20 h4 f5 21 exf5 gxf5 was unclear in Kaidanov-Fedorowicz, Stratton Mountain 1999. Instead 13...②c5 looks logical, with the following possibilities:

c1) 14 0-0-0 has met with three queen moves. 14...♕e8!? 15 ♔b1 a5 16 ♖c1 was played in Hauchard-Ye Jiangchuan, Belfort 1999, and now 16...♖c8 is dynamically balanced. 14...♕a5 15 ♔b1 a6 16 ♖c1 b5 provided Black with enough play in Schutt-Larsson, Correspondence 1999, and 14...♕b8 15 ♔b1 (Alterman-Xu Jun, Cap d'Agde 1994) 15...b5! is given as level by Alterman (*NCO*).

c2) 14 b4 ②a4 15 ②xa4 ♗xa4 (Szeberenyi-Kiss, Budapest 1997) 16 ♖c1 is (again) an edge for White. Meanwhile 15 ②b5 ②e8 16 ♖c1 f5

17 exf5 gxf5 18 ♗g5 ♗f6, Scheffner-Morgado, IECG E-mail 2000 and 15 ♖c1 a6 16 ②xa4 ♗xa4 17 ♗d3 ♕d7 18 ②e2 ♗b5 19 ♖a1 (agreed drawn in Dao Thien Hai-Ye Jiangchuan, Jodhpur 2003) are both interesting.

12 ②h3 ②c5!?

Better than 12...h5?! 13 ②f2 hxg4 14 fxg4 ②c5 15 ♗e3 a5 16 g5 ②h7 17 h4 f5 18 gxf6 ♖xf6 19 0-0-0 with a great position for White in Gaprindashvili-Wang Pin, Subotica 1991.

13 ②f2 a5 14 ♗e3

14 h4 h5 15 ♗e3 ♖fc8 was balanced in Korotylev-Sotnikov, Moscow 1995, but White has better with 15 ♗xf6 ♗xf6 16 gxh5 etc.

14...a4 15 0-0 ♕a5 16 ②b1

16 ②d3 ②xd3 17 ♗xd3 ♖fc8, Korotylev-Beckhuis, Berlin 1995, and now 18 ②e2 keeps White just ahead.

16...♕d8 17 ♖c1 h5 18 h3 ②h7 19 ②a3 f5

The situation is tense. Black is beginning to look menacing on the kingside but White is looking to the e4-square for a source of influence, as well as pressure on the queenside.

20 gxf5 gxf5 21 exf5 ♗xf5 22 ②b5 b6 23 ♔h2 ♔h8 24 ♖g1 ♖g8 25 ♖g2 ♕e7 26 ♖ag1 ♖f6 27 ②c3 ♗h4 28 ♗d1 ♕d7 29 ♖xg8+ ♖xg8 30 ♖xg8+ ♔xg8 31 ♗xc5 bxc5 32 ♗xa4 ♕e7 33 ②fe4 ②g5 34 ②xg5 ♗xg5 35 ♕g2 ♔h8 36 ♗b5 ♗f4+ 37 ♔g1 ♕h4 38 ♗f1 ♕e1 39 ②e4 ♗e3+ 40 ♔h1 ♗xe4?!

40...♗f4!? with equality.

41 fxe4 h4 42 b3 ♔h7 43 ♕e2 ♕g3 44 ♕h5+ ♔g7 45 ♕g4+ ♕xg4 46 hxg4 ♔g6 47 ♔g2 ♔g5 48 ♔f3 ♗d2 49 a4 ♗a5 50 ♗h3 ♗b6 51 ♔e2 ♔f4 52 ♔d3 ♗d8 53 g5 ♔xg5 54 ♔c4 ♔f4 55 ♗f5 h3 56 ♗xh3 ♔xe4 57 ♗g2+ ♔e3 58 ♔b5 e4??

After 58...♕d4! Black can easily draw, e.g. 59 ♔c6 (59 a5 ♗xa5 60 ♔xa5 e4 61 ♔b6 ♔xd5 62 ♔c7 c4) 59...♔c3 60 ♔xd6 ♔xb3 61 ♔xc5 ♔xa4.

59 ♔c6 ♔d4 60 ♔xd6 ♔c3 61 ♔xc5 ♔xb3 62 ♔b5 e3 63 ♗f1 ♔c3 64 a5 ♗c7 65 a6 ♗b8 66 d6 1-0

Summary

Black's best plan is definitely 6...♘a6 without ...h7-h6, dealt with in detail in Games 57-64. Play becomes very complicated and there are enough opportunities for both sides to create interesting scenarios. Not surprisingly this approach is becoming increasingly popular nowadays.

1 d4 ♘f6 2 c4 g6 3 ♘c3 ♗g7 4 e4 d6 5 ♗e2 0-0 6 ♗g5 (D)
6...♘a6

    6...♘c6 (*Game 46*)

    6...c6 (*Game 47*)

    6...♘bd7 7 ♕d2

        7...c6 8 ♘f3 d5 (*Game 48*)

        7...e5 8 d5 ♘c5 9 f3 (*Games 49 & 50*)

    6...h6 7 ♗e3 (D)

        7...♘bd7 (*Game 51*)

        7...c5 (*Games 52 & 53*)

        7...e5 8 d5 (*Games 54-56*)

7 ♕d2

    7 h4 (*Game 57*)

    7 ♕c2 (*Game 58*)

    7 f4 (59)

7...e5 8 d5 c6 (D)

    8...♕e8 (*Games 60 & 61*)

9 ♗f3 (*Game 62*)

9 h4 (*Game 63*)

9 f3 (*Game 64*)

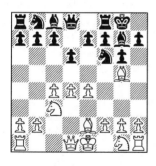

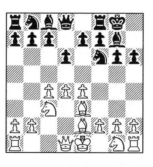

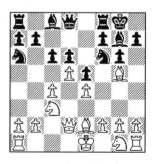

6 ♗g5   *7 ♗e3*   *8...c6*

CHAPTER FIVE

Averbakh System: 5 ♗e2 0-0 6 ♗g5 with ...c7-c5

---

1 d4 ♘f6 2 c4 g6 3 ♘c3 ♗g7 4 e4 d6 5 ♗e2 0-0 6 ♗g5

For many years this treatment was the main line of the Averbakh System, attracting attention amongst analysts and – particularly in the 1970s and early 1980s – frequently seen in international tournaments. As a result many lines have been so thoroughly investigated that some forcing variations 'finish' after the thirty move mark, in the endgame phase!

With a quick advance of the c-pawn Black forces White to make a decision about the centre, and the only chance of obtaining an advantage is by closing the position, after which Black usually plays 7...h6 followed by 8...e6. Then White can retreat the bishop to e3 with more peaceful play, or to f4, hoping to exploit the potential weakness of the backward d6-pawn.

Game 65
Schmidt-Sznapik
Tirnavia Trnava 1984

---

1 d4 ♘f6 2 c4 g6 3 ♘c3 ♗g7 4 e4 d6 5 ♗e2 0-0 6 ♗g5 c5 7 dxc5

This quiet continuation usually steers the game into Maróczy territory. Although Black's position is solid White has more space and can therefore hope to secure a long-term advan-

tage. Black, for his part, might well be expecting some kind of counterplay on the dark squares. The rest of the games in this chapter are devoted to 7 d5.

7...♕a5

After the simple 7...dxc5!? it is difficult to find anything concrete for White. Indeed White must be careful if he is to avoid being worse. After 8 ♕xd8 ♖xd8 9 e5 ♘fd7 White has a number of continuations but none offers an advantage, e.g. 10 f4 ♘c6 11 ♘f3 f6 12 exf6, Savchenko-Paasikangas Tella, Jyvaskyla 1991, when 12...♘xf6!? is good for Black, 10 ♘d5 ♘c6 11 f4 f6 12 exf6 exf6 13 ♗h4 ♘d4 with chances for both sides in Djurovic-Imbert, Meudon 1992 or 10 ♗xe7 ♖e8 11 ♘d5 ♗xe5 (Levin-Bernard, Le Touquet 2000) 12 ♘f3 ♗g7, again with no problems for Black. Uhlmann evaluates the position after 10 ♘f3 ♘c6 11 0-0-0 as being slightly better for White but in our opinion the position is unclear, e.g. 11...h6 (Preinfalk-Gorsek, Correspondence 1978) 12 ♗e3!? e6 13 ♘e4 b6 etc.

White can also try 10 e6. Then 10...♘f6 11 exf7+ ♔xf7 12 ♗e3 ♘c6 13 ♗xc5 b6 14 ♗a3 ♘d4 15 ♗d1 ♗a6 16 ♘f3 ♘xf3+ 17 ♗xf3 ♖ac8 (Olafsson-Istratescu, European Team Championship, Debrecen 1992) 18 0-0 ♗xc4 is given as equal by Hazai. In the case of 10...♗xc3+!? the doubled pawns and Black's

---

superior development will be at least sufficient compensation for the bishop pair – 11 bxc3 ♘f6 12 exf7+ (12 &f3 fxe6 13 &e3, Poschel-Thomas, Monroe 1986, and now 13...e5 14 &xc5 e4 with a good game for Black) 12...♔xf7 13 &e3 (13 ♘f3 ♘e4, or 13 &f3 ♖d6 [Levin-Schebler, Recklinghausen 2002] 14 ♘h3 ♘c6 with a complex position) 13...♘c6!? 14 ♘f3 ♘c6 15 0-0 ♔g7 with good play for Black in Horvath-Mrva, Krynica 1998.

8 &d2

Preferable to 8 ♕d2?! dxc5, e.g. 9 ♘f3 ♘c6 10 0-0 (Heidrich-Bisco, German Correspondence Championship 1993/95) 10...♖d8! and Black can be quite content with life, or 9 e5 ♖d8 10 ♕e3 ♘g4 11 &xg4 &xg4 12 h3 &e6 13 &xe7 ♖e8 14 ♕xc5 ♕xc5 15 &xc5 ♘d7 with an initiative of sorts for Black in Prins-Geller, Amsterdam 1954.

8...♕xc5

Again Black can consider taking with the pawn – 8...dxc5 – with the following position:

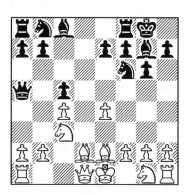

Then 9 ♘f3 ♘c6 10 0-0 &g4 11 ♖e1 ♘d7 12 h3 &xf3 13 &xf3 ♘de5 14 &e2 ♕d8 15 &e3 ♘d4 16 f4 ♘ec6 left both sides with something upon which to build in Uhlmann-Glek, Bad Zwesten 2000. 9 e5 is more direct, e.g. 9...♘e8 (9...♘fd7 10 f4 ♕d8 11 &e3 f6 12 e6 ♘b6 13 ♕xd8 ♖xd8 14 &xc5 &xe6 was unclear in Lukin-Tseitlin, Daugavpils 1978) 10 f4 (10 ♘d5 ♕d8 11 &g5 f6 12 ♘xf6+ ♘xf6 13 exf6, Szczechowicz-Nurkiewicz, Krakow

1996, and now 13...exf6 is level) 10...♘c6 11 ♘f3 f6 12 0-0 (12 ♘d5 ♕d8) 12...fxe5 13 ♘d5 ♕d8 14 fxe5 ♘xe5 15 ♘xe5 ♖xf1+ 16 ♔xf1 &xe5 17 &g5 ♕d7 18 ♘xe7+ ♔g7 19 &f3 &xh2 20 ♘xc8 ♕f5 (20...♖xc8 21 ♕e2 with advantage to White) 21 ♕d8 (21 ♕d5 ♖xc8 22 ♖e1 and White has an initiative) 21...♖xc8 22 ♕e7+ ♔h8 23 ♖d1 &e5 24 ♖d5 ♕b1+ 25 ♖d1 ♕f5 26 ♖d5 and a draw was agreed in Mortensen-Jakobsen, Aarhus 1976, although White could have played for a win after 26 ♖d7. Perhaps 25 ♔f2 is stronger.

9 ♘f3

9 h3 b6 10 ♘f3 &b7 11 &d3 ♘bd7 12 0-0 looks less natural and soon led to a draw in Murshed-Oll, Tbilisi 1983 after 12...♖ad8 13 b4 ♕xb4 14 ♘a4 ½-½, while 9 b4 ♕c7 10 ♖c1 ♘c6 11 ♘d5 ♕d8 12 &d3 ♘e5 was good for Black in Clarke-Battsetseg, Novi Sad 1990.

9...&g4

Also possible is 9...♘c6 10 h3 (10 &e3 ♕a5 11 0-0 ♘g4 12 &d2 ♘ge5 13 ♘d5 [Palus-Dawidow, Polanica Zdroj 1999] 13...♕d8!? 14 ♘xe5 &xe5 15 &c3 e6 and 10 0-0 &g4 11 b3 ♘d7 12 ♖c1 ♕a5, Riemelmoser-Demuth, Austria 1999, are both equal) 10...♘e5 11 ♖c1 ♘xf3+ 12 &xf3 ♕xc4 13 ♘d5 and now Olafsson-Popovic, Groningen 1976 went 13...♕d3 14 ♘xe7+ ♔h8 15 &c3 ♕xd1+ 16 ♔xd1 &e6 17 ♘d5, given in *ECO* as a slight advantage to White. Of course Black can try his luck with 13...♕xa2!? 14 ♘xe7+ ♔h8 15 0-0 ♕e6 (if you want to suffer, at least do so for a pawn!), when White has obvious compensation, but not more...

10 &e3

Other examples demonstrate typical 'dark-square' strategies.

a) 10 0-0 &xf3 11 &xf3 ♘c6 12 &e2 ♕d4!? 13 &e3 ♕xd1 14 ♖fxd1 ♘d7 15 ♖ac1 ♘c5 16 f3 ♖fc8 17 b3 ♔f8 18 &f1 ♘e6 19 ♔f2 &d4 with equality (Hazai) in Petursson-Wojtkiewicz, Komotini 1993.

b) 10 h3 &xf3 11 &xf3 ♘c6 12 &e2 ♕e5 13 ♕c2 ♘d4 14 ♕d3 ♘d7 15 ♖c1 ♘c5 16

♕e3 ♘xe2 17 ♕xe2 f5 and Black was very happy in Jelic-Z.Nikolic, Belgrade 1989

10...♕a5 11 0-0

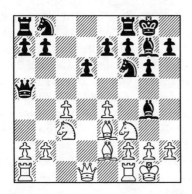

11...♘c6

Black has also played 11...♗xf3 12 ♗xf3 ♘c6 13 ♖c1 ♘d7 14 a3 ♕d8 15 ♗e2 with an edge for White, Almada-Roselli, Uruguay 1988, while 11...♘bd7 should lead to the same assessment, e.g. 12 a3 ♖fc8 13 b4 ♕d8 14 ♕b3 a5 15 ♖ac1 axb4 16 axb4 ♕f8 17 h3 ♗xf3 18 ♗xf3, Bagirov-Damljanovic, Batumi 1999, or 12...a6 13 b4 ♕c7 (Zeihser-Van Meggelen, Correspondence 1984) 14 ♖c1.

12 a3

Other continuations are:

a) 12 ♘d4 ♗xe2 13 ♕xe2 (13 ♘dxe2 ♖fc8 14 ♕d2 a6 15 f3 b5 16 cxb5 axb5 with equality, Karason-Wessman, Reykjavik 1990) 13...♖fc8 14 ♖ac1 ♘e5 (14...♘d7!? with chances for both sides) 15 b3 ♘eg4 16 ♗d2 ♕c5 17 ♘f3 e6 18 ♖fd1 with a pull for White in King-Berthelsen, E-mail 1998.

b) 12 ♖c1 ♘d7 (12...♖fc8 13 b3 ♘d7 14 ♗d2 ♘c5 with a good game for Black, Weinstein-De Firmian, Lone Pine 1976) 13 ♘d2 ♗xe2 14 ♕xe2 ♘c5 15 a3 ♘a4 16 ♘db1 ♘d4 17 ♗xd4 ♗xd4 18 ♖fd1 ♗g7 19 ♘xa4 ♕xa4 20 ♘c3 ♕b3 and Black was fine in Moskalenko-Hazai, Budapest 1991.

c) 12 ♘d2 ♗xe2 13 ♕xe2 ♘d7!? (13...♖fc8 14 ♖ac1 ♕h5 15 f3 ♘d7 16 ♘b3 a5, Ubilava-Petrushin, Barnaul 1984, and 13...♕h5!? 14 f3 ♘d7 15 ♖ac1 f5, Milov-Solak, Saint Vincent

2000 are both unclear, and 13...♖ac8 14 a3 ♕h5 15 f3 ♘d7 16 ♖ac1 b6 17 ♔h1 ♗e5 18 g4 ♕h3 was agreed drawn in Gaprindashvili-Macek, Jajce 1984) 14 ♘b3 ♕a6 15 ♖ac1 ♖ac8 16 a3 (16 f4, Petursson-Hazai, Valby 1994, and now 16...f5 looks fine) 16...b6 with equality, Polovodin-Oll, Tallinn 1983.

12...♖fc8 13 b4

Or 13 ♘d2 ♕h5 (13...♗xe2 14 ♕xe2 ♕h5 with equality) 14 f3 ♗e6 15 ♖c1 ♗h6 16 f4 ♘g4 17 ♗xg4 ♗xg4 with still much to play for in Moskalenko-Roos, Orange 1990.

13...♕d8

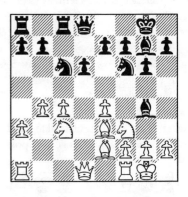

More risky is 13...♕h5 14 ♖c1 ♗h6 15 ♕d2 ♗xe3 16 ♕xe3 a5 as in Rausis-Pedzich, Loewenstein 1997, when 17 b5!? ♘e5 18 ♘xe5 ♕xe5 19 f4 would have secured White an advantage.

14 ♕b3

14 ♖c1 deserves attention. Then 14...a5?! 15 b5 ♗xf3 16 gxf3 ♘e5 17 ♘a4 ♘ed7 18 c5 dxc5 19 ♘xc5 ♘xc5 20 ♕xd8+ ♖xd8 21 ♖xc5 leads to a clear advantage for White in the ending, and 14...♕f8?! 15 ♕d2 ♗xf3 16 gxf3! is equally poor for Black. When Black's queen is not on h5 White can take with his g-pawn, 14...♗xf3 15 gxf3 ♘e5 16 ♘d5 ♘xd5 (L.Bronstein-Garcia, Mar del Plata 1976) 17 ♕xd5!?, with a slight advantage to White. Black's best is 14...♘d7 15 ♘d2 ♗xe2 16 ♕xe2 (Poschel-Bailey, Monroe 1986) 16...a5!? 17 b5 ♘d4 with chances for both sides.

14...♕f8

In some variations Black has ...♗h6 (which cannot be parried by ♕d2) but the main purpose of the text will be revealed later...

Others:

a) 14...♘d7 15 ♖ad1 ♘ce5 16 ♘xe5 ♘xe5 17 f3 ♗e6 18 ♘d5 ♗xd5 19 ♖xd5! ♕e8 20 ♖fd1 was awful for Black in Lalic-Krakops, Linares 1997. 16...♗xe2 17 ♘xe2 ♘xe5 18 c5 is a lesser evil, with an edge for White.

b) 14...♕d7 15 ♖ac1 ♗xf3 16 ♗xf3 ♘e5 17 ♗e2 ♕e6 18 ♘b5 ♘c6 19 f3 ♘d7 20 ♖fd1 with advantage to White, Adamski-Pokojowczyk, Polanica Zdroj 1979.

15 h3

15 ♖ad1 ♗h6 (Sorin-Cativelli, Buenos Aires 1999) 16 ♘d5 is a plus for White, but 15...a5!? is less clear.

15...♗xf3 16 ♗xf3 ♘d7

This is better than 16...♗h6 17 ♘d5, e.g. 17...♘xd5 (Braschi Velasquez-Moreno, Lima 2000) 18 cxd5 ♘e5 19 ♗e2, or 17...♗xe3 18 ♘xf6+ exf6 19 ♕xe3, Jelic-Arsovic, Belgrade 2003, with an edge to White in both cases.

17 ♖fd1 ♘ce5 18 ♗e2 ♘xc4 19 ♗xc4 ♘e5 20 ♗xf7+ ♕xf7 21 ♕xf7+ ♕xf7 22 ♘e2 ½-½

Game 66
Kunsztowicz-Raupp
Bundesliga 1982/3

---

1 d4 ♘f6 2 c4 g6 3 ♘c3 ♗g7 4 e4 d6 5 ♗e2 0-0 6 ♗g5 c5 7 d5

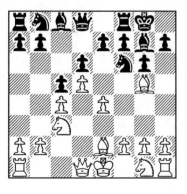

Most games in this variation go down this route, White simply claiming an advantage by virtue of his extra space. Therefore Black must look for something on the queenside.

7...♕a5

One of five options discussed in this chapter.

8 ♗d2

White has also addressed the new arrival on the e1-a5 diagonal with 8 ♕d2, when play might continue as follows: 8...e6 (the preparatory 8...♖e8 was seen in Berriot-Menetrier, Correspondence 1991, when Black's experiment failed miserably after 9 ♘f3 e6 10 0-0 a6 11 dxe6 ♖xe6 12 ♗xf6 ♗xf6 13 ♘d5 ♕d8 14 ♕f4 etc.) 9 ♘f3 exd5 10 exd5 ♗g4 (10...♖e8 11 0-0 ♕b6 12 ♗d3, Castillo-Njirjak, Bratislava 1993, and now 12...♘bd7 is just a slight edge for White) 11 0-0 ♘bd7 (Black should avoid 11...a6 12 ♕f4 ♗xf3 13 ♗xf3 with a poor position indeed in Vlaic-Babic, Kastela 2002) 12 h3 ♗xf3 13 ♗xf3 and White enjoyed a plus in Abramov-Glyanets, Podolsk 1993.

8...e6

In the event of 8...♕b6 9 h3 Black cannot play 9...♕xb2?? as 10 ♖b1 ♕a3 11 ♘b5 is final, which leaves 9...e6 10 ♘f3 exd5 11 exd5 ♗f5 12 ♘h4 ♗d7 13 0-0 with an edge for White (*ECO*) in Lputian-Savon, Yerevan 1982.

9 ♘f3

9 h3 keeps the g4-square out of bounds for Black's pieces but spends a tempo in doing so, and after 9...exd5 10 exd5 ♕d8 11 ♘f3 ♘a6 Black was doing fine in Krizsany-Czebe, Budapest 1994, which went 12 0-0 ♘c7 13 ♗f4 ♖b8 14 a4 ♘a6 15 ♗d3 ♘b4 16 ♗b1 b6 17 ♖a3 ½-½, while 12...♗f5!? 13 ♘h4 ♗d7 also looks perfectly reasonable.

9...exd5

Others:

a) 9...♕d8 10 0-0 exd5 11 exd5 (11 cxd5 with a plus for White) 11...♗g4 12 h3 ♗xf3 13 ♗xf3 with the more pleasant game for White in Uhlmann-Camara, Siegen 1970.

b) 9...♖e8 10 0-0 ♕d8 11 ♕c2 exd5 12 cxd5 ♘a6 13 ♖fe1, Rubinetti-Campos Lopez,

Buenos Aires 1973, and again White is to be preferred.

10 exd5

Not the only recapture:

a) 10 cxd5 and now 10...♗g4 11 0-0 ♘bd7 12 ♗f4 ♗xf3 13 ♗xf3 ♘e8 14 ♕b3 b5 15 ♕xb5 ♗xc3 16 ♕xd7 ♗xb2 17 ♖ab1 ♖d8 (Jensen-J.Christiansen, Denmark Correspondence 1994) 18 ♕b7 spells doom for Black. The alternative is to throw in 10...a6, e.g. 11 0-0 ♕c7, when the game has transposed to the Modern Benoni Defence, with both sides losing a tempo. However, there is a small difference which benefits Black – c7 is a natural position for the queen, whereas d2 is certainly not an appropriate place for the bishop, which also obstructs the knight. A sample line is 12 a4 ♖e8 13 ♕c2 ♗g4 14 h3 ♗xf3 15 ♗xf3 ♘bd7 16 a5 with a choice for Black. 16...♖e7 17 ♖a4 ♖ae8 18 ♗e2, Portisch-Ivkov, Santa Monica 1966, and 16...b5 17 axb6 ♕xb6 18 ♖a2, Rubinetti-Paiva, Sao Paulo 1972, both favoured White, but 16...c4 17 ♖a4 (17 ♗e3!?) 17...♘e5 18 ♗e2 ♘fd7 19 f4 ♘d3 was less clear in Donner-Ivkov, Amsterdam 1974.

b) 10 ♘xd5!? ♕d8 11 ♗g5 ♘bd7 (the move 11...♕a5+?!, as in Zavodny-Licman, Gargulakuv Memorial 1970, runs into 12 b4! etc.) 12 ♘c3 ♖e8 13 ♕c2 h6 14 ♗h4 ♕b6 15 ♖d1 with a slight advantage to White.

With 10 exd5 (see diagram, below) White aims to consolidate what he hopes is a modest but definite lead.

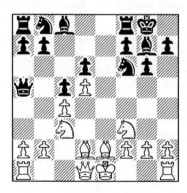

10...♗g4

The light-squared bishop can be a problem piece occasionally, so Black seeks to rid himself of the potential liability before getting on with other matters. An alternative is 10...♖e8 11 0-0 ♕b6 12 h3 (12 ♖e1 ♘bd7 13 ♕b3 with a plus for White, Pachmann-Ujtelky, Bratislava-Prag 1957) and now both 12...a6 13 ♗d3 ♘bd7 14 ♕c2, Forintos-Velimirovic, Bath 1973, and 12...♘e4 13 ♘xe4 ♖xe4 14 ♗d3 ♖e8 15 ♖e1, Gruenberg-Szymczak, Prague 1981, are easier for White. Instead of 11...♕b6 Black drop back to d8 with the queen, although 11...♕d8!? 12 ♕c1!? ♘e4 13 ♘xe4 ♖xe4 14 ♗d3 ♖e8 15 ♗c3 ♗g4 16 ♗xg7 ♔xg7 (Eliskases-Reinhardt, Mar del Plata 1958) 17 ♘g5! favours White.

11 0-0 ♘bd7

11...♖e8 12 h3 and then moving the light-squared bishop doesn't mean Black's development problems have been solved, with White maintaining a definite pull.

12 h3 ♗xf3 13 ♗xf3

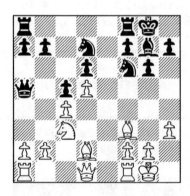

This is a standard position for this variation. Black has no serious weaknesses (the d6-pawn is quite easy to defend) and his pieces are harmoniously developed. There are only two tiny factors that leave him a bit worse: White has the bishop pair and a bit more space. Can these play a significant role in practice? It is quite surprising, but the answer must be yes. White has a simple plan: trade off all the major pieces, push a4-a5 and then b2-b4.

After the exchange on b4 (or c5) he places his bishops on the a3-f8 and a4-e8 diagonals (sometimes the knight might go to a4), usually exerting pressure on the d6-pawn. The final stage combines attack with advancing pawns on the kingside (in fact across the board). This particular game is a good illustration of the execution and realisation of such a strategy.

13...♖fe8 14 ♕c2 ♖e7

14...a6 does not deny White the better game, e.g. 15 ♖ae1 ♖xe1 16 ♖xe1 ♖e8 17 ♖xe8+ ♘xe8 18 b3 ♕d8 19 ♗d1 ♕e7 20 ♕e4 ♔f8 21 ♕xe7+ ♔xe7 22 g4, Petursson-Velimirovic, Novi Sad 1990.

15 ♖fe1

If 15 ♖ae1 ♘e5 16 ♗e2 ♖ae8 17 a4 White has an edge, Sapis-Markowski, Poland 1993.

15...♖ae8 16 ♖xe7 ♖xe7 17 ♖e1

Also effective is 17 ♘b5 ♕b6 18 a4 ♘e5 19 ♗e2 a6 20 a5 ♕d8 21 ♘c3 with a slight edge to White, Szabo-Panno, Portoroz 1958.

17...♖xe1+ 18 ♗xe1 a6

18...♘e5 19 ♗e2 b5 20 cxb5 ♘xd5 21 ♕d2 ½-½, Rost-Berclaz, ICCF E-mail 1996; here 21...♘xc3 22 bxc3 looks good for White.

19 ♗d2 ♕d8 20 a4 ♘e8 21 b3

White has emerged from the opening with a definite advantage.

21...♗d4 22 ♘e2 ♗g7 23 g3 ♘c7 24 ♘c3 ♗d4 25 ♔g2 f5 26 ♘e2 ♗f6 27 ♘f4 ♕e7 28 h4 ♗d4 29 ♗d1 ♘f6 30 ♘e2 ♕e4+?! 31 f3 ♕xc2 32 ♗xc2 ♗e5 33 a5 ♔f7 34 ♔h3 h5 35 b4 cxb4 36 ♗xb4 ♘ce8 37 ♗a4 ♔e7 38 ♘c1 ♗d4 39 ♘d3 ♗e3 40 ♘e5 g5 41 hxg5 ♗xg5 42 f4 ♗h6 43 ♘g6+ ♔d8 44 ♘h4 ♘e4 45 ♘xf5 ♗f8 46 ♗c2 ♘8f6 47 ♔h4 ♔d7 48 ♗xe4 ♘xe4 49 ♔xh5 ♘f2 50 ♔g6 ♗e7 51 ♘xe7 ♔xe7 52 f5 1-0

Game 67
Portisch-Skembris
Tilburg 1994

---

1 d4 ♘f6 2 c4 g6 3 ♘c3 ♗g7 4 e4 0-0 5 ♗e2 d6 6 ♗g5 c5 7 d5 a6

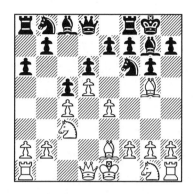

With ...a7-a6 almost part of the furniture in these lines Black chooses to nudge the pawn now before committing himself.

8 a4

8 ♕d2 ♕a5!? 9 ♗d3 looks odd. After 9...b5 10 ♘ge2 ♘bd7 11 cxb5 ♘e5 12 bxa6 ♖b8 13 ♖b1 ♘xd3+ 14 ♕xd3 ♗xa6 Black has compensation, so in Rashkovsky-Loginov, Sverdlovsk 1987 White played 11 f4, when there followed 11...bxc4 12 ♗c2 ♖b8 13 ♖b1 ♖e8 14 0-0 ♕c7 15 h3 e6 16 dxe6 ♖xe6 17 ♘d5 ♘xd5 18 exd5 ♖e8 19 f5, and now 19...♗e5! would have given Black an excellent game.

8...♕a5 9 ♗d2

After 9 ♕d2 e6 10 ♖a3!? exd5 11 exd5 ♖e8 12 ♘f3 ♗g4 13 0-0 ♘bd7 14 ♕f4 ♕b6 15 ♗d1 ♗xf3 16 ♖b3 ♕c7 17 ♗xf3 ♖e5 Black had achieved equality in Borisenko-Tarasov, Kharkov 1956, while 10 ♘f3 invites 10...b5 11 cxb5 axb5 with the following position:

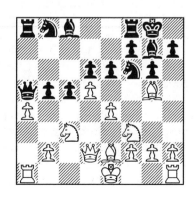

Then 12 0-0 b4 13 ♗xf6 ♗xf6 14 ♘b5 led to a short draw in Farago-Cvitan, Forli 1992, after the subsequent 14...exd5 15 ♘xd6 dxe4 16 ♘xe4 ♗g7 17 ♖ac1 ♕xa4, while 12 ♗xf6 ♗xf6 13 ♘xb5 exd5 14 exd5 (Shirov-Gligoric, Moscow 1989) 14...♗d7 15 0-0 ♕xd2 16 ♘xd2 ♗xb2 is even according to Shirov in *ECO*.

The most interesting move is 12 ♗xb5, with the following options:

a) Black cant play 12...♘xe4? due to the weaknesses of dark squares – 13 ♘xe4 ♕xb5 14 axb5 ♖xa1+ 15 ♔e2 ♖xh1 16 ♗h6 exd5 (16...♗b7 17 ♗xg7 ♔xg7 18 ♕c3+ f6 19 ♘xd6 ♗xd5 20 ♕xc5) 17 ♗xg7 ♔xg7 18 ♕xd5 ♖e8 19 ♔d2 ♗e6 20 ♕xd6 ♘d7 21 ♘xc5 ♘xc5 22 ♕xc5 etc.

b) 12...♗a6 13 0-0 (13 ♖a3 and 13 ♗xa6 have yet to be tested) 13...♗xb5 14 ♘xb5 ♘xe4 15 ♕xa5 (15 ♕d3 ♘xg5 16 ♘xg5 exd5 17 ♕xd5 ♘d7 18 ♘xd6 c4 with equality) 15...♖xa5 16 dxe6 fxe6 17 ♗e7, and now Shirov's recommendation is 17...♖e8 18 ♘xd6 ♖xe7 (18...♘xd6 19 ♗xd6) 19 ♘xe4 ♗xb2? 20 ♖ab1 ♖b7 with equality but in fact 21 ♘d6! ♖b4 22 ♖xb2 ♖xb2 23 ♘c4 ♖xa4 24 ♘xb2 refutes this. Instead Black has 17...d5 18 ♗xf8 ♔xf8 with compensation.

9...e6

Other moves are less energetic:

a) 9...♕c7 10 g4!? e6 (10...♘bd7 11 g5 ♘h5 12 f4 with a menacing initiative) 11 g5 ♘e8 12 h4 and White was having more fun in Smolnyj-Asafov, Schule Leningrad 1956.

b) 9...e5 is illogical as Black deprives himself of any counterplay. White can casually generate a kingside attack, e.g. 10 g4! ♘e8 11 h4 (11 g5! is stronger, meeting 11...f5, as in Szabo-Barczay, Budapest 1958, with the no-nonsense 12 h4) 11...f5 (11...h6!?) 12 h5 f4 13 g5 ♖f7 14 ♗g4 with a strategically winning position in the game Averbakh-Panno, Argentina-USSR match, Buenos Aires 1954. This was one of the first games ever played in this system, White's famous victory popularising the variation.

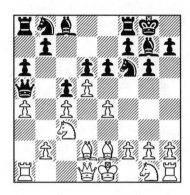

After 9...e6 (see diagram, above) White has two quite different responses to the standard challenge to the centre.

10 ♘f3

The 'normal' treatment, but a flank attack is also possible in the form of 10 g4!?, when 10...exd5 (Ciolcaltea-Gligoric, Moscow 1956) 11 g5! ♘e8 12 ♘xd5 ♕d8 13 h4 is impressive and earns White considerable power to get busy on the kingside. Note that 10...h6 meets with 11 h4 here.

10...♕c7

a) 10...♕d8 11 0-0 (11 h3 exd5 12 exd5 ♖e8 13 0-0 ♗f5 14 ♗f4 ♘e4 15 ♘xe4 ♗xe4 16 ♗d3 ♕f6 17 ♗g5 ♗xf3 18 ♗xf6 ♗xd1 19 ♗xg7 ♔xg7 20 ♖axd1 ½-½, Shamkovich-Schmidt, Polanica Zdroj 1970) 11...exd5 12 exd5 ♖e8 13 ♗d3 (13 ♖e1 ♗g4 14 ♕b3 ♕c7 15 h3 ♗xf3 16 ♗xf3 ♘bd7 17 ♖xe8+ ♖xe8 18 ♖e1 ♖xe1+ 19 ♗xe1 ♘e5 20 ♗e2 ♗h6 was a shade better for White in Kunsztowicz-Cuartas, Hamburg 1980) 13...♗g4 14 h3 ♗xf3 15 ♕xf3 ♘bd7 16 ♕d1 with just an edge for White, Moiseev-Gunsav, Correspondence 1963/70.

b) 10...exd5 11 exd5 (11 cxd5 [see 'a' in the note to White's 10th move in the previous main game – Kunsztowicz-Raupp] 11...♗g4 12 0-0 ♖e8 13 ♕c2 ♕c7 14 ♖fe1 ♘bd7 with chances for both sides, Donner-Hartoch, Amsterdam 1970, while 11 ♘xd5 ♕d8 12 ♗g5 [Balogh-Arnlind, Correspondence 1956]

12...♘bd7 keeps the game well balanced) 11...♗g4 (after 11...♕c7 or 11...♖e8 Black must play ....♗g4 anyway, with positions similar to the main line) 12 0-0 ♘bd7 13 ♖e1 ♕c7 14 h3 ♗xf3 15 ♗xf3 with play along the lines of the main line.

11 0-0

Or 11 a5 exd5 12 exd5 ♘bd7 13 0-0 ♖b8 14 h3 ♖e8 with equality in Litinskaya-Chiburdanidze, Tbilisi 1979.

11...exd5 12 exd5 ♗g4 13 h3 ♗xf3 14 ♗xf3 ♘bd7

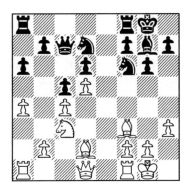

White has a familiar small but long-term advantage. If he realises his plan (outlined in the note to White's 13th move in the main game Kunsztowicz-Raupp, above) he can expect a promising initiative. Note that specific move orders are less important here than appropriate strategy.

15 ♕c2

a) 15 a5 ♖fe8 (15...♔h8 16 ♕a4 ♘g8 17 ♖ab1 ♗h6 18 ♗xh6 ♘xh6 19 b4 with an advantage to White in Farago-Andersson, Cienfuegos 1977) 16 ♕a4 ♖e7 17 ♖fe1 ♘e5 18 ♗e2 ♖ae8 19 f4 ♘ed7 20 ♗f3, as in Borisenko-Yudovich, Gorky 1954, favours White according to *ECO*.

b) 15 ♖e1 ♖ae8 16 ♕c2 ♘e5 17 ♗e2 ♖e7 18 ♗f1 ♖fe8 19 f4 ♘ed7 20 ♖xe7 ♖xe7 21 ♖e1 ♖xe1 22 ♗xe1 with an edge for White in Tramalloni-Belotti, Milan 2001.

15...♖fe8

a) 15...♘e8 16 ♖ae1 ♗e5 (16...♘e5 17 ♗e2

f5 18 f4 ♘f7 19 g4 ♗d4+ 20 ♔g2 ♘g7 21 ♗f3 with advantage to White, Horvath-Rohl Montes, Budapest 1996) 17 ♗e2 ♘g7 18 g4 f5 19 f4 ♗d4+ 20 ♔g2 fxg4 21 hxg4 with a plus for White (*ECO*) in Agzamov-Szekely, Frunze 1986.

b) 15...♖ae8 16 ♖ae1 h5 17 b3 ♖xe1 18 ♖xe1 ♖e8 19 ♖xe8+ ♘xe8 20 ♘e4 ♘e5 21 ♗e2 and Black was worse, Zucchelli-Egger, Arco 2000.

16 ♖fe1

16 ♖ae1 leads to similar play.

16...♘e5 17 ♗e2 ♖e7 18 f4 ♘ed7 19 ♗f3

Also effective is 19 ♗d3 ♖ae8 20 ♖xe7 ♖xe7 21 ♖e1 ♖xe1+ 22 ♗xe1 with a pull for White, Nunes-Schipmann, E-mail 2000.

19...♖ae8 20 ♖xe7 ♖xe7 21 ♖e1 ♖xe1+ 22 ♗xe1 ♕b6 23 ♗d2 ♘e8

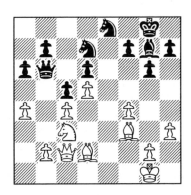

24 g4

White accentuates his advantage by claiming more territory but, already better, such an aggressive and committal thrust might be seen as too risky. In Vioreanu-Djukic, Balatonlelle 2001 White employed the plan highlighted in the previous main game, producing a textbook, methodical win: 24 b3 ♕d8 25 ♕e4 ♘df6 26 ♕e1 (with advantage) 26...♘c7 27 a5 ♘d7 28 ♘a4 ♗d4+ 29 ♔h2 ♘a8 30 ♗g4 ♘f6 31 ♗d1 ♘d7 32 ♕e4 ♘f6 33 ♕e1 ♘d7 34 ♗c2 ♔f8 35 ♕e2 ♕b8 36 ♘c3 b6 37 axb6 ♘axb6 38 ♘e4 ♘f6 39 ♘g5 ♕e8 40 ♕xe8+ ♔xe8 41 ♘f3 ♗b2 42 g4 ♔e7 43 f5 ♘fd7 44

g5 gxf5 45 ♗xf5 ♘f8 46 h4 ♘bd7 47 h5 ♗g7
48 ♔g3 ♗b2 49 ♔f4 ♗g7 50 ♔e4 ♗b2 51
♔d3 ♗a3 52 ♔c2 ♗b4 53 ♗f4 ♗a5 54 ♗e4
♗c7 55 ♘h4 ♘b6 56 ♘f5+ ♔d7 57 ♗f3 ♘c8
58 ♗g4 ♔e8 59 ♔d3 ♘d7 60 ♘g7+ ♔d8 61
g6 hxg6 62 ♗xd7 1-0.

24...h6 25 ♔g2 ♗d4 26 b3 ♕d8

Skembris assesses this position as unclear.
The struggle revolves around the dark squares.

27 ♘e2

The (extremely) careless 27 ♔g3? ♕h4+ 28
♔xh4?? walks into 28...♗f2 mate.

**27...♗f6 28 a5 g5 29 ♘g3 ♘g7 30 ♘e4
♗e7 31 ♕c1 gxf4 32 ♗xf4**

After 32 ♗c3! ♘e5 33 ♕xf4 ♗g5 34 ♘xg5
hxg5 35 ♕e3 White's pieces would have
dominated the whole board, but in missing
this possibility White drifts into a very complex position, albeit one in which we believe
his chances are still better.

32...♕xa5 33 ♕b2

33 ♗xd6!? ♕a2+ 34 ♔g3 ♗xd6+ 35 ♘xd6
♕xb3 36 ♕xh6 a5 37 ♕f4 f6 38 ♘e4 f5 with
initiative (Skembris).

**33...♘e8 34 ♗d2 ♕b6 35 ♗xh6 ♘e5 36
♗e2 ♗f8 37 ♗d2 ♗g7 38 ♕c2 ♕d8 39
♗g5 ♕d7 40 ♘g3 ♗f6 41 ♗c1 ♘g6 42
♕e4 ♘h4+ 43 ♔f1 ♗e5 44 ♗d3 ♘f6 45
♕e3 ♘g6 46 ♘e2 ♘h7 47 ♗f5 ♕d8 48
g5 ♘hf8 49 ♗c2 b5 50 ♕e4 ♕d7 51 ♔g2
bxc4 52 bxc4 ♕b7 53 h4 ♘d7 54 h5
♘gf8 55 ♘g1 ♕b4 56 ♘f3 a5**

57 ♗d2

57 h6! seems to do the trick:

a) 57...♘g6 58 ♕g4 ♘df8 59 ♗xg6 fxg6
(59...♘xg6 60 ♘xe5 dxe5 61 ♕c8+ ♔h7 62
♕f5) 60 ♘xe5 ♕c3 (60...dxe5 61 ♕e4 ♕c3 62
♗e3) 61 ♘f3 ♕xc1 62 ♕c8 and h6-h7 is
coming.

b) 57...a4 58 ♗d2 ♕b2 59 ♗xa4 ♗c3 60
♕c2 ♕xc2 61 ♗xc2 ♗xd2 62 ♘xd2 and
White should win.

**57...♗c3 58 ♗f4 ♘e5 59 ♗xe5 ♗xe5 60
g6 fxg6 61 hxg6**

Why not take the strong bishop? After 61
♘xe5 dxe5 62 hxg6 ♕d2+ 63 ♔f1 the ending
is drawn, e.g. 63...♕f4+ (63...♕d4? 64 ♗xd4
exd4 65 d6) 64 ♕xf4 exf4 65 d6 ♔g7 66 ♔f2
♔f6 (66...a4 67 ♗xa4 ♔xg6 68 d7 ♘e6 69
♗d1 ♔f5 70 ♗f3 ♘d8 71 ♗g2 ♔f6 72 ♔f3
with equality) 67 ♔f3 a4 68 g7 ♔xg7 69 ♗xa4
♔f6 70 d7 ♔e7 71 ♔xf4 ♘xd7 etc.

61...♗f6?!

61...♗g7! with initiative is proposed by
Kotronias.

62 ♘h2

62 ♕e8! ♕b7 with an edge for Black
(Skembris).

62...♕d2+?!

62...a4! is strong (Skembris).

**63 ♔h3 ♕h6+ 64 ♔g2 ♔g7 65 ♘g4
♕xg6**

Skembris gives 65...♕g5!? followed by
...♘xg6.

66 ♕xg6+ ♘xg6 67 ♔f3 ♘e5+ ½-½

After 67...♘e7 followed by ...♘c8-b6 Black
has winning chances.

Game 68
I.Farago-Zaitsev
8th Montecatini Terme 1999

**1 d4 ♘f6 2 c4 g6 3 ♘c3 ♗g7 4 e4 d6 5
♗e2 0-0 6 ♗g5 c5 7 d5 b5**

Saving time by simply investing the pawn,
Black adopts the Benko treatment.

8 cxb5 a6

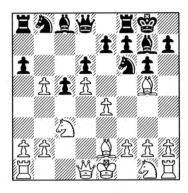

There are differences in comparison with the normal Benko Gambit, for example the location of White's bishops. Although in some cases the position of the g5-bishop might prove awkward or inconvenient for White due to the weakness of certain dark squares (especially b2 and b4), the light-squared bishop is definitely better placed on e2 than in the Benko – Black cannot hinder White's kingside development. Consequently, given a choice of parting with a pawn, we would rather do it under normal Benko circumstances.

9 a4

Other moves are less popular:

a) 9 bxa6 ♕a5 10 ♕d2 (10 f3 ♘bd7 11 ♘h3 ♗xa6 12 0-0 ♖fb8 13 ♖b1 ♘b6 14 ♗xa6 ♖xa6, Hort-Ragozin, Antwerp 1994, and 10 ♗d2 ♗xa6 11 ♘f3 ♕b4 12 ♗xa6 ♘xa6, Popov-Christiansen, Wijk aan Zee 1977 both provided Black with healthy compensation) 10...♘bd7!? 11 ♘f3 ♗xa6 12 ♗xa6 (12 0-0 ♘xe4 13 ♘xe4 ♕xd2 14 ♘fxd2 ♗xe2 was equal in Farago-Rashkovsky, Dubna 1979) 12...♕xa6 13 ♕e2 ♖fb8 14 ♕xa6 ♖xa6 with enough play in Plachetka-Jansa, Havirov 1970.

b) 9 ♕d2 axb5 (9...♘bd7!? 10 f3 ♕a5 11 ♘h3 c4 12 bxa6 ♗xa6 13 0-0 ♖fb8 14 ♘f2 ♘c5 15 ♖fc1 ♖b4 16 ♖ab1 ♕b6, as in Hort-Westerinen, Helsinki 1979, is given as unclear in *ECO*) 10 ♗xb5 ♕a5 11 f3 (11 ♘ge2 ♗a6 12 ♗xa6 ♘xa6 13 0-0 ♖fb8 14 ♖ab1 with an edge for White, Bakalarz-Liebergesell, Ger-

many 1995) 11...♗a6 (11...e6!? with advantage to White in *ECO*) 12 ♗xa6 ♘xa6 (12...♕xa6 13 ♗h6 ♗xh6 14 ♕xh6 ♘bd7 15 ♘ge2 c4 16 ♕e3 ♖fb8 17 ♖b1 ♘c5 18 0-0 and White stood better in Ivasenko-Kolpakchi, Kharkov 2000) 13 ♘ge2 ♖fb8 14 0-0 ♘c7 15 ♖f2 ♖b4 16 ♖c1 with the more pleasant game for White, Skembris-Todorovic, Tuzla 1990.

9...♕a5

The less popular lines are worth a look:

a) 9...axb5 10 axb5 (10 ♗xb5 ♗a6 is fine for Black) 10...♖xa1 11 ♕xa1 ♘bd7 12 ♘f3 ♗b7 (12...♘e8 13 0-0 ♘b6 14 ♕a5 ♘f6 15 ♘d2 h6 16 ♗e3 e6 17 dxe6 ♗xe6, Beliavsky-Petrovic, Nova Gorica 2000, and now 18 b4 looks like trouble for Black) 13 0-0 ♕c7 14 ♕c1 e6 15 dxe6 fxe6 16 e5 (16 ♗h6!?) 16...dxe5 17 ♘d2 with a slight advantage to White, Gaprindashvili-Levitina, Belgrade 1992.

b) 9...h6 10 ♗d2 e6 11 dxe6 ♗xe6 12 ♘f3 axb5 13 ♗xb5 ♘a6 14 0-0 ♘c7 15 ♖e1 (15 ♗e2!? and Black must demonstrate full compensation for the pawn) 15...♘xb5 16 ♘xb5 d5 17 exd5 ♘xd5 18 ♘e5 ♖e8 19 ♘c4 (with advantage to White according to Kasparov in *ECO*) 19...♕h4 20 ♘cd6 ♖ed8 21 ♕c2 ♘b4 22 ♗xb4 ♕xb4 23 ♖xe6 fxe6 24 ♕xg6 ♖f8 25 ♕xe6+ ♔h8 26 ♖f1 ♖xa4 27 ♘c3 ♖a7 28 ♘c8 ♖a8 29 ♘e7 ♖f6 30 ♕d5 ♖fa6 31 ♘d1 ♕b6 (31...♕d4!?) 32 ♘f5 ½-½, Gouw-Schaper, 24th Netherlands Correspondence Championship 1994/95.

10 ♗d2 ♕b4

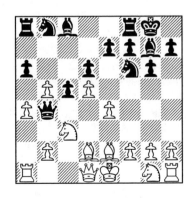

The most principled response, leading to extremely complex positions. Black's queen attacks white pawns but in some variations might run into serious trouble. Unfortunately for Black, accurate play from the opponent leads to a clear advantage for White. Black can find consolation only in the fact that alternatives also fail to equalise, e.g. 10...axb5 (10...♘bd7 11 ♖a3! ♗b7 12 ♘f3 axb5 13 ♗xb5 ♕c7 14 0-0, Kasparov-Spassky, Tilburg 1981 is great for White) and now 11 ♘xb5 ♕b6 12 ♕b1 e6 13 dxe6 fxe6 14 ♘f3 d5 15 exd5 exd5 16 0-0 ♘e4 was unclear in Uhlmann-Szell, Halle 1982, so much stronger is 11 ♗xb5, with the following position:

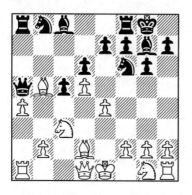

a) 11...♗a6 12 ♘ge2 ♘bd7 (Black shouldn't repeat the ultimately very unpleasant 12...♗xb5 13 ♘xb5 ♕b6 14 ♘ec3 ♘a6 15 0-0 ♘b4 16 ♗g5 ♖fe8 17 ♕e2 ♖a6 18 ♖ad1 ♕b7 19 b3 etc., Seirawan-Youngworth, Pasadena 1983) 13 0-0 ♕b6 14 ♕c2 ♘e5 15 b3 ♖fc8 (15...♘e8 16 ♗xa6 ♖xa6 17 ♘b5, Bagirov-Jojua, Batumi 2002) 16 ♖ab1 ♗xb5 17 ♘xb5 c4 18 b4 ♘d3 19 ♗e3 ♕a6 20 ♘ec3, Damljanovic-Damaso, Leon 1997, with all these lines simply horrible for Black.

b) 11...♘a6 12 ♘ge2 (12 ♘f3 ♘b4 13 0-0 ♗a6 14 ♗g5 h6 15 ♗h4 ♗xb5 16 axb5 ♕c7 17 ♕d2 ♖xa1 18 ♖xa1 ♖b8 19 h3 with advantage to White (*ECO*) in Yusupov-Vogt, Altensteig 1993) 12...♘b4 13 0-0 ♗a6 14 f3 ♕b6 15 ♗e3 ♘e8 16 ♕b3 ♕b7 17 ♗xa6 ♖xa6 18 ♘a2!?, Dao Thien Hai-Morovic Fernandez,

Yerevan 1996 is very good for White.

11 ♗d3!?

White has numerous ways to defend e4.

a) 11 ♕b1!? protects the target pawns, when play can continue as follows: 11...axb5 (11...♘bd7 12 a5 axb5 13 f3) 12 a5! c4? 13 ♘a4! c3 14 ♘xc3 ♘a6 15 f3 ♕c5 16 ♘xb5 ♘b4 (Halkias-Vajda, Varna 1994) 17 ♖a4! ♘c2+ 18 ♔f1 ♘e3+ 19 ♗xe3 ♕xe3 20 ♖a3 and although White has some technical problems he should win. Perhaps the only solution for Black is 12...♖xa5 13 ♘a2 ♕a4 14 b3 ♕xe4 15 ♗xa5 ♕xg2 16 ♗f3 ♕g5 17 ♗c3 ♘xd5 18 ♗xg7 ♔xg7 with a crazy position where Black has four pawns for the rook.

b) 11 f3 ♘fd7 (11...♕xb2?? 12 ♖b1 ♘xd5 13 exd5 ♗xc3 14 ♖xb2 is a disaster, 11...c4?, as in Moskalenko-Piza Cortizo, La Coruna 1993, walks into 12 a5! and 11...♘bd7 12 a5! c4 13 b6 was an unlucky thirteen for Black in Budnikov-F.Portisch, Neuwied 1993) 12 ♕c1! c4 13 ♘d1 (13 a5 axb5 14 ♘a4 ♕b3! 15 ♖a3 bxa4 16 ♖xb3 cxb3 17 ♗c3 ♗xc3+ 18 ♕xc3 ♗a6, and Black was already in hot water in Sorin-Panno, Acasusso 1991) 13...♕c5 14 b6 (the untested 14 ♗xc4! seems to be troublesome for Black, e.g. 14...♗b7 15 ♗e2 axb5 16 ♕xc5 ♘xc5 17 ♗xb5 ♗a6 18 ♖a3 ♗xb2 19 ♘xb2 ♗xb5 20 a5 etc.) 14...a5 15 ♕xc4 with chances for both sides in Uhlmann-Georgiev, Warsaw 1983. Even here 15 ♗xc4!? merits attention.

c) 11 ♕c2 axb5 12 ♗xb5 ♗a6 13 f3

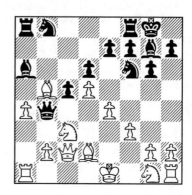

c1) 13...♘fd7?! is poor, e.g. 14 ♘d1 ♗xb5 15 ♗xb4 cxb4 16 ♘e2 ♘c5 17 axb5 ♖xa1 18 0-0 ♘bd7 19 ♕d2 b3 20 ♘d4 ♗xd4+ 21 ♕xd4, Heinig-Penzold, Germany 1996, or 14...♕d4 15 ♗c3 ♗xb5 16 ♗xd4 cxd4 17 ♖a3, Uhlmann-Szell, Zamardi 1980.

c2) 13...♗xb5 14 ♘xb5 ♕xb5! 15 axb5 ♖xa1+ 16 ♗c1 ♘bd7 17 ♘e2 ♖b8 and, according to *NCO*, Black has compensation, but his situation is rather difficult, and he can hardly count on a draw. However, White has considerable technical problems to overcome in order to realise his advantage. Baklanov-V.Andersen, ICCF E-mail 2000 continued 18 ♘c3 (18 0-0!?) 18...♘e8 19 0-0 ♗d4+ 20 ♔h1 ♘c7 21 ♕e2 with a clear advantage to White.

c3) 13...c4 14 ♘ge2 ♕c5 15 ♕c1 ♗xb5 16 ♗e3 ♕b4 17 axb5 ♘bd7 18 0-0 ♘c5 (with compensation according to *ECO*) 19 ♕c2 ♘fd7 ½-½, Meduna-Georgiev, Plovdiv 1982. However, after 19 ♘d4 it is not so simple to prove the correctness of the sacrifice.

11...c4

Others:

a) 11...axb5?? 12 ♘xb5 ♕xb2 13 ♗c3.

b) 11...♘fd7 12 ♘f3 c4 13 ♗c2 ♕xb2 14 ♖b1 ♕a3 15 ♘e2 was clearly better for White in F.Portisch-Biro, Budapest 1999.

c) 11...♘g4 12 ♘f3 c4 13 ♗e2 axb5 14 axb5 ♖xa1 15 ♕xa1 ♕c5 16 0-0 ♘d7 17 h3 ♘ge5 18 ♘d4, Farago-Garcia Martinez, Rome 1990, with a clear lead for White.

12 ♗c2!

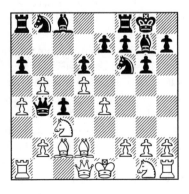

12...♘bd7 13 ♘ge2 ♘e5

Or 13...♘g4 14 0-0 ♕xb2 15 h3 ♘ge5 16 ♖b1 ♕a3 17 b6 ♖b8 (Siegel-Schmezko, Passau 1994) 18 a5 and Black is struggling.

14 0-0 ♘d3 15 b3

The simplest is 15 ♘a2!? ♕c5 16 ♗e3 ♕c7 17 ♗xd3 cxd3 18 ♕xd3 with a very promising advantage.

15...♘g4 16 bxc4 ♕xc4 17 ♗xd3 ♕xd3 18 ♗g5

18 b6 is clearly better for White.

18...♕c4 19 ♗xe7?

19 b6 is again good.

19...♗xc3 20 ♖c1 ♕xe4 21 ♗xf8 ♗e5 22 h3 ♘h2 23 f4?

23 ♗h6! ♘xf1 24 ♔xf1 axb5 25 axb5 with advantage to White.

23...♘xf1 24 ♕xf1 ♗d4+

24...♗b2!? with an edge for Black.

25 ♔h2 ♗e3 26 ♗h6?!

If 26 ♗xd6 ♗xc1 27 ♕xc1 then 27...♕xd5 (27...♕xe2?? 28 ♕c6) 28 ♕c6 ♗b7 29 ♕xd5 ♗xd5 30 b6 ♗b7 is good for Black.

26...♗xc1 27 ♕xc1 ♗xh3! 28 ♕f1 ♕xd5?

28...axb5 29 ♔xh3 ♕xd5 is strong.

29 gxh3 ♖e8 30 ♘g3 ♕d2+ 31 ♕g2 ♕xg2+ 32 ♔xg2 axb5 33 axb5 f5 34 ♔f3 ♖b8 35 ♗g5 ♔f7 36 ♘e2 ♖xb5 37 ♘d4 ♖a5 38 ♗h4 h6 39 ♗f2 g5 40 ♗e3 ♔g6 41 ♘c6 ♖b5 42 ♘d4 ♖b4 43 ♔g3 ♖a4 44 ♘f3 ♖a3 45 ♗c1 ♖c3 46 ♗d2 ♖d3 47 ♗c1 ♔h5 48 ♔g2?? ♖c3 49 ♗d2 ♖c2 50 fxg5 hxg5 51 ♔g3 g4 52 hxg4+ fxg4 53 ♗b4 ♖c4

Not 53...gxf3?? 54 ♗xd6 f2 55 ♔g2 with equality. White must avoid this idea on the 55th move, too.

54 ♗xd6 ♖c3 55 ♔g2 ♖xf3 56 ♗c7 ♖d3 57 ♗e5 ♔g5 58 ♔f2 ♔h4 59 ♔g2 ♖d2+ 60 ♔g1 ♔h3 0-1

Game 69
Pocero-Minguez Guinda
Correspondence 1992

---

1 d4 ♘f6 2 c4 g6 3 ♘c3 ♗g7 4 e4 d6 5

♗e2 0-0 6 ♗g5 c5 7 d5 h6

For many years this move order was the main line of the Averbakh variation. Now we get to see where the bishop goes before embarking on a strategy.

8 ♗f4

This withdrawal looks the most logical because it addresses Black's desired plan of ...e7-e6. 8 ♗e3 features in Games 72 & 73. The h4-square does not fit in well here – 8 ♗h4 and now:

a) 8...a6 appears to guarantee Black counterplay.

a1) 9 ♘f3 b5 10 ♘d2 b4 11 ♘a4 ♘h7 (11...♕a5!? with advantage to Black) 12 0-0 ♘d7 13 ♕c2 g5 14 ♗g3 ♘e5 15 ♖ae1, Ehlvest-Kasparov, Horgen 1995, and now 15...♘g6!? with an edge for Black according to Dokhoian in *ECO*. Instead 15 a3 a5 is approximately equal.

a2) 9 a4 ♕a5 10 ♗d3 (10 ♕d2 ♘bd7, Kristinsson-Olafsson, Reykjavik 1966, and now 11 ♖a3 is unclear) 10...g5 11 ♗g3 ♘xe4 12 ♗xe4 ♗xc3+ (12...f5 13 ♗d3 ♗xc3+ 14 bxc3 ♕xc3+ 15 ♔f1 f4 was equal in Dopino-Muino, Correspondence 1980) 13 bxc3 ♕xc3+ 14 ♔f1 f5 15 ♘e2 ♕f6 16 ♗c2 f4 17 ♖a3 fxg3 18 ♖f3 ♕g7 19 ♖xf8+ ♔xf8 20 ♘xg3, Mirkovic-Poluljahov, Vrnjacka Banja 1996, with compensation (Mirkovic in *ECO*).

b) Also possible is 8...e6 9 dxe6 (9 ♘f3 exd5 10 exd5 ♘a6 11 0-0 g5 12 ♗g3 ♘h5 13 ♘d2 ♘xg3 14 fxg3 f5 was far from clear in

Puc-Ostojic, Yugoslav Championship 1965) 9...♗xe6 (9...fxe6!? 10 ♗g3 e5 followed by ...♘c6-d4) 10 ♘f3 ♘c6 (10...♕b6 11 ♖b1 Kozul-Lenic, Maribor 2003 and now 11...♘h5!? 12 ♗e7 ♖e8 13 ♗xd6 ♖d8 14 e5 ♘f4 is fine for Black) 11 0-0 ♖e8 12 h3 ♕d7 13 ♕d2 ♘h5 14 ♘h2 (Flockert-Wolter, Germany 1989) 14...♘d4 with chances for both sides.

8...♕b6

The idea of this move is to play ...e7-e6 or ...e7-e5 and, after the trade on e6 and ♗xd6, Black has ...♖d8. Unfortunately this plan is a little too slow, which is why we see 8...e6 (Games 70 & 71). Black has also tried:

a) 8...♕a5 9 ♕d2 (better than 9 ♗d2 e6 10 ♘f3 exd5 11 exd5 ♗f5!? 12 ♘h4 ♗d7 13 ♕c1 ♘h7 14 0-0 ♕d8 15 g3 ♗h3 16 ♖e1 ♘bd7 with equality in Kaidanov-Gufeld, Reno 1995) 9...♔h7 10 ♘f3 a6 11 0-0 ♘bd7 (11...b5 12 e5 dxe5 13 ♘xe5 with a plus for White, Rewitz-Lysdal Aarhus 1985) 12 a4 (12 e5!?) 12...♘e8 13 ♗g3 ♘e5 (Alburt-B.Gurevich, Parsippany 2002) 14 ♘xe5 dxe5 15 f4 with a pull for White.

b) 8...♖e8 9 ♕d2 (9 ♘f3 e6 10 dxe6 ♗xe6 11 ♗xd6 transposes to the next main game) 9...♔h7 and now:

b21) 10 h4!? h5 11 ♘f3 a6 (11...♘bd7!?) 12 ♘g5+ (12 e5!? dxe5 13 ♘xe5 with advantage to White) 12...♔g8 13 f3 with a slight advantage to White in Kaidanov-Hernandez, Dallas 1996.

b22) 10 ♘f3 a6 (10...e6 11 dxe6 ♗xe6 12 ♗xd6 ♘c6 13 0-0 ♗g4 14 ♖ad1 ♘xe4 15 ♘xe4 ♖xe4 16 ♗xc5 with advantage to White, Jedrzejowski-Jasinski, Correspondence 1994/5) 11 0-0 e6 12 dxe6 ♖xe6 13 e5 ♘e8 14 exd6 ♘c6, Ruzele-Lapienis, Lietuva 1994 and here 15 ♖ad1 is an edge for White according to Ruzele in *ECO*.

c) 8...♘bd7 9 ♘f3 ♘g4 (9...a6 10 0-0 is given by Yakovich in *ECO* as favouring White, while 9...g5 10 ♗c1 ♘h7 11 0-0 a6 12 a4 also left White with the more pleasant game in Sarosi-Glatt, Hungary 1996) 10 0-0 ♘ge5

11 ♘e1 (11 ♘d2!? followed by ♗g3 and f2-f4 looks good for White) 11...♘b6 12 b3 e6 13 ♖c1 exd5 14 ♘xd5 ♘xd5 (14...f5!? with counterplay) 15 ♕xd5 ♕e7 16 ♘c2 with advantage to White, Volzhin-Velikhanli, Abu Dhabi 2001.

Let's return to the position after 8...♕b6:

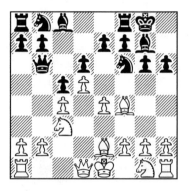

9 ♕d2

White should also emerge with a good game after the alternatives.

a) 9 ♕c1 is not without logic but is not as active or natural as the text, e.g. 9...e6 10 ♘f3 g5 (Dorfman-Rashkovsky, Lvov 1981) 11 ♗e3!?, or 9...♔h7 10 ♘f3 e5 11 ♗d2 ♘h5 12 g3 ♗h3 13 ♘h4 ♘f6 14 ♕c2 ♘a6 15 a3, Farago-Kindermann, Budapest 1987, with a slight advantage to White in either case.

b) 9 ♕c2!? e5 (9...e6 10 ♘f3 exd5 11 cxd5 ♗g4 12 0-0 ♘bd7 13 a4 a6 14 ♘d2 with an edge for White, Lerner-Oll, Ivano Frankovsk 1982) 10 ♗d2 ♘a6 11 a3 ♗d7 12 ♘f3 (12 h3!? followed by g2-g4 looks promising) 12...♘c7 (12...♘h5!? followed by ...♘f4 with counterplay) 13 0-0 a5 14 b3 ♕a7 15 ♖ab1 ♖fb8 16 ♖fc1 with a pull for White, Tukmakov-Murey, Hastings 1982.

9...♔h7

Very dangerous for Black is 9...e5?! 10 ♗xh6! ♗xh6 11 ♕xh6 ♕xb2 12 ♖c1 ♘a6 (12...b5 13 h4! b4 14 ♘d1 and 12...♗g4 13 h4 ♘a6 14 h5 ♗xh5 15 g4 are trouble for Black, while 12...♘h7 13 h4 ♘d7 14 ♕e3!, intending ♖b1 and h4-h5 also looks quite unpleasant) 13

h4 with an initiative in Korotylev-Kurnosov, St Petersburg 2000.

10 h4

White immediately begins active play on the kingside. Also good is 10 ♘f3 e5 11 dxe6 ♗xe6 12 0-0 (but here White should have transposed to the main line after 12 h4!) 12...♖d8 13 ♖ad1 (13 h3 ♘c6 14 ♘d5 ♗xd5 15 exd5 ♘d4 16 ♘xd4 cxd4 17 ♗d3 ♘d7 18 ♖fe1 ♖e8 19 b4 a5 20 a3 axb4 21 ♖xe8 ♖xe8 22 axb4 ♘e5 23 ♗xe5 ♗xe5 ½-½, Ghitescu-Ciolcaltea, Bucharest 1979) 13...♘c6 14 ♘d5 ♗xd5 15 exd5 ♘d4 16 ♘xd4 cxd4 17 ♗d3 ♘d7 18 ♖de1 ♖e8 19 ♗e2 ♘c5 20 ♖fe1 ♖xe2 21 ♖xe2 a5 22 h4 h5 23 ♖e7 ♔g8 24 ♖e1 ♗f6 25 ♗f1 ½-½, Gufeld-Chiburdanidze, Baku 1980.

10...e5

Others:

a) 10...♕b4? was the faulty course of Rensen-Martjukhin, E-mail 2000, when White could have obtained a decisive attack after 11 h5! g5 (11...♘g8 12 hxg6+ fxg6 13 ♘h3 with strategically winning position for White) 12 ♗xg5! hxg5 13 h6 ♗xh6 (13...♔h8 14 ♗d3) 14 ♕xg5 ♘g8 15 ♗d3 f5 16 exf5 ♖f6 17 ♖b1 ♘d7 18 ♘f3 and the g-pawn is coming.

b) 10...♗g4 (Jedrzejowski-Sapa, Correspondence 1992/94) 11 f3 ♗d7 12 g4 h5 13 0-0-0 with advantage to White, who is ready for 13...hxg4 14 h5 etc.

11 dxe6 ♗xe6 12 ♘f3

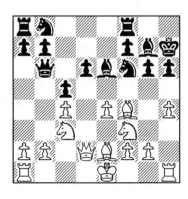

12 h5 g5 13 ♗xd6 ♖d8 14 ♕c2 (14 0-0-0

♘c6) 14...♔g8 15 ♗xb8 ♖axb8 16 ♘f3 ♗g4 17 ♘d2 ♗xe2 18 ♔xe2 ♘g4 (unclear in *ECO*) 19 f3 ♘e5 20 ♘d5 ♕a6! 21 a4 ♘c6 22 ♘b3 ♖xd5! 23 exd5 ♖e8+ with compensation in Uhlmann-Sznapik, Zakopane 1980. Perhaps 19 ♘d5 is an improvement.

12...♘c6

The move that Black would like to play, but he runs the risk of coming under attack. Instead:

a) 12...♘e8 13 0-0 ♘c6 14 ♖ab1 ♘f6 15 ♘d5 ♗xd5 16 exd5 ♘d4 17 ♘xd4 cxd4 18 ♗d3 a5 19 b4 a4 (19...♖fd8 20 bxa5 ♕xa5 21 ♕xa5 ♖xa5 22 ♖xb7 with a technically won position in Tukmakov-Gufeld, USSR 1981) 20 ♖fe1 ♕d8 21 ♗g3 with a clear advantage to White in Jedrzejowski-Marcinkiewicz, Polish Correspondence Championship 1996/8.

b) 12...♘h5 13 ♗xd6 ♖d8 14 e5 ♗xe5 (14...♘c6 15 ♘d5!) 15 ♘xe5 ♖xd6 16 ♘d5! ♗xd5 17 cxd5 clearly favours White, who plans ♘xf7 or ♘c4 (Uhlmann).

13 ♘g5+! hxg5

Otherwise Black loses the pawn: 13...♔g8 14 ♘xe6 fxe6 15 ♗xh6 ♗xh6 16 ♕xh6 ♕xb2 17 ♕xg6+ ♔h8 18 ♕h6+ ♔g8 19 ♖c1 (or 19 ♕c1).

14 hxg5+ ♘h5!

After 14...♔g8 15 gxf6 ♗xf6 16 0-0-0 ♘d4 17 ♗d3 ♖fe8 18 ♖h2 in Uhlmann-Petrushin, Leipzig 1980, White had an attack on the kingside without any counterplay from Black.

15 g4 ♘d4! 16 gxh5 ♗xc4!

An unexpected tactical trick! After other moves White should easily win, e.g. 16...♘xe2 17 ♕xe2 ♗xc3+? (17...♖h8!? 18 0-0-0) 18 bxc3 ♖h8 19 0-0-0 ♕a5 20 ♕c2 ♗xc4 21 hxg6+ ♔g7 22 ♖h7+ ♖xh7 23 gxh7 ♗xa2 (23...♔xh7 24 e5+) 24 ♗xd6! 1-0, Thomas-Bartsch, Correspondence 1990.

17 hxg6+ ♔g8 18 ♗xc4

Others:

a) Premature is 18 gxf7+ ♖xf7 19 g6 (19 ♗d1 ♖xf4 20 ♕xf4 ♕xb2 21 ♖c1 ♘f3+ 22 ♕xf3 ♕xc1 and 19 ♗e3 ♗xe2 20 ♗xd4 ♗xd4 21 ♘xe2 ♖xf2 are both very good for

Black) 19...♗xe2 20 gxf7+ ♔xf7 21 ♖h3 ♖h8 (21...♗g4!?) 22 ♘xe2 ♖xh3 23 0-0-0 ♕a6 with equal chances in Lehmann-Eckermann, East German Correspondence Cup 1985.

b) 18 ♗e3 earns White nothing, e.g. 18...♘xe2 (18...♗xe2 19 ♗xd4) 19 ♘xe2 fxg6 20 ♘c3 ♕a5 and Black was okay in Lerch-Van Willigen, Correspondence 1986.

18...♘f3+ 19 ♔e2

19 ♔d1!? is no worse than the text, e.g. 19...♘xd2 20 ♗xd2 d5 (20...♖fd8 21 ♗xf7+ ♔f8 22 ♗d5 ♖e8 23 f4 ♕b4 24 ♖h7 ♖ac8 25 f5 ♖c7 26 f6 is very good for White) 21 ♘xd5 ♕d6 22 ♔c2 ♖fe8 23 ♘f6+ ♔f8 24 ♗c3 etc.

19...♘xd2 20 ♗xd2 ♖fd8 21 ♘d5!

White has only a bishop and a knight for the queen, yet with amazing calm he is mobilising his pieces for an attack against Black's king. The text is preferable to 21 gxf7+ ♔f8 22 ♘d5 ♕xb2, when 23 ♖ab1 ♕c2 saw Black firmly in the driving seat in Necesany-Dotlacil, Correspondence 1983, while 23 ♘f4 d5! 24 ♖ab1 (24 ♗xd5 ♖xd5 25 ♘xd5 ♕c2 does not save White) 24...♕c2 25 ♗xd5 ♖xd5 26 exd5 ♔xf7 27 ♖xb7+ ♔g8 28 ♖e7 ♕xa2 is also poor. However, after 23 f3! White has still attacking chances.

21 ♗xf7+ ♔f8 22 ♗d5 looks very good, when White should win, e.g. 22...♕a6+ 23 ♔d1 b5 24 f4 b4 25 ♘e2 c4 26 f5 etc.

21...♕xb2 22 ♘f6+! ♔f8 23 ♖ab1 ♕d4 24 ♗d5! ♖ab8 25 ♖b3! ♗xf6

This loses immediately but there are no

useful moves, e.g. 25...♕a4 26 ♖h7 or 25...c4 26 ♖f3 etc.

26 gxf6 ♕xf6 27 g7+ ♔e7 28 ♖f3

28 ♖g1 ♕e5 29 ♖f3 is more to the point.

28...♕xg7 29 ♗g5+ ♔e8

29...♔d7 30 ♖xf7+ ♕xf7 31 ♗xf7 ♖h8 is unpleasant but the lesser evil.

30 ♗f6 ♕g4 31 ♖h4 ♕g8 32 ♖h8 ♕xh8 33 ♗xh8 ♖d7 34 ♗f6 ♖c8 35 ♗c4 a6 36 a4 ♖dc7 37 ♖d3 ♖c6 38 ♖f3 ♖6c7 39 ♔e3 ♔d7 40 ♗c3 ♔e8 41 ♖f6 ♖d7 42 f4 ♖dc7 43 f5 b5 44 axb5 axb5 45 ♗xb5+ ♔e7 46 ♖h6 ♖g8 47 ♗f6+ ♔f8 48 ♖h1 ♖b7 49 ♖a1 1-0

Game 70
Nesis-Metz
Correspondence 1988/95

---

1 d4 ♘f6 2 c4 g6 3 ♘c3 ♗g7 4 e4 d6 5 ♗e2 0-0 6 ♗g5 c5 7 d5 h6 8 ♗f4 e6

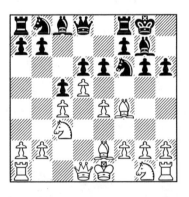

Black carries on regardless, apparently ignoring the fact that the d6-pawn is attacked. The idea is to generate Black considerable play by actively posting his forces. Less accurate is 8...e5 due to 9 ♗d2 (or 9 ♗e3) 9...♘a6 10 g4 ♘e8 11 ♕c1 ♔h7 12 h4 f5?! 13 h5 f4 14 hxg6+ ♔xg6 15 ♘f3 with a clear advantage to White in Pytel-Bellon, Wijk aan Zee 1974.

9 dxe6

White achieves nothing with 9 ♘f3 exd5 10 exd5 ♖e8 11 0-0, e.g. 11...♘e4 12 ♘xe4 ♖xe4 13 ♕d2 ♕f6 14 ♗g3 ♗g4 15 ♗d3 (Pfleger-

Ellrich, Bad Pyrmont 1963) 15...♖e8! 16 ♖ae1 ♘d7 with equality.

9...♗xe6 10 ♗xd6

An alternative is 10 ♕d2:

a) 10...♕a5 11 ♘f3 (11 ♗xh6 ♗xh6 12 ♕xh6 ♘xe4 13 ♖c1 ♘xc3! 14 ♖xc3! ♕xa2 15 ♕c1 ♕a5 was unclear in Sprenger-Halle Allende, Correspondence 1975) 11...♘c6 12 0-0 g5 (12...♔h7 13 a3 ♘d4 14 ♘xd4 ½-½, Kluger-G.Andersson, Eksjo 1977) 13 ♗g3 ♖ad8 14 h3 ♘d4 15 ♘xd4 cxd4 16 ♘b1 ♕a6 17 ♕c2 ♖c8 18 ♘d2 d5 19 exd5 ♘xd5 20 ♖fe1 ♖fd8 21 ♕e4 ♘f6 22 ♕d3 ♘d7 ½-½, Jedrzejowski-Butze, Correspondence 1995 (White has a definite edge here).

b) 10...♕b6 11 ♗xh6 (11 ♘f3 ♘c6 12 0-0 ♘d4! 13 b3 ♘xe2+ 14 ♕xe2 ♘h5 15 ♗d2 ♖fe8 16 ♕d3 ♖ad8 17 ♖fe1, Farago-Menoni, Bratto 1998, and now 17...♘f6 is equal, or 11 0-0-0 ♔h7 12 h4 ♘c6 13 ♘f3 ♗g4! 14 h5 g5 15 ♗g3, Rost-Eberl, Correspondence 1998, when 15...♕a5 is fine for Black) 11...♗xh6 12 ♕xh6 ♕xb2 13 ♖c1 ♘c6 14 h4 with the following position:

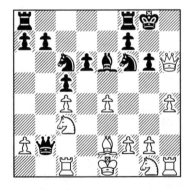

A key position in which both sides have direct threats. 14...♘h7 15 ♘f3 ♘d4! 16 ♘xd4 cxd4 17 ♘b5 ♕xa2 18 ♘xd4 was Farago-Warthmann, Boeblingen 1995, and now 18...♕a5+ 19 ♕d2 ♕xd2+ 20 ♔xd2 is given as unclear by I.Farago in *ECO*, but the position looks nicer for White. After 14...♘b4 White has to do something about 15...♘c2+ and 15...♘g4 – 15 ♘d1 ♕d4 16 a3 ♘d3+ 17

♗xd3 ♕xd3 18 f3 ♗xc4 19 ♘e3 ♗a6 20 h5 ♘d5 21 ♘xd5 ♕f1+ etc. Finally there is 14...♘e5 15 ♘h3 and now both 15...♗xc4, when White must show compensation, and 15...♖ae8 deserve attention, while 15...♖fe8 has been played. Then 16 0-0!? ♗xh3 17 gxh3 ♖e6 was unclear in Dziggel-Jung, Correspondence 1991, which leaves 16 h5:

b1) 16...♗g4?! 17 f3 led Black to a brilliant victory in Obodchuk-Avdeev, Correspondence 1990: 17...♘xe4! 18 ♘xe4 (18 fxe4 ♗e2 19 ♘xe2 ♘d3+ with an attack) 18...♘xf3+! 19 gxf3 (19 ♗xf3 ♖xe4+ 20 ♔f1 ♗xf3 21 gxf3 ♕e2+ 22 ♔g1 ♕xf3 23 ♕h7+! ♔f8! 24 ♕h6+ ♔e7 25 ♘f2 ♖e2 26 ♖h2 gxh5 27 ♕g5+ ♔d7 is very good for Black) 19...♖xe4 20 ♘g1? (20 ♖h2! maintains the balance) 20...♗xf3 21 ♖h2 ♗xh5 22 ♔f1 ♖ae8 etc. However, White has 17 hxg6! ♘xg6 (17...fxg6 18 f3 ♗xh3 19 ♖xh3 is poor for Black) 18 ♗xg4 ♘xg4 19 ♕d2 ♕xd2+ 20 ♔xd2 ♘f6 21 f3 with a slight edge to White.

b2) Black does not have a clear route to equality after 16...♗xh3 – 17 hxg6 ♘xg6 18 ♖xh3 ♘xe4 19 ♖b1 ♕c2 20 ♕h7+ (20 ♖xb7! ♘f6 21 ♕d2 with an edge to White) 20...♔f8 21 ♖xb7 ♕d2+ 22 ♔f1 ♕c1+ 23 ♘d1 ♕xd1+ 24 ♗xd1 ♘d2+ 25 ♔g1 ♖e1+ 26 ♔h2 ♘f1+ ½-½, Lukacs-Hazai, Vrnjacka Banja 1988.

b3) Black should play 16...♘eg4 17 ♕d2 ♕xd2+ 18 ♔xd2 gxh5 19 f3 ♘e5 20 ♘b5 ♖e7 21 ♔e3 with chances for both sides.

10...♖e8

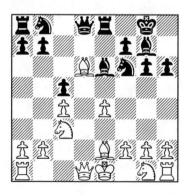

11 ♘f3

This move is usually made automatically. Nevertheless, White has two very interesting alternatives which do not look worse.

a) 11 e5 ♘g4 (11...♘fd7 12 f4! f6, Garriga Nualart-Deslandes, Olot 1994, and now 13 f5!? is interesting) and here theory gives only 12 ♗xb8 ♖xb8 13 ♗xg4 ♗xg4 14 ♕xg4 ♗xe5 15 ♘ge2 ♗xc3+ 16 bxc3 ♕d3 and Black must sooner or later regain the piece with a winning position (Vaulin-Varavin, USSR 1988). However, after 12 ♗xg4! ♗xg4 13 ♕xg4 ♕xd6 14 f4 ♕d4 15 ♘ge2 ♕xc4 16 b3 ♕b4 17 ♕f3 White's position looks nicer.

b) 11 ♗xc5!? is hardly met in the tournament practice but it undoubtedly deserves attention and further practical tests: 11...♕a5 (11...♕c8!? 12 ♗e3 ♗xc4 13 f3, Prokopowicz-Elsness, Norway 1992, and now 13...♗e6!? 14 ♕c1 ♔h7 15 ♘b5 ♕d7 16 ♕c7 ♘a6 17 ♕xd7 ♘xd7 18 a3 with advantage to White) 12 b4 ♕a3 (12...♕a6 13 ♗d4! ♗xc4 14 e5 ♗xe2 15 ♘gxe2 ♘g4 16 b5 ♕e6 17 f4 with a clear advantage for White in Ehrnrooth-Harjunpaeae, Correspondence 1988) 13 ♘b5 ♕b2 14 ♖b1 ♕xa2 15 ♗d4 and Black loses the queen without sufficient compensation, e.g. 15...♘c6 16 ♖b2 ♕a6 17 ♘c7 ♘xe4 18 ♘xa6 ♗xd4 19 ♕c1 bxa6 20 ♘f3 ♗c3+ 21 ♔f1 ♗xb2 22 ♕xb2.

11...♘c6

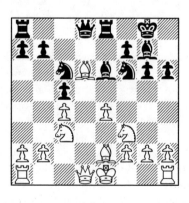

For a long time this move had been the main line but it usually leads to endings in which Black is a pawn down. Although Black should draw there are no winning chances. 11...♕b6 features in the next main game.

12 0-0 ♘d4 13 e5

Not 13 ♗xc5? ♘e2+ 14 ♕xe2 ♕c8 with a great position for Black.

13...♘d7 14 ♘xd4

Others:

a) 14 ♖e1 ♗f5 15 ♘xd4 cxd4 16 ♕xd4 ♘xe5 with equality in Uhlmann-Bielczyk, Polanica Zdroj 1975.

b) 14 ♘b5 ♘xf3+ 15 ♗xf3 ♘xe5 16 ♗xb7 ♖b8 17 ♗xb8 ♕xb8 18 ♗d5 ♘xc4 (Farago-Van Laatum, Dieren 1990) 19 ♗xe6!? with chances for both sides.

14...cxd4 15 ♕xd4

Much weaker is 15 ♘b5 in view of 15... ♘xe5 16 c5 d3!, e.g. 17 ♗xd3 ♖c8 18 ♗e2 ♘c4 19 b3 ♘b2 20 ♕d2? (20 ♕c1 offers some compensation) 20...♖xc5 21 ♕b4 ♖c2 (White is in trouble) 22 ♗d1 ♘d3 23 ♕a4 ♖xf2 24 ♖xf2 ♘xf2 25 ♖c1 ♘d3 0-1, Uhlmann-Schmidt, Bruenn 1975.

15...♘xe5 16 ♗xe5 ♕xd4 17 ♗xd4 ♗xd4 18 ♖ac1

White has secured a comfortable advantage.

18...♖ad8

18...♗xc3 19 ♖xc3 ♖ad8 20 ♖fc1 ♗f5 21 ♗f3 ♗e4 22 ♗xe4 ♖xe4 23 ♖3c2 with a slight advantage to White, Farago-Uhlmann, Austria 1998.

19 b3

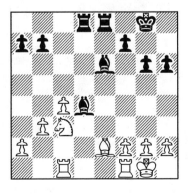

The most popular continuation in the diagram position involves an activation of Black's forces at the cost of surrendering the bishop pair. If White fails to find good moves Black can expect to regain the pawn but, generally, Black has enough play without a pawn to succeed in reducing material, and most games end in a draw. If Kasparov decided to play this ending, then it must be drawn!

19...♗xc3

Another strategy begins 19...♗e5, Black seeking to exploit his bishops. White should certainly avoid 20 ♖fd1? ♗xc3 21 ♖xc3 ♖xd1+ 22 ♗xd1 ♗xc4! (Uhlmann), so play can continue 20 ♗f3 b6 (20...♖d3!? 21 ♘b1! b6 22 ♖fd1 ♖ed8 23 ♗d5! ♖xd1+ 24 ♖xd1 b5 25 ♘d2 bxc4 26 bxc4 ♔f8 27 ♘b3 ♔e7 28 ♘a5 – Uhlmann) 21 ♗c6 ♖e7 22 ♘d5 ♗xd5 23 ♗xd5 (after 23 cxd5!? White could have tried to play for a win) 23...♗d6 24 ♖cd1 ♖e2 25 a4 ♔g7 ½-½, Gralka-Flis, Bydgoszcz 1978.

20 ♖xc3 ♖d2 21 ♗f3 ♖xa2 22 ♗xb7 ♖b8 23 ♗f3!?

a) 23 ♗c6?! ♖a3 24 ♗b5 a6 25 ♗a4 ♖b4 and the weakness of the first rank plays a part, e.g. 26 ♖fc1 ♗xc4 27 ♖xc4 ♖xc4 28 bxc4 ♖xa4 29 c5 ♖d4 ½-½, Nyeman-Hoffmann, Dresden 2000 and 26 ♖cc1 ♗xc4 27 bxc4 ♖axa4 28 c5 ♖b7, which was equal in Uhlmann-W.Schmidt, Polanica Zdroj 1975.

b) 23 ♗e4 ♖a3 24 ♗c2 a5 25 f4 (25 ♖e3 ♖a2 26 ♗xg6 a4! 27 bxa4 ♗xc4 28 ♗b1 ♖ab2 29 ♗d3 ♗xd3 30 ♖xd3 ♖a2 31 h3 ♖xa4 with an eventual draw [66th move] in Uhlmann-Schmidt, Warsaw 1980) 25...a4 26 f5 ♗xf5! 27 ♗xf5 gxf5 28 ♖g3+ ♔f8 29 bxa4 ♖xa4 30 ♖c3 ♖b2 31 ♖xf5 ♖aa2 32 ♖g3 ♖c2 33 h3 (33 ♖g4 h5!) 33...♖xc4 34 ♖f6 h5 35 ♖h6 h4 36 ♖g4 with a level game in Uhlmann-Schmidt, East Germany-Poland 1981.

23...♖a3 24 ♗d1 a5 25 ♖e3

Or 25 ♖c1 ♖c8 26 ♖e1 a4 27 bxa4 ♖xc4 28 ♖xc4 ♗xc4 29 ♗c2 ♗d5 30 h4 ♗c6 31 ♖d1 ♖a2 32 ♗b3 ♖a3 33 ♖d6 ♖xb3 34 ♖xc6 ♖b1+ 35 ♔h2 ♖b4 ½-½, Polugaevsky-Kasparov, Bugojno 1982.

25...♖b4

25...♖d8!? 26 ♖fe1 (26 ♗c2?! ♖d2 27 ♗xg6 a4! was equal in Schuster-Kulczewski, Correspondence 1986/91) 26...♖d2 27 h4 a4 28 bxa4 ♖xe3 29 fxe3 ♗xc4 and Black should draw.

26 h3 ♖a1 27 ♗c2 ♖a2 28 ♗xg6 a4 29 bxa4 ♗xc4 30 ♗b1 ♖ab2 31 ♗d3 ♗xd3 32 ♖xd3 ♖xa4 33 ♖g3+ ♔h7 34 ♖f3 ♔g7 35 ♖c1 ♖b6 36 ♖c7 ½-½

Game 71
Von Rein-Leconte
Correspondence 1999

---

1 c4 g6 2 ♘c3 ♗g7 3 d4 d6 4 e4 ♘f6 5 ♗e2 0-0 6 ♗g5 c5 7 d5 h6 8 ♗f4 e6 9 dxe6 ♗xe6 10 ♗xd6 ♖e8 11 ♘f3 ♕b6

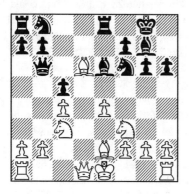

The strongest move. Black has very active counterplay and avoids the trade of queens.

12 ♗xb8

After the aggressive 12 e5 ♘fd7 13 ♘b5 ♘c6 14 ♘c7 Black has excellent compensation for the exchange in all variations, e.g. 14...♘dxe5 15 ♘xe5 ♘xe5 16 ♘xa8 ♖xa8 (16...♕b4+, Petiko-Sfyrney, Correspondence 1989, and now 17 ♔f1! ♘xc4 18 ♘c7 ♖d8 is fine for Black) 17 ♗xe5 ♗xe5 18 0-0 ♗xb2 19 ♖b1 ♗f5 20 ♕d2 ♗xb1 21 ♖xb1 ♗c3 22 ♖xb6 ♗xd2 23 ♖xb7 ♖e8 24 ♔f1 a5 25 g3 ♔f8 26 a4 ♖e7 27 ♖xe7 ♔xe7 ½-½, Yatneva-Ershova, Serpukhov 2003. Instead of sending the knight into c7 White can play 13 0-0 ♘c6

14 ♘a4 ♕a5 15 a3 ♘dxe5 16 ♘xe5 ♘xe5 17 b4 cxb4 18 axb4 ♕d8 as in Schmidt-Gdanski, Slupsk 1987, with an assessment of unclear in *ECO*.

12...♖axb8

Less convincing is 12...♘d7 13 ♕c2 ♖axb8 14 ♘d2 ♖bd8 15 0-0 with advantage to White in Norri-Nouro, Vantaa 1991.

13 ♕c2 ♘h5 14 g3

14 0-0 ♘f4 15 ♖fe1 ♘xe2+ 16 ♖xe2 (16 ♕xe2 ♕b4 17 ♘d5 ♕xb2, Lputian-Petrushin, Krasnodar 1980, and now 18 ♕e3!? is unclear) 16...♗xc4 17 ♖d2 ♗xc3 18 bxc3 ♕c6 19 ♖e1 ♖e6 ½-½, Ryskin-Sutovsky, Ljubljana 1994.

14...♗xc3+

After 14...♗h3 Black has good compensation for the pawn, e.g. 15 ♘d2 (15 0-0-0 ♘f6 16 ♖d2 ♕c6 with an edge for Black in Szymczak-Sznapik, 1981) 15...♗xc3! 16 bxc3 (16 ♕xc3 ♗g2 17 ♖g1 ♗xe4, intending 18 ♗xh5 ♗f5+ 19 ♔d1 gxh5) 16...♘g7 with compensation in Leuner-Fessling, Correspondence 1984.

15 bxc3

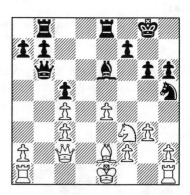

15 ♕xc3 ♗h3 16 e5 ♗g2 17 ♖g1 ♗xf3 18 ♗xf3 ♕d6, Tukmakov-Gufeld, Moscow 1983, with equality according to *ECO*.

15...♗g4

15...♘f6!? 16 ♘d2 ♗h3 was interesting in Grivas-Howell, Sharjah 1985.

16 h3

This exchange helps White more than 16 ♘d2 ♗xe2 17 ♔xe2, e.g. 17...♕e6 18 f3 ♖bd8

19 ♖hf1 ♕h3 20 ♖f2 f5 21 ♖e1 fxe4 22 fxe4 ♗e6 23 ♔d1 ♘f6 24 e5 ♘g4 25 ♖fe2 ♕h5 and in this favourable (for Black) position Chekhov took the draw in Agzamov-Chekhov, Telavi 1982.

16...♗xf3

16...♗d7!? followed by ...♗c6 looks okay for Black.

17 ♗xf3 ♕e6 18 0-0-0

18 0-0 ♕xh3 19 ♖fe1 ♘f6 20 e5 ♘g4, Kummer-Stummer, Aschach 1992, and now 21 ♗xg4 ♕xg4 is a shade better for Black.

18...b5 19 ♖he1

After 19 cxb5 ♖xb5 Black has an initiative, but perhaps this is nevertheless White's best.

19...bxc4!?

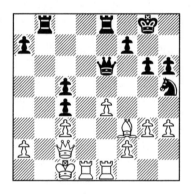

19...b4 20 e5 ♕a6, Yermolinsky-Kindermann, Groningen 1997, and now 21 ♖d3 is given as unclear in *ECO*.

20 e5

20 ♗xh5 gxh5 21 e5 ♕a6 is complex, White having problems with his king but at least damaging Black's pawn structure.

20...♕a6 21 ♖d2 ♘g7 22 ♗d5 ♖ed8

Both 22...♘e6!? and 22...♖b6!? (intending ...♖eb8) deserve attention.

23 ♔d1 ♘e6 24 ♖e4

Now an unpleasant surprise is awaiting White...

24...♘d4! 25 ♗xc4

25 ♗xf7+ ♔xf7 26 cxd4 c3! with an attack (Leconte).

25...♕xc4 26 cxd4 ♕f1+ 27 ♖e1 ♕xh3

28 d5

Neither 28 dxc5 ♕g4+ 29 ♔c1 ♖xd2 30 ♕xd2 ♕a4 with a very good game for Black, nor 28 ♕xc5?? ♕g4+ 29 ♖ee2 ♖dc8 30 ♕xc8+ ♖xc8, with a decisive advantage for Black, can be recommended.

28...♕g4+ 29 ♖ee2 ♖b4 30 a3 ♖d4 31 ♕xc5 ♖xd2+

31...♖8xd5 32 ♕xd5! ♖xd5 33 ♖xd5 ♕a4+ 34 ♔e1 ♕xa3 is unclear, but 31...♖c4!? is interesting, when Leconte gives 32 f3 ♖xc5 33 fxg4 ♖cxd5 34 ♖xd5 ♖xd5+ 35 ♔c2 ♔f8 36 e6 f6 37 e7+ ♔e8 38 ♖e6 ♖g5 39 ♖xf6 ♖xg4 with a big lead for Black.

32 ♔xd2 ♖c8 33 ♕e3

Not 33 ♕xa7?? ♕c4 and White comes under heavy fire.

33...♕c4 34 ♔e1 ♕xd5 35 f3 ♕a5+ 36 ♔f2 ♖c3 37 ♕xh6 ♕xa3 38 ♕f4 ♕c5+ 39 ♔g2 ♖c2 40 ♕e4 ♖xe2+ 41 ♕xe2 a5 42 e6 fxe6 43 ♕xe6+ ½-½

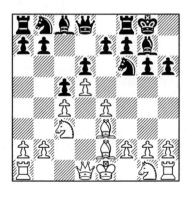

Game 72
Alterman-Shirov
Elista Olympiad 1998

1 d4 ♘f6 2 c4 g6 3 ♘c3 ♗g7 4 e4 d6 5 ♗e2 0-0 6 ♗g5 c5

The actual move order (6...h6 7 ♗e3 ♘bd7 8 ♕d2 c5 9 d5) has been altered in order to better accommodate variations.

7 d5 h6 8 ♗e3

This move is apparently less aggressive than

8 ♗f4. White does not attack the d6-pawn and therefore allows Black to open the e-file. However, the situation can be tricky. White still can press on the kingside and, after the trade ...e6xd5, e4xd5 and a possible ...♘e4 Black's rook does not attack the bishop (as would happen after ♗f4).

8...♘bd7

Alternatively:

a) 8...b5 9 cxb5 a6 10 a4 and the position resembles Farago-Zaitsev but with the pawn on h6 instead of h7. 10...♕a5 (10...axb5 11 axb5 ♖xa1 12 ♕xa1 e6 13 dxe6 ♗xe6 14 ♘f3 ♖e8 15 0-0 ♗b3 16 ♕c1 with a clear advantage to White, Kollberg-Espig, Frankfurt/Oder 1977) 11 ♗d2 axb5 12 ♗xb5 ♘a6 (12...♕b4 13 f3 is clearly better for White but 13...♗a6?? 14 ♘ce2 ♕xb2 15 ♗c3 1-0 was all over in Wagner-Kunsztowicz, Correspondence 1973) 13 ♘f3 ♘b4 14 0-0 ♗a6 15 ♖e1 (15 ♗xa6!? ♖xa6 16 ♕e2 with an edge for White) 15...♕b6 (Deze-Benko, Novi Sad 1972) 16 ♖e2 ♖fb8 17 ♖a3 with the more pleasant game for White.

b) 8...a6 9 a4 (9 ♕d2 b5 10 f3 b4 11 ♘d1 e6 12 ♘f2 exd5 13 cxd5 h5 14 ♘gh3 a5 15 ♘g5 ♗a6 16 ♗xa6 ♘xa6, Maga-Wojtkiewicz, Manila 1991 with equality according to Byrne & Mednis in *ECO*, but 10 cxb5 improves) 9...♕a5 10 ♗d2 and we have a position that can arise after 8 ♗f4. Instead after 10 ♕d2 ♔h7 11 ♘f3 Black has 11...b5 12 cxb5 axb5 13 ♗xb5 as in Morchat-Dykacz, Mikolajki 1991, when 13...♘xe4! 14 ♘xe4 ♕xb5 15 axb5 ♖xa1+ is very good for Black. Returning to 10 ♗d2, Black has a couple of options:

b1) 10...e6 11 ♘f3 (11 dxe6 fxe6 12 ♘f3 ♕c7 13 ♘h4 ♕f7 14 ♗e3 g5 15 e5 dxe5 16 ♘f3 ♘bd7 17 0-0 with a slight advantage to White in Bellmann-Haag, Correspondence [Germany] 1995) 11...exd5 12 exd5 ♗g4 (12...♕c7!? 13 0-0 ♖e8 14 ♕c1 ♔h7 15 ♗d3 ♘bd7 16 h3 ♘e5 17 ♘xe5 dxe5 18 ♕c2 ♘h5 19 ♖fe1 ♗d7 20 a5 ♘f4 was unclear in Twardon-Pojedziniec, Lubniewice 1981) 13 0-0 ♕c7 14 a5 ♘bd7 15 h3 ♗xf3 16 ♗xf3 ♖fe8

(16...b6 17 axb6 ♕xb6 18 ♘a4 ♕c7 19 ♕c2 ♖fe8 20 ♖fe1 ♖xe1+ 21 ♖xe1 ♖b8 22 ♗d1 with advantage to White, Uhlmann-Vogt, Zinnowitz 1971) 17 ♕a4 ♘e5 18 ♗e2 ♖e7 19 ♖fe1 ♖ae8 20 ♗f1 ♔h7 21 ♖e2 ♘ed7 22 ♖ae1 (Uhlmann-Andersson, Skopje 1972) with a plus for White in *ECO*.

b2) After 10...♕c7 White can hardly achieve even a minimal advantage, e.g. 11 ♘f3 (11 ♕c1 ♔h7 12 h4 h5 13 f3 ♘bd7 14 ♘h3 ♘e5 15 0-0 ♗xh3 16 gxh3 ♘e8 17 ♔h2 ♗f6 18 ♗g5 ♘d7 19 ♗xf6 ½-½, Sapi-Dely, Budapest 1970; 11 f3 e6 12 ♕c1 ♔h7 13 g4 exd5 14 cxd5 ♖e8 with chances for both sides, Prieto-Bibiloni, Buenos Aires 2002) 11...♗g4 12 0-0 ♘bd7 13 ♕c2 (13 a5, Reithel-Campbell, Correspondence 1978, and now 13...♖fe8 followed by ...e7-e6 guarantees counterplay) 13...♖fe8 14 h3 ♗xf3 15 ♗xf3 e6 16 ♗e2 exd5 17 exd5 ♖e7 18 f4 ♖ae8 19 ♗d3 ♘f8 20 ♖ae1 ♖xe1 21 ♖xe1 ♘h5 22 ♘e2 f5 23 ♗f2 ½-½, Sanguinetti-Jones, Nice 1974.

The immediate 8...e6 is Black's choice in the next main game.

9 ♕d2 ♔h7

Not 9...♕a5? 10 ♗xh6! ♗xh6 11 ♕xh6 ♘xe4 12 ♖c1 ♘df6 13 h4! ♕b4 (13...♘xc3 14 bxc3 ♘e4 15 h5 was decisive in Petursson-Demirel, Katerini 1993) 14 ♗f3 ♗f5 (14...♘xc3 15 bxc3 ♕xc4 16 h5 with a clear advantage to White) 15 ♘ge2 ♕xb2 16 h5 and White was well in control in Horvath-Hassan, Cairo 1997.

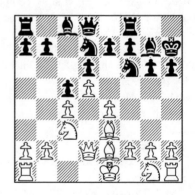

10 h3!?

After 10 ♘f3 a6! 11 a4 ♛a5 12 0-0 Black has 12...♘g4, e.g. 13 ♗f4 (13 ♘g5+ hxg5 14 ♗xg4 ♘e5 15 ♗e2 g4 was equal in Garcia Vicente-Llaneza Vega, Empuriabrava 1997) 13...♘ge5 14 ♛c2 (14 ♘xe5 ♘xe5 with equality in Avrukh-Krakops, Szeged 1994) 14...♘xf3+ 15 ♗xf3 ♘e5 16 ♗e2 f5 17 ♗d2 f4 18 f3 g5 19 ♔h1, Uhlmann-Lanka, Zillertal 1993 when 19...♔h8 followed by ...♛d8, ...e7-e6 is enough for equality according to Lanka in *ECO*. The aggressive 10 g4 can be met with 10...b5 11 cxb5 a6 12 f3 ♛a5 13 a4 ♘b6 14 ♖a3 ♘fd7 with chances for both sides in Beliavsky-Nevednichy, Herceg Novi 2000. Black also has 10...a6, e.g. 11 g5 hxg5 12 ♘f3 g4 13 ♘g5+ ♔g8 14 h3 ♘e5 which was unclear in Raceanu-Istrate, Bucharest 2000. However, 11 h4!? b5 12 g5 b4 13 ♘d1 ♘xe4 14 ♛c2 f5 15 gxh6 ♗xh6 16 ♘f3 looks like an improvement, with a pull for White.

10...b5

Or 10...♛a5 11 ♘f3 a6 12 0-0 b5 13 a3! bxc4 14 ♗xc4, Bareev-Wahls, Germany 1992, given as slightly better for White in *ECO*.

11 cxb5 a6 12 ♘f3

12 bxa6 ♛a5 13 f4 can be messy, e.g. 13...♗xa6 14 ♗xa6 ♖xa6 15 ♘ge2 ♛b4 16 ♛c2 ♖b8 17 ♗c1 c4 18 0-0 ♘c5 19 e5, Tukmakov-Von Gleich, Bern 1992.

12...♛a5 13 b6

After 13 bxa6 ♗xa6 14 ♗xa6 ♛xa6 15 ♛e2 ♖fb8 Black has compensation for the pawn.

13...♘xb6 14 0-0

Nothing is achieved by 14 ♖c1 ♘a4 15 ♗d3 ♘xc3 16 bxc3 ♖b8 ½-½, Luft-Roos, Germany 2000, but 14 a3!? deserves attention, e.g. 14...♘fd7 (14...♘a4? 15 b4 is decisive) 15 ♛c2 (15 0-0 ♘a4!) 15...♘a4 16 ♗d2 ♘xc3 17 ♗xc3 ♗xc3+ 18 bxc3 with an edge for White.

14...♘a4! 15 ♗d3

Black has good counterplay after both 15 ♘d1 ♛xd2 16 ♘xd2 ♘d7 17 ♖b1 f5, Cvek-Oral, Usti nad Labem 1996 and 15 ♛c2 ♘xc3 16 bxc3 e6 17 c4 exd5 (17...♖e8!? unclear) 18

cxd5 ♗d7 19 a4 ♘h5 20 ♖a2 f5 with chances for both sides in Petursson-Lanka, Debrecen 1992.

15...♘xc3

An interesting continuation is 15...c4 16 ♗xc4 (16 ♘xa4 ♛xd2 17 ♘xd2 cxd3 18 ♖ac1 e6 with chances for both sides) 16...♘xc3 17 ♗d3 ♛a4 18 bxc3 ♘xe4 19 ♗xe4 ♛xe4 and Black is holding his ground.

16 bxc3 ♗d7 17 c4 ♛xd2

17...♛c7!? 18 ♖ab1 with advantage to White.

18 ♗xd2 ♗a4 19 ♖ab1 ♖fb8

Alterman gives 19...♖ab8 20 ♗a5 ♖fc8 21 ♘d2 ♘d7 22 f4 with advantage to White.

20 ♖xb8?!

Better are:

a) 20 ♗a5 ♘d7 21 ♗c7 ♖b4 22 a3 ♖b3 23 ♖xb3 ♗xb3 24 ♖b1 ♖a7 25 ♖xb3 (25 ♗xd6?! ♗a2) 25...♖xc7 with a slight advantage to White.

b) 20 e5 dxe5 21 ♘xe5 ♘xd5 22 ♘xf7 ♘c3 23 ♖xb8 ♖xb8 24 ♖e1 ♘xa2 25 ♖xe7 and again White stands better.

20...♖xb8 21 ♖b1 ♖xb1+ 22 ♗xb1 ♘d7 ½-½

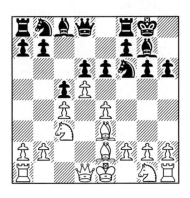

Game 73
Snajdr-Nitsche
Correspondence 1987

1 d4 ♘f6 2 c4 g6 3 ♘c3 ♗g7 4 e4 d6 5 ♗e2 0-0 6 ♗g5 c5 7 d5 h6 8 ♗e3 e6

The most typical reaction. Black wants to open the e-file.

9 h3

Securing the e3-square for the bishop. Other continuations are:

a) 9 ♕d2 exd5 10 exd5 and now 10...♘g4 11 ♗xg4 ♗xg4 12 ♗xh6 ♖e8+ 13 ♔f1 ♗xh6 14 ♕xh6 ♘d7 15 ♕d2 ♕f6 16 b3 b5 17 cxb5 c4 18 h3 ♗f5 19 ♘f3 cxb3 20 axb3 ♖ac8 21 ♘d4 ♘c5 ½-½, Sorin-Barria, Cascavel 1996, but 15 h3!? ♗f5 16 ♘f3 is interesting, e.g. 16...♗d3+ 17 ♔g1 ♗xc4 18 h4 ♕f6 19 h5 with an attack. Instead of ...♘g4 Black has played 10...♔h7. After 11 0-0-0 (Frederiks-Fay, Corr. 1992) 11...b5! 12 ♘xb5 ♘e4 13 ♕c2 a6 14 ♘a3 ♕a5 Black has enough activity. Or 11 h3 ♘a6 (11...♖e8 12 ♘f3 ♗f5 13 ♗d3 ♘e4 14 ♗xe4 ♗xe4 15 ♘xe4 ♖xe4 with equality in Bronstein-Quinteros, Corrientes 1985) 12 ♘f3 ♗f5!? 13 ♗d3 ♕d7 14 0-0 ♖fe8 15 ♖fe1 ♘b4! 16 ♗xf5 ♕xf5 17 a3 ♘c2 18 ♘h4 ♕h5 19 ♕xc2 ♕xh4 20 ♘b5 (Johansen-Haugseth, Correspondence 1990) 20...♖ed8 with equality, or 20 b3 with equality in Uhlmann-Fischer, Siegen 1970.

b) 9 dxe6 ♗xe6 10 ♕d2

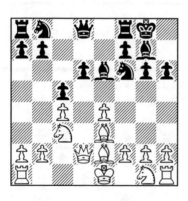

b1) 10...♕b6 11 0-0-0! ♕b4 (otherwise Black loses a pawn without any compensation – 11...♔h7 12 ♕xd6, or 11...♘g4 12 ♗xg4 ♗xg4 13 f3 ♗e6 14 ♗xh6) 12 ♗xh6 ♗xc4 13 h4 (13 ♗xg7!? ♔xg7 14 a3 ♕b3 15 ♕xd6 and White has the upper hand) 13...♗xe2 14 ♘gxe2 ♘c6 (14...♘xe4 15 ♘xe4 ♕xe4 16 h5

with an attack) 15 h5 with an initiative in Grechkin-Seger, Correspondence 1970/73.

b2) 10...♔h7 11 h3 ♘c6 12 ♘f3 ♕a5 and:

b21) 13 0-0!? (Sax's recommendation) 13...♘d4!? (neither 13...♖ad8 14 ♖fd1 a6 15 ♕c2 ♘e8 16 ♘d5, as in Portisch-Sax, Hungary 1984 nor 13...♖fd8 14 ♖fd1 a6 15 ♕c2 ♖ac8 16 a3 ♖d7 17 ♖d2 ♘e5 18 ♖ad1 ♘xc4 19 ♗xc4 ♗xc4 20 e5 ♘e8 21 ♕a4 ♕xa4 22 ♘xa4 ♗b3 23 ♘b6 ♗xd1 24 ♖xd1 ♖cd8 25 ♘xd7 ♖xd7 26 ♗xc5, Uhlmann-Schmidt, Warsaw 1983 is enough to give Black equality) 14 ♘xd4 cxd4 15 ♕xd4 ♘d5 and according to Sax the position is level. Nevertheless after the forcing variation 16 ♕d3 ♘xc3 17 bxc3 ♕xc3 18 ♕xc3 ♗xc3 19 ♖ac1 ♗g7 20 ♖fd1 ♖fd8 21 g4 White has the superior prospects.

b22) 13 ♖d1 ♘d7 (13...a6 is perhaps the best plan, e.g. 14 0-0 ♖fd8 followed by ...♖ab8, ...b7-b5 etc.) 14 ♕xd6 ♖ad8 15 0-0 ♕b4 16 ♖b1 ♖fe8 with compensation in Portisch-Nunn, Brussels 1988. 13...♖ad8!? 14 0-0 ♖fe8 15 ♗f4 ♘e5 16 b3 a6 (Ditt-Kotka, Correspondence 1972/81) 17 ♕c2 ♘fg4!, intending 18 hxg4 ♘xf3+ 19 ♗xf3 ♗xc3.

b3) 10...♕a5!?

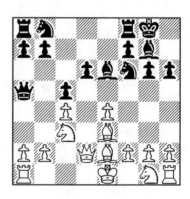

Now 11 ♗xh6 ♗xh6 12 ♕xh6 was covered in our annotations to Nesis-Metz, Game 70 after 10 ♕d2 ♕a5. Castling 'into it' is not the best idea – 11 0-0-0 (Bukhman-Lukin, USSR 1973) 11...b5! 12 ♗xh6 b4 13 ♗xg7 ♔xg7 14 ♘b5 ♕xa2 15 ♘xd6 ♘c6 with a dangerous initiative, or 12 cxb5 ♗xa2 13 e5

dxe5 14 b4! cxb4 15 ♘xa2 ♘a6! with compensation. 11 ♘f3 ♘c6 12 0-0 ♗g4 13 ♗f4 g5 (13...♘d4!? 14 ♘xd4 cxd4 15 ♘d5 ♕xd2 16 ♗xd2 ♘e5 is unclear) 14 ♗g3 ♘ge5 15 ♘xe5 dxe5 was unclear in Rejfir-Bobotsov, Sarajevo 1962.

9...exd5 10 exd5 ♖e8

10...♗f5 is provocative, e.g. 11 g4 ♗c8 12 ♕d2 b5!? 13 ♗xh6 (13 cxb5!?) 13...b4 14 ♗xg7 ♔xg7 15 ♘d1 ♘e4 16 ♕f4 ♖e8, Hort-Polgar, Munich 1991. In *ECO* Hort gives Black compensation, but thus far no repeat has been made of this experiment.

11 ♘f3 ♗f5 12 g4

Others:

a) 12 ♗d3 ♘e4 13 ♘xe4 ♗xe4 14 0-0 ♘d7 15 ♗xe4 ♖xe4 16 ♕c2 ♖e8 with equality, Wunsch-Legahn, Germany 1990.

b) 12 ♕d2 ♘e4! 13 ♘xe4 ♗xe4 14 ♗xh6?! ♗xh6 15 ♕xh6 ♗xf3 favours Black according to Gufeld.

12...♗e4

Black also has good counterchances after 12...♗d7 13 ♕d2 ♔h7 14 ♗d3 b5, e.g. 15 cxb5 a6 16 bxa6 ♘xa6 17 ♔f1 ♘b4 18 ♗e2 ♗c8 19 ♔g2 ♗b7 20 ♗c4 ♘e4 21 ♘xe4 ♖xe4, Afanasiev-Korotylev, Moscow 1998.

13 ♕d2

13 0-0 ♗xf3 14 ♗xf3 ♘bd7 was equal in Averbakh-Geller, USSR 1974.

13...♘bd7

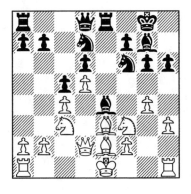

14 0-0-0

GM Gufeld's idea. Other moves are:

a) 14 ♖g1 ♗xf3 (14...b5!? 15 cxb5 ♘b6 with an edge for Black) 15 ♗xf3 b5 (15...♘b6!? 16 b3 ♘h7 17 ♗g2 ♕f6 18 ♖c1 ♘g5 was unclear in Lorin-Cavril, Correspondence 1995) 16 cxb5 (16 ♘xb5 ♘e5 17 ♗e2 ♘e4 is okay for Black) 16...a6 (16...♘b6!? with chances for both sides) 17 bxa6 ♖xa6 18 ♔f1 ♘e5 and Black had healthy compensation in Mikenas-Plachetka, Lublin 1972.

b) In the event of 14 0-0 g5!? Black clears the way for ...♗g6, 15 ♘xe4 ♘xe4 16 ♕d3 (16 ♕c2 ♘g3) 16...♕f6 securing equality. 14...♗xf3 15 ♗xf3 h5 16 g5 ♘h7 was interesting in Lputian-Gufeld, Moscow 1983.

14...♘e5?!

Black wins the exchange but finds himself under considerable pressure. There are two very promising alternatives:

a) 14...b5! 15 ♗xh6 (15 cxb5 a6 16 bxa6 ♖b8 17 a7 ♖b4 18 ♗xh6 ♗xh6 19 ♕xh6 ♕b6 looks good for Black, while after 15 ♘xb5?! ♘b6 White has no good way to defend the c4-pawn, e.g. 16 ♘a3 ♘xg4 17 hxg4 ♘a4 or 16 g5 ♗xf3 17 gxf6 ♗xe2 18 ♕xe2 ♕xf6 etc.) 15...b4 16 ♗xg7 ♔xg7 17 ♘xe4 ♘xe4 18 ♕e1 ♕a5 19 ♔b1 ♖ab8 and ...♖b6-a6 is the plan.

b) 14...♘b6 15 b3 ♘fxd5! 16 ♘xe4 (16 cxd5?? ♕f6 and 16 ♘xd5?? ♘xd5 17 cxd5 ♕f6 are disastrous) 16...♘xe3 17 ♕xe3 d5 18 cxd5 ♘xd5 19 ♗b5 (19 ♖xd5 ♕xd5 20 ♗d3 ♕c6 with an edge for Black, and 19 ♕d3? runs into 19...♕a5) 19...♘xe3 20 ♖xd8 ♖axd8 21 ♗xe8 ♖xe8 22 ♘d6 ♖e6 23 ♘xb7 with an excellent position for Black.

15 ♘xe5 ♗xh1 16 ♘xf7 ♔xf7 17 ♖xh1 ♖h8?

If you play the King's Indian you must avoid taking even one step back! Black should opt for the aggressive 17...b5 18 cxb5 ♘e4 19 ♘xe4 ♖xe4 20 a3 c4! with a very complex position.

18 ♗d3

Now White stands clearly better.

18...♘d7 19 f4 ♕e7 20 ♘e2

This time White should be more active, 20

♖e1 ♖he8 21 ♘b5 ♘f8 22 f5 promising a clear advantage.

20...♖he8

The immediate 20...b5 looks effective.

21 ♗f2 b5 22 ♕c2 ♕f6 23 g5?

Better was 23 cxb5.

23...hxg5 24 ♖g1?

24 cxb5!? gxf4 25 ♖f1 is very good for Black.

24...bxc4 25 ♗xc4 ♖ab8 26 b3 gxf4 27 ♖g4 ♘e5 0-1

Game 74

Petursson-Larsen

Holstebro playoff 1989

1 d4 ♘f6 2 c4 c5 3 d5 d6 4 ♘c3 g6 5 e4 ♗g7 6 ♗e2 0-0 7 ♗g5 e6

Black does without ...h7-h6, getting straight to business in the centre.

8 ♕d2

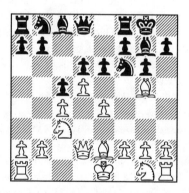

Others are rare:

a) 8 dxe6 ♗xe6 (8...fxe6 9 ♘f3!? ♘c6 10 0-0 ♕b6 11 ♕d2 ♘d4, Rasmussen-Jensen, Denmark 1980 and now 12 ♖ad1 with advantage to White) 9 ♘f3 ♘c6 10 0-0 ♖e8 11 ♘d5 ♗xd5 12 exd5 ♘e5, as in Mirkovic-Zaichik, Belgrade 1988 is unclear according to *ECO*.

b) 8 h3 exd5 9 exd5 h6 10 ♗f4 ♖e8 11 ♕d2 ♔h7 12 0-0-0 (12 ♘f3 ♗f5 13 0-0 with equality) 12...♘e4 (12...b5! with an initiative) 13 ♘xe4 ♖xe4 14 ♗d3 ♖e8 was well balanced in Meyer-Rich, Correspondence 1967.

8...exd5

An alternative is 8...♕a5 9 ♘f3 a6 (9...exd5 10 exd5 ♗g4 11 0-0 ♘bd7, Kachiani Gersinska-Berger, Germany 2001, and now 12 h3 ♗xf3 13 ♗xf3 favours White) 10 a4 exd5 11 exd5 ♗g4 12 0-0 ♘bd7 13 h3 ♗xf3 14 ♗xf3 ♖fe8 (14...♘e5 15 ♗e2 ♕c7 16 ♖ae1 was slightly better for White in Amura-Chaves, Merida 1997) 15 ♕c2 ♕c7 16 ♖fe1 ♖xe1+ 17 ♖xe1 ♖e8 18 ♖xe8+ ♘xe8 19 ♗e2 with advantage to White, Polak-Tesar, Czechoslovakia 1997.

9 exd5 ♕b6

Black plays 9...♖e8 in the next main game. Others:

a) 9...♘a6 10 ♘f3 ♘c7 (10...♖e8 11 0-0 ♕b6 12 ♖ae1 ♗g4 13 h3 ♗xf3 14 ♗xf3 with a slight advantage to White in Hutchings-Ojanen, Skopje 1972) 11 0-0 a6 (11...♗f5 12 ♘h4 ♗d7 13 ♖fe1 ♖e8 14 ♕f4 was good for White in Kaidanov-Chudnovsky, Philadelphia 1993) 12 a4 ♖b8 13 ♕f4 ♘ce8 14 a5 with the more pleasant game for White, Vaganian-Velimirovic, Budapest 1973.

b) 9...a6 10 ♘f3 (10 a4 ♖e8 11 ♘f3 ♗g4 12 0-0 ♕c7 13 h3 ♗xf3 14 ♗xf3 ♘bd7 15 ♖fe1 h5 16 ♖xe8+ ♖xe8 17 ♖e1 ♘e5 18 ♗e2 ♘h7 19 ♗e3 with a pull for White in Portisch-Istratescu, Budapest 1993) 10...♕c7 (10...b5 11 cxb5 axb5 12 ♗xb5 ♗a6 13 ♗xa6 ♖xa6 14 0-0 ♘bd7 15 ♗h6 ♗xh6 16 ♕xh6 and Black's play had backfired in Zhukhovitsky-Dementiev, Voronezh 1971, while 10...♖e8 11 0-0 ♗g4 12 ♖ae1 ♘bd7 13 ♕f4 ♗xf3 14 ♗xf3 was an edge for White in Ulms-Neumann, Schoeneck 1996) 11 0-0 ♗g4 12 h3 ♗xf3 13 ♗xf3 ♘bd7 14 a4 b6 15 ♗d1 (15 ♖fe1 ♖fe8 16 ♗f4 ♖xe1+ 17 ♖xe1 ♖e8 18 ♖xe8+ ♘xe8 19 ♘e4 ♗d4 20 ♕e2 with slight advantage to White, Cherek-Fiensch, Correspondence 1980) 15...♔h8 16 ♗c2 ♘g8 17 ♖ae1 ♖fe8 (17...♘e5 18 b3 f6 19 ♗f4 favoured White in Mendez-Berdichesky, Correspondence 1983) 18 b3 with advantage to White, Polugaevsky-Shaw, Siegen 1970.

10 ♘f3

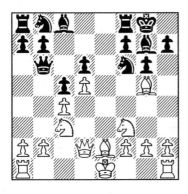

10...♗g4

10...♗f5 11 ♘h4 ♘e4 12 ♘xe4 ♗xe4 13 f3 ♕xb2 14 ♖c1 h6 (14...♗f5 15 ♘xf5 gxf5 16 ♕xb2 ♗xb2 17 ♖c2 ♗e5 18 f4 ♗d4 19 ♗d3, Bukhman-Nezhmetdinov, Daugavpils 1973 and 14...♕xd2+ 15 ♔xd2 ♗xd5 16 cxd5 ♖e8 17 ♖b1, Lputian-Yurtaev, Volgograd 1985 were both very good for White) 15 ♗xh6 ♕xd2+ 16 ♗xd2 ♗f6 17 g3 ♗xh4 18 gxh4 ♗f5 19 ♗f4 with an edge for White, Boleslavsky-Balendo, Minsk 1970.

11 0-0 ♘bd7 12 ♖ac1

12 h3 is very good, e.g. 12...♗xf3 13 ♗xf3 or 12...♗f5 13 ♘h4 ♖ae8 14 ♘xf5 gxf5 15 ♖ab1 ♘e4 16 ♕f4, Mohr-Larsen, Palma de Mallorca 1989 with a modest lead for White in either case.

12...♖ae8 13 h3 ♗f5 14 ♖fe1 ♘e4 15 ♘xe4 ♗xe4 16 b3 a5 17 ♘h2

Now Black loses material, although he fails to equalise after both Yrjola's recommendation 17...f6 (intending ...g6-g5), e.g. 18 ♗f4 g5 19 ♗g3, or 17...♘e5!? 18 ♘f1 ♗f5 19 ♗h6 ♗xh6 20 ♕xh6 with a slight edge to White.

18 f3 ♗d4+ 19 ♔h1 ♗f5

Black could have prolonged the resistance after 19...♕xd2!? 20 ♗xd2 ♘f6 21 ♘g4 (21 fxe4 ♘xe4 22 ♘f1 ♘xd2 23 ♘xd2 ♗f2 24 ♘b1 ♗xe1 25 ♖xe1 with an excellent game for White) 21...♗f5 22 ♘h6+ ♔g7 23 ♘xf5+ gxf5 24 ♗d3 and White is clearly better.

20 g4 f6

20...♖e5 21 ♗f1! (Petursson).

21 ♗h6 ♖f7

21...♕xd2 22 ♗xd2 ♗xg4 23 hxg4 ♗f2 is a lesser evil, but the end is approaching.

22 ♗f1 ♖xe1 23 ♕xe1 ♗b2 24 ♗d2

Petursson gives 24 ♕xb4 axb4 25 ♖e1.

24...♕a3 25 gxf5 ♗xc1 26 ♗xc1 ♕xa2 27 ♘g4 ♘e5 28 ♘h6+ ♔g7 29 ♘xf7 ♘xf7 30 fxg6 hxg6 31 ♕e3 ♕c2 32 ♗d2 b6 33 ♗c3 ♘e5 34 f4 ♘f7 35 ♗g2 g5 36 fxg5 1-0

Game 75
Polugaevsky-Uhlmann
Amsterdam 1970

---

1 c4 ♘f6 2 ♘c3 g6 3 e4 d6 4 d4 ♗g7 5 ♗e2 0-0 6 ♗g5 c5 7 d5 e6 8 ♕d2 exd5 9 exd5 ♖e8 10 ♘f3

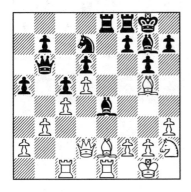

17...♕b4?

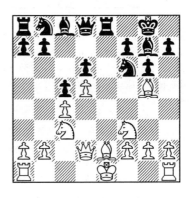

10...♗g4

Black has also tried:

a) 10...♕b6 11 0-0 ♗g4 12 h3 ♗xf3 13 ♗xf3 ♘bd7 14 ♖fe1 a6 15 ♖ab1 ♖xe1+ 16 ♖xe1 ♖e8 17 ♖xe8+ ♘xe8 18 ♘d1 and White was better in Olivera-Donoso Velasco, Buenos Aires 1978.

b) 10...♕e7 11 0-0 ♕f8 12 h3 ♘a6 13 ♗d3 ♗d7 14 a3 h6 15 ♗f4 and Black's pieces occupied unnatural posts in Bareev-Dyachkov, Azov 1996.

11 0-0 ♘bd7 12 h3

Other moves do not alter the character of the position, e.g. 12 ♖ae1 a6 13 h3 ♗xf3 14 ♗xf3 ♖xe1 15 ♖xe1 ♕f8 16 ♗f4 with an edge for White, Kozma-Stulik, Podebrady 1956, or 12 ♖fe1 a6 13 h3 ♗xf3 14 ♗xf3 ♕c7 15 ♗f4 h5 16 a3 ♘h7 17 ♘e4 ♘e5 18 ♗e2 ♖e7 19 ♗f1 ♖ae8 with a niggling pull for White, Cuellar Gacharna-Reshevsky, Sousse 1967.

12...♗xf3 13 ♗xf3 a6

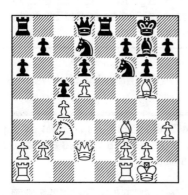

This structure is very similar to that discussed in Kunsztowicz-Raupp (Game 66), and indeed the plans for both sides are also similar (see the annotation after White's 13th move).

14 a4

14 ♗e2 ♕b6 15 ♕c2 (15 ♖ae1!? with a plus) 15...h6 16 ♗h4 ♘h7 17 f4 ♗d4+ 18 ♔h1 ♘hf6 19 ♗d3 ♔g7 20 ♖f3 ♖e3 and Istratescu in *ECO* evaluates this position as equal but after 21 ♖xe3 ♗xe3 22 ♖f1 ♖e8 (Oral-Istratescu, Canakkale 1994) 23 ♘e2 White is better. Instead 15...♖e7 16 f4 (Hort-

Fernandez, Decin 1977) 16...♖ae8!? looks fine.

14...♕e7

Black has also tried:

a) 14...♘e5 15 ♗e2 ♕a5 16 ♕c2 h6 17 ♗d2 ♕c7 18 f4 ♘ed7 19 ♖ae1 with a slight advantage to White, Gulko-Radjabov, Wijk aan Zee 2001.

b) 14...♕a5 15 ♕c2 ♖e7 (15...♖ab8 16 ♗d2 ♕c7 17 a5 ♖e7 18 ♖fe1 ♖be8 19 ♖xe7 ♖xe7 20 ♘a4 ♘e8 21 ♖b1 ♗d4 22 b4 with the more pleasant game for White in Olafsson-Peralta, Bled 2002) 16 ♗d2 ♕c7 17 ♖ae1 ♖ae8 18 ♖xe7 ♖xe7 19 ♖e1 ♘e5 (19...♖xe1+ 20 ♗xe1 favours White) 20 ♗e2 ♘e8 21 g3 f5 22 f4 with a slight edge to White (*ECO*) in Mochalov-Vaganian, USSR 1973.

c) 14...♕c7 15 a5 (15 ♕c2 ♖e7 16 ♖ae1 ♖ae8 17 ♖xe7 ♖xe7 18 ♗e2 h6 19 ♗d2 ♘e8 20 g4!, Polugaevsky-Gufeld, Tbilisi 1966 and 15 ♖ae1 h5 16 ♕c2 ♖xe1 17 ♖xe1 ♘e5 18 ♗e2 ♘h7 19 ♗d2 followed by launching the f-pawn, Horvath-Todorov, Val Thorens 1995 are both pleasant for White) 15...h5 16 ♕c2 ♘h7 (16...♖ab8!? followed by ...b7-b6 looks okay) 17 ♗d2 ♖e7 (17...♕d8 18 ♖fe1 ♘e5 19 ♗e2 f5, Lukacs-Velickovic, Belgrade 1984, and now 20 ♗f1 favours White) 18 ♗d1 ♖ae8 19 f4 ♗d4+ 20 ♔h1 with a slight advantage to White in Habermehl-Kratochvil, Correspondence 1999.

d) 14...♕b6 15 ♕c2

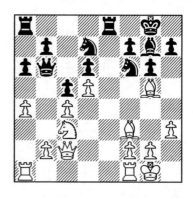

Now 15...♖e7 16 ♖ae1 ♖ae8 17 ♖xe7 ♖xe7 (Horvath-Strikovic, Niksic 1991) 18 ♗d2 is

enough to secure White an advantage according to Polugaevsky in *ECO*, while 15...♖e5 16 ♗f4 ♖e7 17 ♗d2 ♖ae8 18 ♖ae1 h5 19 ♖xe7 ♖xe7 20 ♗d1 was also a plus for White in Pogorelov-Paunovic, Zaragoza 2001. This leaves 15...h5, e.g. 16 ♗d2 (16 ♗e2 ♘h7 17 ♗d2 ♕d8 18 ♖ae1 ♕h4 19 ♗d3 f5, Bagaturov-Velickovic, Kavala 1998, and now 20 f4! looks good for White) 16...♘h7 17 ♖ae1 ♗d4 (17...h4 18 ♗d1 ♘df8 19 b3 with a pull for White, Aleksandrov-Damljanovic, Herceg Novi 2001) 18 b3 ♕d8 19 ♖xe8+ ♕xe8 20 g3 (20 ♖e1!?) 20...♕f8 21 ♔g2 ♖e8 22 ♗d1 ♖e7 23 ♖e1 ♖xe1 24 ♗xe1 and White had succeeded in hanging on to the lead in Petursson-Vragoteris, Katerini 1993.

15 ♖ae1

15 ♖fe1 (15 a5 ♕f8 16 ♖ab1 ♘e5 17 ♗e2 ♘ed7 18 ♗e3 ♘e4 19 ♘xe4 ♖xe4 20 ♗d3 ♖e7 21 b4 with a slight edge to White, Kindermann-Karl, Zurich 1984) 15...♕f8 16 ♖xe8 ♖xe8 17 ♖e1 h6 18 ♖xe8 ♘xe8 19 ♗e3 (19 ♗f4!?) 19...f5 20 ♗e2 with the more pleasant game for White, Kaidanov-Fedorowicz, Lexington 1995.

15...♕f8 16 ♗d1

The bishop is going to the b1-h7 diagonal. White can play along the lines of Kunsztowicz-Raupp (Game 66) or try to generate an initiative on the kingside, retaining at least one pair of rooks and gaining space through g2-g4 and f2-f4 etc. White often plays 16 a5 in order to increase his stock on the queenside, e.g. 16...♖xe1 (16...h5 17 ♗d1 ♖xe1 18 ♖xe1 ♖e8 19 ♖xe8 ♕xe8 20 ♗c2 with advantage to White in Damljanovic-Popovic, Belgrade 1997) 17 ♖xe1 ♖e8 18 ♗d1 ♖xe1+ 19 ♕xe1 ♕d8 (19...♘e5 20 ♕e2 ♕d8 21 ♘e4 with a small plus for White, Pein-Paavilainen, Helsinki 1990) 20 ♘a4 and White had something in Korchnoi-Karl, Lugano 1985.

16...♖xe1

16...h6 17 ♗f4 ♘h7 18 ♗c2 ♘hf6 (18...♘e5 19 b3 f5 20 ♗g3 ♕f6 21 ♘e2 with advantage to White, Yusupov-Zapata, Saint

John 1988) 19 a5 b6 20 ♖xe8 ♖xe8 21 axb6...♘xb6 22 b3 and White stood better in Bellmann-Da Silva Filho, ICCF E-mail 1999.

17 ♖xe1 ♖e8 18 ♖xe8

18 ♗f4 ♖xe1+ 19 ♕xe1 ♕e8 20 ♗d2 ♔f8 21 ♕xe8+ ♘xe8 with the well-known better ending for White in Chernin-Mohr, Portoroz 1997.

18...♕xe8 19 ♗c2

19 ♗f4 ♕e7 20 ♕e2 ♔f8 21 ♕xe7+ ♔xe7 22 a5! ♘e8 23 ♗d2 h5 24 ♔f1 ♗d4 25 b3 and again Black is not quite comfortable enough, Uhlmann-Gligoric, Hastings 1971.

19...♘b6

Other moves fall short of equality.

a) 19...h5 20 ♗f4 (20 f4!?) 20...♘e5 21 ♕e2 ♔h7 22 ♗d2 ♘ed7 23 f4 (23 ♕xe8!? ♘xe8 24 a5) 23...♕xe2 24 ♘xe2 with advantage to White, Doroshkievich-Liberzon, Riga 1970.

b) 19...♘e5 20 ♕e2 ♘ed7 21 ♕xe8+ ♘xe8 22 ♗d2 ♘e5 23 b3 ♘d7 24 g4 ♔f8 25 ♔g2 ♔e7 26 f4 ♗d4 27 ♘e4 b5 and Black was still worse in Mohr-Gheorghiu, Switzerland 2000.

20 b3 ♘bd7 21 ♗f4! ♕e7 22 ♕e2 ♔f8 23 ♕xe7+ ♔xe7 24 a5 h5 25 ♗d2 ♘e8 26 g3 ♗d4 27 ♔g2 ♘g7 28 f4 ♘f5 29 ♘d1 ♘h6 30 ♔f3 f5

Although this move creates a new weakness on g6 it is Black's best try. Otherwise White simply gains space, e.g. 30...♘g8 31 g4 hxg4+ 32 hxg4 ♗g7 33 g5 etc. (Belov).

31 ♗d3 ♔d8 32 ♘e3 ♔e7 33 ♘c2 ♗b2 34 ♔e3 ♘f6 35 ♘e1 ♗d4+ 36 ♔f3 ♗b2 37 ♘g2 ♘d7 38 ♘h4 ♔f6 39 ♔e3 ♘f7 40 ♗c2 ♗a1?

Now or on the next two moves Black should have played 40...♘h6 to address the advance of White's g-pawn.

41 ♔e2 ♗b2 42 ♗e1

Missing 42 g4! hxg4 43 hxg4 fxg4 44 ♘xg6 ♘h6 45 ♘h4 ♗d4 46 ♔f1 with a decisive advantage (Belov).

42...♗a1? 43 g4 hxg4 44 hxg4 fxg4 45 ♘xg6 ♔g7 46 ♘h4 ♔f8 47 ♗f5 ♘f6 48 ♗c8 ♘d8 49 ♘f5 ♘h5 50 ♗d2 ♗d4 51 ♘xd4 1-0

Summary

The most interesting variations arise after 7...h6 8 &f4 (or 8 &e3) 8...e6, with Black reacting quickly in the centre. 8 &f4 is the most demanding move because Black has to sacrifice the d6-pawn (otherwise he is too passive), leading to complicated situations that offer decent compensation for the pawn. These are encountered in Games 70 & 71, the latter being Black's best. However, it is important in these lines that both sides are well acquainted with the (very) long variations, and not everybody likes starting the game around the thirtieth move! This is why numerous other moves are played. 8 &e3 shouldn't be a problem for Black, as is demonstrated in Game 73.

1 d4 &f6 2 c4 g6 3 &c3 &g7 4 e4 d6 5 &e2 0-0 6 &g5 c5 (D)
7 d5

7 dxc5 (*Game 65*)

7...h6

7...&a5 (*Game 66*)

7...a6 (*Game 67*)

7...b5 (*Game 68*)

7...e6 8 &d2 exd5 9 exd5 (*Games 74 & 75*)

8 &f4

8 &e3

8...&bd7 (*Game 72*)

8...e6 (*Game 73*)

8...e6 (D)

8...&b6 (*Game 69*)

9 dxe6 &xe6 10 &xd6 &e8 11 &f3 (D)

11...&c6 (*Game 70*)

11...&b6 (*Game 71*)

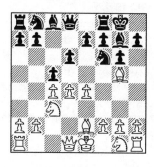
6...c5

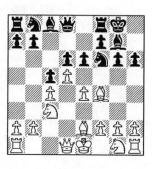
8...e6

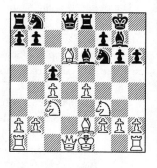
11 &f3

INDEX OF COMPLETE GAMES